FRENCH NUCLEAR DIPLOMACY

FRENCH NUCLEAR DIPLOMACY

BY WILFRID L. KOHL

PRINCETON UNIVERSITY PRESS
PRINCETON, NEW JERSEY
1971

LC Card: 71-153846
ISBN: 0-691-07540-9

This book has been composed in Linotype Caledonia

Printed in the United States of America by
Princeton University Press

For Kay

Preface

THIS is a study of the French nuclear force, its origins under the Fourth Republic, and the policy shifts which guided its development under the Fifth Republic of General de Gaulle. Nuclear weapons have had an important impact on postwar international politics. Nowhere have they appeared to cause greater discord than in Europe during the sixties when France set out to develop her own independent nuclear deterrent. A central objective of this book is to explore the interrelationship between French nuclear armament and French foreign policy, especially during the de Gaulle years when the two were so closely intertwined. The role of French nuclear diplomacy in France's relations with her key alliance partners—the United States, Great Britain, and West Germany—is particularly important in this investigation.

An interest in the interaction of strategy and politics, conceived during the period of heated NATO nuclear debates in the early 1960's, led me to this subject. My desire to understand the European perspective on questions of Western strategy and defense was spurred by a fascination and curiosity about General de Gaulle and the motivations for his policies. In retrospect, the transatlantic nuclear discussions of those years take on an esoteric and sometimes superficial cast. At the start of the 1970's, the context has changed. Ostpolitik and the pursuit of détente, superpower negotiations on the limitation of strategic arms, and talk about a European security conference mark the current scene. Yet Soviet troops continue to occupy Central Europe, and any change in the aims of Soviet policy remains uncertain. European nuclear forces persist, France's in ever growing strength. The challenge of finding a common framework for French, British, and U.S. nuclear deterrence is still with us. As

French nuclear capability increases, and as Britain edges close to entry into the European Community, nuclear diplomacy may reemerge as a pivotal issue in Western alliance politics and offer important opportunities for influencing Europe's future evolution. It is my hope that this study will provide the perspective necessary for understanding and dealing with the defense and nuclear policies of post–de Gaulle France, a subject on which some comments are made in the concluding chapter.

For support and assistance while this study was in preparation, a number of debts should be acknowledged: to the Fulbright program and Columbia University, which made possible my initial research in Europe during 1965-66; to the Brookings Institution for a research fellowship and congenial surroundings when the first draft was written in 1966-67; to the Fondation nationale des sciences politiques, my working base in Paris, for kind hospitality and access to its clipping files; to the Deutsche Gesellschaft für Auswärtige Politik and the library of the German Bundestag in Bonn for use of their research facilities; and to the library of the Institute for Strategic Studies in London. A study group on European security and arms control organized by Columbia University's Institute of War and Peace Studies provided lively discussion when this book was taking final form.

Over a hundred Europeans and Americans were interviewed in the course of my research. Many government officials, past or present, will remain anonymous at their own request, except for the few who are cited in the footnotes. Some others must be singled out for special thanks. In Paris, Professor Jean-Baptiste Duroselle gave helpful guidance in the early phases of the project. Professors Raymond Aron, Alfred Grosser, Pierre Hassner, and Serge Hurtig offered many valuable suggestions, as did journalists André Fontaine, Nicolas Vichney, Jean Planchais, and Jacques Isnard. At the Assemblée nationale, Joël le Theule was especially generous with his time and insights. For stimulating conversations I am also indebted to Generals André Beaufre, Paul Stehlin, Pierre Gallois, and Paul Ély. For assistance in the German aspects of this study, I wish to thank Dr. Wolfgang Wagner, Uwe Nerlich, and Theo Sommer. In London Alastair Buchan, Brigadier Kenneth Hunt, Kenneth Younger, and Curt Gasteyger (then at the Institute for Strategic Studies) were particularly helpful.

For support and encouragement from the beginning, I am grateful to Professors Philip E. Mosely and William T. R. Fox of Columbia University. For critical comments on the manuscript I wish to express appreciation to Lawrence Scheinman, Robert Gilpin, Mark Kesselman, Robert McGeehan, Arnold Kramish, Catherine Kelleher, and Andrew Pierre. Hilda Shakin and Bess Heitner undertook a large part of the typing task. Joanna Hitchcock of Princeton University Press applied her editing skill to the final manuscript and guided me in preparing it for publication with patience and good cheer. My wife, to whom this book is gratefully dedicated, gave valuable editorial assistance, as well as moral support at all stages of this venture.

Earlier discussions of some of the issues treated in this book appeared in two articles: "The French Nuclear Deterrent," *Proceedings of the Academy of Political Science*, XXIX, no. 2 (November 1968), 80-94; and "Die Zukunft der französischen Atomstreitmacht," *Europa Archiv*, XXIV, no. 7 (April 1969), 229-39.

To avoid any misunderstanding, I wish to make it clear that this study was drafted and essentially completed, except for final editing and updating, before I began an assignment with the staff of the National Security Council in 1970. Responsibility for the facts and judgments herein is obviously mine.

February 1971

Contents

TWO

The Force de Dissuasion: Its Rationale and Evolution

THREE

France and Her Allies: The International Implications of Gaullist Strategy

FRENCH NUCLEAR DIPLOMACY

Introduction

Charles de Gaulle's *politique de grandeur* was characterized by actions of boldness and defiance in the international arena. Among his many controversial policies, the decision to develop a French nuclear deterrent was perhaps most symbolic of the general's determination to achieve an independent role for France in world politics. Inspired more by political considerations than by concern for military security, the *force de frappe* became the mainstay of Gaullist foreign policies in the West, as well as toward the East. Yet the original French decision to produce atomic weapons was not de Gaulle's. It was made before his return to power. Moreover, it is noteworthy that the nuclear program has been reaffirmed by the first government of post–de Gaulle France led by Georges Pompidou.

The French nuclear force has several important implications for world political stability. First, it serves as a model for other countries which might be tempted to seek a nuclear capability. By developing atomic weapons on their own, as they did, the French demonstrated that membership in the world's nuclear club was obtainable, and may thereby be encouraging further nuclear proliferation. Secondly, French nuclear armament poses grave questions for the cohesion of the Atlantic alliance. Nuclear disagreements with the United States underlay much of de Gaulle's hostility toward NATO, for example, and this eventually led to France's withdrawal from the organization's military commands in 1966. Thirdly, the existence of small nuclear forces such as the French could complicate the chances of United States–Soviet agreement on measures of superpower arms control. Finally, the French nuclear deterrent will continue to have significant consequences for European integration and the organization of West European defense;

it will also affect prospects for forming an all-European security system and attaining a European settlement.

This study does not deal with all of these questions. Its purpose is twofold: first, to describe how the French nuclear force was conceived and subsequently developed, especially under General de Gaulle; and secondly, to analyze its role in Gaullist foreign policy and its effects on France's relations with her principal Western allies and, therefore, its consequences for the Atlantic alliance. Previous works by several authors have focused on the origins and history of the French atomic program under the Fourth Republic.[1] Other books and articles have treated particular aspects of the Gaullist *force de frappe* and some of its strategic and political consequences for European and Atlantic relationships.[2] But no work deals with French military nuclear development in its entirety and investigates in detail its relationship to foreign policy, especially under the Fifth Republic. This is the task of this book.

It should be stressed that the focus here is confined to the evolution of the French nuclear deterrent and its implications and consequences. Although students of nuclear proliferation may find this book of interest, no systematic effort has been made to extract theoretical conclusions of a more general nature about the applicability of French military nuclear development to other nations which may in the future seek a similar capability. Those readers interested pri-

[1] See Lawrence Scheinman, *Atomic Energy Policy in France Under the Fourth Republic* (Princeton: Princeton University Press, 1965); Bertrand Goldschmidt, *L'Aventure atomique* (Paris: Arthème Fayard, 1962) and *Les Rivalités atomiques, 1939-1966* (Paris: Arthème Fayard, 1967); and the late General Charles Ailleret, *L'Aventure atomique française* (Paris: Éditions Bernard Grasset, 1968). Despite its title, the recent study by Wolf Mendl, *Deterrence and Persuasion: French Nuclear Armament in the Context of National Policy, 1945-1969* (New York: Praeger, 1970), also concentrates on the period of the Fourth Republic. Unfortunately it came to the author's attention too late to be incorporated in this book.

[2] See, e.g., the writings of Raymond Aron, Alfred Grosser, Stanley Hoffmann, Henry Kissinger, and Cyro Zoppo, as cited in the bibliography.

marily in international relations may find insights in this study regarding the interaction of strategy and politics in the nuclear age—especially the effects of nuclear weapons on an alliance. No attempt has been made, however, to explain the France-NATO case in terms of a particular model of international relations theory or behavior. Many subjects treated in this work relate to questions of how to organize European and Atlantic security. These are matters that have provoked much controversy in the American foreign policy debate over the past decade. While not primarily intended as a policy study, some comments are offered in this book on past American policies when they relate to questions of the main analysis.

Previous studies have emphasized continuity between the Fourth and Fifth Republics in the area of nuclear policy. Indeed, as Chapter 1 describes, there is considerable continuity between the two Republics with respect to the decision to produce atomic weapons and the existence of a nuclear research and development program to accomplish this aim. The French civilian atomic effort began immediately after World War II and serious studies of military applications date from about 1954. Although at the level of official policy a clearcut decision for a nuclear weapons program was postponed until four years later, studies and developmental work on the first atomic bomb proceeded anyway under the leadership of a bureaucratic cadre. The military nuclear program was carried forward not by directives from the premier and his cabinet, but by second-rank officials—mainly technocrats and military officers centered in the atomic energy agency, the Commissariat à l'énergie atomique (CEA). Finally, in April 1958, shortly before the fall of the Fourth Republic, Premier Félix Gaillard issued the official order setting the 1960 target date for the first French atomic test. When General de Gaulle resumed power a few months later, he reconfirmed that decision and accelerated the atomic development program he had inherited.

There is, however, a substantial discontinuity between the role which nuclear weapons played in de Gaulle's foreign and defense policies and the intentions of leaders of the Fourth Republic. This shift in motivation for a nuclear force furnishes the basis for this study. Supporters of the military nuclear program before 1958 sought to enhance France's political status and military role within the existing framework of the North Atlantic alliance. They assumed that the nuclear force to follow would be related to the NATO military structure. General de Gaulle, on the other hand, proceeded to develop French atomic armament primarily as a political instrument to support his independent foreign policies which sought to change the European and international system and France's role in it. This was first evident in 1958 when he attempted to transform NATO by proposing a British-French-American triumvirate at the top of the Alliance to elaborate world strategy. Later, after this plan was rebuffed, the general made use of the nascent French nuclear arsenal to support his efforts to form an independent West European grouping of states under French leadership, on the model of the Fouchet plan. Still later, French nuclear weapons underpinned de Gaulle's withdrawal from NATO military commands in 1966—a move carefully synchronized with the launching of his policy of rapprochement with the Soviet Union and Eastern Europe aimed at replacing Western Europe's Atlantic defense alignment with a new framework of pan-European security.

For de Gaulle, then, the *force de frappe* was a tool which he employed in pursuit of his larger foreign policy objectives, and these were much bolder and more grandly conceived than those of French leaders before 1958. In brief, the general's foreign policy aims included the restoration of French *grandeur* through the achievement of a global role for France and—so far as possible—coequal status with the United States and Great Britain; the subordination of West Germany to France and the preservation of French leadership in Western Europe; reunification of the two halves of the European continent in a loose association of states "from the Atlantic to the Urals"; and an independent role for this "European" Europe in world politics.

The incentives for the development of nuclear weapons under the Fourth and Fifth Republics should be viewed in relation to their quite different political systems and policy-making processes, as well as their foreign policy perspectives. The Fourth Republic was characterized by unstable coalition governments. Cabinets and premiers changed frequently in response to fluctuating party alliances in the French parliament. The coalition character of the numerous governments severely limited their ability to reach firm policy decisions and, as a result, policies were often framed in noncommittal terms. As a number of observers have pointed out, the role of the administration and the bureaucracy in the policy-making process was strengthened by the instability of the system at the top.[3] This was true in many fields, and atomic policy is an especially good example, as Lawrence Scheinman ably demonstrated in his revealing study.[4] Parliamentary control was also weak, and it is noteworthy that under the Fourth Republic there was little real political debate on the implications of the military nuclear program that was developing.

The absence of a firm government policy decision in favor of nuclear weapons development until the very end of the Fourth Republic, plus the covert nature of the process by which atomic policy was formulated, complicate a discussion of nuclear incentives. Different groups—such as the CEA technocrats, military officers, and those politicians who were concerned with the problem—advocated the development of an atomic bomb for different reasons. In general, incentives for atomic weapons under the Fourth

[3] See, e.g., Philip M. Williams, *Crisis and Compromise: Politics in the Fourth Republic*, 3rd ed. (Hamden, Conn.: Shoe String Press, 1964).

[4] Scheinman, *Atomic Energy Policy in France under the Fourth Republic*, cited.

Republic included a variety of political and military-strategic factors ranging from France's declining influence in NATO and the frustrations caused by the loss of her colonial territories to a desire for the most modern weapons for the French army to restore its morale, to offset the effects of German rearmament, and to diminish France's dependence upon American military protection. As will be explained, the idea of a *force de frappe* began to appear in certain military planning circles only in the last years before the Fourth Republic's demise. But it was meant to be coordinated with France's NATO allies and not to be totally independent of the Alliance as General de Gaulle later directed.

In contrast to the Fourth Republic, the motivations underlying the Fifth Republic's nuclear policy are readily discernible because of the stability of its presidential political system and the fact that for over a decade important foreign and defense policy decisions were made essentially by one man. Bureaucratic politics certainly continued during the Gaullist period, but the Élysée dominated the policy-making process in the foreign and defense fields (the *domaine réservé*), often to the extent of informing ministries after decisions had been made instead of seeking their views and discussing their recommendations at cabinet meetings. The influence of parliament and public opinion on de Gaulle's foreign and security policies was minimal, although many of the president's decisions and initiatives were the object of lively debate in the National Assembly and the press.

A project closely supervised by General de Gaulle himself, the nuclear striking force was not an ordinary weapons program. It went far beyond defense. Although no single Gaullist document or pronouncement entirely revealed the general's philosophy on the nuclear force, its rationale can be pieced together from comments scattered throughout the speeches of de Gaulle and his official spokesmen. It must be viewed in the overall context of Gaullist foreign policy perspectives. For the nuclear force was intrinsically related to the general's political goals of ensuring France's independence and augmenting France's freedom of action in world affairs.

The preceding themes relating to the change in motivations behind the nuclear policies of the Fourth and Fifth Republics are treated in the first two parts of the book. Part I reviews the period of the Fourth Republic and the early years of the Fifth Republic, during which the Gaullist nuclear force was conceived. Particular attention is paid to external factors and the diplomatic setting that faced General de Gaulle. In Part II the various assumptions of and justifications for the *force de dissuasion*—political-diplomatic, military-strategic, and economic-technological—are analyzed, as is the force's relationship to Gaullist foreign policy. An effort is made to assess the rate of development of the French force during de Gaulle's tenure and to estimate the financial costs. Considered especially in this connection is the impact of France's economic crisis of 1968 on the French nuclear program. The effects of the Soviet invasion of Czechoslovakia on the force's role and utility in Gaullist foreign policy are also discussed.

Implications of the French nuclear deterrent and Gaullist independent strategy for alliance politics in the West are assessed in Part III. Over the past decade questions of nuclear strategy have taken on enormous political significance and have appeared to exert considerable influence on relationships within the Atlantic alliance, notably among the United States, Great Britain, France, and the Federal Republic of Germany. Nuclear issues have divided France from her three principal alliance partners, and the resulting discord has been especially great in her relationship with America.

The task of this section is to evaluate the impact of the *force de dissuasion* on France's relations with the United

States, and hence with NATO, since those two relationships were so intermeshed. Likewise, we shall investigate the role played by nuclear questions in Franco-German relations in the context of European integration efforts, and in French-British relations as a corollary issue to British entry into the European Communities. Two kinds of conclusions emerge. First, nuclear weapons and questions about their control or their use have not been the real source of the irritation or estrangement that has frequently plagued France's recent relations with her principal European and Atlantic partners. Moreover, they were not the fundamental cause of France's withdrawal from NATO in 1966. Rather, French disagreements on defense and security issues were rooted in more basic political differences, in large part explained by de Gaulle's ambitious foreign policy objectives in the European and Atlantic arena. Discord over nuclear issues merely served to amplify already existing political divergences.

A second conclusion from Part III concerns the measure of success or failure of Gaullist nuclear policy. Here there are short-run and long-run problems involved and the author's findings are necessarily more tentative, since final judgment must be based on history which has yet to unfold. In the period under review it would appear that de Gaulle's independent nuclear policy had more failures than successes in relation to the general's overall foreign policy goals. Indeed, it tended mainly to isolate France. Seen in a long-run perspective, however, a French nuclear capability does give France important political cards in the future organization of Europe. De Gaulle's insistence on European independence during the period of his rule may have increased France's—and Europe's—political leverage and influence in the longer term.

These points are discussed in the concluding chapter, which also considers the prospects for French nuclear armament in the period after de Gaulle. The key factors that will most immediately determine these prospects are the defense and nuclear policies adopted by the government of Georges Pompidou; possible French-British nuclear co-operation following likely British entry into the European Community; and developments in superpower weapons technology and arms control.

ONE

THE BACKGROUND

1 · *The Nuclear Program of the Fourth Republic*

A FEW months after his return to power in 1958, General Charles de Gaulle declared in one of his first press conferences: "Everybody knows that we now have the means of providing ourselves with nuclear weapons and the day is approaching when we, in our turn, will carry out tests." He went on to indicate that, while the United States, the Soviet Union, and Great Britain possessed atomic arms, "France will not accept a position of chronic and overwhelming inferiority." The message was clear—that France would soon become an atomic power and would then have "all the greater means at her disposal for making her action felt in fields that are precious and useful to all mankind: those of world security and disarmament."[1]

General de Gaulle could not have uttered these words with any assurance, nor would France have achieved her first atomic explosion a year and some months later, in early 1960, had it not been for the extensive program of atomic research carried out under the Fourth Republic. Indeed, this program provided the foundation for the French nuclear strike force, or *force de frappe*, developed later under de Gaulle—a politico-military instrument destined to become a symbol of the independent policies of the Fifth Republic and to have considerable impact on France's relations with her allies. In order to put that development in perspective, it will be useful first to review the history of France's atomic program under the Fourth Republic.[2]

[1] Press conference of Premier Charles de Gaulle, Paris, October 23, 1958, *Major Addresses, Statements and Press Conferences of General Charles de Gaulle, May 19, 1958–January 31, 1964* (New York: Ambassade de France, Service de presse et d'information, 1964), pp. 27-28.

[2] This subject is best described in Lawrence Scheinman, *Atomic Energy Policy in France Under the Fourth Republic* (Princeton:

Later in this chapter the motivations behind the military nuclear program will be considered, as will the extent of thinking about nuclear strategy under the Fourth Republic and the origins of the idea of a *force de frappe*.

THE FOURTH REPUBLIC'S ATOMIC POLICY

France's entrance into the postwar atomic field dates from October 18, 1945, when General de Gaulle as president of the provisional government issued an ordinance establishing an atomic energy agency: the Commissariat à l'énergie atomique (hereafter referred to as CEA). This agency was entrusted "with the mission of developing the uses of atomic energy in various fields of science, industry, and national defense."[3] It was given considerable administrative autonomy and placed under the direct authority of the prime minister.

The founding of the CEA was not France's first experience with atomic energy. French scientists such as Henri Becquerel and the Curies had played an important role in early atomic research prior to 1900. Later, in the 1930's, the Frenchman Frédéric Joliot-Curie discovered artificial radioactivity and led research teams which worked on the neutron bombardment of uranium and the concept of a chain reaction. After the outbreak of World War II the French government acquired the entire Norwegian stock of heavy water and, from Belgium, the uranium oxide necessary to fuel an atomic device. But the fall of France cut short further progress in nuclear research. During the war a number of French atomic scientists left the country to participate in the Anglo-Canadian nuclear programs.

Princeton University Press, 1965). For general treatment by a participant-observer, see also Bertrand Goldschmidt, *L'Aventure atomique* (Paris: Arthème Fayard, 1962) and *Les Rivalités atomiques* (Paris: Arthème Fayard, 1967).

[3] *France's First Atomic Explosion*, French White Paper (New York: Ambassade de France, Service de presse et d'information, 1960), p. 5.

After the Liberation the scientist Frédéric Joliot-Curie and Raoul Dautry, who had been minister of armaments in 1940, urged General de Gaulle to reestablish an atomic energy program. At a time when France faced the immense tasks of postwar reconstruction, the economic advantages offered by atomic power as a potential energy source were probably paramount in the decision to undertake a new program. However, the military implications of atomic energy cannot have escaped de Gaulle and must have weighed heavily in his decision to establish the CEA.[4]

The history of the Fourth Republic's atomic program can be viewed in three phases. The first or *scientific* phase spanned the years 1946-52; it was a formative period concerned with acquiring the necessary atomic raw materials, training needed scientists and technicians, and building an infrastructure of basic laboratories.[5] Initial resources were few: ten tons of uranium oxide hidden in Morocco during the war, some heavy water obtained from Norway on the basis of prewar purchase rights, and the experience of the small number of French physicists and chemists who returned to France after having participated in the Anglo-Canadian wartime atomic project. Most of the British and American research and development work on the atomic bomb during the war had been kept secret and was therefore unavailable to France. Among the activities of the CEA in the early postwar years were the establishment of the Chatillon research center, where the first reactor went critical in 1948, prospecting for uranium, large deposits of which were soon discovered in metropolitan France, and initial work on the establishment of a second nuclear research center at Saclay.

Administratively the CEA was and still is headed by both an administrator-general and a scientist, who holds the post

[4] Scheinman, pp. 5-7.

[5] See Scheinman, pp. 20-57; Bertrand Goldschmidt, "The French Atomic Energy Program," *Bulletin of the Atomic Scientists* (September 1962), pp. 39-40.

of high commissioner. The dominant figure during the initial period was the high commissioner, Frédéric Joliot-Curie. These years were characterized by scientific control over the management of atomic policy and a high degree of autonomy of the CEA vis-à-vis the government. The orientation of the program, conditioned by both the peacetime circumstances and the low level of available infrastructure, was toward basic research and peaceful uses of atomic energy. This was emphasized in a government declaration delivered by M. Parodi before the United Nations in 1946; it was also the will of most of the scientists who were involved in the CEA.[6]

In 1950 Joliot-Curie was relieved of his post because of his Communist affiliations and his statements against military uses of atomic research. This led to a reorganization of the CEA in 1951. Pierre Guillaumat was appointed administrator-general, and the balance of control over atomic policies shifted from the scientists to the government administrators.

The second or *industrial* phase of the nuclear program began in 1952 with the approval by parliament of the first Five Year Plan for atomic development.[7] Under this plan the CEA budget was increased to allow for the construction of two high-power plutonium-producing reactors at Marcoule in the Rhone Valley: G_1—which went into operation in 1956, and G_2—which was completed in 1958. The plutonium from these reactors was intended primarily for use in secondary reactors to produce electrical power for propulsion, but the possibility of conversion to military purposes was clearly recognized.

In this second period French industry was mobilized to

[6] One of the interesting differences between French atomic development and that of the United States, Great Britain, and the Soviet Union is the fact that for almost a decade the French program was oriented entirely toward peaceful rather than military uses of atomic energy.

[7] Goldschmidt, "The French Atomic Energy Program," pp. 40-41; Scheinman, pp. 58-89.

move France into the business of applying atomic energy. It was a period in which atomic policy was made by the administrative elites and by scientists of more conservative political leanings. (Many of the scientists in the CEA who were Communists had been removed.) Especially dominant was the leadership of the administrator-general, Pierre Guillaumat, who served in this position for seven years. The scientist who became high commissioner, Francis Perrin, held this post until 1970. With the start of the industrial production phase, the possibility of military atomic applications was opened for France, since the quantities of fissionable material necessary for such applications would soon be at hand.

The third or *military* phase cannot be dated from a specific governmental decision or political act. Rather, it was the result of a series of incremental decisions—and the postponement of other decisions—beginning in 1954 within the French bureaucracy during a period of frequently changing governments and cabinet ministers. On April 11, 1958, just before the demise of the Fourth Republic, Premier Félix Gaillard signed the official order authorizing the manufacture of an atomic bomb and preparations for the first French atomic tests in the spring of 1960.[8] But, as Scheinman explains, this order only ratified what was already a *de facto* policy. The following passage presents the central conclusion of the Scheinman study:

> The action of responsible political leadership was the last in a long chain of events—a response to protracted internal pressure combined with the force of the external military and political environment. Guidance and direction for nuclear policy came not from the French Government or the French Parliament, but from a small, dedicated group of administrator-technocrats, politicians and military officers whose activities centered on and emanated from the CEA. This group exhorted successive

[8] *France's First Atomic Explosion*, p. 11.

governments at least to prepare the groundwork for an eventual decision to create an atomic arsenal, and their persuasiveness increased in direct proportion to the decline of French influence and prestige in the international environment.[9]

Convincing confirmation of Scheinman's analysis is found in a speech by a high French government official concerned with atomic matters, François de Rose, in November 1958, before the French War College. In discussing the background of the French nuclear program, de Rose stated that "on the political level there had been no doctrine of French nuclear armament." In his words, "the manufacture of an atomic bomb . . . wedged itself into our public life as a sort of by-product of an officially peaceful effort, there existing no overview of the problems involved, nor of the means necessary to solve them, nor of the results to be expected." De Rose termed this a "paradoxical situation," since considerable sums of money were spent on the development of nuclear arms before the government really made the decision to produce them and before that decision had been debated and approved in parliament.[10] In his posthumous memoirs, General Charles Ailleret made the same point and, given his position as a strong advocate of French atomic armament, criticized the "oscillating politicians" of the Fourth Republic for having held up the military program by not making up their minds earlier.[11]

There is not space here to trace in detail the history of military atomic policy in the last years of the Fourth Republic, but some of the main steps in this interesting development can be highlighted. The trend probably started

[9] Scheinman, p. 215.

[10] François de Rose, "Aspects politiques posés par l'armement nucléaire français," speech delivered at the Institut des hautes études de défense nationale, November 18, 1958 (Paris: Institut des hautes études de défense nationale, no. 1043), p. 3 (mimeographed).

[11] General Charles Ailleret, *L'Aventure atomique française* (Paris: Éditions Bernard Grasset, 1968), pp. 393-95.

with the first Five Year Plan for atomic energy passed in 1952. As Bertrand Goldschmidt, an important figure in the CEA over the whole postwar period, has pointed out, the 1952 plan "mentioned no eventual use of plutonium for military purposes, a decision on this subject not having been taken for several years; but it is certain that this aspect of the atomic problem was present, and *undoubtedly predominant,* in the mind of those who inspired and were responsible for the plan."[12] It was also in 1952 that a small group of army officers under the direction of Colonel Charles Ailleret, then *commandant des armes spéciales,* began preliminary studies on requirements for the development of an atomic bomb and the time it would take to achieve the first atomic explosion.[13]

The problem of military atomic applications began to be raised seriously in 1954. At the beginning of that year, the councils of National Defense held serious discussions on atomic questions. In May the minister of armed forces officially consulted the heads of the three services about an atomic national defense program. A number of projects were considered, and several military groups were set up to study them.[14]

In the public forum the issue of military atomic applications was broached for the first time in the 1954 debate on the European Defense Community (EDC), since the proposed EDC treaty contained provisions regulating the whole question of atomic weapons.[15] This issue was not the central focus of public attention, however, which was directed more to the broader questions of German rearmament and the prospective relinquishment of French sovereignty that the project would entail. France's defeat in the Indochina war also reinforced some military pressures for

[12] Goldschmidt, *L'Aventure atomique,* p. 86. (Italics added.) This and all subsequent foreign language quotations have been translated by the author, unless otherwise noted.

[13] Ailleret, p. 79ff.

[14] *France's First Atomic Explosion,* p. 8.

[15] See Scheinman, pp. 103-16.

atomic weapons. During the course of the year Colonel Charles Ailleret and other military advocates began arguing the virtues of atomic armament in a series of articles, many of which appeared in the pages of the *Revue de défense nationale*.[16] In the 1954 parliamentary debate on the military budget, the question why the budget did not include provisions even for the study of atomic weapons was seriously raised for the first time. The minister of defense, René Pleven, expressed government interest in further study of the question, recognizing the potential role of atomic weapons for France. But the most important step was the high-level consideration of the issue by the premier at the end of the year.

On December 26, 1954, the question of the military applications of atomic energy was addressed in a lengthy meeting of a cabinet-level interministerial committee convened by Premier Mendès-France. Previously, Mendès-France had put two questions to a group of atomic experts, through his secretary of state for scientific research, Henri Longchambon. The questions were: Given the existing state of French atomic development, how long would it take before France could manufacture an atomic bomb and a nuclear-powered submarine? How soon must the government make a definite decision for a military program in order to achieve the objectives stated? The answers: that it would be five years before France could possess a nuclear bomb, and that the last two years of this program "would have to be devoted exclusively to the manufacture of the bomb itself, without any benefit to research or industry."[17] With these facts in hand, the interministerial committee, which included Guillaumat and Perrin of the CEA and military

[16] As described in his book, Ailleret's writing on the subject during 1954-56 was part of a campaign to convince politicians and government officials that France should make a firm decision to mount a nuclear armament program. *L'Aventure atomique française*, pp. 151-64.

[17] Editorial by Pierre Mendès-France, *Les Cahiers de la République*, no. 24 (March–April 1960), p. 6; quoted in Scheinman, p. 112.

officers as well as cabinet members, discussed the problem. The results were not conclusive. The prime minister decided only to reserve final decision on a military atomic program for a later time, and that any studies to be undertaken would be under the direction of the CEA.[18]

With the apparent acquiescence of Mendès-France, but without an official order, the CEA proceeded anyway to lay the groundwork for a military atomic program. This was due in no small part to the special interest in military applications of the CEA administrator-general, Guillaumat; he was supported by a small group in the military services. Thus, after the Mendès-France interministerial meeting in December 1954, France began to move toward the development of an atomic bomb without official sanction, and the timetable predicted by the premier's advisers was to be accurately met.

In December 1954 also, General Albert Buchalet agreed to head a secret atomic weapons unit within the CEA, the Bureau d'études générales (BEG). Established in May 1955, this unit was to play an important role in the military program. It later became the Direction des applications militaires (DAM) in 1958.[19]

By the spring of 1955 Edgar Faure had become premier; both he and Guy Mollet, his successor, fluctuated on the military atomic issue. In March Faure first declared that France should consider making a nuclear weapon. A short time later, however, he had shifted and expressed his intent to eliminate research related to the construction of an

[18] Referring to this 1954 sequence of events during a television debate with Maurice Schumann in December, 1966, Mendès-France gave the same account of the time estimates for atomic development. However, he insisted that he was *not* "one of the fathers of the atomic bomb," that he ordered only the first phase of the program—the first three years—and that he reserved decision on the second military phase for a future time. He said that he personally was very much against the idea of a French atomic bomb, and that he had intended to propose a prohibition of atomic tests at the U.N. at the end of 1954. See text of the debate in *Le Monde*, December 7, 1966.

[19] Scheinman, pp. 116-17; *France's First Atomic Explosion*, p. 10.

atomic or hydrogen bomb. Yet on May 20, 1955, a secret protocol was signed which recorded agreement between the CEA and National Defense on a joint program for the 1955-57 period to be carried out by the CEA, to extend basic nuclear infrastructure and conduct technical research. Under the terms of the accord the Ministère des armées provided financial support for the CEA program, including construction of a third plutonium reactor; in return, the CEA agreed to produce fissionable material for later joint use and to pass on information from its study program relating to the development of a prototype weapon.[20]

This important accord suggests either that Faure was not in complete control of the situation, or that he was acquiescing to the continuation of a study program and had postponed final decision on military uses until a later date. During the Faure regime the BEG began its operations, and the French Navy transferred substantial funds to the CEA for the construction of an atomic submarine. Indeed, according to the French White Paper, "The Armed Forces budget for 1955-56 included for the first time considerable appropriations specifically assigned to the national defense atomic program."[21] Thus, a coordinated military atomic program was being launched at the same time that the government declared itself officially opposed to such a development.

A similar sequence occurred under Premier Guy Mollet when negotiations were under way concerning the establishment of Euratom. In his investiture speech in early 1956, and in a second statement soon thereafter, Mollet indicated that he favored a Euratom devoted only to peaceful purposes, exclusive Euratom ownership of all nuclear material, and a renunciation of military uses of the atom by all member states of the proposed organization. The issue of a French renunciation of the right to make nuclear weapons caused concern, especially in certain military circles

[20] *France's First Atomic Explosion*, pp. 8-9; Scheinman, pp. 122-23.
[21] *France's First Atomic Explosion*, p. 9.

and the CEA. By the time of the parliamentary debate on Euratom in July, Mollet had shifted to the position that Euratom must not in any way hamper France's right and ability to construct nuclear weapons later, if she should choose to do so. Pressures from the military and the pro-weapons cadre of the CEA had obviously been brought to bear on the Mollet government, and considerable parliamentary reaction had also had its effect.[22]

Although personally not in favor of a military atomic program, it is clear that Mollet did not hinder such a program and wanted to leave the option open for future governments. Indeed, it was under his administration that the most important steps, up to that time, were taken along the path toward development of the French atomic bomb. Some of these steps were as follows:

1. In the summer of 1956 Mollet's minister of defense, Bourgès-Maunoury, who favored atomic weapons, called an important meeting attended by top military officers, ministers, and other government administrators to hear a talk by General Pierre Gallois, one of the leading military proponents of French nuclear armament. Gallois argued that France would not always be able to rely on American nuclear protection, and he evidently advocated a one-way nuclear striking force as the most feasible kind of French deterrent (a two-way force would either require larger, more expensive planes or aerial refueling). The result of this meeting was not a final consensus, but there was recognition on the part of most of the military commanders that eventually a firm decision for or against atomic weapons would be required.[23]

[22] Scheinman, p. 136ff.

[23] The army high command was not yet decided on the question. It was still strongly influenced by the view that guerrilla wars were the most likely form of future conflict, and should therefore be given priority in military planning (the doctrine of *la guerre révolutionnaire*). There was also concern that conventional weapons not be slighted in the military budget.

2. The military bureau of the CEA, the Bureau d'études générales, continued to receive financial support from the Ministry of Armed Forces during this period and evidently grew sufficiently in size to warrant transformation from a bureau into a department. It became the Département de techniques nouvelles (DTN) in May 1956.[24]
3. Soon after the Suez crisis in the fall of 1956 a new CEA–National Defense protocol was signed, which replaced the earlier 1955 protocol and established a definite military program for the period 1957-61, inclusive. The aims of the program were enumerated and the responsibilities divided between the CEA and National Defense. According to the French White Paper:

> The Commissariat à l'Énergie Atomique was made responsible for conducting the preliminary studies for the experimental atomic explosions and for the preparation of the scientific parts of the tests; for supplying the necessary plutonium; and, in implementation of possible decisions of the Government, for making prototypes and for carrying out experimental atomic explosions. Besides, the Commissariat was made responsible for studies leading to the construction of a factory for the separation of uranium 235 (an isotope separation plant) and to the supplying of highly enriched uranium.
>
> The Armed Services were put in charge of the preparation for experiments concerning nuclear explosions.[25]

In December 1956, the Comité des applications militaires de l'énergie atomique was created, under the chairmanship of the *chef d'état-major général des armées,* General Paul Ély. It brought together the high commissioner and administrator-general of the CEA, high military officers, and technical directors to consult on joint research and

[24] *France's First Atomic Explosion,* p. 10.
[25] Ibid., p. 9.

development programs and the allocation of funds between the CEA and the armed forces.[26]

4. In 1956 also, Colonel Charles Ailleret, one of the most vocal military partisans of atomic weapons, was elevated to the rank of general and his unit, the Commandement des armes spéciales, was put in charge of studies and technical preparations for the first atomic tests. In November of that year, General Ailleret again outlined his views on a national military atomic program in an article in the *Revue de défense nationale*.[27] Much of his plan was adopted in 1957 by the État-major général.

By the end of 1956 the military atomic program was, for all intents and purposes, fully under way. An official government decision had not yet been taken, "but everything was launched as if it were already made and in a manner that, once it had become definitive, everything could proceed without loss of time."[28] In March 1957, even closer cooperation between the CEA and the armed forces was achieved through the creation of two new combined groups to prepare for nuclear tests.[29] In May, Defense Minister Bourgès-Maunoury announced a military policy based on the premise that "the new conditions of war, our adversary's possession of a substantial stock of atomic weapons . . . require that on the list of studies to be undertaken, the strategic reprisal weapon must have priority. . . ."[30] The only remaining steps were a formal government decision and the necessary budget appropriations. The French navy, meanwhile, had set up a special school in Cherbourg for atomic submariners and continued to supply funds to the

[26] Ibid., pp. 9-10; also Ailleret, p. 181; Goldschmidt, *Les Rivalités atomiques*, p. 222.

[27] General Charles Ailleret, "De l'Euratom au programme atomique nationale," *Revue de défense nationale* (November 1956), pp. 1319-27.

[28] Ailleret, *L'Aventure atomique française*, p. 181.

[29] *France's First Atomic Explosion*, pp. 10-11.

[30] *Le Monde*, May 12-13, 1957; as quoted in Scheinman, pp. 183-84.

CEA for the study of a nuclear submarine. Technical discussions between Guillaumat of the CEA and the armed services concerning problems connected with the bomb and atomic tests were increasing in number.

In July 1957, the Second Five Year Plan was presented to parliament and approved with very little discussion. Covering a variety of research and development projects relating to both defense and electricity production, this plan included important allocations of 25 billion francs to begin work on an isotope separation plant, although it was still somewhat open to question whether the plant would be national or European. This plant was crucial to the military program, and there were important CEA and military pressures behind its establishment on a national basis.[31] In July the French parliament also ratified the Euratom treaty. Care had been taken to assure that in its final form no part of the treaty limited France's right to proceed with military applications of atomic energy, and fissionable material was to be Euratom property only in the area of peaceful uses.

As can be seen from this brief account, Premier Félix Gaillard's action on April 11, 1958, ordering final efforts to prepare for the first atomic tests in the first quarter of 1960, only gave his official sanction to a program long since established as a result of a consensus reached among a number of interested subministerial groups, notably the CEA and the relevant civilian defense organs and the army. As Scheinman notes at the end of his study:

> Governments . . . were not strong enough to underwrite a military atomic policy or courageous enough to stop the trend towards a French atomic bomb which originated as early as 1952. It is vain to argue that Mendès-France, or Faure or Mollet, adopted one position or another; in truth, each of them reserved decision for a future Government while France steadily progressed toward the

[31] Scheinman, pp. 180-82.

> atomic bomb under the tutelage of the military atomic cadre . . .[32]

The nature of the political system of the Fourth Republic was most responsible for this phenomenon of indecisiveness on atomic policy. Constantly changing cabinet coalitions rendered ministers impotent and ineffective and the bureaucracy became the principal source of policy-making. However, by the time of the Gaillard decision in 1958 a general parliamentary consensus had developed in support of such an action by the government. Underlying this new broader political consensus was agreement on a combination of political and strategic requirements for France, as will be discussed in a moment.

This review should be sufficient to demonstrate that French interest in nuclear weapons and the French decision to construct an atomic bomb predate General de Gaulle. The next questions to be examined concern the motivations behind the military atomic policy of the Fourth Republic and the extent of thinking about nuclear strategy, i.e., about the *mode d'emploi* of the bomb that was under development.

Motivations and Incentives

The motivations behind the military nuclear policy that had developed by the end of the Fourth Republic are somewhat difficult to assess, in view of the covert nature of the process by which this policy was formulated and the fact that the groups responsible operated largely outside directly accountable government and parliamentary circles. It is not easy to weigh the influence of attitudes held in different sectors, e.g., parliamentary opinion, the press, pronouncements of government leaders, and the views of certain elements in the CEA and the military. Yet this is the task confront-

[32] Ibid., p. 210.

ing the analyst. As will be explained, the motives of those responsible for the initial elaboration of this policy were a complex mixture of political, military, and economic-technological factors.

An awareness of the military advantages of nuclear weapons can be traced back as early as 1952. However, the military services were never united on the question, and it was not until 1956 that the weight of military authority began to favor atomic weapons and to gain the support of cabinet ministers. The absence of an all-out military campaign for nuclear armament was rooted in the fact that France's principal military preoccupation during the mid-1950's lay in defending her colonial interests in costly wars outside Europe—first in Indochina, then in Algeria. Atomic weapons were not appropriate for these guerrilla conflicts; rather, they called for conventional weapons in large quantities, a requirement which was already straining French defense budgets. A further consideration reinforcing military doubts about the need to spend money on atomic arms in the early 1950's was the fact that France's defense needs in Europe were being adequately fulfilled by the Brussels Pact and NATO, especially the latter, which provided France with the nuclear protection of the American Strategic Air Command. Nevertheless, the foundation for the army's later interest in atomic weapons began to be laid in 1952 in studies conducted by a small group of officers headed by Colonel Charles Ailleret, then *commandant des armes spéciales.*

Ailleret became a key military protagonist for nuclear weapons in the years to follow. His memoirs confirm that his passionate interest in atomic arms was based on a rather narrow view of their military advantages as the most modern weapons. His advocacy of a nuclear program did not emerge from notions of nuclear strategy, with which he simply did not concern himself (beyond a rudimentary concept of proportional deterrence).[33]

[33] Ailleret, *L'Aventure atomique française*, passim.

Ailleret argued that nuclear weapons were cheaper than the equivalent amount of conventional explosives and far more effective on the battlefield. In his own mind he had reflected on the tactical advantages of nuclear arms much more thoroughly than on their strategic or political implications. Nevertheless, he was aware that nuclear armament would allow France "to assert herself with much more weight in alliances" and would also give France distinct military superiority over Germany, where he had been a prisoner of war.[34]

It is interesting to note his clear expression of the latter point, which must have been important in the minds of many Fourth Republic supporters of nuclear weapons, yet seldom received public expression.

> But for someone like me who had been in the Resistance, then at Buchenwald, there was always the risk that Germany would become again one day, at the sound of music, the people who suddenly start to impose their domination on the rest of the world by conquest and, to begin with, their neighbors. If France had some atomic arms and the means of delivering them, she would be protected from the terrible experiences of 1914 and 1940. It is in large part with this thought in mind that I have fought in order that France constitute this effective umbrella against the storms coming regularly from the other side of our eastern frontiers.[35]

Although recognizing the postwar decline of hostility in Franco-German relations, he nevertheless saw protection against the uncertainty of future German policies in French nuclear arms.

Other arguments offered by Ailleret for an atomic weapons program included its benefits for civilian science and technology, a point often disputed by scientist opponents. He also believed atomic armament was becoming a requirement for great powers, and that it would contribute to,

[34] Ibid., p. 114. [35] Ibid.

rather than undermine, world peace. Beginning in 1954, Ailleret and his colleagues defended their ideas in numerous articles, as already noted.[36]

Although ardent military advocates of atomic weapons were few in number, there can be little doubt that the prolific writings of Ailleret—the leader of this group—must have had influence in the years which followed. His persuasiveness was surely enhanced by the adoption of a NATO strategy in December 1954, calling for a tactical nuclear response to conventional aggression in Europe.[37] By 1956, Bourgès-Maunoury, speaking as minister of defense, had clearly accepted Ailleret's thesis at the time of the Euratom debate: "A number of years hence . . . an army not vested with atomic weapons will be an outmoded force. . . . The option which we face is not between classic weapons and nuclear arms, but between the possession of the latter and the abandonment of the national defense. . . ."[38]

Increasing interest in nuclear arms on the part of some army circles can also be traced to changes in French military doctrine. After the war in Indochina there emerged a theory of revolutionary warfare which saw the principal Russian threat to the West as a kind of outflanking movement via Asia, Africa, and Latin America, rather than a

[36] See General Ailleret's book *L'Aventure atomique française*, pp. 151ff., for an account of his motivations in writing his articles, some of which are: "L'Arme atomique, arme à bon marché," *Revue de défense nationale* (October 1954), pp. 314-25; "Applications 'pacifiques' et 'militaires' de l'énergie atomique," ibid. (November 1954), pp. 421-32; "L'Arme atomique; ultima ratio des peuples," ibid. (December 1954), pp. 553-63; "L'Arme atomique, facteur de paix?" ibid. (January 1955), pp. 34-41.

[37] See Robert E. Osgood, *NATO, The Entangling Alliance* (Chicago: University of Chicago Press, 1962), pp. 116ff. Osgood says that "the principal effect of NATO's nuclear strategy upon French military policies was to intensify France's concentration upon developing a nuclear capability instead of collaborating with NATO's forces" (p. 132).

[38] *Journal officiel*, Assemblée nationale, no. 80, July 11, 1956, p. 3443, quoted in Scheinman, p. 160.

Cold War confrontation in Europe itself.[39] This theory, coupled with the army's preoccupation after 1954 with Algeria, shifted the army's primary attention away from Europe to Africa. The consequence was a relative vacuum in Europe due to the absence of forces committed there, and the conclusion (reinforced by impending German rearmament and the new NATO nuclear strategy) that this vacuum should be filled by nuclear weapons. In this manner certain elements of the air force and some military technicians became attached to the idea of a French nuclear force.[40]

A further consideration was the French army's sagging morale after the serious defeat in Indochina and the increasing difficulty of its assignment in Algeria. "The military felt seriously out of touch with the nation and unable to exercise its civil prerogatives; a genuine inferiority complex had set in."[41] This complex also extended to the military's dealings with allies in NATO, where the British, with their nuclear capability, outshadowed the French in their impact on policy-making. Some military and political authorities felt that low military morale would be bolstered by the acquisition of atomic weapons.

Concern for France's scientific and technological advancement was another motivation behind the military nuclear program of the Fourth Republic. In one sense the development of atomic energy in postwar France was part of a broader change in the importance assigned to economic progress and technological innovation.[42] Although true that

[39] For an explanation of the doctrine of *la guerre revolutionnaire*, see John Stewart Ambler, *Soldiers Against the State* (Garden City, N.Y.: Doubleday & Co., 1968), pp. 333-65; also Paul Marie de la Gorce, *The French Army* (New York: George Braziller, 1963), chs. 16, 17.

[40] Wolf Mendl, "The Background of French Nuclear Policy," *International Affairs*, XLI (January 1965), 31-32.

[41] George A. Kelly, "The Political Background of the French A-Bomb," *Orbis*, IV (Fall 1960), 293-94.

[42] For a general discussion of scientific and technological change under the Fourth Republic, see Robert Gilpin, *France in the Age of the Scientific State* (Princeton: Princeton University Press, 1968), ch. 6.

many scientists did not concur, military applications of atomic energy were undoubtedly viewed by a large number of engineers and administrator-technocrats as a natural extension of, and a benefit to, civilian atomic development. This line of reasoning is the most probable explanation of Pierre Guillaumat's intense interest in military atomics. As administrator-general of the CEA over the whole period 1952-58, Guillaumat's role in promoting military nuclear research and development and providing continuity in atomic policy at a time of governmental indecision was of capital importance. A fierce supporter of the military atomic program, he successfully retained CEA control over it, in spite of pressures from National Defense to place the program under its authority.

Guillaumat's devotion to military applications has not been publicly explained. However, his training at the École polytechnique and his experience as an engineer-administrator in the petroleum industry (he later returned to this activity and became head of France's largest petroleum combine) support the conclusion that the growth and industrialization of atomic energy in France was his first interest. But the implications of a military nuclear capability probably did not escape this astute technocrat. "Indifferent to governmental fluctuations, he had always pursued the same essential goal: the creation of a powerful national nuclear industry, the indispensable condition to allow the country to engage in civilian development but also the military phase."[43] As a confident and highly successful CEA administrator, Guillaumat may also have been driven by considerations of bureaucratic politics to preserve control over the important area of military atomic applications, as well as to succeed in its development.

As studies proceeded secretly on the development of an atomic bomb, led by the CEA and military planners, political-diplomatic factors took on increasing importance in arguments for the French nuclear effort. These factors

[43] Goldschmidt, *Les Rivalités atomiques*, p. 210.

were directly related to the growing foreign policy frustrations felt by governments of the Fourth Republic, both within NATO and in the colonial world. During the years 1954-58 France's principal foreign policy goal was the preservation of her prewar status as a great power, in spite of her internal weaknesses and lack of adequate resources.[44] Yet in the face of political *immobilisme* at home and costly and unsuccessful struggles to retain the remnants of her colonial empire abroad, France was having difficulty in achieving this objective. Forced by events into a series of withdrawals from her extra-European commitments, she simultaneously felt her influence declining with her NATO allies. Officials began to conclude that the development of a French nuclear capability would help France regain some of her lost prestige and diplomatic influence.

In the colonial area France had been forced into a series of retreats, in Indochina in 1954, at Suez in 1956, and then in Tunisia and Morocco, only to find herself embroiled in 1957-58 in a long conflict in Algeria. At the same time French and American interests in the third world began to diverge sharply, as the United States took positions in favor of movements for national independence. The result was a growing French awareness of the dangers created by excessive strategic dependence on the United States. The French defeat in the Indochina war in 1954, after negotiations had failed to obtain American military aid, helped to create an atmosphere favorable to a military atomic program, for it raised the question of the extent to which France could rely on U.S. support to defend national interests which were peculiarly French.[45] During that same year the first arguments were heard in the French parliament in favor of atomic weapons and articles began to appear in French military reviews advocating nuclear arms.

The failure of her allies to support her during the 1956

[44] See, e.g., Edgar S. Furniss, Jr., *France, Troubled Ally* (New York: Frederick A. Praeger, 1960), pp. 246-50.

[45] See Kelly, p. 287.

Suez crisis had a strong impact on French thinking; indeed, many observers cite Suez as the turning point in France's decision to "go nuclear." Although it may not have been the right one, the lesson drawn in France has been stated as follows:

> At the time of the Suez affair, the French leaders (first the government, then the parliament) came to realize to what extent France would be at the mercy of the Russians in case she were abandoned by the Americans (this despite the reassuring words of SACEUR). France either could rely on American bombs for protection (but then she would be at the mercy of the Americans in Africa and would be forced to abandon Algeria), or else, if she wished to keep Algeria, she would have to acquire atomic weapons and thus be in a position to resist Soviet pressures alone. The Suez affair clearly showed the parliament members the profound divergencies between American and French policy in the Mediterranean and Africa and the necessity of acquiring an atomic arsenal if France was not to be compelled to align her policy with that of the United States.[46]

Bertrand Goldschmidt, a CEA official, reinforces this view in his second book where he notes that France "found herself terribly alone" after Suez, just when the Algerian conflict was entering its most difficult phase. "An autonomous defense, based on national nuclear equipment, appeared to many as the only response to the defeat and the humiliation [that France had] undergone. . . . More than any other, the Mollet government, which had set itself to preparing the operation in utmost secrecy, resented the affront to which it had been subjected; its hostility to atomic

[46] Christian de la Malène and Constantin Melnik, *Attitudes of the French Parliament and Government toward Atomic Weapons*, RM-2170-RC (The Rand Corporation, Santa Monica, Calif., May 14, 1958), p. 33.

armament, a result of its European passion, was transformed immediately into a definite interest."[47]

France's declining influence within the Atlantic alliance had several causes. One was the revival of German power and influence on the Continent as a result of German rearmament and admission to NATO. In the aftermath of World War II France had sought to prevent such a revival, as she pursued her traditional policy of security and supported efforts to limit German armament and political influence. But with the evolution of East–West relations that produced the cold war and—especially after Korea—the specter of possible aggressive Soviet action in Europe, American policy intervened in support of German rearmament. The French response was to submerge Germany in European organizations in the hopes of channeling Germany's economic power and political orientation away from strictly national ends. In the military field, however, the problem was more difficult to handle. Compelled to pull out most of her ground forces assigned to NATO for service in Algeria, France's military, and hence political, position in the Alliance was steadily weakening. In security terms, atomic weapons were evoked as a way to preserve France's superiority over Germany, since the latter was denied the possibility of developing a nuclear capability under the 1954 Paris agreements.[48] However, the long-run political advantages that nuclear weapons would afford France in her efforts to preserve leadership on the Continent must have been apparent to French officials. (As will be seen later, this factor continued to play an important, though unstated, role in the reasoning behind the nuclear policy of the Fifth Republic.)

A persisting Anglo-American special relationship in deci-

[47] Goldschmidt, *Les Rivalités atomiques*, pp. 221-22. See also C. L. Sulzberger's article, "Where the Trouble Started," *New York Times*, Paris ed., July 27, 1966.

[48] See Kelly, p. 293; Mendl, pp. 33-34.

sion-making and nuclear matters was a second cause of France's diminished status in the Alliance, and one about which French leaders became increasingly indignant. France began to view NATO as an Anglo-American show. The success of Great Britain in obtaining special treatment from the United States in the area of nuclear sharing by 1956 (as illustrated by the "*Nautilus* affair") was a particularly sensitive point with the French, since they failed to gain similar access to American atomic secrets.[49] France saw herself becoming a second-class ally. This discrimination spurred French efforts to become a nuclear power. As Jacques Chaban-Delmas, then minister of national defense, noted in his press conference of November 22, 1957: "For France, for Europe to accept discrimination in the matter of weapons and especially atomic weapons would be equivalent to self-condemnation to permanent decadence."[50]

A similar point was made by Premier Félix Gaillard just a few months before he issued the final order to prepare for the first French atomic test:

> If in the division of tasks within NATO in research and manufacture, and if, in the precise conditions of use of these arms, France has the feeling of being treated as a subordinate partner, it is evident that this will lead France much more easily to undertake her own effort. Such an effort would not be undertaken if France were to find herself in practice on a footing of equality in the interdependence which has been approved in principle by the NATO conference.

The premier then went on to describe France's intention to proceed with Germany and Italy in the formation of a Eu-

[49] See, e.g., Harold L. Nieburg, *Nuclear Secrecy and Foreign Policy* (Washington, D.C.: Public Affairs Press, 1964), pp. 166-70.

[50] *Revue militaire d'information*, no. 287 (December 1957), p. 77, as quoted in Scheinman, pp. 188-89. See also the comment of Maurice Schumann in "France and Germany in the New Europe," *Foreign Affairs*, XLI (October 1962), 75-76.

ropean consortium, to be discussed in the next chapter, "so that they can benefit from a position of equality in NATO."[51]

Furthermore, there were French misgivings about the degree of American domination of NATO affairs and the American monopoly of key positions in the NATO staff. As one analyst wrote: "Under his [General Norstad's] reign, SHAPE has become largely what the man on the street thinks it is: an American *état-major* . . . The important decisions and the most vital information remain in American hands."[52]

Toward the end of the Fourth Republic a strategic development which amplified the aforementioned political arguments for developing French nuclear arms was the ending of the American monopoly of nuclear weapons and means of delivery. As long as the United States possessed a preponderant nuclear advantage over Russia, France had felt confident of the protection of the American umbrella for her security in Europe. When Russia acquired long-range bombers that could reach the United States, the credibility of the American commitment to defend Europe against a Soviet attack with nuclear reprisals began to be questioned. But it was the launching of the Soviet Sputnik in October of 1957 that seriously raised the issue of the validity of the American promise. For the first time it became clear that Russia could threaten the territory of the United States with intercontinental missiles. This strategic shift stimulated further French thoughts about the need for an independent French nuclear force which could trigger the American nuclear arsenal, and thus reestablish a stable balance of deterrence in Europe.

One influential analyst, Jacques Vernant (secretary-general of the Centre d'études de politique étrangère), com-

[51] Interview with Robert Kleiman, *U.S. News and World Report*, January 3, 1958, p. 63. See also Furniss, pp. 248-50; Osgood, pp. 218-19.

[52] Jean Planchais, *Le Malaise de l'armée* (Paris: Plon, 1958), p. 53.

mented as follows on the passing of the "massive retaliation" advantage the West had enjoyed in the days when it held an edge over the Soviet Union in the ability to deliver nuclear reprisals: "From the day when this superiority disappears, when American territory tends to become as vulnerable as Soviet territory, the menace of this reprisal becomes less convincing for the adversary."[53] Vernant continued:

> European anxiety can be explained and justified by the fact that the use of the weapon which guarantees the integrity of European territory is controlled by the United States, and secondarily by Great Britain, two powers which are not—at least the former—European. Thence proceeds the idea that the situation would be fundamentally modified if the European powers themselves, individually or collectively, held high-powered atomic arms for the discouragement of aggression; an aggressor would then be better persuaded of the inevitable use of these weapons by those powers whose integrity had been violated.[54]

Generals Pierre Gallois and Paul Stehlin, among other French observers, were thinking similar thoughts.[55]

Parallel to this strategic development was the influence felt in France of the British White Paper issued in the spring of 1957 (even before Sputnik), a document which concluded there was no effective way to defend Great Britain except by a British nuclear deterrent. An indication of the French reaction can be found in the following passage from a 1958 speech by François de Rose, an official of the

[53] Jacques Vernant, "Stratégie et politique à l'âge atomique," *Revue de défense nationale* (May 1958), p. 859.

[54] Ibid., p. 861.

[55] See, e.g., General Gallois' "Les Conséquences stratégiques et politiques des armes nouvelles," *Politique étrangère*, no. 2 (1958), pp. 167-80; General Stehlin, "Réalités stratégiques en 1939 et vingt ans après," *Revue de défense nationale* (May 1959), pp. 749-62.

Quai d'Orsay, where he reviewed the history of the French nuclear program:

> The publication of the White Paper demonstrated that the British effort, above all a political effort and an effort for prestige with the aim among other things of reestablishing the privileged cooperation with the United States which had existed during the war, responded in 1957 to a *military necessity.* The intervention of the U.S. being no longer certain, England had to have at her disposal the means of strategic reprisal, in the event that she should be threatened by nuclear annihilation.
>
> For France this was the moment when more and more vigorous pressures intervened on the part of political and military elements in order that a decision be taken to produce the atomic weapon.[56]

To summarize, the fact that there was no one French "decision" to undertake a military nuclear program, but rather a cumulation of small "decisions" by many different subcabinet officials in the atomic policy process before Premier Gaillard's final governmental commitment in 1958, renders difficult the task of judgment on the weight of particular motivations at particular times. As the reader has seen, a combination of political, economic-technological, and military-strategic considerations led the Fourth Republic to lay the basis for the production and testing of nuclear arms.

When by 1958 a government consensus on the question had finally emerged, the political arguments in favor of developing atomic weapons appeared paramount in the minds of political leaders. Although military factors may have motivated a small group of officers to press for atomic armament as early as 1952, their influence at the time on cabinet ministers and parliamentary deputies was small. Although their voices had greater effect later, it was the evolution of the international situation in the middle and late 1950's that

[56] François de Rose, "Aspects politiques des problèmes posés par l'armement nucléaire français," p. 6. (Italics added.)

brought the question to the fore in the high councils of government, as France sought to compensate for her diplomatic isolation and her successive defeats in colonial conflicts. The development of a French nuclear capability was seen primarily as a way to preserve France's status and respect as a front-rank ally within the Atlantic alliance, along with Great Britain and the United States, the other atomic powers. Military incentives were supplemental, rather than central, factors in the government's final choice.

In this conclusion the author shares the view of Lawrence Scheinman, although the question of nuclear incentives was not at the center of his analysis.[57] A corroborative statement by two French authors underscores the importance of political considerations for nuclear armament in the French parliament by the spring of 1958.

> . . . the question of the utility of an atomic arsenal from the strictly military point of view has never been examined. The currents in favor of an atomic arsenal have been motivated by diplomatic concerns far more than by purely military interest. . . .
>
> There is no doubt that the motive of the trend toward nuclear armament in France has been, not "to produce a modern and powerful army," but "to make France politically respected," "to enable France to carry on an independent policy." The causal relationship between the two has been forgotten. Vague notions of power not directly related to military affairs also enter into the picture, and notions of prestige as well. . . .[58]

There is a further important point, central to the argument of this study. As stated by Maurice Schumann, who held important posts in several Fourth Republic governments, "The decision to provide France with atomic weapons was first taken by governments that firmly believed in

[57] Scheinman, pp. xxiii-xxiv, 218-19.

[58] De la Malène and Melnik, pp. 66-67.

the Atlantic alliance and favored European integration."[59] In spite of France's declining influence with her allies and her grievances concerning the organization and operation of NATO affairs, French governments at the end of the Fourth Republic continued to base their foreign and defense policies on participation in the Western alliance. The preceding statements by Premier Félix Gaillard also confirm this point, which was amplified in an interview he gave the author shortly before his death in a boating accident in 1970. France still relied on NATO for her security against any possible Soviet aggression in Europe, even if this appeared less likely in 1958 than in 1950, and most French military officers were loyal to the NATO framework.[60] France's weakened condition offered her no alternative. She also saw in NATO an effective instrument for the containment of West Germany, since all German forces were integrated into NATO structures.

French governments did hope, of course, for changes in the Alliance. Even before Suez, suggestions had been made to broaden the scope of NATO to allow the formation of common Western strategy against Communist threats in Asia, the Middle East, and Africa.[61] It was hoped that discrimination against France could be rectified—especially in nuclear matters—by France's acquisition of a nuclear arsenal. And France did want less dependence on the United States than she had had up to 1958. But in none of these cases did France make her future participation in Al-

[59] Schumann, p. 75. He became, of course, foreign minister in the first post-de Gaulle government of President Georges Pompidou.

[60] The point was emphasized in several interviews with military officers who held important posts in this period. It is confirmed by John Stewart Ambler in his book, cited, p. 301, and by Paul Marie de la Gorce, cited, pp. 527ff.; the latter makes the point that many officers of the *guerre révolutionnaire* school supported the overall strengthening of the West against Communism and therefore favored strengthening the Atlantic alliance along with maintaining French Algeria.

[61] See Furniss, pp. 278-81.

liance activities contingent upon the fulfillment of demands for reform.[62] Rather, France looked forward to exerting greater influence in the councils of the West after she had surmounted the Algerian crisis and could turn her full attention once more to Europe. It was in this context, i.e., of strengthening France's role in the Alliance, that the idea of a French nuclear striking force, or *force de frappe*, originated in the last years before the Fourth Republic's demise.

Origins of the Idea of a Force de Frappe

The need for more modern weapons and the advantages—both political and military—associated with nuclear arms were becoming accepted ideas by the end of the Fourth Republic. But the strategic implications of the atomic weapon were not generally understood, much less discussed. Yet it is interesting to note that a start was made in this area by certain secret military planning groups which began to address the question of *mode d'emploi* of the bomb that was being developed and basic ideas of deterrence strategy that might govern its use.

In 1956 when General Paul Ély returned to France after service in Indochina, to become *chef d'état-major général* for the second time, he established a committee to study strategic questions and nuclear weapons. Out of these studies emerged the idea that a French national nuclear force could augment the amount of deterrence (dissuasion) available to France and the West by increasing the number of nuclear centers of decision in the Alliance, thus multiplying the uncertainty facing an enemy contemplating an attack. Such a force would remain in the context of the Atlantic alliance and would be a part of NATO's nuclear capability. But, at a time when the American pledge to defend

[62] It should be noted, of course, that some Gaullists—especially Michel Debré—were already espousing a doctrine of strict national control over future French atomic weapons. See Guy de Carmoy, *Les Politiques étrangères de la France, 1944-1966* (Paris: La Table Ronde, 1967), pp. 62, 71.

Europe was becoming less certain as a result of Soviet gains in intercontinental nuclear capability, a French nuclear force would, it was thought, reinforce the deterrent balance by allowing less room for errors in judgment by the Soviet adversary on the extent of the American commitment to European defense. A French force, albeit a small one, could bring nuclear weapons immediately to bear to counter a Soviet attack. This would increase the stakes involved and force the Soviet Union to face the possibility of a larger nuclear conflict from which the United States could not hold itself aloof.[63]

An article published in 1957 gave a glimpse of what General Ély had in mind. He argued that France had to be able to act militarily anywhere in the world, to meet a threat wherever it should occur; that she should possess a flexible structure of forces for different kinds of conflict; and, thirdly, that she must possess a means of atomic retaliation, which would be placed "fully within the military framework of NATO." In proposing a threefold organization of French forces which presaged remarkably the scheme adopted by de Gaulle's government in 1960, Ély listed first a *capacité de dissuasion*, to consist primarily of a strategic air force, missiles, and nuclear submarines.[64]

The term *force de frappe*—a translation from the English "strike force"—was also coined by General Ély, although he later regretted the phrase. But, as he explained to the author, it was meant to denote a broader military concept including both conventional and nuclear forces designed both to deter and to intervene in offensive or defensive missions beyond the nation's borders.[65] But sometime later the

[63] These early French thoughts on simple deterrent strategy resemble some of the more theoretical concepts developed later in the 1960's by General André Beaufre.

[64] General Ély, "Notre Politique militaire," *Revue de défense nationale* (July 1957), pp. 1040-47.

[65] Interview with General Ély, Paris, September 28, 1966. That General Ély first used the term was also confirmed by another interview source.

term entered the vocabulary of the press and the politicians, referring to the idea of a French nuclear deterrent, even though because of its ambiguities it was quickly dropped by military circles in favor of *force de dissuasion* (the literal translation of "deterrent force") or *force nucléaire stratégique* (which became the official designation of the French deterrent). However, the phrase *force de frappe* continues to be used in public discussion, despite its offensive rather than deterrent connotation.

In addition to General Ély, the idea of a nuclear force was promoted by certain officers in the French air force (called the "Young Turks" by one French general reflecting on that period). Among this group were Generals Maurice Challe and Paul Stehlin. Other military officials who favored it included Generals Jouhaud, Lavaud, and Buchalet. It is probably correct to say that the first real nuclear strategist in France was General (then Colonel) Pierre M. Gallois, whose lectures to military groups and writings during the 1956-58 period undoubtedly had influence. He was the first person to think broadly about the general strategic and political consequences of nuclear weapons.

In late 1956, as a result of the studies previously mentioned, two actions were taken by the *chef d'état-major général* in preparation for development of a French nuclear force. The first was a decision to begin research work on a long-range missile program, although it was recognized that France was starting with little technological know-how in the missile field and that the road would be a long one unless foreign help could be enlisted. A second decision was made to proceed with the construction of the first prototype Mirage IV aircraft, a plane which, it was hoped, would fill the gap in a future nuclear arsenal until such time as missiles would be ready. The Mirage IV was envisaged primarily as a tactical aircraft in 1956, although with a nuclear capability; only later under the Fifth Republic was consideration given to extending its range to allow long-range strategic nuclear missions.[66]

[66] The prototype Mirage IV plane was first flown in 1959.

Although its precise form had yet to be determined, Defense Minister Bourgès-Maunoury and his advisers decided in the spring of 1957 to create a nuclear force. Militarily, such a force would keep France abreast of the technology of modern warfare. Politically, it would allow her to continue as a great power, to make her voice heard vis-à-vis both her enemies and her allies. Most important, it would enable France to meet her commitments in the Atlantic alliance.[67] Those military officers concerned with nuclear arms were deeply committed to the Alliance and envisaged a French nuclear force coordinated closely in NATO with other allied nuclear forces. This was also the general thinking of political leaders at the end of the Fourth Republic who favored the development of French atomic armament, but who had not yet had to focus on exactly how it would be employed. Both groups sought to enhance France's role in the Alliance and accepted the NATO framework.

As will become clear in later chapters, the nuclear force actually developed under the Fifth Republic of General de Gaulle was to have a substantially different orientation. It became a highly political instrument at the service of independent Gaullist foreign policy outside the Atlantic alliance system. Indeed, it was used by de Gaulle in his efforts to change that system, and, when that failed, to undermine it by withdrawing France from NATO's military structures. In this respect, then, de Gaulle's *force de frappe* was a fundamental departure from the thinking of the French leaders at the end of the Fourth Republic who started France down the nuclear path.

[67] Claude Delmas, "La France et sa défense nationale," *Revue de défense nationale* (October 1957), pp. 1446-48.

2. *From the Fourth to the Fifth Republic*

THE DIPLOMATIC SETTING, DE GAULLE'S TRIPARTITE PROPOSAL, AND THE NUCLEAR ISSUE IN 1958

ON May 13, 1958, a demonstration in Algiers unleashed events which brought about the downfall of the Fourth Republic, as Algerian settlers and certain military officers conspired against the government in Paris to keep Algeria French. After two weeks of political turbulence, General de Gaulle was installed as prime minister of an interim government on June 1. To him fell the task of designing a new constitution and constructing a new republic.

Although faced with the enormous problems of restructuring France's political system and settling the Algerian conflict, de Gaulle found time almost immediately after his return to power to deal with issues of defense and foreign relations. These were areas where he had long held a keen interest and had already formulated many of his own ideas, as a reading of his memoirs will attest. During his first few months in office de Gaulle moved quickly to define his nuclear policy and his position on NATO and the Atlantic alliance. As this chapter will demonstrate, his views on France's political-strategic relations with her Western allies, anchored in his vision of an independent global role for France and equal status with the Anglo-Saxon powers, were considerably bolder and more far-reaching than those held by the leaders of the Fourth Republic. Before describing de Gaulle's first steps in nuclear diplomacy toward the West, it will be useful to review the diplomatic setting he inherited from the Fourth Republic, which provided the context for his early decisions on nuclear policy and alliance relations.

The Diplomatic Setting upon de Gaulle's Return to Power

In the year before de Gaulle's return to power, France had joined with Germany in two major new efforts toward European integration. The treaties establishing the European Common Market and Euratom were signed in Rome on March 25, 1957; they were ratified later in the year by the six member countries and came into force in January 1958. France had insisted on modifying a clause in an earlier draft of the Euratom treaty that would have required her to renounce fabrication of atomic weapons. The final Euratom treaty placed no restrictions on the French military nuclear program.

The year 1957 also saw two important strategic developments to which we have already alluded. The publication of the White Paper on defense in April had ushered in a "new look" in British defense policy focused on the construction of a nuclear deterrent and the reduction of British conventional forces stationed on the Continent. In support of this policy the government contended that, given limited British resources, it was an economic necessity to concentrate on the building of the nuclear deterrent to prevent war rather than on maintaining a conventional capability to wage war if the deterrent failed. But British Defense Minister Duncan Sandys also stressed the strategic factor, arguing that a British nuclear force was necessary to reinforce overall deterrence as the United States became more vulnerable to direct Soviet attack and developed long-range, intercontinental missiles, making her less dependent on European bases. However, in February 1958, the British retreated from military-strategic arguments and came to justify their nuclear striking force entirely on political grounds in terms of national prestige and diplomatic influence. Prime Minister Macmillan said in a television interview at that time:

> The independent (nuclear) contribution gives us a better position in the world, it gives us a better position with

> respect to the United States. It puts us where we ought to be, in the position of a great power. The fact that we have it makes the United States pay a greater regard to our point of view, and that is of great importance.[1]

Meanwhile, Great Britain had already exploded her first hydrogen bomb on Christmas Island in the Pacific on May 15, 1957.

The second strategic development was the launching of the first Soviet Sputnik on October 4, marking the beginning of the intercontinental missile and space age. This event became the symbol of a new strategic era in East–West relations, since American territory would soon be vulnerable to direct Soviet missile attack. The new potential of Soviet military power raised anxieties about future Soviet intentions toward the Western alliance.

Later in the same month, on October 25, President Eisenhower and Prime Minister Macmillan issued a lengthy "Declaration of Common Purpose" after talks in Washington that must have appeared in the eyes of French observers to reincarnate the close Anglo-American wartime partnership. The declaration spoke of several common tasks, one of which was to "regard our possession of nuclear weapons power as a trust for the defense of the free world." Another paragraph stated that the U.S. president would request the Congress to amend the Atomic Energy Act of 1946 (the McMahon Act) to enable a closer nuclear cooperation between Great Britain, the United States, "and other friendly countries."[2]

Although the 1946 Atomic Energy Act had ended the special wartime Anglo-American cooperation in atomic matters so as to protect America's atomic monopoly, in fact Great Britain had already reestablished her privileged position

[1] *The Times* (London), February 24, 1958, p. 3; as cited in Robert E. Osgood, *NATO, The Entangling Alliance* (Chicago: University of Chicago Press, 1962), p. 243.

[2] Paul E. Zinner, ed., *Documents on American Foreign Relations, 1957-58* (New York: Harper and Brothers, 1959), pp. 132-36.

by receiving American nuclear assistance under the amendments to the McMahon Act in 1954. The atomic policy provision in the Eisenhower-Macmillan declaration led to the presentation of new McMahon Act amendments to the Congress in the spring of 1958. After approval by the Congress and the president, these amendments became law on July 2; they authorized the transfer of technical information and material help for the manufacture of nuclear devices to countries that had already made "substantial progress in the development of atomic weapons."[3] In spite of the reference to possible cooperation with "other friendly countries" in the 1957 Anglo-American declaration, the 1958 amendments served to perpetuate discriminatory treatment in favor of Great Britain. Only Britain met the legal requirements set forth in the amendments, and it was clear that the Congress—especially the Joint Committee on Atomic Energy (JCAE)—did not intend to extend nuclear cooperation later to other countries.[4]

On July 3, 1958, a British-American Agreement for Cooperation on the Uses of Atomic Energy for Mutual De-

[3] See U.S. Congress, House, *Amendment to the Atomic Energy Act of 1954, As Amended,* 85th Cong., 2nd sess., June 5, 1958, H. Report no. 1849 to accompany H.R. 12716, written by Mr. Durham of the JCAE. The JCAE was responsible for inserting the language of the "substantial progress" clause into the AEC draft language of the amendments. It is interesting to note the Committee's interpretation of that clause: "With regard to the words 'substantial progress' in the second proviso of subsection 91c (4) it is intended that the cooperating nation must have achieved considerably more than a mere theoretical knowledge of atomic-weapons design, or the testing of a limited number of atomic weapons. It is intended that the cooperating nation must have achieved a capability on its own of fabricating a variety of atomic weapons, and constructed and operated the necessary facilities, including weapons research and development laboratories, weapon-manufacturing facilities, a weapon-testing station, and trained personnel to operate each of these facilities" (p. 12).

The report also indicates the Joint Committee's intention "that the language not be interpreted to promote or encourage the entry of additional nations into the atomic weapons field" (p. 20).

[4] See William B. Bader, *The United States and the Spread of Nuclear Weapons* (New York: Pegasus, Western Publishing Co., 1968), pp. 26-33.

fense Purposes was signed in Washington. Providing for the exchange of classified information concerning the development, fabrication, and employment of atomic weapons, it also authorized the sale to the United Kingdom of one complete nuclear submarine propulsion plant with related information concerning its design and operation, plus the necessary quantities of enriched U-235 needed to fuel the plant for a period of ten years.[5]

The provision of an American nuclear submarine engine for Great Britain was part of a broader American offer for nuclear sharing with European allies made at the NATO ministerial meeting in December 1957. At that meeting, attended by both President Eisenhower and Secretary of State Dulles, the latter announced an American plan to participate in a NATO atomic stockpile system in Europe "to assure that nuclear warheads will be readily available to NATO forces in event of hostilities." He also indicated that in order to strengthen the NATO deterrent, the United States was "prepared to make available to other NATO countries intermediate-range ballistic missiles, for deployment in accordance with the plans of SACEUR."[6] The U.S. proposal seemed to be motivated by at least two considerations: first, a desire to protect the United States against a possible "missile gap" in ICBM capabilities by placing medium-range missiles on allied soil; and second, a concomitant concern to move toward joint allied control of nuclear weapons in order to meet allied suspicions regarding the reliability of American strategic power and to head off new national nuclear forces in Europe.

At the same time Secretary Dulles had also announced the intention of the American administration to seek legislation from Congress to permit cooperation with interested NATO allies in the development of atomic submarines. Aside from Great Britain, three countries were interested

[5] See the text of the agreement in *Documents*, pp. 68-77.

[6] Statement by Secretary of State Dulles, December 16, 1957; text in *Documents*, pp. 101-102.

in the submarine offer: France, Italy, and the Netherlands. France, already at work on a submarine reactor using natural uranium, was eager to obtain the highly enriched uranium fuel used in American submarines. Thus, the French government of Premier Gaillard had quickly begun negotiations with the United States to obtain an agreement.[7]

On the matter of the IRBM proposal, however, France and other European allies had doubts and objections about the placement of missiles on their soil. For this reason, the NATO communiqué could express no more than agreement in principle. Only Britain and Turkey were willing to accept missiles under this arrangement. In February 1958, the U.S. Government went ahead to sign an agreement providing for the supply of IRBMs (Thor missiles) to Britain, to be controlled by a "double-veto" arrangement.[8] (Later, in 1959 and 1960, agreements were negotiated with Italy and Turkey to establish batteries of Thor and Jupiter missiles in those countries.)

As for France, Defense Minister Jacques Chaban-Delmas had "reserved" the question of installing allied missiles on French soil. The issue was linked to the receipt of American assistance for the French nuclear weapons program, a possibility of much interest to his government. An interagency debate was already shaping up in Washington on this question, and certain elements in the Pentagon and the State Department favored assistance. The French government appeared ready for a deal. Conversations were initiated with American defense officials regarding nuclear aid. According to one source, the French even requested purchase rights for the guidance system of the Polaris missile. France also wanted to share in the decision to fire any American

[7] See Harold L. Nieburg, *Nuclear Secrecy and Foreign Policy* (Washington, D.C.: Public Affairs Press, 1964), p. 141.

[8] See the texts of the exchange of Notes between the U.S. and the U.K., February 22, 1958, in *Documents*, pp. 65-68. In fact, this establishment of missiles in Great Britain had already been agreed to in principle by the president and the prime minister at their meeting in Bermuda in March 1957.

missiles stationed on French soil. Negotiations continued with the United States but did not resolve any of these issues.[9] This is where the matter stood when General de Gaulle came to power; it became one of the first items on his diplomatic agenda.

The 1957-58 Franco-German "Nuclear Flirtation"

Another immediate policy decision facing de Gaulle upon his accession was whether or not to continue diplomatic efforts initiated by the last governments of the Fourth Republic toward European cooperation on armaments production, including nuclear weapons. The issue had been raised especially in the context of possible cooperation with the Federal Republic of Germany. Not all the details of this episode are known, but the evidence that is available, plus interview information, are enough to confirm the existence of this Franco-German "nuclear flirtation," a controversial affair which may prove to be an important precedent for future developments.

As early as 1955 France had approached Germany regarding possible collaboration on the construction of an isotope separation plant to produce enriched uranium, which has both civilian and military atomic applications. But the Messina conference in June of that year interrupted these preliminary negotiations and transferred the issue to a European scale.[10] During 1956 and 1957 France pressed for acceptance of an isotope separation plant as a common European project during the Euratom negotiations, primarily for financial reasons, but the other European part-

[9] The request for the Polaris guidance system was turned down. See John Newhouse, *De Gaulle and the Anglo-Saxons* (New York: The Viking Press, 1970), pp. 21-25, for a discussion of these questions; also *New York Times*, January 24 and February 8, 1958.

[10] Lawrence Scheinman, *Atomic Energy Policy in France Under the Fourth Republic* (Princeton: Princeton University Press, 1965), pp. 176-77.

ners lost interest in the idea, especially after the United States offered U-235 for sale at cheaper prices.[11] Thus, the French made a "decision in principle" to construct a national isotope separation plant and budgeted accordingly in the Second Five Year Plan passed in July 1957. But even then the question of a possible European project had not been finally settled, and an interim committee of the new Euratom organization was still examining the question, with French support.[12]

Against this background rumors circulated in 1957 about Franco-German nuclear cooperation, for which the basis had reportedly been laid in January talks between German Defense Minister Franz-Josef Strauss and his French counterpart, Maurice Bourgès-Manoury.[13] Accompanied by General Heusinger and a delegation of advisers, Strauss had extended discussions with the French defense minister in Paris and then toured French military installations, including the rocket test center at Colomb-Béchar in the Sahara. The result of these talks was a series of accords on Franco-German cooperation in the development and production of "modern weapons." A permanent expert committee was also set up, and it was decided that the Bonn government should have the "right of recourse" to the French military research center at Saint-Louis in Alsace. Reports soon followed that France had or would soon obtain German financial and technical assistance for joint atomic development on French soil. Although no details of these accords are available, they were probably only "exploratory" in nature.

[11] See Goldschmidt, *L'Aventure atomique*, pp. 131-32.

[12] *Scheinman*, pp. 181-82.

[13] *Frankfurter Allgemeine Zeitung*, January 16, 1957, and Edmund Taylor, "The Powerhouse of German Defense," *The Reporter*, April 18, 1957, pp. 25-27, as cited in Catherine Kelleher, "German Nuclear Dilemmas, 1955-1965" (M.I.T. doctoral diss., 1967, on the development of German attitudes and policy on nuclear weapons, now being revised for publication). The following summary of the 1957-58 episode relies heavily on Catherine Kelleher's dissertation, unless otherwise cited.

In subsequent comments Strauss indicated that any talk of European atomic production was "premature," but that such a project was not "excluded" from the Franco-German program. He emphasized that Germany would stand by its 1954 obligation not to produce atomic weapons, but issued the reminder that the 1954 declaration did not prohibit participation in nuclear research. It was also possible that the Federal Republic might one day construct "elements" of atomic missiles under some sort of WEU control arrangement.[14]

The French then issued a general call for increased European military cooperation in November 1957. Jacques Chaban-Delmas, the new defense minister, made contact with his Italian counterpart, Tarrani, and then with Strauss on the possibility of a "significant activation and expansion" of the earlier Franco-German accords. The French proposal called for a pooling in all spheres of armament production, which implied also atomic armament.[15] Chaban-Delmas was apparently motivated by a desire to secure economic and technical assistance for the French nuclear weapons program. The issue was postponed, however, until after the December NATO ministerial meeting because of German hesitation about French intentions and general uncertainty concerning the American position on the sharing of nuclear and other weapons. Another reason for the postponement of the French proposal for a French-Italian-German (F-I-G) pool was to allow use of the "threat" of a European consortium as a lever to extract concessions from the United States.

After the NATO meeting French premier Gaillard commented on the proposed F-I-G pool, indicating that the three nations had not yet gone beyond an "agreement in principle." He confirmed, however, that joint atomic development was being considered:

[14] See Kelleher for a more detailed discussion.
[15] See, e.g., *Le Monde*, December 14, 1957, as cited in Kelleher.

The three countries are ready to pool their efforts to a certain extent on research and manufacture of arms so that they can benefit from a position of equality in NATO . . . Germany can contribute scientific cooperation or certain manufactures not in themselves nuclear but which enter into the construction of atomic missiles.[16]

In late January 1958, the three defense ministers met in Bonn and formally announced the F-I-G agreement. It included "common development, production, and standardization of weapons," and was reportedly reached with "the knowledge and approval of the NATO allies."[17] Emphasis was to be placed first on cooperation in the area of short-range rocket systems and vehicles for ground forces, including a new European tank. Joint efforts in the field of nuclear weapons received no mention. Subsequently, Chaban-Delmas indicated that the question of possible F-I-G atomic production was, for the moment, "reserved."[18] It seemed that only German hesitation was holding up broader cooperation in this area.

Rumors continued to circulate throughout the spring, especially on the subject of German intentions. These were fed by several ambiguous statements from Strauss.[19] When

[16] Interview with Premier Félix Gaillard, "Plain Talk by France and the United States on World Problems," *U.S. News and World Report*, January 3, 1958, pp. 60-63.

[17] See the *New York Times*, January 22, 1958; cited in Kelleher.

[18] *New York Times*, January 24, 1958.

[19] In a controversial interview with the British socialist leader, Richard Crossman, Strauss was quoted as saying: "We [meaning the West German government] have nothing to do with the French H-bomb." He also reiterated that West Germany does not have the right to fabricate nuclear arms, nor the desire to possess such arms or to control those tactical nuclear weapons in Germany in American hands. "But," he continued, "I must warn you that this situation cannot continue indefinitely" (*New Statesman*, April 12, 1958, pp. 460-62). Later, in a portion of the same interview published elsewhere, but denied by Strauss, the German defense minister reportedly said: "I can guarantee that for three, four, or even five years there will be no German nuclear weapons. After that, however, if other states, espe-

on March 25, 1958, the German government was faced with questions from the SPD opposition in the Bundestag on the subject of the F-I-G tripartite accords and the extent of Franco-German military cooperation, it simply did not answer.[20]

In early April a second meeting of the three F-I-G defense ministers was held in Rome. The communiqué indicated agreement on the desirability of further talks, and a short time later a list of joint conventional armament projects was presented.[21] This is about where the matter stood at the time of de Gaulle's accession; a willingness had been expressed to harmonize national plans in the matter of armaments production, but the actual modes of cooperation had not been hammered out.

There were signs, however, that Franco-German discussions were proceeding at a more rapid pace. During the course of the April F-I-G talks, and at other times during March, April, and May, Strauss met with his French counterpart, Chaban-Delmas, to pursue further the possibilities of Franco-German military cooperation. The exact content of their conversations remained a guarded secret even to other members of their governments, and the only record of the talks is reported to be the personal notes left by the men themselves in their respective defense ministries. According to one account by a person who must have been involved on the French side, the last meeting took place on May 13, 1958, and examined the possibility of "extensive cooperation in all kinds of armaments." West Germany was

cially France, produce their own atomic bombs, Germany could also be inspired to do the same" (*Daily Mirror*, April 2, 1958). Gerald Freund asserts in his book that Strauss told him approximately the same thing at about the same time. See *Germany Between Two Worlds* (New York: Harcourt, Brace and Co., 1961), pp. 154-55.

[20] See Nicole Deney, *Bombe atomique française et opinion publique internationale*, series C, no. 6 (Paris: Fondation nationale des sciences politiques, Centre d'étude des relations internationales, 1962), pp. 85-86.

[21] *Frankfurter Allgemeine Zeitung*, April 5, 1958, and *The Times* (London), April 16, 1958; as cited in Kelleher.

considering a variety of decisions relating to future weapons production, and French industry was particularly interested in cooperation—presumably in order to expand its export market.[22] According to another source, the French proposed that West German capital, researchers, and technology be associated with the construction of the French atomic bomb. That source also revealed that Strauss and Chaban-Delmas had already signed an accord on March 31, 1958, under which the Bonn government agreed to invest several million deutschmarks in the military research institute at Saint-Louis in Alsace and to pay half of the operating costs, in return for sharing the results of the research program.[23]

Interviews conducted by the author with both French and German officials confirm that Franco-German conversations did indeed take place on French initiative concerning possible West German financial and technical contributions to the "common production of nuclear weapons." Potential German access to these weapons for use in case of crisis was presumably touched on, although this aspect remained unclear. The talks, however, did not proceed beyond an exploratory stage. Although the two defense ministers had intended to pursue the matter further, they were cautioned by their foreign offices and political leaders that the question of possible nuclear cooperation was sensitive and premature.[24] Of the two participants themselves,

[22] General Paul Stehlin, *Retour à zero—l'Europe et sa défense dans le compte à rebours* (Paris: Robert Laffont, 1968), pp. 229-30.

[23] *Der Spiegel*, August 26, 1959, pp. 17-18. The French institute at Saint-Louis had taken on some German scientists after World War II. Contrary to many rumors after the 1958 Franco-German accord, the institute's research was reported to be limited to conventional weapons and to ballistic studies on small rockets.

[24] Support for the existence of a substantial "agreement in principle" between the French and German defense ministries on nuclear cooperation can be found in several articles by C. L. Sulzberger. See, e.g., the *New York Times* on November 16, 1964, where he mentions a secret agreement that promised German access to French weaponry in exchange for financial and technical help; also his articles on November 21, 1964, November 17, 1965, and July 27, 1966.

Chaban-Delmas has—to the knowledge of this writer—maintained complete silence on the whole affair; Strauss has been more outspoken but cautious and not always consistent.[25]

As Catherine Kelleher points out, the Franco-German discussions at the end of the Fourth Republic did not progress very far because of some basic uncertainties on both sides.[26] For the French, cooperation with Germany on a matter as sensitive as nuclear arms was politically an explosive issue. Any decision would have required the mustering of a domestic political consensus. Moreover, the government in Paris still hoped for an agreement with the United States on assistance to the French nuclear program;[27] any collaboration with Bonn in this area might have impeded chances for American aid, which was even more desirable. On the German side hesitation was also present. The reasons seemed to range from lack of support by Adenauer and his advisers for any cooperation that might be opposed by the United States, to the possibility of American assistance to German nuclear research for civilian purposes (a cheaper and safer bet on which to build claims for more extensive cooperation in the future), and Strauss's apparent private conviction that American warheads would soon be transferred directly to Europe anyway. At any rate, this is where the matter rested when General de Gaulle returned to power. The possibility of cooperation with Germany

[25] Strauss said in an interview in 1966 that the focus of the 1957-58 discussions had been ". . . the use of nuclear energy in the military sphere but not for the production of weapons. In this we had two things in mind. First the development of small reactors. . . . Their purpose was not to produce fissionable material for weapons manufacture but rather . . . to provide electric energy through small reactors, similar to the way the Canadians had developed them for radar stations in the Arctic. The second thing . . . would have been the development of nuclear ship propulsion." Interview with Hans Gresmann and Theo Sommer, *Die Zeit*, April 8, 1966. This statement does not seem to correspond to all of the available evidence.

[26] See Kelleher.

[27] This point is supported by Alfred Fabré-Luce, *Le Monde*, December 5, 1959.

(and other European countries) was an option he had to consider in his approach to future French nuclear weapons development; the groundwork had already been laid if he desired to explore further that course of action.

General de Gaulle's First Steps in Nuclear Diplomacy

De Gaulle's basic foreign policy attitudes had been well formed by June 1958. They were readily discernible from his wartime actions as leader of the Free French resistance, his early writings and the two published volumes of his war memoirs, and from his statements during the years of his political "retirement" at Colombey-les-deux-Eglises.[28] The general's concern for the prestige and international political standing of his country was already legend from World War II. His aspirations for France are best summarized in his own words: "La France n'est réellement elle-même qu'au premier rang . . . la France ne peut être la France sans la grandeur."[29]

For some time de Gaulle had been hostile to NATO and dissatisfied with France's position in the Atlantic alliance. Indeed, he is reported to have said just a few months before his return to power:

> I would quit NATO if I were running France. NATO is against our independence and our interest. Our membership in NATO is said to be for the reason of protecting France against a Russian attack. But I don't believe that the Russians will attack at this time. . . . NATO is no longer an alliance. It is a subordination. . . . After France has

[28] Particularly important among de Gaulle's early writings is *Le Fil de l'épée*, published during the 1930's, in which he reveals his philosophy of leadership. The English translation is *The Edge of the Sword* (London: Faber & Faber, 1961). For an interesting account of de Gaulle's wartime diplomacy, see Milton Viorst, *Hostile Allies* (New York: Macmillan, 1965).

[29] *Mémoires de guerre*, I, *L'Appel* (Paris: Plon, 1954), 5.

regained her independence, perhaps she will be linked with the Western countries in formal alliances. . . . But we cannot accept a superior, like the United States, to be responsible for us.[30]

The quality of French national defense had been a subject close to de Gaulle's heart since his days as a young colonel in the 1930's. In one of his early books, he had written critically of French strategy and advocated the concept of a mobile striking force based on fast moving armored vehicles and a highly trained professional army corps.[31] His postwar statements on NATO had emphasized the political significance, and therefore the necessity of a "national" defense, even when coordinated with allies. Not much is known about the general's early views on nuclear weapons. His desire that France become a nuclear power was manifest from his founding role in the CEA in 1945. Later in a press conference in 1954 he suggested that he had supported the CEA in order to provide France with atomic weapons. He also revealed his sensitivity to the political importance of French nuclear development when he spoke of France's mission to promote "coexistence between the two blocs" in order to save the world from the cataclysm of nuclear war. To further that goal, France, in his view, had to become "an atomic power" and possess a system of defense which, although associated with that of her allies, would be "autonomous" and "balanced" (*équilibré*). In the same press conference, de Gaulle complained of France's excessive dependence on the United States for defense and asserted that French governments "had not demanded for France her part in plans and decisions concerning atomic war."[32]

Whether or not de Gaulle had specific ideas in June 1958,

[30] Interview with C. L. Sulzberger, February 20, 1958, as quoted in Sulzberger's book, *The Last of the Giants* (New York: Macmillan, 1970), pp. 61-62.

[31] *Vers l'armée de métier* (Paris: Éditions Berger-Lerrault, 1934).

[32] *Le Monde*, April 9, 1954; *New York Times*, April 8, 1954.

about the kind of nuclear force he envisaged to deploy French atomic bombs, still two years from reality, is uncertain. But the notion of a deterrent or strike force would seem a logical extension of his earlier thinking about mobile, armored tank units in the 1930's and his perception of the political implications of nuclear weapons, as hinted in his 1954 press conference.

At any rate, de Gaulle turned his attention to atomic questions soon after he assumed office. During his first few weeks he reviewed the state of the French atomic program, to which he gave his full support. On July 22, 1958, he formally reaffirmed the decision made by Premier Gaillard in April, authorizing preparations for the first French atomic test in early 1960.[33] But before doing so, de Gaulle considered the question of possible collaboration with West Germany in the nuclear field and the prospects for American atomic assistance. Presumably he was briefed both on the Strauss–Chaban-Delmas conversations of 1957-58 and on the new amendments to the U.S. McMahon Act, which favored atomic aid to Great Britain and not to France.[34]

When told of the F-I-G discussions and the bilateral Franco-German talks, the general immediately rejected the option of West German collaboration in the French nuclear weapons program. According to one interview respondent, a high government official close to the situation at the time, de Gaulle had not even bothered to study the matter; the

[33] *France's First Atomic Explosion*, French White Paper (New York: Ambassade de France, Service de presse et d'information, 1960), p. 11.

[34] According to Richard Goold-Adams, de Gaulle approached Washington almost immediately after his accession to power "with the request that the administration should intervene with Congress, in order to have the amendments to the 1954 Atomic Energy Act altered in France's favor." But Ambassador Alphand had then reported that the Senate and House of Representatives had already passed the amendments, which were awaiting presidential signature. Thus, Dulles had to explain the situation to de Gaulle, after the new laws had been signed by President Eisenhower, during his visit to Paris on July 5. See *John Foster Dulles: A Reappraisal* (New York: Appleton-Century-Crofts, 1962), p. 269.

official was indignant at the way the general simply issued a flat "no." Undoubtedly he was moved by a firm conviction that French nuclear weapons had to be exclusively "national" in their command and control, in order to enhance the national *grandeur* of France, and that Germany should be given no role in military nuclear technology. As will be seen later, this decision against any nuclear sharing with Germany remained de Gaulle's policy throughout his presidency.

The decision against any Franco-German cooperation on nuclear weapons was communicated to Strauss during his visit to Paris in July, ostensibly for the inspection of the Mirage III plane.[35] Strauss saw Pierre Guillaumat, then French minister of defense, and also General de Gaulle himself. It was made clear to the German defense minister that future military cooperation with Germany would extend only to the sphere of conventional armament.[36]

Having discarded the "German option," General de Gaulle was nevertheless interested in obtaining assistance from the United States to accelerate the French atomic effort. He discussed this question in an important meeting with Secretary of State Dulles in Paris on July 5. A few days before this encounter (on July 2) the 1958 amendments to the McMahon Act were signed by President Eisenhower in Washington and the Anglo-American bi-

[35] Kelleher; also Stehlin, pp. 229-30.

[36] Of the written accounts previously cited, Sulzberger, Fabré-Luce, and *Der Spiegel* agree with French and German officials interviewed by Catherine Kelleher and myself that it was General de Gaulle personally who administered the final blow to the 1957-58 Franco-German nuclear flirtation.

One question which might logically be posed regarding this episode is how Chaban-Delmas, a "Gaullist," could have gone so far in the direction of collaboration with Germany against the apparent wishes of his "chief." The answer is probably that the general was not in close contact with Chaban-Delmas during this period, since de Gaulle scorned "Gaullists" who participated in the governments of the Fourth Republic. Apparently Chaban-Delmas was forgiven, however, since he became an important official in the new Republic as president of the National Assembly.

lateral agreement on atomic cooperation had been concluded, which—as already described—provided for new favored treatment of Great Britain in the area of atomic weapons secrets. The discriminatory nature of the McMahon Act amendments and the new bilateral agreement with Britain did not go unnoticed in the French press, which suggested that de Gaulle should claim equal treatment when Secretary of State Dulles visited Paris.[37]

Secretary Dulles was himself aware of French feelings. He said at a news conference a few days before his departure:

> I have no doubt that will be one of the topics of our discussion at that time and that General de Gaulle will want to have an exposition as to the impact of these amendments on possible exchanges of information with the French. I hope to be able to give him such an explanation.[38]

The secretary's "talking points," which he drafted himself, reveal that the explanation he was prepared to give de Gaulle was highly negative, and that any earlier intentions Eisenhower and Dulles may have had to share nuclear secrets with allies other than the British had been shelved. After explaining to Dulles that he planned to proceed with the development of French nuclear weapons with or without American help, the general then asked whether the United States would be willing to assist France in this area. In response Secretary Dulles must have told the French leader that the Atomic Energy Act did not give the American government authority to extend assistance directly to the French nuclear weapons program. The secretary's explanation presumably included the following points:

> The United States would have no objection to France becoming a nuclear power, if the nuclear race would stop

[37] See, e.g., Roger Massip in *Le Figaro*, July 5-6, 1958; *L'Information*, July 5, 1958; *La Croix*, July 4, 1958.

[38] *Department of State Bulletin*, 39, no. 995 (July 21, 1958), 109.

> there. . . . We did not encourage or help the U.K. nuclear program, believing that if each allied nation seeks independently to develop itself into a nuclear power, there would be bankruptcy everywhere and no real strength anywhere. . . .
>
> We believe that the utmost importance should be given to trying to devise a system which will assure that the free world will have adequate and dependable nuclear capacity both in terms of quantity and quality, and do this on terms that would deny nuclear power where it might be subject to possible irresponsible use.[39]

What Dulles did suggest to de Gaulle was that the United States might assist France in building a nuclear submarine-propulsion reactor and provide enriched uranium fuel.[40]

The de Gaulle–Dulles meeting marks a major turning point toward deterioration in Franco-American relations. It is probably the only time when the general personally raised the question of American nuclear assistance to France with an American official. In the spring of 1966 Premier Georges Pompidou referred with obvious bitterness to this exchange in a debate before the National Assembly on France's withdrawal from NATO. Replying to an assertion by René Pleven that France, after having constituted a nuclear force, could have asked the United States

[39] *Dulles Papers*, Category IX, Conference Dossiers, Special Subjects, dated June 30, 1958, as quoted in Bader, p. 34. This quotation clearly implies an American view that French nuclear weapons might be subject to possible "irresponsible use."

[40] See the *New York Times*, July 6, 1958, p. 1; also Osgood, p. 226; Nieburg, pp. 184, 189-90. France was interested by this offer of help in the area of submarine propulsion. However, when it was made public, opposition developed in Congress and at the Pentagon to the Dulles plan. Senator Clinton P. Anderson let it be known he was opposed to the Dulles offer on grounds that the stability of the French government was still unproved and the French might be tempted to use an atomic submarine for military ventures in Africa. As an important member of the JCAE, he promised to mobilize the Congress against such assistance to France.

for nuclear assistance under the McMahon Act, as Britain had done, Pompidou said:

> That is no longer politics, but wishful thinking. You will excuse me if I give the Assembly some precise details. I will mention a simple personal recollection. I happened to be present at a meeting during which this kind of question was raised, between General de Gaulle and M. Foster Dulles in—remember this date—June 1958. [Actually, it was July.] I will say simply that I came away with the firm and definite conviction, not without some surprise —I had your naïve innocence, M. Pleven—that never would the American leaders ever permit the subject to be raised. Since that time I have never had occasion to change this view.[41]

A second important area where the de Gaulle–Dulles meeting marked the divergence of French and American views was NATO and the Atlantic alliance. On the issue of stationing NATO atomic stockpiles and IRBMs on French soil, de Gaulle declined the American offer made in December 1957 (which Britain had already accepted under a dual control arrangement). "He emphasized that nuclear weapons could be located in France only under French control and disposition, could be used in accordance with NATO plans provided France had the same plans, and that this required an arrangement at the summit for French participation in planning for world security and armament."[42] In this manner the general broached the subject that was to become the focus of his famous September 1958 letter and

[41] Speech before the National Assembly, *Journal officiel*, Débats parlementaires, Assemblée nationale, April 21, 1966, p. 813.

[42] "Statement of the Department of State Recording the Events Surrounding General de Gaulle's 'Directorate' Proposal of 1958 and the U.S. Response to It," transmitted to Senator Jackson, August 11, 1966, in U.S. Congress, Senate Subcommittee on National Security and International Operations of the Committee on Government Operations, *Hearings, The Atlantic Alliance*, 89th Cong., 2nd sess., 1966, p. 228. (Hereafter this document will be referred to as "Statement of the Department of State, 1966.")

memorandum to President Eisenhower, to which we will return in a moment—his desire that NATO be transformed through the establishment of a Franco-British-American grouping at the highest level to plan world strategy and security policy.

According to David Schoenbrun, who first published details of the de Gaulle–Dulles meeting, based on private conversations with Dulles, de Gaulle's desire to elevate France's alliance status and participate with the Anglo-Saxon powers in summit planning on world security was motivated by at least two reasons: that France had worldwide interests and responsibilities and was therefore different from other continental powers, and that the French people, torn in spirit and morale by defeat in Indochina and the Algerian rebellion, "have the need to believe in themselves and the right to believe in themselves." De Gaulle is reported to have told Dulles that at the crucial moment of strain brought on by the liquidation of the French Empire in Africa, "there is nothing more important for the French people than to be made to believe again that France is a great power."[43] Dulles expressed understanding for de Gaulle's concern about the French people, but warned him that Germany and Italy might not accept his efforts to set up France in a superior position in the Atlantic alliance. In effect, Dulles told the general that any formalized French role in Western global strategic planning was unrealistic.[44] This conversation portended severe disagreement between France and the United States in the months and years to come.

Undiscouraged by the resistance of the American secretary of state, de Gaulle formulated his strategy on this question in the ensuing months. The emergence of a major crisis in the Middle East provided new arguments. In the

[43] As quoted in David Schoenbrum, *The Three Lives of Charles de Gaulle* (New York: Atheneum, 1965), p. 293.

[44] See also George W. Ball, *The Discipline of Power* (Boston: Little, Brown and Co., 1968), pp. 128-29.

aftermath of a military coup in Iraq, President Eisenhower ordered the landing of American marines in Lebanon in mid-July and two days later British paratroopers went into Jordan to bolster the regime of King Hussein. International tension mounted in the face of threats of Soviet intervention, and the United Nations Security Council went into continuous sessions. Although warned by Dulles in early July about the tense situation in the Middle East and the possibility of an American intervention, de Gaulle felt he had been "informed" rather than "consulted" about American plans for the oncoming crisis. In the wake of these events the general sent his foreign minister, Couve de Murville, on exploratory visits to Rome and Bonn for consultations which must have included soundings on his plans for the Alliance. De Gaulle then met with Chancellor Adenauer for the first time on September 14 at Colombey-les-deux-Églises.

The French president seized the opportunity of this meeting to win Adenauer's confidence and support. From the general's standpoint, it was an immensely successful encounter. He completely captured the West German leader. In his memoirs Adenauer revealed satisfaction at finding de Gaulle to be very frank and not a nationalist, as he had been described in the press. The two men had a most friendly and wide-ranging exchange of views. They agreed on the importance of increased Franco-German cooperation as the basis for European unity and on the need to reform NATO to strengthen Europe's position vis-à-vis the United States. In return for a promise of regular French consultations with West Germany, de Gaulle skillfully gained Adenauer's assent for an expanded French role in extra-European problems and matters of worldwide security.[45] With this firm indication of German support, the general then went

[45] Konrad Adenauer, *Erinnerungen, 1955-1959* (Stuttgart: Deutsche Verlags-Anstalt, 1967), pp. 424-36. For de Gaulle's account of this meeting, see Charles de Gaulle, *Mémoires d'espoir: Le Renouveau, 1958-1962* (Paris: Plon, 1970), pp. 184-90.

ahead to send his famous letter and memorandum to President Eisenhower and Prime Minister Macmillan a few days later.

The September 1958 Memorandum

The de Gaulle Memorandum dated September 17, 1958, is the basic document of the first phase of the general's policy toward the United States and NATO. Taken together with subsequent exchanges, the Memorandum underlay Franco-American disagreements until the early 1960's. Although the text remains secret, most—if not all—of its substance has been revealed. In order to understand de Gaulle's alliance policy and his views on nuclear force, it is essential to examine its main points and arguments.[46]

The document sent by General de Gaulle to President Eisenhower consisted of two parts.[47] The first part was a personal letter to Eisenhower in which the general said that events subsequent to his talks with Secretary of State Dulles in July had "served to affirm certain views" which were described in the attached "memorandum," the second part of the document. De Gaulle assured Eisenhower of his personal esteem, but expressed concern about the mutual problems facing France and the United States and the difficulties he saw in the functioning of the Alliance.

The "memorandum" was sent as an attachment to the letter, evidently to ensure that it be considered an official gov-

[46] The following summary of the letter and memorandum is based on these accounts by writers who have had access to the document: David Schoenbrun, pp. 295-300; James Reston, "Why the U.S. and de Gaulle Have Disagreed," *New York Times*, May 1 and 3, 1964; André Fontaine, "Un Memorandum 'connu' mais non 'publié,'" *Le Monde*, October 28, 1960. It is corroborated by the summary issued by the U.S. State Department. See the "Statement of the Department of State, 1966," p. 228.

[47] For a long time the date was believed to be September 24, 1958. Later it was revealed that the document was dated September 17. The question remains open, however, as to whether it was sent immediately, or whether it was held up—perhaps until September 24.

ernment-to-government communication by a succeeding president of the United States. (Eisenhower was nearing the end of his term of office.) It first reviewed the crises of the previous summer in the Middle East and the Formosa Straits (the latter crisis erupted when Communist China began shelling Quemoy in late August), observing that there had been a danger of an explosion into general war. De Gaulle contended that these events had demonstrated the risks incurred by France as an ally of the United States, since the North Atlantic Treaty pledged joint action by all members if one were attacked. Decisions taken by the United States which could lead to hostilities anywhere in the world were therefore of concern to its allies. In this connection, de Gaulle expressed his dissatisfaction with the structure of NATO, an organization he saw as too limited in its geographic scope in view of the global nature of the Communist menace.

Further, the general complained about the dispersed and often contradictory actions taken by NATO members outside the NATO area, and also about the fact that only two powers in the Alliance (the United States and Great Britain) were evidently "qualified" to take major decisions on global security problems. France, in his opinion, did not benefit from sufficient advance information and consultation regarding these Anglo-Saxon decisions in many areas of the world. Moreover, he continued, "France is a power with worldwide interests and responsibilities," in addition to being an ally whose own security could be vitally affected by American actions. After a difficult period of postwar recovery, France, argued de Gaulle, was now ready in 1958 to assume once again "its historic role in world affairs."

The thrust of de Gaulle's contention was that France no longer accepted an exclusive American or Anglo-Saxon authority to make vital decisions on free world defense. In his view, it would be more realistic to create a tripartite organization to take "joint decisions" on global problems. The general therefore proposed "l'organisation d'une direction anglo-franco-américaine de l'alliance occidentale,"[48] capable of elaborating political and military strategy for all the free world and, if necessary, of taking the decision to use nuclear weapons. He further suggested the constitution of combined commands for operational theaters throughout the world on the pattern of World War II. The point about nuclear weapons was especially important, since it meant that France demanded, in effect, a veto right over the use of Anglo-Saxon nuclear weapons. De Gaulle did agree that if the United States, Britain, or France were attacked directly, they could use any weapons in retaliation, but short of that the United States should not use nuclear arms in any other situation unless France and Britain concurred.[49]

Finally, and most important, de Gaulle declared that France would "subordinate" her participation in NATO to the "recognition of French worldwide interests" and "equal participation" by France in global strategy. This meant that France's subsequent cooperation in NATO would depend upon acceptance of de Gaulle's demands for a formal tripartite organization to elaborate world security policy. De Gaulle went further and suggested that, if necessary, he would propose a revision of the North Atlantic Treaty.[50]

[48] As quoted by Fontaine.

[49] The sharing of atomic secrets was not specifically mentioned in the document, but it was certainly implied. See the discussion which follows.

[50] There has been disagreement about the relationship of de Gaulle's proposed tripartite organization to NATO and the Atlantic alliance. According to some sources, an earlier draft of the Memorandum linked the proposed organization directly to NATO and may even have mentioned revision of the NATO Standing Group. Advisers to the French president are said to have warned him, however, that such an arrangement would probably raise trouble with other NATO allies, so the final draft was vaguer on this point. It does seem clear, though, that what de Gaulle intended was a triumvirate grouping at the highest level to make strategy and security policy for the entire world, *including* the NATO area. But the emphasis was on arrangements for the non-NATO areas.

The Memorandum ended with an appeal for tripartite consultations on his proposals.

For many years the French encouraged the belief that the United States did not reply to de Gaulle's September 1958 Memorandum, and this myth contributed to considerable Franco-American misunderstanding. The truth is that President Eisenhower did respond on October 20, 1958.[51] Eisenhower agreed with the French leader that the threat to the free world was global in scope, but explained that the United States had already recognized this fact and adapted policies to meet it through a series of bilateral and regional defense pacts, in only two of which both France and the United States were present (NATO and SEATO). He defended previous American efforts to use the NATO Council "to inform or consult with our allies on the threat facing the free world in the Far East and the Middle East." At the same time he admitted the need for continual improvement in the "habit of consultation."

De Gaulle's principal demand that a tripartite organization be set up at the summit to evolve security policy on a global scale was refused by the American president, who said: "We cannot afford to adopt any system which would give to our other allies, or other free world countries, the impression that basic decisions affecting their own vital interests are being made without their participation." Although acknowledging serious problems in any attempt to extend the geographical scope of NATO, Eisenhower did express a willingness to consult on how to adapt the organization to make it more useful "in the face of changing conditions."

Eisenhower's letter of reply was, however, not the end but the beginning of a long series of exchanges between the

[51] Eisenhower's response was made public in the summer of 1966 by Senator Jackson, the chairman of the Senate subcommittee on National Security and International Operations. The text of the letter from President Eisenhower to General de Gaulle, dated October 20, 1958, is annexed to the "Statement of the Department of State, 1966," pp. 230-31.

United States and France on de Gaulle's tripartite proposal. As will become clear, this dialogue remained at the center of Franco-American relations even after a new American president entered the scene.

Interpretations of de Gaulle's Tripartite Proposal and Its Relation to Nuclear Force

What was the meaning of de Gaulle's 1958 tripartite directorate proposal? Did it represent a serious foreign policy objective of the French president, or was it a tactical maneuver designed to achieve other ends? On the one hand, it can be argued that the Memorandum was merely a continuation of efforts begun by de Gaulle during the war when he tried to persuade President Roosevelt to include France as one of the three great powers of the West, along with Britain. Moreover, as several French observers have pointed out, the General's grievances regarding Anglo-Saxon domination of NATO and the organization's limited geographic scope had been felt by governments of the Fourth Republic; and many of them had substance. The idea that France ought to increase her role in Western global strategic planning had been prominent in French military circles for some time, rooted in the military doctrine of "revolutionary war" in response to a perceived worldwide Communist threat. The Lebanon and Formosa Straits crises in the summer of 1958 further supported the French case that greater consultation was needed with the United States on international crises outside Europe which conceivably could erupt into a global conflagration.[52]

[52] On these points see, e.g., René Pleven, "France in the Atlantic Community," *Foreign Affairs* (October 1959), p. 22; General Ély, "Perspectives stratégiques d'avenir," *Revue de défense nationale* (November 1958), pp. 1631ff.; André Fontaine, "What is French Policy?" *Foreign Affairs* (October 1966), pp. 65-66.

It can also be argued that de Gaulle viewed the tripartite proposal not so much as a means for coordinating Western global strategy but rather as a way to divide the world outside Europe into spheres of

Extending this line of reasoning, some observers who take the Memorandum seriously have concluded that the United States should have been more receptive to it. They tend to accept the proposition that America, by its unwillingness to consult seriously with France on sharing global power, must bear a large part of the responsibility for the disarray that ensued in the Atlantic alliance as a result of de Gaulle's subsequent intransigeance.[53]

There is, however, another interpretation that conforms more closely to the available evidence. If the general's gambit had succeeded and Eisenhower and Macmillan had granted France some kind of institutionalized global role, this would have gone far toward restoring France to the rank of a global power and giving her equal status with the Anglo-Saxons. Serious disagreements with London and Washington might have been postponed for a time, at least until the Algerian war was terminated and the general had turned to another phase in his foreign policy. But it is difficult to believe that the French leader could have held out much hope for an affirmative American response to his proposal, especially to so extravagant a demand as a veto power over the use of American nuclear weapons anywhere in the world. This, after all, was more influence on Washington than that enjoyed by Great Britain, the "privileged" American ally. The demand seems all the more preposterous when it is recalled that France had just emerged from a period of chronically unstable government under the Fourth Republic, was still bogged down in the morass of

influence. The French were particularly interested in guarding their influence in Africa. The Near East would presumably have been left mainly to Britain, and the Far East to the United States.

[53] This has been the position, for example, of Robert Kleiman in some of his writings; see "Reports Differ on U.S.–French Rift," *New York Times* (European ed.), August 29, 1966, and an editorial (presumably written by Kleiman) in the same paper on the same day; also his *Atlantic Crisis* (New York: W. W. Norton & Co., 1964), pp. 38-39, 44, 138-42. A similar argument was made by Bernard Brodie in "How Not to Lead an Alliance," *The Reporter* (March 9, 1967), pp. 18-24.

the Algerian conflict, and had not yet tested her first atomic device.

Having had extensive firsthand experience with American leaders during World War II, de Gaulle must have been well aware of the United States' reluctance to share its enormous power. Moreover, as previously noted, during his years out of office the general made no effort to conceal his negative feelings about NATO, which he regarded as an instrument to ensure American hegemony in Europe. The directorate proposal, it would appear, was in essence a tactical ploy which, once rejected by Washington and London, could then be used (as it was) to justify the general's subsequent actions reducing France's NATO participation. In the words of one French expert on de Gaulle:

> De Gaulle placed the Americans before an unceasing dilemma: either they accepted the propositions of the memorandum of September 1958, and consented to the complete transformation of the Atlantic system, or France would hold herself aloof from that system because she judged it to be a bad one and was unsuccessful in obtaining its reform.[54]

An American author, John Newhouse, has also argued this thesis:

> In establishing that London and Washington had denied France's insistence upon playing a global role, he would legitimize the tough, independent policy designed to revive and expand French influence, to free France, and thus, by his lights, restore her soul. . . . De Gaulle, in short, was setting up the context for his long-range dealings with the Anglo-Saxons.[55]

More important, this is the explanation which de Gaulle

[54] Paul Marie de la Gorce, *La France contre les empires* (Paris: Éditions Bernard Grasset, 1969), pp. 71-72. See also Guy de Carmoy, *Les Politiques étrangères de la France, 1944-1966* (Paris: La Table Ronde, 1967), pp. 332, 338.

[55] Newhouse, *De Gaulle and the Anglo-Saxons*, p. 78. Newhouse based his interpretation in part on several quotations attributed to

himself has left us. Writing in the first volume of his postwar memoirs, which appeared shortly before his death in 1970, the general confirmed that he had not expected a favorable response to his tripartite démarche, and that it was the key to his plan for a step-by-step French disengagement from NATO, an objective he had already clearly formulated in 1958.[56]

Viewing de Gaulle's directorate proposal in the context of his overall foreign policy design as later elaborated does reinforce this interpretation. Unlike the policy of the Fourth Republic, Gaullist policy was aimed at a radical revision of the European and Atlantic system. Analyzed in detail in Chapter 4, this revision was to take place in several phases. After testing the Anglo-Saxon powers with his tripartite demand, de Gaulle concentrated his later efforts on seeking a position of leadership in a loosely organized grouping of states in Western Europe, while maintaining French membership in both the Atlantic alliance and—although at a declining level—in NATO. France needed the protection of alliance defense arrangements in this second period to preserve French security in the face of a persisting hostile attitude toward Europe on the part of the Soviet Union. At the same time, however, de Gaulle's tripartite demands indicated his dissatisfaction with the prevailing system and his insistence on changing it to allow France a global role and the prestige of equal status with the United States and Great Britain. As Alfred Grosser has pointed out, the claim of "equality in the Alliance, while waiting for the world to cease being divided into two camps" was the fundamental goal of Gaullist foreign policy during this first phase of the revisionist design.[57]

---

de Gaulle but from unidentified sources, taken from J. R. Tournoux, *La Tragédie du Général* (Paris: Plon, 1967), pp. 320-22. Tournoux is a French journalist and diligent student of de Gaulle. His account portrays the general's intent in 1958-59 to lay the basis for his later withdrawal from NATO.

[56] De Gaulle, *Mémoires d'espoir*, pp. 214-15.

[57] Alfred Grosser, *La politique extérieure de la Ve République* (Paris: Seuil, 1965), p. 143.

Whether or not de Gaulle's demands for reform of the Atlantic alliance were accepted, however, the general would probably have abandoned NATO later anyway, as he did in 1966, since his European policy eventually called for the reunification of the two halves of Europe and the replacement of NATO and Atlantic defense ties with some form of all-European security system, presumably buttressed by a nascent French nuclear arsenal. His tripartite proposal was a clever tactical instrument to help justify France's eventual withdrawal from NATO (and possibly from the Atlantic alliance as well, although the 1968 Soviet invasion of Czechoslovakia and the general's resignation in 1969 foreclosed this action) under conditions of a much reduced Soviet threat in Western Europe. This disengagement from the Western alliance system was a prerequisite for the third phase of de Gaulle's foreign policy design—the pan-European vision, as will be contended later.

That France was becoming a nuclear power was an important factor in any claim de Gaulle could make for French equality with Britain and the United States in a restructured Atlantic system. The general stressed France's nuclear intentions in a press conference shortly after dispatching the Memorandum. Affirming that the day was approaching when France would test her first atomic bomb, he admonished that as long as the United States, the Soviet Union, and Great Britain continued to possess enormous stockpiles of atomic weapons, France would not accept "a position of chronic and overwhelming inferiority." Soon France would be an atomic power and would then possess the means that would strengthen her influence in world security and in discussions of arms control and disarmament.[58]

[58] Press conference of Premier Charles de Gaulle, October 23, 1958, in *Major Addresses, Statements and Press Conferences of General Charles de Gaulle, May 19, 1958–January 31, 1964* (New York: Ambassade de France, Service de presse et d'information, 1964), pp. 27-28.

The relationship of Gaullist nuclear ambitions to the general's 1958 tripartite proposal was illuminated in a speech delivered later that year at the École militaire by a high official of the Quai d'Orsay, François de Rose:

> Finally, on the level of general policy, it is probably that the realization of nuclear armament is likely to be immediately exploitable for France on the political level perhaps even before its exploitation in the field of national defense. I mean that it will perhaps facilitate our accession to this role of *codirecteur de l'alliance* which is necessary for the protection of our interests.[59]
>
> The possession of the deterrent contributes to the solution of two essential problems of a policy for national defense. It guarantees us, if the doctrine is correct, against the risk of abandonment by our stronger allies. It gives us legitimate reasons to think that we will not be drawn into a global conflict without our agreement, because it constitutes a supplementary element which justifies our participation in worldwide strategy.[60]

In his quest for equal French status with the Anglo-Saxons in 1958, de Gaulle sought a tripartite organization which would not only plot global strategy but also take "joint decisions" on the employment of nuclear weapons anywhere in the world. As clarified later, this meant a French right of veto over the use of British and American nuclear weapons, except if these nations were attacked directly.[61] If taken seriously, it is interesting to note the im-

[59] François de Rose, "Aspects Politiques posés par l'armement nucléaire français." Speech delivered at the Institut des hautes études de défense nationale, November 18, 1958 (Paris: Institut des hautes études de défense nationale, no. 1043), p. 8 (mimeographed). (Italics added.)

[60] Ibid., p. 18.

[61] According to David Schoenbrun, Secretary Dulles asked de Gaulle at his meeting with him in December 1958 about this point, and was deeply distressed by de Gaulle's demand for a veto power. Schoenbrun quotes Foreign Minister Couve de Murville as telling him in an interview at about the same time: "Yes, in effect, it does amount to

plication of this demand that France would submit to a similar allied veto over French nuclear weapons when they became a reality. In the general's view, apparently, this was the basis of fair play among great powers with equal rights.[62]

De Rose's speech is of further interest for its clarification of Gaullist attitudes toward collaboration with other countries in the nuclear field. Like de Gaulle, de Rose opposed any collaboration with West Germany which might result in German access to nuclear arms. He also rejected the alternative of a jointly controlled European nuclear force because such a force would require total political integration in Europe in order to have deterrent value and, especially, because such a force would not support French political objectives outside Europe.[63] The link between a French nuclear force and France's political aims was clearly fundamental to the whole Gaullist nuclear venture.

In his conversation with Dulles in July, de Gaulle had expressed interest in receiving nuclear assistance from the United States. This point was also implicit in the Memorandum sent to Eisenhower and Macmillan in September, as we have noted. De Rose's November speech further underscored the French desire for American nuclear aid. His extensive analysis of the 1958 amendments to the U.S. Atomic

---

a veto on the use of nuclear weapons anywhere in the world. . . . If China attacks Taiwan, America may have to strike back with atomic weapons. This could lead to world war if Russia reacts. As your allies we could be plunged into war with you, without ever having been consulted or having participated in the chain of events. Do you think this is reasonable?" (*The Three Lives of Charles de Gaulle*, p. 300.)

[62] In one of his intriguing but undocumented quotations, J. R. Tournoux quotes de Gaulle in 1959 as saying: "I do not want to hear talk of Atlantic cooperation as long as I do not have my atomic force. When I have this force, then we will combine our strategies. On the condition that the Americans give us as many rights concerning their strategy as we will give them on ours. We will deal as equals. And if they do not want to permit us to control their strategy, well, we will not permit them to control ours." (*La Tragédie du Général*, p. 320.)

[63] De Rose, pp. 13-15.

Energy Act demonstrated complete understanding that American nuclear assistance could be granted only to countries which had already made "substantial progress" in the nuclear field. Harboring no illusions about the unpredictability of the American Congress, de Rose was nevertheless enticed by the possibility of France's obtaining American atomic assistance if she could first make the necessary progress on her own.

> . . . it is certain that our effort will soon place us in a position to lay claim to this cooperation and that we are the only ones in this situation. This is an important element in the hands of the Government, an element which is the fruit of twelve years of nuclear policy.[64]

The 1958 McMahon Act amendments clearly offered an additional incentive for the French military nuclear program, rather than discouraging that program as the U.S. Congress had intended.

[64] Ibid., p. 19.

3 · *The Genesis of the Gaullist* Force de frappe *and France's Entry into the Nuclear Club*

French atomic development was accelerated from the autumn of 1958 to the end of 1960 under General de Gaulle's leadership, and culminated in the first atomic tests. In an historic speech in 1959, the French president unveiled plans for the *force de frappe*, a controversial political-military project finally passed into law a year later by the French parliament after much heated debate and the failure of several censure motions. Meanwhile, the area of Franco-American political disagreement widened as de Gaulle made several unsuccessful attempts to gain American acceptance of his 1958 tripartite plan. These differences were further exacerbated by the persistence of a special Anglo-American nuclear relationship and continuing United States reluctance to share nuclear secrets with France. This chapter, which describes these developments, focuses on the Atlantic diplomatic context from which (and into which) the *force de frappe* emerged.

On the Road to Reggane—the French Military Nuclear Program, 1958-60

"The advent of the Fifth Republic transformed the character of French atomic development by the decision of the government to give priority and the necessary funds not only to the rapid completion of the first bomb, but also to a true program of studies and, later on, to the production of perfected atomic weapons."[1] In this manner a high official of the CEA described the impact of the de Gaulle gov-

[1] Bertrand Goldschmidt, *L'Aventure atomique* (Paris: Arthème Fayard, 1962), p. 143.

ernment on the atomic program created by the Fourth Republic.

After signing a resolution on July 22, 1958, setting the target date for the first experimental atomic explosion in the first quarter of 1960, Premier de Gaulle underscored his keen interest in the military nuclear program by transferring Pierre Guillaumat, who had been administrator general of the CEA, to the post of minister of the armed forces. This led to some further administrative changes, especially in the army and the CEA. In September 1958, a new body was created at the CEA—the Direction des applications militaires (DAM). It replaced the former Département de techniques nouvelles and subsequently, in early 1959, absorbed the Section atomique previously attached to a military unit, the Direction des études et fabrications d'armement of the Ministère des armées.[2]

The main technical problems to be solved were the manufacture of the bomb and the planning and execution of tests. The CEA was responsible for the manufacture of the device, a task assigned primarily to the DAM. A second section, the Direction industrielle, was in charge of managing the Marcoule reactors and providing plutonium. The construction of the Reggane test center in the Sahara was executed by the Commandement interarmées des armes spéciales headed by General Charles Ailleret, with the cooperation of various divisions of the armed forces. The tests themselves, being of both a scientific and military nature, were jointly planned and supervised by the DAM of the CEA and the Commandement interarmées des armes spéciales through a joint body known as the Groupe mixte des expérimentations militaires. This was the general administrative structure developed to achieve the first French atomic explosion in February 1960.[3]

[2] *France's First Atomic Explosion*, French White Paper (New York: Ambassade de France, Service de presse et d'information, 1960), pp. 10-11.

[3] Ibid., pp. 11-12. For a personal account of his role as *commandant interarmées des armes spéciales*, see General Charles Ailleret,

The plutonium for the first French atomic bombs was obtained from the nuclear reactors at Marcoule, of which there were three. The first, G_1, had gone critical in January 1956, and began operation at full power later the same year. G_2 and G_3 were dual purpose reactors designed for both plutonium and electricity production. G_2 went critical in July 1958, and rose to full power in March 1959. G_3 went critical in June 1959, but did not reach full-scale operation until early in 1960. All these reactors were designed to use natural uranium and produce plutonium by a chemical extraction process.[4] Production of enriched uranium (U-235) necessary for a thermonuclear bomb as well as miniaturized tactical atomic weapons began much later in France. The decision to construct the isotope separation plant required for this endeavor was reached in July 1957, and it became a part of the Second Five Year Plan; but construction of the plant at Pierrelatte was not started until 1960.[5]

According to a former CEA official, "The years 1958-59 were a period of intense work, during which measures which had been taken earlier yielded their results. Theoretical and experimental work in nuclear physics, metallurgy, and ballistics led to the conception and finally the realization of the first experimental devices. Completely immersed in its own activities, the CEA hardly concerned itself with the military policy to which they could lead."[6]

The Diplomatic Stage for the Force de Frappe

Although President Eisenhower had essentially rejected General de Gaulle's tripartite proposal in his letter of October 20, 1958, the door was left open for further discussion

---

L'Aventure atomique française (Paris: Éditions Bernard Grasset, 1968), pp. 267ff.

4 *France's First Atomic Explosion*, p. 15.

5 See *Pierrelatte: Usine de séparation des isotopes de l'uranium* (Paris: CEA, 1964).

6 Marc de Lacoste Lareymondie, *Mirages et réalités: l'arme nucléaire française* (Paris: Éditions de la SERPE, 1964), p. 32.

of the matter. De Gaulle continued to press for acceptance of his plan; indeed, it became the dominant issue in Franco-American relations until the end of President Eisenhower's term of office in 1960, and also during the early period of the Kennedy administration.

In an apparent gesture toward de Gaulle's proposal, and in order to determine exactly what the French president had in mind, Eisenhower instructed Dulles to set up a "tripartite committee," but one below cabinet level. Dulles made arrangements for such a committee in November 1958, and two tripartite discussions were held in Washington in December 1958, with the French and British ambassadors and Deputy Undersecretary of State Robert Murphy participating.[7] At that time, French ambassador Hervé Alphand indicated that France sought joint strategic war planning on a worldwide scale by tripartite combined staffs.

Later Secretary Dulles flew to Paris for the NATO ministerial meeting and saw de Gaulle on December 15 for an exchange of views on Premier Khrushchev's November ultimatum on Berlin and the need to formulate an allied position on maintaining allied rights in that divided city. On the subject of the Washington tripartite discussions, de Gaulle told Dulles that the world situation was too critical for "playing political games with committees." The general was concerned by the absence of careful advance planning on the part of the Alliance in case of war, for example over Berlin.[8] According to the State Department account, "Secretary Dulles indicated that the United States was ready

[7] "Statement of the Department of State, 1966," p. 229; James Reston, *New York Times*, May 3, 1964; David Schoenbrun, *The Three Lives of Charles de Gaulle* (New York: Atheneum, 1965), pp. 302-303. Schoenbrun relates that Secretary Dulles had already made two moves which enraged de Gaulle, namely, the appointment of Robert Murphy as the American representative—a man who had had bitter wartime relations with the general—and subsequently his report to the Germans and Italians (who had promptly passed the information back to de Gaulle) that the committee would "discuss" de Gaulle's proposals but not "carry them out."

[8] Schoenbrun, p. 303.

for a program of consultations on problems around the world but would not go beyond an exchange of views; that it was simply not possible to establish an organic directorate either over NATO or the rest of the world."[9]

A series of tripartite discussions on African problems were held in April 1959, preceded by two conferences in February on the Far Eastern situation. All these meetings were conducted on the same level as the December talks, with the addition of military staff officers.[10] After the April talks on Africa, the United States and the United Kingdom indicated to France their willingness to continue to participate in discussions on African military questions. However, according to the State Department's account, the French government did not respond to this proposal and no further talks took place. Other accounts indicate that the French ambassador Hervé Alphand had pressed for contingency strategic planning by all three nations, which would lead to specific military plans arrived at by the respective military staffs. But this step was not agreed to by the United States.[11]

Meanwhile General de Gaulle had taken his first steps to reduce France's commitment to NATO, moved ostensibly by what he considered an unsatisfactory American response to his tripartite proposal. At the NATO meeting in December 1958, it had been revealed that France was unwilling to integrate French tactical fighter aircraft into a European air defense command, as General Norstad had requested. France continued to oppose the installation on French soil of IRBM launching sites, unless they were under complete French control. Then, on March 11, 1959, General de Gaulle notified the NATO Council that he was withdrawing French naval units previously committed to NATO's Mediterranean command in case of war. In his press conference

[9] "Statement of the Department of State," p. 229.

[10] "Statement of the Department of State," p. 229.

[11] James Reston, *New York Times*, March 3, 1964; Robert Kleiman, *New York Times*, August 29, 1966.

of March 25, he explained his action by saying that France had interests in Africa and the Middle East, i.e., outside of the defined NATO area, which she had to be prepared to defend. He therefore wished to have the French fleet available at all times for action in these areas. He went on to indicate his dissatisfaction with the principle of *integration* in the Alliance and his preference instead for a basis of *cooperation* among the great powers.[12]

On March 15 de Gaulle sent Eisenhower his second secret letter, warning the American President to stand firm against Khrushchev's maneuvering on Berlin. It repeated several themes from the September 1958 Memorandum, especially the "vital need to cooperate everywhere in the world on political, diplomatic, and strategic joint planning." The timing of his letter, coming immediately after his announcement of the withdrawal of the French Mediterranean fleet from NATO, suggested a direct link between that action and his triumvirate proposal. De Gaulle was carrying out his warning that French NATO cooperation would be reduced if his three-power directorate were not accepted.

President Eisenhower responded later the same month, stating that he attached "the greatest importance to maintaining our military posture through the fullest, closest cooperation . . . *in NATO*."[13] Eisenhower's emphasis on NATO as the instrument for allied cooperation, and his unwillingness to contemplate major changes in the organization to raise France's status, must have prompted de Gaulle's first public attack against NATO integration in his March 25 press conference. The drama was unfolding as the general had probably anticipated it would. At any rate, basic political differences about the organization of the Alliance and

[12] First press conference held by General de Gaulle as president of the French Republic, Paris, March 25, 1959, in *Major Addresses, Statements and Press Conferences of General Charles de Gaulle, May 19, 1958–January 31, 1964* (New York: Ambassade de France, Service de presse et d'information, 1964), p. 49.

[13] As cited in Schoenbrun, p. 305 (italics added); see also Reston, cited.

the sharing of American power were now dividing the United States and France.

This growing French-American disagreement over France's role was aggravated by the evolution of American policy on nuclear sharing. Nuclear discrimination was further extended in favor of Great Britain and atomic assistance refused to France—even for the development of a nuclear submarine as promised by Eisenhower in December 1957 and by Dulles in July 1958. The French were interested in the submarine offer and had sent a mission to the United States in February 1959 to negotiate. They quickly learned that American aid would be limited to the sale of enriched uranium fuel for use in a French land-based prototype submarine reactor, as confirmed in a Franco-American bilateral agreement signed on May 7 and ratified a few months later by the Congress. A French request to purchase an American nuclear submarine power plant and to receive classified information relating to nuclear submarine design was not honored because of congressional hostility toward the sharing of submarine secrets. This refusal to fulfill an earlier promise of assistance in nuclear submarine technology provoked obvious bitterness in France.[14]

The limited nature of the 1959 agreement with France was particularly clear when compared with accords reached the same year with Britain and other NATO members. An amendment to the July 1958 cooperation agreement with the United Kingdom was especially far-reaching: it provided for the transfer of all parts of nuclear weapons systems except the nuclear component itself, about which restricted design information could, however, be shared. In effect, this agreement all but integrated British nuclear weapons development with that of the United States, and

[14] See Bertrand Goldschmidt, *Les Rivalités atomiques, 1939-1966* (Paris: Arthème Fayard, 1967), pp. 242-43. Goldschmidt reveals this bitterness as follows: "The American government refused to treat France as a true partner, not only at the level of the direction of the Alliance, as General de Gaulle proposed, but even in the context of an offer made seriously by President Eisenhower" (p. 242).

it seemed to confirm once again the Anglo-American special relationship in atomic matters. One article of the accord required that information, materials, and equipment received by the British could not be transferred to a third country or to an international organization unless so authorized by the United States.

A bilateral American agreement with Canada for mutual defense purposes also covered a broad range of atomic information and material. Other agreements with West Germany, the Netherlands, Turkey, and Greece permitted the communication of certain types of nuclear weapons information for the training of military personnel and the stockpiling of these weapons in the respective countries. Such an agreement was finally signed with France, but much later —in 1961.

American nuclear policy at this time was beginning to confront the dilemma of reconciling the objective of alliance cohesion with an evolving distaste for the spread of nuclear weapons. In the aftermath of Sputnik, President Eisenhower and Secretary of State Dulles had laid the groundwork for a policy of maximum flexibility in the use of American nuclear weapons resources, which was to include sharing with France as well as Great Britain.[15] They were moved by their perception of hostile Soviet intentions toward Europe and the need to bolster NATO's defenses in the post-Sputnik period. The powerful Joint Committee on Atomic Energy of the Congress, however, had other concerns. It lacked confidence in the stability of the French government and its security arrangements, since many members of the French scientific establishment had Communist political affiliations. Moreover, its members had heard the voice of Admiral Rickover, the father of the nuclear submarine, who admonished in early 1958 that the United States should exercise extreme caution in sharing nuclear submarine data with any country other than Great

[15] See William B. Bader, *The United States and the Spread of Nuclear Weapons* (New York: Pegasus, 1968), ch. 1, passim.

Britain in order to preserve America's lead over Russia in nuclear submarine technology, America's most advanced weapons system.[16] But perhaps most important was the committee's intention, noted in the previous chapter, that the language of the 1958 McMahon Act amendments not be used to encourage other countries to become nuclear powers.

In the State Department this last point seemed to be gaining predominance among the political arguments raised against extensive nuclear sharing with France. As Philip Farley, special assistant to the secretary of state for atomic energy and disarmament, testified before the JCAE: "The bar to our cooperation with France in her own nuclear weapons development program has not been security in the French defense establishment, but has been our own national policy of not assisting fourth countries to become nuclear powers."[17]

Another factor was the bad political climate in Washington as a result of the withdrawal of the French Mediterranean fleet from NATO, as well as France's refusal to accept NATO IRBMs and atomic stockpiles on French soil without French control over their use. These "acts of infidelity" to the Alliance, coupled with de Gaulle's continuing pressure for an equal French role in tripartite political direction of NATO and extra-NATO strategy, had caused the State Department to wonder whether the tactic of nuclear submarine assistance would suffice to head off increasingly independent French policies. Ivan B. White, deputy assistant secretary of state for European affairs, commented: "In my judgment, France—the de Gaulle administration and

[16] See Harold L. Nieburg, *Nuclear Secrecy and Foreign Policy*, (Washington, D.C.: Public Affairs Press, 1964), p. 190.

[17] U.S. Congress, JCAE, Subcommittee on Agreements for Cooperation, *Agreements for Cooperation for Mutual Defense Purposes, Hearings on the Exchange of Military Information and Material with the United Kingdom, France, Canada, the Netherlands, Turkey, Greece, and the Federal Republic of Germany*, 86th Cong., 1st sess., 1959, p. 46.

General de Gaulle specifically—would not be satisfied with anything short of an agreement which would enable France to become a nuclear power."[18]

In June 1959, France announced its final decision against NATO atomic stockpiles on French territory unless French conditions were met regarding control over use of the weapons.[19] Official government spokesmen linked this position directly to General de Gaulle's earlier demands for a greater French role in Western global strategy and consultation on the use of nuclear weapons. Moreover, France remained the only important opponent of NATO plans to establish an integrated air warning and defense system for Western Europe. As a result of the French decision on the stockpile question, General Norstad resolved to transfer some two hundred American fighter-bombers with nuclear delivery capability (F-100 Super Sabres) from France to other bases in Great Britain and West Germany where atomic weapons stockpiles would be available.[20]

These developments, coupled with new French-American tension over the Algerian issue and the announcement that Premier Khrushchev would soon visit the United States, accentuated the need for a face-to-face meeting between General de Gaulle and President Eisenhower. Eisenhower visited de Gaulle in Paris on September 2 and received a warm welcome as the general's wartime comrade. Their talks ranged over a variety of subjects, including Algeria. President Eisenhower agreed to support de Gaulle's forthcoming offer of self-determination (announced in his broadcast on the future of Algeria on September 16, 1959). The two leaders had an important exchange of views on NATO and on de Gaulle's tripartite proposal, especially during their stay at Rambouillet.

According to President Eisenhower's memoirs, de Gaulle reasserted his view that NATO was no longer organized to meet worldwide defense problems, and that instead an or-

[18] Ibid., p. 9. [19] *New York Times*, June 9 and 21, 1959.
[20] Ibid., July 9, 1959.

ganization was needed to coordinate the political policies of the United States, Britain, and France in every corner of the world. Eisenhower wrote that he wanted these matters discussed in private rather than in public, so as not to antagonize other allies and neutral nations. In his view, "any attempt to organize a coalition of the 'Big Three' nations would be resented by all the others to the point that NATO itself might disintegrate. He [de Gaulle] discounted this possibility but did not seem too disturbed even at the prospect of its coming about."

Eisenhower tried to convince de Gaulle that he was ready to coordinate French and American policies around the globe, especially when the two countries had important interests at stake. He even expressed his willingness "to organize a permanent staff, representing the heads of all three governments, to look into such problems as alleged arms shipments from Tunisia to the Algerian rebels."[21] But this did not satisfy the general, who persisted in his demands for a formal three-power organizational structure at the summit where France's equal role would be visible to the world. No agreement was reached on the question.

In a general discussion of defense questions with the American president, de Gaulle had also emphasized that each nation, in the last analysis, must be responsible for its own security. In the general's view, the low morale of Frenchmen could only be boosted by national, and not multinational, organizations.

> In that spirit he [de Gaulle] had set the development of a French nuclear capability as a matter of first priority, and he seemed determined to develop all three of

[21] Dwight D. Eisenhower, *Waging Peace, 1956-1961* (Garden City, N.Y.: Doubleday and Co., 1965), p. 427. Eisenhower said later in an interview with David Schoenbrun in August 1964 that he had offered (exactly when was not specified) to set up a special tripartite staff in London, where both the U.S. and France had large embassies, with high-level political and military representatives to coordinate and plan global policies. But de Gaulle evidently did not accept this suggestion. See Schoenbrun, p. 339.

> France's armed services to an extent that the nation might be considered "in business for itself" from a military point of view.[22]

In Eisenhower's eyes this idea seemed needlessly expensive, militarily ineffective, and politically fragmenting.

The École militaire Speech

Unable to gain Eisenhower's assent to a revamping of NATO and the institutionalizing of tripartite consultation, and unwilling to compromise with him, de Gaulle launched an attack on NATO. In a major speech on November 3, 1959, at the École militaire, the general refuted the NATO tenet of "integration" and then formally unveiled his own concept of a French nuclear *force de frappe.*[23] De Gaulle began by enunciating what was to him a sacred principle: "It is necessary that the defense of France be French." To him, *national* defense was the indispensable foundation of any sovereign state, a theme he emphasized by references to appropriate periods of French history.

Starting from this premise, the general went on to say:

> . . . the concept of a war or even of a battle in which France would no longer be herself and would not act on her own accord, following her own goals, such a concept cannot be admitted. The system which is known as "integration" and which was inaugurated and even to a certain extent practiced after the great trials which we have undergone, while one believed that the free world was faced with an imminent and unlimited threat, and that

[22] Eisenhower, p. 428.

[23] Although the full text of this speech was not published by the French government at the time, it did receive extensive quotation immediately in the press. See, e.g., *Le Monde*, November 6, 1959. The text did become available in the information bulletin of the Defense Ministry on November 13.

> we had not yet recovered our national personality, *this system of integration has lived.*

The defense of France could be combined (*combinée*) with that of other countries, and French strategy could be associated (*conjugée*) with the strategy of others; "but each country must play its own part."

Having expressed these thoughts on the system of NATO integration, de Gaulle then explained how the defense of France would be undertaken in an age of atomic weapons:

> Consequently, it is evident that what is necessary and what we must achieve during the coming years is a force capable of acting exclusively on our behalf, a force which has been conveniently called a *force de frappe* susceptible to deployment anywhere at any time. It goes without saying that the basis for such a force will be atomic armament—whether we manufacture it or buy it—but one which belongs to us; and since France could be destroyed on occasion from any point in the world, it is necessary that our force be designed so that it can act anywhere on earth.
>
> You are aware as I am of the scope of this undertaking. . . . As a nation we must have the courage to face up to it; the whole nation must be associated with it. We must have the courage and the will to achieve it. It will be our great work for the coming years in the area of defense.[24]

The École militaire speech was without doubt de Gaulle's personal handicraft; at the time it confounded many of his closest military advisers and even his minister of defense, who apparently had not been consulted about it before-

[24] These quotations have been taken from the text appended to a document of the Defense Committee of the National Assembly in 1960: *Avis sur le projet de loi de programme (no. 784) relative à certains équipements militaires*, by M. Le Theule, no. 882, Assemblée nationale, annexe au procès-verbal de la séance du 13 octobre, 1960, pp. 49-52.

hand.[25] The passage referring to the possible purchase of atomic arms, a direct hint to American policy-makers, was probably intended to indicate de Gaulle's interest in assistance for the development of delivery vehicles and thermonuclear weapons, since the first French atomic bomb was already in its final stages of development. De Gaulle's definition of the French nuclear deterrent surprised many in France, where even the advocates of French atomic weapons had, for the most part, a much more modest conception of their use.[26]

De Gaulle's notion of a national *force de frappe* was not only consistent with his belief in the fundamental importance of *national* defense; it was also a key element, as we have noted, in his bid to obtain coequal status with the Anglo-Saxons in a Western global strategic directorate. On the one hand, it added weight to the French case for an equal role in a tripartite consultative arrangement, since without a national deterrent the French demand for a veto power over the use of British and American nuclear weapons was meaningless. On the other hand, the fact that the United States and Britain had not accepted the General's tripartite proposal gave him the pretext he needed for his sharp attack on NATO integration in the École militaire speech and his vigorous assertion of a French national nuclear force, which he undoubtedly planned anyway. With French atomic tests a few months away, the proper time seemed at hand.

Whether or not he really believed he could attain the tripartite scheme, a national nuclear deterrent fitted into de Gaulle's broader foreign policy designs. These will be analyzed more thoroughly in a later chapter, but a glimpse of

[25] Several French interviews confirmed this point. Most of de Gaulle's military advisers were committed to NATO defense arrangements and favored continued French participation in them.

[26] See, e.g., Jean Planchais's article in *Le Monde*, November 6, 1959; Raymond Aron in *Le Figaro*, November 18, 1959.

them was visible in a press conference he gave a few days later in which he stressed that French nuclear weapons would further world equilibrium between the existing superpower blocs.

> Probably the sort of equilibrium that is establishing itself between the atomic power of the two camps is, for the moment, a factor in world peace, but who can say what will happen tomorrow? Who can say, for example, whether some sudden advance in development—particularly in the field of space rockets—will not provide one of the two camps with such an advantage that its peaceful inclinations will not hold out? Who can say whether, in the future, if basic political facts should change completely, as has already occurred on the earth, the two powers that would have a monopoly of nuclear weapons might not make a deal with each other to divide the world between them. . . . In truth, France, by equipping herself with nuclear armaments, is rendering a service to the equilibrium of the world.[27]

In this exposition, which reveals his basic distrust of America and his fear of "another Yalta," we can see the outlines of de Gaulle's vision aimed at breaking down nuclear bipolarity and promoting the formation of a greater "European" Europe independent from both the Soviet and Anglo-Saxon camps.

In the same speech de Gaulle broached the question of disarmament and the impending French nuclear tests in the Sahara, which were provoking anti-French attacks in the United Nations. He argued that if the Anglo-Saxon powers and the Soviet Union were to agree to halt nuclear tests, France could not concur and suspend her own tests so long as other countries were in possession of large quantities of nuclear bombs. This point, which had often been articulated by Jules Moch, the French disarmament representa-

[27] *Major Addresses, Statements, and Press Conferences*, p. 61.

tive at the United Nations, formed the basis of Gaullist doctrine on disarmament for years to come.[28]

Several weeks later General de Gaulle, together with Prime Minister Michel Debré and atomic adviser Jacques Soustelle, visited a Paris laboratory of the DAM to view a model of the first French atomic bomb. De Gaulle is said to have remarked at the time:

> I congratulate you for what I have seen. . . . Certainly the Russians and the Americans, with their enormous bombs, can kill people a hundred times, or even a thousand times. As for us, our goal is more modest; it will suffice to be able to kill them once. This is the only ambition of France.
>
> And besides, you see, the most important thing about what we have done is that we have accomplished it all by ourselves, I say entirely on our own.[29]

Meanwhile other official spokesmen in de Gaulle's government raised their voices during 1959 in defense of the French nuclear weapons program. Thus, Minister of Information Roger Frey contended before an audience of British and American journalists that France's possession of thermonuclear arms would soon justify her demand for a position of parity with the United States and the United Kingdom in NATO.[30] In a similar vein, Premier Debré argued that "to avoid being crushed by agreements between very

[28] Just a few days before Moch had defended the forthcoming French nuclear tests before the U.N. Political Commission by saying: "In the absence of a general decision for nuclear disarmament applying to all without distinction, France proclaims its will for nondiscrimination. . . . France will abandon with enthusiasm all military atomic tests the day the three first atomic powers renounce their nuclear armament, i.e., agree to halt, with controls, the production of fissile materials for military purposes, begin the reconversion of their stocks, and eliminate the vehicles to carry these explosives" (*Le Figaro*, November 5, 1959).

[29] As quoted in de Lacoste Lareymondie, p. 34.

[30] *Combat*, February 5, 1959.

great powers, a nation like France must have the power to make herself heard and understood."[31] Louis Joxe, a secretary of state in the office of the prime minister, emphasized that as long as members of the atomic club refused to give up their stocks of nuclear arms, France intended to join them and to have her own atomic weapons. France, in his words, desired "to be associated in the discussions and decisions concerning the use of nuclear weapons" by the Western powers.[32] And Jacques Soustelle, a former minister-delegate for atomic research, stated: "I regret that for a nation such as ours, possession of such a weapon is still necessary for entry into a sort of world 'Jockey-club.' But in the present state of affairs we must devote part of our research to [atomic] weapons which constitute an admission card among the truly Great Powers."[33] Later Joxe used other arguments to defend the French program—that the bomb would also protect the French community, that its development was necessary for the independence of the country, and that if France did not master nuclear technology, "we would soon be no more than a *nation secondaire*."[34]

In another speech before the Institut des hautes études de defense nationale in January 1960, François de Rose of the Quai d'Orsay again stressed the political aspects of French atomic armament. In his view, a French nuclear force would "give the necessary authority to our voice in the great international conferences where world policy is formulated."[35] Although he saw no prospects for European nuclear cooperation, de Rose once again expressed interest in American nuclear assistance and predicted that France

[31] *The Times* (London), August 19, 1959.

[32] *Combat*, October 21, 1959.

[33] *Le Méridional* (Marseille), May 27, 1959, as cited in Lawrence Scheinman, *Atomic Energy Policy in France Under the Fourth Republic* (Princeton: Princeton University Press, 1965), p. 195.

[34] *Le Monde*, November 5, 1959.

[35] François de Rose, "Les Aspects politiques des problemes nucléaires," speech delivered at the Institut des hautes études de défense nationale, January 26, 1960 (Paris: Institut des hautes études de défense nationale, no. 0328/DE), p. 18 (mimeographed).

would soon fulfill the conditions of the McMahon Act and thus qualify for American aid. He continued:

> If we conclude such an accord [with the United States], it is logical to conceive of a settlement of the problems which have been posed between America and us during recent years. I mean to speak of what one has called our participation in nuclear strategy. If we have such arms, it is evident that we will have to accept that the United States have the same right of consideration over their use which we have asked to have over theirs. It is necessary to understand that it will be impossible to turn our backs and not admit that the nuclear factor is going to play a capital role in the evolution of our relations with America.[36]

De Rose also listed several strategic arguments for French atomic weapons: doubts about the American nuclear guarantee to defend Europe in light of Soviet nuclear parity; an option for the future in case of an American troop withdrawal from Europe; the principle of proportional deterrence; the uncertainty created for the Soviet Union, which would have to contemplate the possibility that the French force might trigger the American nuclear arsenal in case of a conflict in Europe from which the U.S. first decided to remain aloof. But de Rose admitted that the doctrine of the French deterrent had never been the subject of a detailed government statement in France, and that he had seen no official documents on the rationale for French nuclear armament, either military or political. Thus, he was explaining the government's position only as he saw it.[37]

In the arena of public debate, the pros and cons of the Gaullist atomic program were frequently discussed in the press by the fall of 1959, and many of the themes to be elaborated at great length a year later, at the time of the vigorous parliamentary debates on the *force de frappe*, were beginning to emerge. The position taken in 1959 by one par-

[36] Ibid., p. 17. [37] Ibid, pp. 5-7.

ticularly thoughtful commentator is of special interest. Raymond Aron, then professor of sociology at the Sorbonne and a regular writer for *Le Figaro,* was one of the few who combined support for the development of a French atomic bomb with skepticism about de Gaulle's designs for its use. Aron favored the construction of French atomic weapons for strategic reasons, as a counter to any eventual threat of Soviet aggression or blackmail (he used the argument of "proportional deterrence"), and also as a political trump card in France's relations with her allies. He believed that only by possessing her own atomic bombs could France stand a chance of obtaining atomic secrets and other nuclear assistance from the United States.[38]

However, Aron clearly preferred that France use her nuclear status, once the bomb had been acquired, to press for some form of solution of the nuclear control problem within the Atlantic alliance. The solution he suggested was that of *le double contrôle*—dual control under which atomic arms and delivery vehicles would be usable only with the consent of the atomic power supplying the weapons and the state on whose territory they were stationed or installed. Under certain conditions of direct threat, the European state might receive exclusive national control. After de Gaulle's announcement of his conception of a *force de frappe* at the École militaire, Aron argued for the more modest "dual control" solution and criticized the *force de frappe* as a project beyond attainment, given French resources, and not in the French national interest.[39]

Hardware for the Force de Frappe

Even before the École militaire speech, important technical decisions had already been taken concerning hardware for the Gaullist nuclear force. During the months of July and August the question of the proper basic aircraft for the first

[38] *Le Figaro,* August 14, 1959.
[39] *Le Figaro,* November 18 and 27, 1959.

phase of the *force de frappe* was debated at high levels of government. The essential choice lay between the new Mirage IV, which had made its maiden flight a few months before and had originally been designed to replace the Vautour tactical bomber, and the Super-Vautour 4060, a much larger and more expensive plane but one with a longer range. After heated cabinet debate the advocates of economy won out, and de Gaulle decided in favor of the Mirage IV in August.

Under study since 1956, the Mirage IV aircraft was originally conceived for a tactical mission within NATO; its first prototype was ordered in 1957. The plane can fly over twice the speed of sound (Mach 2.2) and at an altitude of about 18,000 meters. Without in-flight refueling, it has a range of 2,500 kilometers, half of which can be traversed at supersonic speeds. This range is considerably superior to that of the Mirage III or the F-104 used by the West Germans, thus making the Mirage IV a natural complement of these other two fighter bombers within NATO.[40] However, the choice of the Mirage IV plane for the strategic missions of the *force de frappe* meant that in-flight refueling would be necessary if the aircraft were to be able to reach targets in the Soviet Union and return. Such refueling would be all the more essential because, in order to avoid enemy radar, the planes would have to fly at low altitudes where fuel consumption would be greater. Apparently no decision was taken at this time on the support aircraft needed to perform in-flight refueling, but the Transall (a Franco-German plane under development) and some French planes were potential candidates. There was also the possibility that tanker planes might be acquired from the United States. (KC-135 tanker planes were later purchased from the United States for this refueling mission.)

As a result of the August 1959 decision, three preproduction Mirage IV aircraft were ordered by the French gov-

[40] See the "Note sur le Mirage IV," in Assemblée nationale, *Avis* (no. 882) by M. Le Theule, p. 48.

ernment, to be built by a consortium of some ten French companies. The 1960 military budget included funds for fifty Mirage IV aircraft, as will be discussed later.

In the missile field, where France was starting from far behind and had only initiated preliminary studies, steps were also taken in 1959 to accelerate research and development. In May a private consortium operating under government auspices, the Société d'études et de recherches sur les engins balistiques (SEREB), was created to coordinate and supervise all missile work. It was to be concerned with the development of launch vehicles for military and space research applications. At first SEREB had hopes of gaining American cooperation. Preliminary accords were signed in 1959 with the Boeing Aircraft Company and the U.S. government for cooperation in the development of inertial guidance systems and other aspects of missile launch vehicles. However, both agreements were annulled a few months later when the U.S. State Department refused its approval.

Late in 1959 France attempted to form a continental consortium with West Germany, the Netherlands, and Belgium, and sought American aid for the development and manufacture of IRBMs by such a group. A consortium was formed for the production of the defensive antiaircraft Hawk missile. But the United States and Great Britain resisted other demands at the December 1959 NATO Council meeting for cooperation in IRBM development.[41] The French SEREB organization continued to hope for a multilateral NATO missile program in the first half of 1960. But when it became clear that U.S. policy remained opposed to cooperation in the development of missile launchers, the director of SEREB was instructed by the minister of the armed forces in August 1960 to concentrate on a strictly national program for missile development.

[41] Nieburg, p. 188.

France's First Atomic Tests

In the early morning hours of February 13, 1960, the first French atomic bomb was exploded from the top of a 336 foot-high tower at the Reggane test center in the Sahara. The power of the explosion was rated at between 60 and 70 kilotons, or roughly four times that of the first Hiroshima bomb. Extensive precautions had been taken to minimize the spread of radioactive fallout on sensitive neighboring African countries which had been highly critical of the test. The test was successful, and France had thus made her entry into the nuclear club. President de Gaulle's glee was reflected in an immediate public announcement:

> Hurrah for France! Since this morning she is stronger and prouder. From the bottom of my heart, my thanks to you and to those who have obtained for her this magnificent success.

He also issued a brief communiqué expressing the country's gratitude to those responsible; it concluded with these words:

> Thus France, thanks to its own national effort, can reinforce its defensive potential, that of the Community and that of the West. On the other hand, the French Republic is better able to make its action felt for the conclusion of agreements between atomic powers with a view toward realizing nuclear disarmament.[42]

Pierre Messmer, the new minister of the armed forces, told the press:

> We have just taken a very important step, but we have not yet attained our goal. We will continue to work in order to give France a *force de frappe* disposing of both nuclear warheads and the necessary means to transport

[42] Quotations from *Le Monde*, February 14-15, 1960.

them, thus giving our armed forces the capacity to accomplish their permanent mission which is to insure respect under all circumstances of national independence.[43]

A month and a half later France exploded a second device, a much smaller plutonium bomb of about 20 kilotons. This ground-level test on April 2, 1960, demonstrated that France was already moving in the direction of miniaturizing her bomb with an eye on eventual production of tactical atomic weapons.[44]

French press reactions to the first atomic test reflected a complete spectrum of opinion. Thus, an editorial in *Le Monde* commented that France would derive increased pride and prestige from the atomic test, but expressed doubt that France would be better protected and warned of the dangers of nuclear proliferation. It was suggested that France might gain equal or greater prestige by concentrating on a program of peaceful uses of atomic energy.[45] Another writer in the same paper stressed the hope that the atomic test would demonstrate France's scientific capabilities to the United States and thus open the way for negotiations to obtain American atomic secrets, so as to reduce the enormous expenses of nuclear development which lay ahead.

Writing in *Le Figaro*, Raymond Aron expressed satisfaction at the French bomb, but underlined the difficult tasks which remained before France would have an operational deterrent. France, he predicted, could pay the cost of producing operational atomic bombs and delivery vehicles if she wanted to. But Aron again voiced his disagreement with de Gaulle's reasons for constructing a French nuclear force. Aron did not concur with the general's belief in a strictly *national* defense, nor in his hope to use a French force for an ambitious independent diplomacy. "France will

[43] As quoted in *Combat*, February 15, 1960.

[44] *Le Monde*, April 2, 1960.

[45] *Le Monde*, February 14-15, 1960.

never be able to brandish her bombs to solve minor [diplomatic] problems, such as those of the Suez Canal."[46]

According to an article in *La Croix*, a Catholic daily, the French bomb would assure that France was treated with respect by the United States. "In short, France has constructed the atomic bomb and is preparing to construct an H-bomb not in order to use it against those who could become her adversaries, but to be able to be respected in the camp to which she belongs."[47] A writer in the left wing *Observateur* commented, on the other hand, that the French bomb had served only to isolate France internationally by provoking worldwide criticism, especially that of the Soviet Union and Africa. Arguing that one atomic test was not sufficient to give France access to American atomic secrets under the McMahon Act, he suggested that it would be better to renounce the bomb now in favor of disarmament and concentrate on the industrial uses of atomic energy.[48]

Michel Bosquet offered a comparison of the French and British nuclear programs in *L'Express*. He pointed out the grave financial problems which Britain faced, as described in the 1960 White Paper on defense, in trying to acquire both a nuclear deterrent and a modern conventional armed force. In his view this posed grave questions concerning the value of the French atomic program, which was being undertaken with even less money than the British effort. Military returns were nonexistent, he concluded, until missiles were obtained in the distant future; the political objectives seemed therefore to be the overriding ones. Bosquet seriously doubted that France could achieve a credible independent deterrent force.[49]

Although voicing pride at the French accomplishment, several papers picked up the disarmament theme and ex-

[46] "La Bombe," *Le Figaro*, February 15, 1960.
[47] "La Bombe du respect," *La Croix*, February 29, 1960.
[48] *Observateur*, February 18, 1960.
[49] *L'Express*, February 25, 1960.

pressed hope that France would now participate in the Geneva disarmament talks.[50] The Communist party issued a resolution denouncing the French atomic tests as against the wishes of the United Nations and French national interest. It called for a ban on further tests and an abolition of all nuclear stockpiles.[51] A short time later a group of ninety professors in the science faculty of the University of Paris sent a declaration to President de Gaulle demanding that the French atomic program be directed toward peaceful ends and scientific research instead of nuclear weapons development.[52]

The International Context in 1960

In early 1960 hopes were raised momentarily in France by signs from Washington that seemed to augur fundamental changes in American nuclear policy. On the eve of the first French atomic test, President Eisenhower suggested in a news conference that he favored amending the Atomic Energy Act to allow sharing of atomic information and weapons already in the hands of the Russians with France and other American allies.

> I have always been of the belief that we should not deny to our allies what the enemies, what your potential enemy, already has. We do want allies to be treated as partners and allies, and not as junior members of a firm who are to be seen but not heard. So I would think that it would be better, for the interests of the United States, to make our law more liberal, as long as . . . we are confident, by our treaties and everything else [that the recipient countries would] stand by us in time of trouble.[53]

[50] *Le Populaire, Paris-Jour, Paris-Presse, Combat*; see articles on February 15, 1960, and the days following.
[51] *L'Humanité*, February 15, 1960.
[52] *Combat*, March 3, 1960.
[53] As quoted in the *New York Times*, February 4, 1960.

These remarks provoked enthusiastic French reactions. But shortly thereafter warnings were issued by the JCAE that the president would not be allowed to violate the 1958 atomic energy law. Soon the White House had to deny any intention of changing the Atomic Energy Act or previous American practice on nuclear sharing.[54]

The French atomic test also raised hopes in Paris that France would at last qualify for American nuclear assistance. But these hopes, too, were quickly dashed by Senator Clinton P. Anderson, the chairman of the JCAE, who stated immediately after the first French explosion: "One test does not necessarily mean substantial progress. When the French conduct a few more tests, if they elect to do so, and develop a diversity of weapons and, perhaps manufacturing facilities, then the situation might be changed."[55] However, Senator Anderson's statement still held out the carrot of further nuclear progress as the requirement for American atomic aid. A few days later Eisenhower and his secretary of state again emphasized that France had not yet achieved full entry into the nuclear club and the American administration had no intention of requesting from the Congress any changes in the McMahon Act.[56] In fact, Eisenhower had wanted to change the nuclear sharing law, but he felt he could not overcome the opposition of the powerful Joint Committee.[57]

[54] Ibid., February 7, 1960.

[55] *New York Herald Tribune*, European ed., February 15, 1960; also *Le Monde*, February 15, 1960.

[56] *New York Times*, February 18 and 19, 1960.

[57] In an interview with David Schoenbrun after his retirement, Eisenhower stressed his wish for broader nuclear sharing and his hostility to the restrictions imposed by the McMahon Act. He said, *inter alia:*

> Look, I could have reached a satisfactory agreement with de Gaulle on the atom thing except for the law. I told de Gaulle time and again. I said, look, Mr. President, I'll go as far as I can today and I'm going to try to get Congress to change some of the provisions in the atomic-energy law. He believed me and I did do it. I

During the rest of 1960 American policy-makers continued to search for ways to provide increased nuclear sharing with European allies and at the same time to satisfy the Congress and others who were increasingly worried about the dangers of nuclear proliferation.[58] In March General Lauris Norstad, NATO's supreme commander, suggested a NATO nuclear force to include both land-based MRBMs and tactical nuclear weapons in highly mobile multinational units under a NATO commander. Interest in dispersing IRBMs in Europe along the lines of the 1957 Eisenhower proposal had been reactivated by the approaching operational status of the Polaris missile, and the next month Secretary of Defense Thomas S. Gates, Jr., proposed another variation on that theme—the deployment on barges and flatcars in Europe of hundreds of these missiles when they became available a year or two later. Speaking before the NATO defense ministers, he also suggested that the system of dual control be modified to give the NATO supreme commander authority to fire the missiles. De Gaulle was attracted to neither of these plans; he is reported to have advised Norstad that France would only accept Polaris installations on French soil if one-third of them (about fifty) were given to France for use at her discretion and with her own nuclear warheads. Talks conducted by NATO Secre-

---

> changed the law twice, but we never did get all we needed. The atomic-energy act ought to be repealed, because it's a futile thing —those restrictions on the president. But there's a joint committee there in Washington, a very powerful one, and it became an emotional issue.

See Schoenbrun, p. 335. Eisenhower repeated essentially the same position in his letter to Senator Henry M. Jackson of May 17, 1966, at the time of hearings on the 1966 NATO crisis, reprinted in U.S. Congress, Senate, *The Atlantic Alliance, Hearings before the Subcommittee on National Security and International Operations of the Committee on Government Operations*, 89th Cong., 2nd sess., August 15, 1966, part 7 (supplement), pp. 225-27.

[58] See e.g., Robert E. Osgood, *NATO, The Entangling Alliance* (Chicago: University of Chicago Press, 1962), pp. 230-34.

tary-General Paul-Henri Spaak with the French president on such a deal produced no agreement.[59]

Nothing having come of the Norstad and Gates plans, attention focused later in the year in government circles on another idea—a seaborne multilateral nuclear force. Suggested first by Professor Robert R. Bowie, director of the Harvard Center for International Affairs and a State Department adviser, this answer to the problem of forming a collective NATO deterrent called for two kinds of actions. First, the United States would assign to NATO twelve Polaris submarines, to be under joint allied control; later a mixed-manned fleet was to be created to assure that no nation could withdraw its contingents in time of crisis. This MLF concept was endorsed and officially presented for allied discussion by Secretary of State Christian Herter at the NATO ministerial meeting in Paris in December 1960. It was picked up and advocated with varying degrees of enthusiasm by the Kennedy and Johnson administrations until the end of 1964, and we shall return to its later elaboration and the French response to it in another part of this study.[60]

Meanwhile, the British government continued its independent nuclear effort, although pains were taken to explain the compatibility of that effort with the cohesion of NATO (the British force would be a "contribution" to the deterrent posture of the West) and Britain's special relationship with the United States.[61] There was one major change—the cancellation of the liquid-fuel Blue-Streak missile program in April 1960 because of rising costs and its minimal utility (it was both vulnerable and slow-firing). Many French commentators took note of this event and urged that France draw the consequences, but the French

[59] C. L. Sulzberger, *New York Times*, June 25, 1960, and the *New York Times*, July 23, 1960, as cited in Osgood, p. 232.

[60] See, e.g., Alastair Buchan, "The Multilateral Force: An Historical Perspective," *Adelphi Papers*, no. 13 (London: Institute for Strategic Studies, October 1964).

[61] Osgood, pp. 250-52.

government continued its own missile program. To replace Blue-Streak the British government reached an agreement with the United States whereby the latter would undertake the development of the air-launched Skybolt missile and sell it to Great Britain minus the warheads in 1965, or whenever the development program was completed, to prolong the life of the obsolescent British V-bomber force.

In October Britain launched her first nuclear submarine, constructed with American cooperation as part of a program expected to lead to British missile-launching submarines. (The French nuclear submarine program had received some reactor fuel but no design information from the United States, and it was in a much earlier stage of development.) By this time, however, the success of the American Polaris had considerably diminished the effect of Britain's military arguments for a nuclear force and had revealed the important underlying political motivations, i.e., the desire to preserve British political influence—especially in the field of arms control and relations with the East.[62] The French government must have taken note of this fact as it prepared its 1961 military budget, which provided the basis for the first developmental phase of the *force de frappe*.

During the summer of 1960 de Gaulle raised once again the question of his tripartite directorate and pressed for its acceptance. At the Paris summit conference in May, which aborted over the U-2 affair, de Gaulle had stood faithfully behind President Eisenhower in the face of Soviet Premier Khrushchev's hostile demands; de Gaulle even tried to mediate to save the conference. After the summit meeting the French leader emphasized the solidarity that had existed between the Western powers, but insisted that France's role was still inadequate.

> Our alliance appeared a living reality. In order for it to become even more so, France must have her own role in

[62] Ibid., p. 251.

> it, and her own personality. This implies that she too must acquire a nuclear armament, since others have one; that she must be sole mistress of her resources and her territory; in short, that her destiny, although associated with that of her allies, must remain in her own hands. It goes without saying that such autonomy must be coupled with ever closer coordination among the Western powers in their policy and their strategy.[63]

The General then proceeded to send a new secret letter to Eisenhower on June 10 in which he argued that the existing system of political consultations was not enough and did not "meet the essential aspect of our problem, which is global strategic cooperation."

De Gaulle made it unmistakably clear in this letter that France would settle for nothing less than "an equal voice in joint (presumably tripartite) decisions on the use of nuclear weapons." This point had been touched on in the September 1958 Memorandum and subsequently, but never so specifically. It confirmed the French desire for a veto right over American and British atomic arms. De Gaulle proposed that a "high-level planning group" be created for joint planning on the employment of nuclear weapons.[64] Later in October 1960, he made even more explicit his demand for a veto power over the use of Anglo-American nuclear weapons in a public speech at Grenoble: "France intends that if, by misfortune, atomic bombs were to be dropped in the world, none should be dropped by the free world's side unless she should have accepted it."[65]

On August 2 President Eisenhower replied to de Gaulle's letter of June 10, "recalling that the offer of military talks

[63] Address on May 31, 1960, following the failure of the Summit Conference, in *Major Addresses*, p. 77.

[64] The quotations are found in Schoenbrun, p. 309; the date and general substance are confirmed in the "Statement of the Department of State," August 11, 1966.

[65] French text in André Passeron, *De Gaulle parle*, I (Paris: Plon, 1962), 373. See also André Fontaine's comments in *Le Monde*, October 9, 1960.

on Africa the year before had not been followed up by the French." According to the State Department, "He suggested another approach that would not contemplate formal combined staff planning, but rather talks among military representatives on all strategic questions of interest to France in various parts of the world, primarily outside the NATO area."[66] Another version states that President Eisenhower "assumed the Africa talks of 1959 had not been followed up by France because the basis had not met the French desire."[67]

General de Gaulle did not find satisfaction in President Eisenhower's suggestion for a renewed attempt at organizing three-power military talks. He (de Gaulle) wanted "a tripartite meeting at the heads of government level, to work out a joint plan for organizing united action on world problems and for reorganizing the Atlantic Alliance."[68] Although by now well aware of American objections to any such public formalization of a special status for France in the Alliance, de Gaulle persisted in his demands for an augmented French role. In addition, he added the inflammatory issue of NATO reorganization as a subject for tripartite discussions.

These suggestions were not well received by President Eisenhower. Though agreeing in principle that a meeting with the French president might be useful (but without reference to a summit meeting), he requested on August 31 that de Gaulle first set forth his views on NATO in a memorandum, as he had promised to do twice before, in order to expedite preparations.

The general's response to Eisenhower's last letter came publicly in his press conference on September 5, 1960; he argued that the North Atlantic Treaty had to be revised to provide an organized structure to coordinate the political

[66] "Statement of the Department of State," p. 229.

[67] From a 1964 account, as cited by Robert Kleiman, *New York Times*, August 29, 1966.

[68] Ibid., p. 229; see also Schoenbrun, p. 310.

and strategic conduct of the Western powers outside of Europe, especially in the Middle East and Africa. He also renewed his attack on the principle of NATO "integration" and reiterated that French defense must have a national character. After explaining again that France had withdrawn her Mediterranean fleet from NATO in 1959 to protect her responsibilities in Africa, the French president reaffirmed that if atomic weapons were to be stockpiled on French territory, they had to be under French control. "Given the nature of these weapons and the possible consequences of their use, France obviously cannot leave her own destiny and even her own life to the discretion of others."[69] The Gaullist themes of "national defense," plus the need for a national nuclear deterrent and a French veto power over the use of Free World nuclear weapons, were further amplified in several speeches the general made in the provinces a short time after his September press conference.[70]

Whether the French president had believed he could persuade Eisenhower, his wartime friend, to accept his bid to elevate France's status through participation in a formal tripartite directorate at the top of the alliance, or whether—as is more likely—he persisted in raising the question only as a tactical decoy, by the autumn of 1960 the negative American response was clear. A political gulf had developed between America and France. The United States was unwilling to risk offending its other European allies by accepting de Gaulle's demand for a formal triumvirate over NATO and unprepared to share America's world power to the extent sought by France. Under the circumstances, Washington—which had tried to increase consultation with de Gaulle—could probably not have done otherwise.

[69] Third press conference held by General de Gaulle, September 5, 1960, in *Major Addresses*, p. 96.

[70] See the speeches at Pontivy (early September), and at Grenoble, Saint-Julien-en-Genevois, Chambéry, and Briançon (all in October), as quoted in Passeron, *De Gaulle parle*, I, 373-74.

Failing to obtain American agreement on the issue, de Gaulle, on the other hand, had stepped up his attacks against NATO and repeatedly demonstrated his unwillingness to continue France's cooperation with the organization in its existing form. At the root of this divergence were sharply different conceptions of alliance policy and of each country's global role. This was the setting at the beginning of the October parliamentary debates on the *loi de programme* which was to provide the basis for development of an independent French nuclear force.

The 1960 Program Law

The government began preparing the defense-program law for 1960-64 during the spring of 1960, and its broad outlines were presented in preliminary fashion to the Defense Committee of the National Assembly (Commission de la défense nationale et des forces armées) in April by Minister of Defense Pierre Messmer. Some discussion ensued and a special study group was formed by the committee to hear testimony from Messmer and General Lavaud, the chief of staff of the armed forces. Approved in final form by the Council of Ministers at the end of June, the proposed law went to the National Assembly in July. Intensive examination of the bill by the Defense Committee began in mid-September, when private presentations were given by Premier Michel Debré and Defense Minister Messmer, followed later by General Gallois (for) and General Valluy (against), as well as other experts. There was heated debate within the committee and several blunt questions were put to the government for clarification. Finally, the committee approved the government bill with amendments and submitted its report to the National Assembly on October 13.[71] Reports were also delivered by the Committee on Foreign Affairs, which had been unable to reach agreement on the proposed law, and the Finance Committee, which had barely accepted it.

[71] Assemblée nationale, *Avis* (no. 882) by M. le Theule.

Although it bore the innocuous title "Projet de loi de programme relative à certains équipements militaires," in the words of the French chief of staff, General Lavaud, "a revolution rather than an evolution" in the French system of defense was at stake with this law. The new law reflected the decision of the government to give priority to the development of an atomic *force de frappe*, that is "an advanced instrument representing an enormous potential of massive destruction capable of instant use anywhere on the globe and without preliminary mobilization."[72] Estimated to cost in the neighborhood of NF6 billion, the nuclear force was part of an overall military budget of about NF11.8 billion for the five-year period. However, observers were quick to point out that the nuclear program would probably cost much more and that other costs were undoubtedly hidden in other budgets; for example, the costs of the Pierrelatte isotope separation plant were partly absorbed by the CEA.

The program law authorized the production of fifty Mirage IV nuclear bombers and atomic bombs, plus further research on missiles and one nuclear submarine. With respect to the missiles, provision was made to allow for purchasing them from abroad or licensing their fabrication by foreign companies in France, should this become possible (i.e., if American policy on sharing nuclear and missile technology changed) before French prototypes could be successfully developed. The goal was a national thermonuclear armament which would "guarantee the independence of the country and allow French forces to cooperate more effectively at the side of allied forces, in the defense of the free world." The possibility of "technical collaboration" or "strategic cooperation" with France's allies was not to be excluded.[73]

[72] General Lavaud, as quoted in *Le Monde*, August 18, 1960.

[73] Assemblée nationale, *Projet de loi de programme relative à certains équipements militaires*, Annexe au procès-verbal de la séance du 18 juillet 1960, no. 784 (Paris, 1960).

Formal parliamentary debate on the *loi de programme* opened with the government's presentation by Premier Michel Debré in the National Assembly on October 13 and lasted two months, during which time the bill followed a tortuous parliamentary path. The subject of two censure motions in the Assembly, it was rejected twice by the Senate, failed to obtain agreement from two mixed parliamentary commissions, and finally became law only after a third censure motion in the National Assembly did not receive the necessary absolute majority vote.

Opponents of the bill seemed to come from all the opposition parties and included a few Gaullists as well. Lengthy speeches were delivered by former Socialist Premier Guy Mollet and Maurice Faure, a Radical. The opposition attacks were multifarious. Some argued on technical grounds, i.e., that the proposed *force de frappe* would never deter, that it would be obsolete when it became operational, or that the proposed financial credits would be insufficient to construct it. Others were concerned that conventional armed forces might be slighted by the priority given by the government to credits for nuclear arms. But the debates reached their most acrimonious pitch over the foreign policy implications of a national nuclear force. Although many deputies were willing to provide France with nuclear weapons, they were unwilling to sanction a national defense policy that would weaken NATO. Thus, the censure motion in the Assembly on October 20 called for negotiations with France's allies to obtain an integrated *force commune de dissuasion* in place of a national atomic force.[74] Reference was made to discussions under way at the time in the United States and among members of the Alliance regarding the possibility of creating a NATO nuclear force (e.g., Norstad's proposal, the Gates plan, Bowie's proposal). Other deputies urged that the nuclear force be constructed

---

The technical and financial aspects of the *loi de programme* will be discussed in greater detail in Chapter 5.

[74] From the text as quoted in *Le Figaro*, October 21, 1960.

with France's European allies; they saw a European force as the only viable framework for an adequate nuclear deterrent.[75]

One amendment to the bill, proposed by Valentin—a Gaullist—and accepted by the government, inserted a preamble (which became article 1 of the final program law) stating that: "The defense policy of the Republic is founded on the willingness to assure the national independence and to reinforce the effectiveness of the alliances which guarantee the security of the free world. It has as its object the meeting of the commitments which derive from these alliances. . . ."[76]

Throughout the period of parliamentary debates the French press carried column after column discussing the pros and cons of the *force de frappe*; most of these articles were critical of the proposed government program. For example, Generals Béthouart and Valluy attacked the vulnerability of the Mirage IV system and supported the creation of a force within a European or Atlantic framework. Both generals based their critique on the necessity of continued French participation in NATO.[77] Similarly, Alfred Fabré-Luce preferred the alternative of a NATO nuclear force.[78] Jules Moch argued that France could not afford a credible nuclear arsenal, and that she was not a country of sufficient size to play any meaningful role in deterrence, since her territory could be quickly destroyed by a small

[75] The reader is referred to the debates, which are published in the *Journal officiel.* A summary of some of the arguments was presented in *Le Figaro*, October 24, 1960. See also Walter Schütze, "Die französische Atombewaffnung im Spiegel der parlamentarischen Debatten," *Europa Archiv*, no. 9 (1961), pp. 207-18.

[76] From the "Texte définitif" of the *Projet de loi de programme*, Assemblée nationale, no. 211, December 6, 1960.

[77] General Béthouart, "La force de frappe: oui, mais integrée à l'OTAN," *Le Figaro*, October 11, 1960; General Valluy, "Le grand problème de la force de frappe," *Le Figaro*, October 15-16, 1960, an extract from his book *Se Défendre* (Paris: Plon, 1960).

[78] "L'Espoir subsiste d'un accord interallié," *La Vie Française*, October 21, 1960.

Soviet missile attack.[79] The Communists persisted in their opposition to any kind of nuclear force, national or European, and urged disarmament instead.[80]

Writing in his column in *Le Figaro*, Raymond Aron defended the French *force de frappe* as an option against an uncertain future and as the only apparent way to qualify for American atomic secrets under the McMahon Act. But he criticized the planned Mirage IV force, or even the projected IRBM force, as an inadequate deterrent. Instead, he favored French participation in a collective nuclear solution for the Alliance, which he believed would remain the necessary basis of French security for at least another decade. To Aron, de Gaulle's concept of military independence was utter folly, although he did suggest that a national atomic force would have some diplomatic value.[81]

On December 1, 1960, after rejection for the second time by the Senate, the *loi de programme* was returned to the National Assembly for a final round of debate. Once again Premier Debré pledged the responsibility of his government on the bill, and again a censure motion was offered by the opposition. The final vote took place on December 6. As had happened twice before, the opposition failed to obtain the requisite absolute majority vote (277 votes—based on the total membership of the Assembly and not just the number of members present and voting) and the motion failed, although it did receive 215 votes. Under the procedure set down in Article 49 of the Constitution of the Fifth Republic, the *loi de programme* thus became law, in spite of the strong parliamentary opposition it had encountered.[82] The

[79] *Le Monde*, December 7, 1960.

[80] See the resolution of the French Communist party in *L'Humanité*, October 17, 1960.

[81] *Le Figaro*, October 20 and November 21, 1960.

[82] Under Article 49 of the French Constitution, a bill upon which the government has pledged its responsibility automatically becomes law if a censure motion fails to receive an absolute majority of the members of the Assembly. Only votes in favor of censure are counted. The government thus gets the benefit of those deputies who abstain or are absent.

constitutional procedure which the government had used to its advantage came under sharp attack from the deputies. The feeling of many seemed to be summarized in the following passage from *L'Année politique*: "One can scarcely speak of a 'passing of the bill,' since the amendments were not really discussed and appraised. The military policy of the government is thus the act of the executive, without real collaboration with the legislature."[83]

[83] *L'Année politique*, 1960, p. 122.

TWO

THE *FORCE DE DISSUASION*

ITS RATIONALE AND EVOLUTION

4 • *Nuclear Weapons and Gaullist Foreign Policy*

POLITICAL AND STRATEGIC ASSUMPTIONS OF THE FORCE DE DISSUASION

Two basically contradictory visions motivated General de Gaulle's foreign and security policies.[1] The first vision stemmed from the Gaullist perception of the international system as an unstable system, dominated by the two superpowers. As a consequence, the general sought to change that system into another that would provide a more stable world balance. His efforts were directed primarily at transforming the existing state system in Europe and encouraging the emergence of a new Europe which would act as a third world power. According to his second vision, de Gaulle was determined that France be recognized once again as a great power with an important global role. Thus the general attempted to expand French influence in Asia and Latin America, and to retain it in Africa. But Europe remained his chief concern and it was there that he devoted his greatest energies. He sought a union of European states under French leadership, through which, he hoped, Europe would regain its importance on the world political stage and speak with an independent voice among the super-powers. At the same time this expanded European role would serve as a vehicle to augment France's global influence.

This chapter examines how these two visions were reflected in de Gaulle's policies, especially toward Europe and the Atlantic alliance. Against this background the po-

[1] The late Chancellor Adenauer remarked in his memoirs: "I would rack my brains over the general's way of thinking. I believe that two ideas struggled against each other inside de Gaulle: France as a great nation and Europe." (Konrad Adenauer, *Erinnerungen, 1959-1963* [Stuttgart: Deutsche Verlags-Anstalt, 1968], p. 56.)

litical role of French nuclear armament, which supported each of these visions, will be explained. Since under the Gaullist regime foreign and defense policies were very much the personal handicraft of the president, and because de Gaulle displayed remarkable consistency in the elaboration of his policies, the main source of this analysis is the body of statements made by the general himself. Later in the chapter we shall address the strategic aspects of the French atomic force and Gaullist policy on disarmament and arms control, both of which were closely related to Gaullist political objectives and perceptions of the international system. The economic and technological aspects of French atomic armament will be dealt with in the next chapter.

The Bases of Gaullist Foreign Policy

France under de Gaulle's rule saw the international system as dominated by the bipolar strategic balance between the Soviet and American superpowers.[2] However, a multipolar diplomatic order was also perceived, consisting of various bilateral and multilateral relationships between all the states in the system along both regional and global lines. In the Gaullist view this system was inherently unstable. Because of their enormous strategic power and global interests, the two superstates structured all international conflict and, as a result, determined to a great extent the balances and relationships of small and middle powers. Security relationships in Europe, France's primary concern, were seen to depend on superpower conflict or cooperation. In order to influence this situation, Europe—according to the Gaullist view—would have to develop its own identity and a global strategy. This was all the more necessary in

[2] For a lucid treatment of the Gaullist perception of the international system and its impact on French policy, see Edward A. Kolodziej, "Revolt and Revisionism in the Gaullist Global Vision: An Analysis of French Strategic Policy," *Journal of Politics* (May 1971), pp. 448-77.

order to avoid what was seen as an inexorable tendency on the part of the international system toward superpower conflict or superpower condominium. Either the superstates would clash, and their rivalry would entangle all the states of the system whether they wished it or not, or they would unite in efforts to limit the power and influence of other states. Both prospects were seen as menacing to the status and political independence of France and other smaller nations.

Gaullist France demonstrated both status quo and revisionist tendencies in her foreign and security policies.[3] On the one hand, she was a status quo power in the sense of having no territorial ambitions or conflicts of interests with other nations, i.e., no "possession goals." De Gaulle also adhered to an essentially nineteenth-century view of the stability of the international system, based on the preservation of the nation-state as the fundamental unit of world politics. All efforts to downgrade national sovereignty, especially in the direction of supranational integration, were doggedly opposed. Moreover, de Gaulle's diplomacy and diplomatic style conformed to the pattern of the traditional realist school: power is the key to influence; ideologies are only the cloaks of national ambitions; national security is best pursued by traditional methods—balance of power, cabinet diplomacy, coalitions, a concert of the great powers.[4]

More fundamentally, however, Gaullist France was a revisionist power. In accordance with his view of the instability of the prevailing international system, de Gaulle sought to reshape that system by creating a new European and world equilibrium. Although his tactics in pursuing this objective were often unpredictable, the general defined his overall aims with considerable clarity and pursued them

[3] See, e.g., Pierre Hassner's discussion in his "Change and Security in Europe, Part I: The Background," *Adelphi Papers*, no. 45 (London: Institute for Strategic Studies, 1968), pp. 9-11.

[4] See, e.g., Stanley Hoffmann, "De Gaulle's Memoirs: The Hero as History," *World Politics*, XIII (October 1960), 140-55.

with remarkable consistency in his policies. Starting with the division of Europe, each half of which was under the strong influence of a superpower, de Gaulle sought a reunification of the European continent in a loose confederation—a "Europe of the states." According to his design, this would be a "European" Europe independent of the two superpower hegemonies. Such a transformation of the European system would require, on the one hand, removal of the American military presence (and therefore direct political influence) from Western Europe, and on the other, a Soviet troop withdrawal from the states of Eastern Europe coupled with Moscow's consent to an evolution toward liberalization and national autonomy in its former satellite countries. In de Gaulle's view, a new system of pan-European security would then be created—presumably "balanced" by the Soviet Union in the East and France in the West, and buttressed by the nascent French nuclear force. This new European security equilibrium would then be the basis of a global realignment of power along multipolar lines.

The broad outlines of this Gaullist vision for the future of Europe are visible in an often quoted passage from the third volume of the general's war memoirs (written during the years 1957-58). De Gaulle described his goals for French policy as follows:

> To ensure France's security in Western Europe by preventing a new Reich from menacing her again. To collaborate with the West and the East, constructing alliances with one side or the other as necessary, without ever accepting a position of dependence. . . . To encourage the political, economic, and strategic grouping of the states bordering on the Rhine, the Alps, and the Pyrenees. To establish this organization as one of the three world powers and if it should one day be necessary, the arbitrator between the Soviet and Anglo-Saxon camps. Since 1940, my every word and act has been dedicated to establish-

ing these possibilities; now that France is on her feet again, I am going to try to realize them.[5]

The general also wrote of a broader "image of Europe," presumably a longer-term objective. He hoped that Europe would eventually find peace and equilibrium "by an association among Slavs, Germans, Gauls, and Latins." This would provide the basis for a unity of the European peoples "from Iceland to Istanbul, from Gibraltar to the Urals."[6]

The second vision inspiring Gaullist foreign policy was that of French *grandeur* (i.e., prestige, greatness): de Gaulle insisted that France once again be fitted for special international status as a global power. This idea, which was in continuous tension with his revisionist design, was stated on the first page of his memoirs.[7] In de Gaulle's eyes the condition of French *grandeur* was the maintenance of France's independence.[8] This was presumably his meaning when he wrote that France should "collaborate with the West and the East, constructing alliances with one side or the other as necessary, without ever accepting a position of dependence."[9] On another occasion he explained that inde-

[5] Charles de Gaulle, *Memoires de guerre, Le Salut* (Paris: Plon, 1959), pp. 210-11.

[6] *Le Salut,* pp. 57-58.

[7] Charles de Gaulle, *Memoires de guerre, L'Appel* (Paris: Plon, 1954), p. 5. "Toute ma vie, je me suis fait une certaine idée de la France. Le sentiment me l'inspire aussi bien que la raison. . . . Bref, à mon sens, la France ne peut être la France sans la grandeur."

De Gaulle did not define *grandeur.* He simply argued that France was destined for greatness and that "vast enterprises" were necessary to compensate for the internal divisions that characterize the French people.

[8] In Stanley Hoffmann's words, "Independence is the condition of grandeur. Grandeur itself consists of playing as active and ambitious a role in the world as the nation's position and resources allow. The substance of such a policy depends on and varies with the circumstances of the international system. In today's world, French grandeur is defined by de Gaulle as an attempt to play the role of Europe's awakener and leader." Stanley Hoffmann, "De Gaulle, Europe, and the Atlantic Alliance," *International Organization,* XVIII (Winter 1964), 2.

[9] De Gaulle, *Le Salut,* p. 210.

pendence is the "essential goal" of France's policy.[10] This point raises a serious question whether it is possible for a country to work for the achievement of a goal such as the transformation of the European system, which involves cooperation and alliances with other states, without accepting some dependence and loss of freedom of action.

These two Gaullist visions and the tension between them—the revisionist design for the European and world international system and the quest for French *grandeur* and an independent global role—explain the essence of de Gaulle's foreign and strategic policies, their constructive contribution, and their failure. French nuclear armament was an important element in both of these visions.

Gaullist assumptions on nuclear force derived from the general's view that the nation-state is and must remain the fundamental unit of world politics and that the indispensable characteristic of any sovereign state is *national defense.* This point was made succinctly in his 1959 speech at the École militaire, discussed earlier. For de Gaulle, the general, an effective defense had to include the most modern armaments; in this respect the *force de frappe* was the logical postwar extension of his efforts in the 1930's to modernize the French army and French strategy on the basis of a mobile, mechanized armored corps of professional soldiers, as described in one of his early books.[11] But even more im-

[10] Press conference, October 28, 1966, *Speeches and Press Conferences*, no. 253A (New York: Ambassade de France, Service de presse et d'information), p. 1.

According to André Fontaine, Couve de Murville is reported to have said at one time that the aim of Gaullist policy is *indépendance en soi.* Fontaine argues the contrary and contends that de Gaulle developed a "constructive and original policy" centered on his efforts to achieve European reunification and the disengagement of the blocs. See Fontaine's article, "What is French Policy?", *Foreign Affairs*, XLV (October 1966), 68ff.

[11] *Vers l'Armée de métier* (Paris: Éditions Berger-Levrault, 1934). Referring to these events of his military past, the general said in a speech in 1963: "In sum, our country, perpetually threatened, finds itself once again faced with the necessity of possessing the most powerful weapons of the era unless, of course, others cease to possess

portant for de Gaulle, the statesman, were the political consequences of atomic armament. He saw nuclear weapons as a fundamental ingredient of a nation's political power and influence in the present era of world politics: "A great State which does not possess them, while others have them, does not command its own destiny."[12]

On another occasion he elaborated further on the same theme as follows:

> . . . the countries which do not have an atomic arsenal believe that they have to accept a strategic and consequently a political dependency in relation to that one of the two giants which is not threatening them. In these conditions France, . . . as soon as she was able to be herself, judged it necessary to begin the desired effort in order to become an atomic power in her turn.[13]

In de Gaulle's eyes, however, nuclear weapons were also the key to his attempt to modify the bipolar structure of world politics based on the strategic predominance of the Soviet and American superpowers. As the general said in 1959 in a speech noted in Chapter 3, "Probably the sort of equilibrium that is establishing itself between the atomic power of the two camps is, for the moment, a factor in world peace, but who can say what will happen tomorrow?"[14] Obsessed soon after his return to power by the specter of a Soviet–American conflict enveloping the world, and later by the possibility of a Soviet–American political deal on a European settlement as the Cold War diminished, de Gaulle asserted that France, in equipping herself with

---

them" (radio and television address, April 19, 1963, *Major Addresses, Statements and Press Conferences of General Charles de Gaulle, May 19, 1958–January 31, 1964* [New York: Ambassade de France, Service de presse et d'information, 1964], p. 226).

[12] Speech at Strasbourg, November 23, 1961, as quoted in André Passeron, *De Gaulle parle*, I (Paris: Plon, 1962), 357.

[13] Press conference, July 23, 1964, *Speeches and Press Conferences*, No. 208, p. 8.

[14] Press conference, November 10, 1959, *Major Addresses*, p. 61.

an atomic force, was promoting world equilibrium by according Europe once again the means for her own security and an independent political role. He implied, of course, that French nuclear weapons were at the service of Europe.

In justifying the French atomic force soon after his announcement of France's withdrawal from NATO military commands in 1966, de Gaulle made the following statement:

> The world situation in which two super-States would alone have the weapons capable of annihilating every other country . . . this situation, over the long run, could only paralyze and sterilize the rest of the world by placing it either under the blow of crushing competition, or under the yoke of a double hegemony that would be agreed upon between the two rivals.
>
> In these conditions, how could Europe unite, Latin America emerge, Africa follow its own path, China find its place, and the United Nations become an effective reality? As America and the Soviet Union failed to destroy their absolute weapons, the spell had to be broken. We are doing so, insofar as we are concerned, and with our resources alone.[15]

According to the Gaullist view then, French nuclear armament was seen as the foundation for France's independent foreign policy and global role, as well as a factor of stability in a new multipolar world order growing out of a new strategic and political equilibrium in Europe. As de Gaulle's foreign and strategic policies were elaborated and implemented, the main focus of his attention was on the European and Atlantic area.[16]

[15] Press conference, October 28, 1966, *Speeches and Press Conferences*, no. 253A, p. 6.

[16] In addition to the role of the French nuclear force in Gaullist foreign policies, brief mention should be made of another kind of political purpose ascribed to French nuclear armament. Some observers, such as the late Edgar S. Furniss (*De Gaulle and the French Army—a Crisis in Civil-Military Relations*, New York: The Twentieth Century Fund, 1964), saw the *force de frappe* primarily as an instru-

The Elaboration of Gaullist European and Atlantic Policies and the Role of Nuclear Armament

De Gaulle's policies as they were elaborated over the years can be viewed retrospectively in four phases. Variables which influenced the contours and timing of these phases included French perceptions of the rise and decline of militaristic Soviet policies in Europe and of indirect American threats to French sovereignty and status, the course of West European integration and U.S. Atlantic policy, the development and deployment of French nuclear armament, and French domestic political and economic constraints (e.g., first, the Algerian war; then, in 1968, France's economic and political crisis).

Beginning in 1958, the first phase of Gaullist European-Atlantic policy centered on the tripartite proposal to extend the scope of NATO and elevate France's role and status in the Alliance; it also saw the first reduction in France's NATO participation when these demands were not met. The second phase began about 1961 and focused on de Gaulle's efforts to construct an independent confederal grouping of states in Western Europe on the model of the Fouchet plan. During this period France combated the alternative American vision for an Atlantic-oriented Europe linked closely with the United States and stepped up her attacks against NATO. In the third phase, with widespread recognition of a much-reduced Soviet threat against Western Europe, de Gaulle turned his attention in 1965 to his Eastern policy of détente and rapprochement with the So-

---

ment to give the French army a new sense of mission and purpose after the bitter defeats in successive colonial wars, culminating in Algeria. It is true that de Gaulle himself referred to this point. (See his press conference, July 23, 1964, *Speeches and Press Conferences*, no. 208, p. 10.) But this author views such an explanation only as a supplementary motivation for French nuclear armament. As this study argues, the thrust of Gaullist reasoning for a French nuclear capability lay elsewhere—and principally in its contribution to de Gaulle's international policies.

viet Union and the East European states aimed at the eventual formation of a Europe "from the Atlantic to the Urals" and a system of pan-European security. His efforts were reinforced by the announcement of France's withdrawal from NATO in 1966. Finally, in the fourth and final phase, 1968-69, the invasion of Czechoslovakia caused a reassessment of Soviet policy and a postponement of de Gaulle's pan-European design, while France's domestic and monetary crisis raised doubts about the stability of the Gaullist regime, all of which undermined France's ambitious foreign policy objectives. The following examination of these phases reveals the continuous tension between de Gaulle's twin visions of a reordered European system and a restored global role for France, each of which was served in different ways by the evolving French nuclear force.

The initial phase, centering on de Gaulle's efforts to achieve Anglo-American acceptance of his 1958 tripartite proposal, has already been described in large part. However, Franco-American exchanges on this question continued through 1961, as we will see in Chapter 6. The persistence of a hostile Soviet attitude toward Western Europe —as revealed, for example in the 1958 and 1961 Berlin crises —made it necessary for de Gaulle to rely heavily on the United States and NATO to preserve French security, especially since France was then weakened domestically by unrest caused by the Algerian war. But the general had made clear his dissatisfaction with the organization and scope of the Atlantic alliance and had demanded coequal status with the United States and Great Britain in the formation and conduct of global strategy. As we have noted, one of his objectives may have been Anglo-Saxon acceptance of a French sphere of influence in Africa. Probably anticipating that his demands would not be met, de Gaulle had at the same time planted the seeds for his withdrawal from NATO later on when the reduction of the Soviet threat in Europe would allow it.

In this first phase of Gaullist policy French nuclear armament was only in the planning stages. It was argued, however, that the forthcoming French nuclear arsenal would put France on an equal footing with the Anglo-Saxon powers and thus justify her participation in a special triumvirate grouping of the Big Three to oversee Western security interests around the world. Had the tripartite scheme been accepted, the result would have been the consolidation of a system of East-West bloc politics. France, however, would have achieved special status in the Western bloc.

An Anglo-French-American directorate would have institutionalized discrimination within the Atlantic alliance and probably destroyed all hope of West European unity. In this respect, the Gaullist national objective of reinstating France as a great power with worldwide interests, based on the development of French nuclear capability, would have been served; it appeared that the objective of French *grandeur* and special international status took precedence during this phase over the idea of transforming the East-West power alignment in Europe into a different European equilibrium based on an independent European role. If the tripartite proposal is viewed, however, primarily as a tactical instrument whose acceptance de Gaulle never really expected, but which provided the foundation for France's later withdrawal from NATO and the pursuit of a pan-European policy, then it also served the longer-range Gaullist objective of revision of the European system following French disengagement from the Western military bloc.

By 1960 de Gaulle had begun to speak of his design for a "European entente from the Atlantic to the Urals," but he concentrated initially on achieving an "organized cooperation between states" in Western Europe in the fields of politics, economics, culture, and defense.[17] In his view, a strong grouping of states in Western Europe was a prerequisite for a new all-European equilibrium that would include the states in both halves of Europe. This concept led him actively to encourage the construction of a political union in

[17] See, e.g., his address of May 31, 1960 in *Major Addresses*, p. 78.

Western Europe on the model of the Fouchet plan during 1961-62,[18] the beginning of *the second phase* of his policy, and to resist President Kennedy's grand design for an integrated, Atlantic-oriented Europe in close partnership with the United States.[19] After the Fouchet negotiations failed in April 1962, when Belgium and the Netherlands refused further discussion until Great Britain had secured entry into the Common Market, de Gaulle's response was to make a start toward West European organization on a more modest scale on the basis of the Franco-German treaty of January 1963, which was the Fouchet plan writ small.

De Gaulle explained how West European unity fitted into his long-range pan-European design as follows:

> . . . the union of the Six, once achieved and all the more if it comes to be supplemented then by new European memberships and associations, can and must be, toward the United States, a valid partner in all areas, I mean powerful and independent. The union of the Six can and must also be one of the piers on which will gradually be built first the equilibrium, then the cooperation and then, perhaps one day, the union of all of Europe, which would enable our continent to settle its own problems peacefully, particularly that of Germany, including its reunification, and to attain, inasmuch as it is the main hearth of civilization, a material and human development worthy of its resources and its capacities.[20]

As part of his plan for a West European grouping of states, de Gaulle urged the creation of a European defense system around the nucleus of the French atomic force. The French government implied that French atomic arms would

[18] See Chapter 7 for a discussion of the Fouchet plan.

[19] See Chapter 6.

[20] From his press conference, February 21, 1966, *Speeches and Press Conferences*, no. 239.

be placed at the disposal of Western Europe when the necessary degree of political cooperation was attained, and on this basis he attempted to woo West Germany and the other European allies away from close defense ties with the United States. As Chapter 7 describes, the concept of Europeanization of the French force was left purposely ambiguous.[21] There was never any indication of French willingness to share control of the *force de frappe* with her European neighbors. Rather, it became clear that de Gaulle's primary aim was to use the advantage of an evolving French nuclear capability as a political card in her relations with Germany and other European states. If any serious discussion of the organization of West European defense ever developed, France would clearly assume the leading role as the only continental nuclear power. Thus, de Gaulle's concern for special French status took precedence over his concern for a coherent European role in a revised international system.

The Gaullist pursuit of *grandeur* and French leadership in Western Europe was manifested in other ways. France continued to oppose trends in the direction of supranational integration in the European Communities, as reflected by her resistance to expanding the authority of the EEC Commission during the 1965-66 crisis over agriculture[22] and her refusal to support increased cooperation in Euratom when it threatened French national control.[23] The Gaullist stand on European integration also had implications for the future of European defense, since it was unlikely that a loose European confederal structure which based its defense on

[21] The French position never was defined further than the following comment from an official government statement in 1964: "If a political Europe were formed with real responsibilities, France would be willing to study how this French deterrent could be used within the framework of the Europe of tomorrow." *The First Five Years of the Fifth Republic of France, January 1959–January 1964* (New York: Ambassade de France, Service de presse et d'information, 1964), p. 19.

[22] See John Newhouse, *Collision in Brussels: The Common Market Crisis of June 30, 1965* (New York: W. W. Norton, 1967).

[23] See Lawrence Scheinman, "Euratom: Nuclear Integration in Europe," *International Conciliation*, no. 563 (May 1967).

the coordination of national contributions could deal satisfactorily with the problem of nuclear control. Furthermore, de Gaulle resisted the enlargement of the European Community—as demonstrated in his 1963 veto of British entry (followed by another veto in 1967); he was undoubtedly moved not only by a fear of Britain's serving as a Trojan horse for expanding American influence on the Continent but also by a concern that France retain a preeminent position in Western Europe, which the United Kindgom would be in a position to challenge were she admitted to the Community.[24] Yet there was a contradiction here, too, in the Gaullist design, since without Great Britain it would be difficult to form a "European" Europe sufficiently strong to play an independent role between the superpowers.

By pursuing a highly nationalistic policy in Europe and blocking further steps toward West European integration, de Gaulle encouraged nationalist tendencies in the German Federal Republic and, indeed, in other countries of the European Community. This contributed to a politically fragmented Western Europe, rather than the increased West European cooperation which de Gaulle sought; the fragmentation guaranteed the perpetuation of the kind of strong American influence on the Continent that the general wanted to combat.

While maintaining France's participation in the Atlantic alliance during this period, de Gaulle resisted American military domination of Europe by opposing NATO and arguing that the American commitment to defend the Continent with nuclear weapons in case of Soviet attack was no longer credible. In his words, the Alliance had to be maintained "so long as the Soviets threaten the world. . . . If the free world were attacked, on the old or the new continent, France would take part in the common defense at the sides of her allies, with all the means that she has."[25] But NATO,

[24] See Chapter 8 for a discussion of the role of defense issues in Franco-British relations and the question of British entry into Europe.

[25] Press conference, May 15, 1962, *Major Addresses*, p. 179.

the Alliance's organization for military preparedness, was another matter; the general continued to attack the organization on grounds of its limited geographic scope, its domination by the Americans, and its "over-integration," which undermined national sovereignty in defense.[26] Similarly, as Chapter 6 describes, the American proposal for a multilateral nuclear force (MLF) was opposed as a device aimed at undermining the strategic and diplomatic utility of the French national *force de frappe* and denying Western Europe a fully independent voice over her own defense, since it was to remain subject to an American veto.

French strategy supported Gaullist diplomatic objectives. De Gaulle contended eloquently that, given recently acquired Soviet strategic power, "no one in the world—particularly no one in America—can say if, where, how, and to what extent the American nuclear weapons would be employed to defend Europe. . . . American nuclear power does not necessarily and immediately meet all the eventualities concerning Europe and France."[27] In this manner he justified the creation of France's independent atomic force. The general realized he needed, and indeed benefited from, the presence of the American nuclear umbrella to deter a major Soviet aggression against France and Western Europe. However, the French nuclear arsenal was held out as a "trigger" of American nuclear power in case of lesser provocations against which the United States might not be willing to muster a nuclear response. More fundamentally, however, French nuclear armament was presented as the core of a future West European defense independent from American control, the necessary basis for the Gaullist revisionist design for eventual disengagement from the Western bloc and the formation of an independent West European —and later all-European—political and security identity. Gaullist France had concluded that the American "flexible response strategy," which became the *de facto* strategy of

[26] *The First Five Years*, p. 18.
[27] Press conference, January 14, 1963, *Major Addresses*, p. 217.

NATO, not only contained great risks in its emphasis on conventional forces as the first counter to aggression in Europe and American monopoly of nuclear control, but that it also condemned Europe to a secondary strategic role.[28]

Unsuccessful at rallying West Germany and other members of the Six to his concept of a West European confederation, de Gaulle turned his attention beginning in 1965 to developing his Eastern policy of détente, entente, and cooperation, and to his pan-European design; thus began *the third phase* in Gaullist European and Atlantic diplomacy. Several factors provided the basis for this initiative. There was growing evidence that the Soviet Union had decided on a less militaristic policy toward Western Europe. American-Soviet dialogue was on the decline because of differences over the Vietnam war and the MLF, yet the nuclear stalemate between the two superpowers continued and showed signs of preventing any military confrontation (the dangers of which had been highlighted by the 1962 Cuban missile crisis). In the East, the Sino-Soviet conflict had grown more acute and produced further fragmentation within the Soviet bloc, while in the West, France continued to differ with her European allies about the future organization of Western Europe and its relations with the United States. French and Soviet views were converging on a number of issues: Vietnam, Cuba, American intervention in the Dominican Republic, the Congo, the MLF, U.N. financing. Furthermore, Russia seemed to be included in de Gaulle's pan-European concept of a Europe "from the Atlantic to the Urals," and worsening Franco-German relations together with continued French hostility to NATO simplified Franco-Soviet dialogue.

The initial basis for a warming up in Franco-Soviet relations was the general's statement on the German problem in February 1965, when he spoke of the reunification of Germany as a purely European problem, dependent upon

[28] For more on the Franco-American strategic conflict, see Chapter 6.

the recognition of Germany's present Eastern frontiers and the limitation of its armament (the implication being that Germany must not have nuclear weapons).[29] Evidence of Moscow's approval of these views was quickly forthcoming during the friendly visit of Soviet Foreign Minister Gromyko to Paris in May. His visit was followed by the appointment of a new high-ranking Soviet ambassador to Paris, Valerii Zorin, who in a lecture given soon after his arrival spoke of the Soviet Union and France as "the great continental European powers . . . called upon by their very location to play an important role in guaranteeing European security."[30] Meanwhile, Franco-Soviet trade was increasing and a Franco-Soviet agreement was signed in March 1965 on the joint exploitation of the French system of color television.

A fundamental step in this new phase of Gaullist policy was the French withdrawal from NATO military structures, first announced in the general's press conference on February 21, 1966. This move, which de Gaulle contemplated for a long time, was necessary for France's pursuit of a pan-European policy that included among its aims the creation of an all-European security system. It had finally become possible because of what de Gaulle termed "new conditions," in particular the reduction of the Soviet threat in Western Europe and new trends toward a peaceful and polycentric evolution in Eastern Europe. As de Gaulle observed, "the Western world is no longer threatened today as it was at the time when the American protectorate was set up in Europe under the cover of NATO."[31] In place of a threat from the East, the French leader spoke instead of the danger that America's involvement in extra-European conflicts, especially Vietnam, might engulf Europe in a con-

[29] Press conference, February 4, 1965, *Speeches and Press Conferences*, no. 216.

[30] As quoted in W. W. Kulski, *De Gaulle and the World* (Syracuse: Syracuse University Press, 1966), p. 304.

[31] Press conference, February 21, 1966, *Speeches and Press Conferences*, no. 239.

flagration, given American domination of NATO strategy and the American military presence on European soil. Another new condition noted by the French leader was the fact that France was now becoming an atomic power (the first-generation weapons of the *force de frappe*, atomic bombs carried by Mirage IV aircraft, were almost fully deployed) and would now begin "to assume itself the very extensive strategic and political responsibilities that this capacity involves."[32]

A further factor behind Gaullist policy in this phase was the French perception, not limited to Gaullists, that the United States had become the dominant world power and would automatically seek to extend its hegemony.[33] Based in part on persisting U.S. strategic power, this view was now reinforced by growing American economic and technological strength, which was expanding rapidly into European markets. American superiority in high-technology industries, such as computers, and in the management of large-scale international corporations was making it difficult for French and other European firms to compete.[34] In French eyes the international system was seen as gravitating toward a unipolar system, which was menacing the international balance. In place of a Soviet military threat, the de Gaulle Republic now saw subtle new forms of indirect threat in rising American power; the Gaullist response was to combat American influence wherever possible. Thus, "the

[32] Ibid.

[33] See the speech by de Gaulle reported in *Le Monde*, July 15, 1967; a similar view was expressed by critics on the French Left, such as Maurice Duverger, "America the Superpower," *Interplay*, I (October 1967). For a similar view from a scholar sympathetic to the French position, see George Liska, *Imperial America* (Baltimore: The Johns Hopkins Press, 1967). Raymond Aron assessed this thesis in a series of articles titled "Le gigantisme américain," *Le Figaro*, October 7, 12, 19, 1966.

[34] See J. J. Servan-Schreiber, *The American Challenge*, trans. Ronald Steel (New York: Atheneum, 1968); also Robert Gilpin, *France in the Age of the Scientific State* (Princeton: Princeton University Press, 1968).

struggle against the ally" became an overriding French objective and differences between France and the United States multiplied and encompassed almost every area of their foreign relations.

France's withdrawal from NATO seemed timed to underpin de Gaulle's eleven-day trip to the Soviet Union in June 1966, the high point in the French flirtation with Moscow. Despite a lavish reception and the spirit of growing détente which it fostered, the general's journey to Moscow achieved only modest results. No new ground was broken on the German question; the Soviet leaders repeated their insistence on recognition of the DDR and de Gaulle refused to go along. The principal fruits of the trip were a Moscow–Paris "hot-line," plus new Franco-Soviet cooperation in trade, science, and technology, peaceful uses of atomic energy, and outer-space exploration.

At the end of 1966 de Gaulle acclaimed: "The cold war that lasted for twenty years is in the process of disappearing." "Continental rapprochement," he said, was the goal of France's Eastern policy. Its purpose was the creation of a "European Europe" in order to "re-establish the peaceful equilibrium indispensable to the world" and to allow Europe to "take its place once again at the forefront of human progress."[35] In the months which followed, the French president and his senior officials continued to expand France's contacts and relations with Eastern Europe through a number of visits to many of the East European states.

French strategy during this period seemed intent on keeping open France's military options in order to preserve her independence and support her political efforts aimed at détente and cooperation with the East. Thus, France remained aloof from NATO and refused to commit herself in advance on the conditions under which French forces might cooperate with NATO troops in any European conflict. Talks between French Chief of Staff Ailleret and NATO

[35] New Year's message, December 31, 1966, *Speeches and Press Conferences*, no. 255.

Commander Lemnitzer, which were designed to clarify this situation, produced no result. Gaullist leaders frequently reiterated that France would not be drawn into any Soviet-American hostilities in Europe that might develop out of the Vietnam conflict, which the French government severely condemned.

In this new context the French nuclear force became an instrument to preserve France's freedom of action and support her intention to refuse participation in any defense activities of the Atlantic alliance with which she did not directly concur. The point was underscored by General Ailleret at the end of 1967 when he asserted that France should develop a system of defense worldwide in scope (*tous azimuts*) based on megaton warhead ballistic missiles with intercontinental range.[36] As discussed further on, this call for a bold extension of the French nuclear arsenal was consistent with de Gaulle's efforts to create a system of pan-European security and to fit France for the role of primary West European guarantor.

The main points of Ailleret's exposition were confirmed in the following months by President de Gaulle himself and by Defense Minister Messmer.[37] France appeared to be laying the groundwork for an ambitious new phase in her nuclear weapons program in the 1970's and for eventual withdrawal from the Atlantic alliance—the logical next step toward de Gaulle's espoused objective of French leadership of an all-European grouping of states independent of the two superpowers.

The Gaullist design for a reconstituted European system based on a reunited Europe independent of the superpowers contained positive elements for any future Euro-

[36] "Défense 'dirigée' ou défense 'tous azimuts,'" *Revue de défense nationale* (December 1967), pp. 1923-32. An English translation appeared in *Survival* (February 1968), pp. 38-43.

[37] See de Gaulle's speech at the École militaire, reported in *Le Monde*, January 30, 1968; Pierre Messmer, "L'Atome, cause et moyen d'une politique militaire autonome," *Revue de défense nationale* (March 1968), pp. 395-402.

pean settlement. However, it was also beset with a number of contradictions, stemming especially from de Gaulle's insistence on a special French status in the new European order that was clearly beyond French capabilities.

On the positive side, the Gaullist vision—in contrast to several alternative Atlantic designs—called for a developing West European identity free from direct military ties to the United States as the first step toward interesting the Soviets in the process of all-European engagement (i.e., removal of Soviet troops from Eastern Europe, to be followed by increased cooperation between the states in both halves of Europe and eventually some kind of all-European confederation). This diplomatic strategy does have merit, for it is difficult to understand why the Soviet Union should ever disengage itself from the Eastern half of Europe as long as the Western half remains dominated militarily by the United States. France's expansion of contacts with the East European states aimed at "breaking down the blocs," described here as the third phase of the general's European policy, was also an important contribution to the development of East–West détente politics in the middle 1960's. In several respects Gaullist initiatives helped prepare the way for the *Ostpolitik* launched by West Germany's Grand Coalition government in 1967, as well as President Johnson's policy of "bridge-building" with Eastern Europe.

But the Gaullist pan-European vision of a "Europe of states" extending "from the Atlantic to the Urals" was weakened by inconsistencies and paradoxes. First, the Soviet Union's position in this new European system was not altogether clear. De Gaulle often spoke of a "European" Europe independent of the superpowers. In this formulation Russia would seem to be excluded from the system (just as the United States would be) in order that the new pan-European grouping could wield an independent policy. On the other hand, if this Europe were to extend "to the Urals," Russia would necessarily be included in the new system. Other Gaullist utterances bear out such a conclusion and are based on the assumption that Russia was expected to play a balance-of-power role, along with France, in containing Germany and preserving the stability of the new European order.[38]

Among other ambiguities in the general's pan-European design, it is not clear how a loosely organized European confederal system could contain Germany. As Pierre Hassner has pointed out, "The overall weight of Germany as compared to France, and the other medium European states, constitutes the disruptive factor in any continental European system, and most strikingly so in such a system based on control by a Franco-Soviet concert."[39] It seems much more probable that the European balance will be determined by the nature of the relationship between Germany and Russia and that France, given her slender resources, will play a less important role. Developments in German-Soviet relations in the post–de Gaulle period tend to confirm this point.

Furthermore, the general's tactics and blunt diplomatic style frequently infuriated his allies, left France in isolation, and generally worked against the realization of his European design. During a period when Western Europe's defenses (including the French nuclear force) were generally weak, France had to rely as much as her neighbors on the protection provided by American troops stationed on West European soil, as well as on the American nuclear umbrella, in

[38] André Fontaine commented in 1966: "In the Elysée it is increasingly clear that the entente must embrace all Europeans, including the Russians. Like all French schoolboys, de Gaulle learned that Europe extends 'from the Atlantic to the Urals.' But since he went to Novosibirsk he has been forced to persuade himself that the Urals, which are practically invisible from an airplane, are no more significant as an ethnic or political barrier than as a geographical one. Thus in his toast at the farewell reception in the Kremlin, he spoke of Europe 'from one end to the other.' This is more vague and cuts short many speculations caused earlier by his too-scholastic vocabulary." See his "What is French Policy?" p. 73.

[39] Pierre Hassner, "Change and Security in Europe, Part II: In Search of a System," *Adelphi Papers*, no. 49 (London: Institute for Strategic Studies, 1968), p. 30.

order to guarantee European security in case of a change in Soviet policy. In order to achieve first a strong, independent, West European group of states, and later his longer-range goal of all-European reconciliation, de Gaulle also required American cooperation. Yet the French leader engaged in a series of Olympian actions over a period of several years, always without prior consultation, that served only to alienate the United States. These actions were marked by opposition to and public contempt for American policies everywhere in the world.

The Gaullist pan-European vision, plus the hope that through it France would achieve a special European and global role, were abruptly jolted by two events in 1968. The domestic economic and political crisis which shook France as a result of the events of May weakened the stability of the Gaullist regime and undermined France's international standing, and hence her claim to leadership on the Continent. The Soviet invasion of Czechoslovakia was sudden proof that the general's pan-European design was premature and based upon an overly optimistic assessment of Soviet policy toward the Eastern bloc. These events caused several shifts in French positions toward Europe and the Atlantic and marked the beginning of *the fourth and final phase* of Gaullist foreign policy. Among the most important changes were the postponement of the Gaullist pan-European vision, a reassessment of France's relations with her European partners, and a warming-up in French policy toward NATO and the United States.

The Soviet intervention challenged several assumptions of de Gaulle's all-European policy of détente, entente, and cooperation. It raised serious concern about a new militaristic attitude in the Kremlin, and doubts about Soviet tolerance of liberalization and national autonomy in the Eastern European states, and of greater independence in their relations with the West. De Gaulle first condemned the Soviet invasion as a return to the policy of the two blocs begun at Yalta. He reasserted his intention to proceed with his efforts aimed at dismantling the blocs and working toward détente and European engagement, despite the setback of Czechoslovakia.[40] It was soon clear, however, that progress toward a European reconciliation along Gaullist lines would be postponed for a long time to come. De Gaulle's premise that contacts could be expanded and good relations developed simultaneously with Moscow and the East European states had been proved false. In the months which followed, French government statements, although indicating that the goals of France's Eastern policy remained unchanged, nevertheless admitted to a major revision in the time-perspective necessary before they might be realized.[41]

The domestic crises which shook France in 1968 weakened her political strength in the eyes of the world, thus affecting the means for carrying out French foreign policy and the chances for its success. Student revolts and industrial strikes shook the very foundations of the regime. De Gaulle survived the crisis with an impressive victory in the June elections by appealing for law and order in the face of an exaggerated Communist threat. He increased industrial salaries and promised reforms ("participation") in French government and university structures. But then he fired the man who had done most to surmount the disorder, Premier Georges Pompidou. When in November the French franc came under heavy speculative pressures and the government was forced to take new measures of eco-

[40] See de Gaulle's press conference, September 9, 1968, *Speeches and Press Conferences*, no. 1128.

[41] See the speech by Foreign Minister Michel Debré before the National Assembly on October 2, 1968, in *Le Monde*, October 3, 1968; Debré's speech at the U.N. General Assembly, October 7, 1968, *Speeches and Press Conferences*, no. 1141; and his speech before the National Assembly, November 7, 1968, *Le Monde*, November 9, 1968. Also Defense Minister Messmer's speech to the National Assembly, December 5, 1968, *Le Monde*, December 7, 1968.

nomic retrenchment, this added to the declining trust of Frenchmen in the stability of the Gaullist regime.

For a time after Czechoslovakia de Gaulle suspended all Franco-Soviet contacts, but he resumed them in January 1969, when a Soviet delegation headed by Deputy Premier Vladimir A. Kirillin visited Paris to discuss questions of trade and scientific cooperation. This was followed by the visit of French Minister Galley to Moscow in May for more detailed talks on cooperation in the area of atomic and space research and other scientific projects. An agreement was also signed the same month which called for a doubling of French-Soviet trade in the period 1970-74. Nevertheless, there were new limits to how far the Gaullist regime was willing to go in relations with Russia after the Czech crisis. No further forays by French leaders were made in Eastern Europe. In April 1969, at the twentieth anniversary meeting of the North Atlantic Treaty Organization in Washington, French Foreign Minister Debré agreed with the United States position that the time was not ripe to accept the Budapest appeal issued the previous month by the Warsaw Pact states for the convocation of an all-European security conference.

The invasion of Czechoslovakia and the new French domestic difficulties led to a reappraisal of Soviet intentions and an unequivocal statement that France planned to remain in the Atlantic alliance. Liaison with NATO was stepped up, and there were renewed efforts to cooperate with NATO forces in Europe and the Mediterranean. Friendlier relations were also reestablished with the United States, spurred by an apparent American decision to negotiate a settlement to the Vietnam war, American backing of de Gaulle's decision not to devalue the franc, and the advent of the Nixon administration.[42]

Although declared aims of French defense policy, like France's Eastern policy, were unchanged at the end of 1968,

[42] These changes are discussed further in Chapter 6.

there was a setback in the timetable of several military programs. The budgetary pressures arising out of France's domestic crisis of May and June, plus the international monetary crisis in November, forced a reduction in the military budget and the postponement of the 1969 nuclear tests. Officially, it was admitted that ongoing nuclear programs would be delayed about a year and that long-range plans for the period 1971-80 (which were to include intercontinental ballistic missiles) would be "revised and amputated."[43] The development of ICBMs was postponed indefinitely.

A significant change in French strategy announced in March 1969 seemed to underline French interest in a new kind of relationship with NATO. Lecturing before the Institute of Higher Defense Studies at the École militaire, General Michel Fourquet, the new chief of staff, announced that henceforth French military doctrine would contemplate a "series of graduated actions" to test out the strength of an eventual aggressor before recourse was made to a "strategic response."[44] This meant that French strategy was now moving toward "flexible response" based on the use of tactical nuclear weapons, a concept which NATO had adopted many years earlier despite French opposition. General Fourquet made no mention of the *tous azimuts* strategy of his predecessor, the late General Ailleret; instead he spoke specifically of an enemy "coming from the east." French forces would act "in close coordination" with allied forces in meeting an aggressor. Thus, France reverted to a much more modest strategy and laid the foundation for future defense cooperation with NATO and the United States.

[43] Defense Minister Pierre Messmer before the National Assembly, as reported in *Le Monde*, November 1 and December 7, 1968. See Chapter 5.

[44] "Emploi des differents systèmes de forces dans le cadre de la stratégie de dissuasion," *Revue de défense nationale* (May 1969), pp. 757-67; an English translation appeared in *Survival* (July 1969), pp. 206-11.

If the Gaullist concept of a Europe from the Atlantic to the Urals had been shaken by the Soviet occupation of Prague, other events in 1968 had moved de Gaulle to reassess his relations in Western Europe. In particular, the refusal of West Germany to revalue the deutschmark at the international monetary conference in Bonn in November was a sharp reminder to a weakened France of the growing political influence of the Federal Republic, based on her economic strength. It was probably this realization that moved de Gaulle to make a substantial overture to Great Britain in his talk with the British ambassador in Paris, Christopher Soames, in February 1969. De Gaulle's suggestion that Britain and France discuss the idea of a more loosely organized and broadly based economic association in Europe with an inner political council of four (France, Britain, Germany, and Italy) was misunderstood in London. However, the general, it appears, was seeking a way to promote British entry into an *Europe des États*, unhampered by traces of supranationality, in which Britain could help provide a counterbalance to Germany's fast expanding economic, and hence political, power.[45]

To summarize, sudden changes in France and in Europe during his last year in office had severely undermined the prospects for de Gaulle's twin visions mentioned at the outset of this chapter. The Soviet intervention in Prague all but destroyed the vision of a new pan-European grouping of states that might exert its own influence in world affairs, independent of the superpowers, and provide the basis for a new multipolar international order. The economic and social disruptions inside France revealed new instabilities in the Gaullist regime and undercut France's image abroad. Clearly, France was not capable of the leadership of Europe through which she had hoped to regain the status of an independent global power. Moreover, the new domes-

[45] See the revealing account of the "Soames affair" by André Fontaine, "Comment avorta le dialogue Franco-Britannique," *Le Monde hebdomadaire*, no. 1064 March 13-19, 1969.

tic strains on France's limited resources had postponed the realization of a panoply of nuclear weapons and was proof that a worldwide nuclear capability—the linchpin of de Gaulle's French and European visions—was beyond France's means. For a man so preoccupied with France's place in the world, the collapse of these foreign policy designs must have had a strong bearing on the general's decision to resign from office after his referendum defeat in April 1969.

French Strategy

In contrast to the United States, France has seen the development of only a small body of "strategic thought" since the initial Gaullist decision to develop the national deterrent. De Gaulle and his government spokesmen confined themselves to a few rather vague strategic notions in defending the *force de frappe*. These received little detailed elaboration and tended to be *ex post facto* explanations in military terms of earlier political choices. With few exceptions, detailed analysis of the strategic rationale for the French deterrent can only be found in the public writings of a few military analysts whose influence on the government, and especially on General de Gaulle, was known to be limited.[46]

As reorganized under the Fifth Republic, French armed forces are grouped in three categories. The first, which has clear priority, is the nuclear force: *la force nucléaire stratégique*. It is responsible for nuclear deterrence.[47] The

[46] The writings of some of these analysts will be discussed later in this chapter. One of them told the author a revealing anecdote in 1966. He had sent a copy of his book on nuclear strategy to General de Gaulle. The French president later sent a letter of reply, thanking the man for his interesting analysis of strategic questions, but stressing that for him the central and clearly the only important issue was: "Est-ce que la France restera la France?"

[47] See Chapter 5 for discussion of the elements of the nuclear strike force and its technical evolution.

second, *les forces de manœuvre*, are intervention forces charged with the task of opposing an enemy attack against France or one of her allies. They are composed of five army divisions, plus most of the forces of the navy and air force, and must be prepared for action on the Continent or outside of Europe. The forces of *la défense opérationnelle du territoire*, the third category, have the mission of resisting an enemy invader within the national territory. Made up primarily of army units, these forces are also available to maintain internal order in the country. The general objective of French defense policy was stated in 1964 as follows: "to maintain peace, without conceding anything which compromises the independence, security, and integrity of the country. Intended first of all to deter (*dissuader*) an eventual aggressor by the threat of an atomic riposte, the means of this policy affirm our will to fight if war should be imposed on us."[48]

Within this framework, the officially stated mission of the nuclear force was: "to deter, and if deterrence does not work, to strike in the shortest possible time at the designated enemy targets with the most powerful nuclear explosives." In consideration of her capabilities, France's nuclear weapons would be targeted on population centers.[49] As with other French forces, the action of the nuclear force would in principal be coordinated (*conjuguée*) with the forces of France's allies.[50]

[48] From the "Exposé des Motifs" of the 1964 program law, Assemblée nationale, *Projet de loi de programme relative à certains équipements militaires*, annexed to the record of the debates of November 6, 1964, no. 1,155 (Paris: Imprimerie nationale, 1964), p. 7. See also the following on the general organization of the French armed forces: Pierre Messmer, "Notre politique militaire," *Revue de défense nationale* (May 1963), pp. 754-61; *France and Its Armed Forces* (New York: Ambassade de France, Service de presse et d'information, December 1964); "Les Moyens de la dissuasion," *Note d'information*, no. 4 (Paris: Ministère des armées, Service d'information, d'études et de cinématographie, 1965).

[49] Messmer, "Notre Politique militaire," pp. 745-47.

[50] *Projet de loi de programme, 1964*, p. 7.

Among de Gaulle's few statements on strategy, the following remark defending the French nuclear force in terms of proportional deterrence is illustrative:

> We are in a position to think that six years from now our deterrent means will reach a total instantaneous power of 2,000 Hiroshima bombs. . . . The field of deterrence is thus henceforth open to us. For to attack France would be equivalent, for whomever it might be, to undergoing frightful destruction itself. Doubtless the megatons that we could launch would not equal in number those that Americans and Russians are able to unleash. But, once reaching a certain nuclear capability, and with regard to one's own direct defense, the proportion of respective means has no absolute value. Indeed, since a man and a people can die only once, the deterrent exists provided that one has the means to wound the possible aggressor mortally, that one is very determined to do it and that the aggressor is convinced of it.[51]

Another allusion by the general was in even simpler terms:

> . . . the French atomic force, from the very beginning of its establishment, will have the sombre and terrible capability of destroying in a few seconds millions and millions of men. This fact cannot fail to have at least some bearing on the intents of any possible aggressor.[52]

The idea of proportional deterrence was developed in greatest detail by General Pierre M. Gallois and adopted by President de Gaulle.[53] It is, however, the only one of Gallois's controversial theories which the French president accepted, a point to which we will return later in this chapter. The heart of the proportional deterrence principle is that

[51] Press conference, July 23, 1964, *Speeches and Press Conferences*, no. 208, p. 9.

[52] Press conference, January 14, 1963, *Major Addresses*, p. 218.

[53] See Gallois's book, *Stratégie de l'âge nucléaire* (Paris: Calmann-Lévy, 1960); English translation, *The Balance of Terror* (Boston: Houghton Mifflin Co., 1961).

a small national atomic force designed for use in a "massive retaliation" strategy has a deterrent value against a potential great power aggressor nation, since the consequences such a force could inflict on the great power would exceed the value to the latter of taking over or destroying the small or medium-sized state. Thus, "The thermonuclear force can be proportional to the value of the stake it is defending."[54] This principle is the cornerstone of the strategic rationale for the French deterrent. As many analysts have noted, the argument is essentially valid if the small atomic force is safe from surprise attack, i.e., relatively invulnerable (which the French force certainly is not in its first-generation weapons based on Mirage IV aircraft), and if the medium-sized state can convince potential great power aggressors that under certain conditions it would accept annihilation rather than surrender.

The most detailed presentation of French "massive retaliation" strategy is General Ailleret's speech in 1964, intended as a rebuttal to the American "flexible response" doctrine. Ailleret rejected as inadequate a purely conventional defense of Europe and argued that even an early recourse to tactical nuclear weapons was unsatisfactory to Europeans, in view of the widespread destruction it would cause. As he explained, "Even a purely tactical nuclear exchange would completely wipe out Europe over a depth of eighteen hundred miles from the Atlantic to the Soviet frontier." His conclusion was that only strategic nuclear weapons were capable of defending France and Europe without local devastation and loss of territory. Moreover, only the threat of immediate strategic retaliation with nuclear arms would have a sufficiently strong deterrent effect on Moscow to prevent Soviet aggression in Europe.[55] Ailleret's speech struck a sympathetic cord among many other Europeans who

[54] Gallois, English ed., p. 137.

[55] "Opinion sur la théorie stratégique de la 'flexible response,'" speech delivered before the NATO Defense College, June 26, 1964, reprinted in the *Revue de défense nationale* (August 1964), pp. 1323-40.

viewed the shift in American strategy ushered in by the Kennedy administration with some alarm—notably because the new U.S. emphasis on conventional defense promised to turn Europe once more into a battlefield, if hostilities ever occurred.[56]

Another basic assumption of official French strategy is that the French nuclear force could serve, in case of an extreme provocation against France or Western Europe, as a "trigger" of the American nuclear arsenal. The scenario runs as follows: If the Soviets threatened or actually began an invasion, France would threaten to use her atomic force. Moscow would probably counterthreaten the annihilation of France with Soviet missiles. This, it is contended, would force the United States into a declaration of solidarity with France, if one had not been forthcoming already. The uncertainty of this kind of chain of events actually occurring would be enough to deter the Russians from any attack, or threat of aggression. Thus, deterrence in Europe is actually strengthened by the presence of the French atomic force.[57]

Although never detailed in official French statements, there have been several allusions to this kind of reasoning; and it became a part of the strategic rationale for the *force de frappe*. In a speech in 1964 at Strasbourg, de Gaulle spoke of the desirability of establishing a European defense system (presumably organized around a French nuclear core) in order to assure "the *initial safeguard* of the Old Continent," implying that the United States would have to

[56] France played on this European concern in defending her own strategy as an alternative to the frequently shifting American doctrine. The French government also continued to voice its dissatisfaction with the adoption of "flexible response" as the *de facto* strategy of NATO, in spite of French protests. See, e.g., Defense Minister Messmer's interview in *U.S. News and World Report* (September 24, 1962), p. 72; also the statement explaining the reasons for the French force in "Les Expériments nucléaires dans le Pacifique," *Note d'information*, no. 14 (Paris: Ministère des armées, May 1966), p. 2.

[57] Stanley Hoffmann has termed this concept "preventive triggering." See his "De Gaulle, Europe, and the Atlantic Alliance," p. 9.

come to the rescue in case of major conflict.[58] Similarly, Premier Pompidou stated a month later before the National Assembly that the Atlantic alliance "still provides today . . . the certitude of *final victory*; it no longer provides that of not being attacked."[59] He argued that the French nuclear force provided the only certain deterrence in Europe, although admitting that it was insufficient, by itself, to defeat the Soviet Union; he implied it could deter Moscow because of the likelihood that its use would engage the superior American nuclear arsenal. Finally, Jacques Baumel, secretary-general of the Gaullist party, the UNR-UDT, referred to the French nuclear force as "le *parachute de sécurité* de la France face aux hésitations de ses alliés dans le monde."[60]

The most sophisticated treatment of this concept is found in the writings of General André Beaufre, by far the most creative and interesting French nuclear strategist of the Gaullist period. In his book *Dissuasion et stratégie*, first published in 1964, Beaufre wove a subtle fabric of strategic logic around the idea of "multilateral deterrence."[61] His theory is based on his concept of deterrence, which he analyzed on several levels, the nuclear level being the most important one. Beaufre's principal concern was that nuclear deterrence in Europe had become too stable, in view of the deterrent strength of NATO and the evolution that had led to less aggressive policies in the Soviet Union. Worried that the threat of using nuclear weapons over a conflict in Europe had lost credibility for either superpower, Beaufre argued that the uncertainty of a possible nuclear confrontation should be stepped up through the addition of other independent centers of nuclear decision-making.

[58] Speech at Strasbourg, November 22, 1964, *Speeches and Press Conferences*, no. 212, pp. 3-4. (Italics added.)

[59] *Journal officiel*, Assemblée nationale, Débats parlementaires (December 3, 1964), pp. 5780-81.

[60] As quoted in *Le Monde*, October 8, 1963.

[61] André Beaufre, *Dissuasion et stratégie* (Paris: Armand Colin, 1964).

National nuclear forces in Europe, he concluded, would strengthen overall deterrence. From the standpoint of his deterrence theory, therefore, independent forces such as the French *force de dissuasion* are desirable, although it is implicit in his argument that these forces should be coordinated in some fashion with the American deterrent.

According to Beaufre, a framework of multilateral deterrence results when there are more than two nuclear powers involved in a strategic relationship. He defended the French force on the basis of "proportional deterrence" and because it could serve to increase the level of uncertainty faced by the Soviet Union over potential aggression in Europe, a zone of possible "marginal interest" for the United States. Underlying Beaufre's reasoning was the notion that the French nuclear force might "trigger" the use of the American nuclear deterrent in case of a major conflict, or at least that the Soviet Union would have to live with this uncertainty. Thus, the existence of the French force would increase Western deterrence vis-à-vis Moscow and further discourage any Soviet attack against Europe or any sort of nuclear blackmail.

Although Beaufre supported the French nuclear deterrent, he was not a spokesman for General de Gaulle, who did not concern himself with such strategic nuances. Beaufre's ideas received wide attention in French military circles, however. They provided the basis for a paper entitled "French Deterrence" in early 1965 which was reprinted several times by the French government and therefore must be taken as one of the few official statements of French strategic policy. Without using Beaufre's term of "multilateral deterrence," his reasoning was employed to explain how middle nuclear powers such as France could play a role in deterrence in case their vital interests were challenged and they represented a zone of possible "marginal interest" for the superpowers. The French nuclear striking force was said to represent a *jeton de présence* that would permit France to have its own voice in international affairs insofar as its destructive power was sufficiently credible to have a *valeur de pression.* Moreover, and most importantly, the existence of the independent French force would strengthen nuclear stability in the world because it would increase the element of uncertainty faced by each superpower with regard to the other in time of crisis.[62]

In the second half of the 1960's, French strategy evolved primarily in accordance with de Gaulle's shifting foreign policy objectives as outlined in the first part of this chapter. Thus, in the third phase of Gaullist policy—highlighted by a reduced Soviet threat in Europe, France's withdrawal from NATO military commands, new initiatives toward the East, and the deepening American involvement in Vietnam —the notion of the nuclear *détonateur* ("trigger") became less relevant. For then France's immediate concern was to guard her independence and to keep from being drawn into any future hostilities in Europe that might grow out of a superpower confrontation elsewhere—in Vietnam, for example. The French government declared itself ready to join with its Atlantic allies to meet an aggression against one of them only if it considered that aggression "unprovoked" (*non provoquée*). Paris retained the option of defining any aggression in its own way and refused participation in NATO defense structures until after a conflict had broken out and France had decided to apply Article 5 of the North Atlantic Treaty. In this context the French nuclear force became an instrument to help France stay aloof from any defense activities of the Alliance with which she did not directly concur.

[62] See XX, "La dissuasion française," *Revue de défense nationale* (June 1965), pp. 985-94; reprinted as a *Note d'information*, no. 3 (May 1965), by the Service d'information, d'études et de cinématographie des armées, and later as *Notes et études documentaires*, no. 3343 (December 6, 1966). This document is also reproduced under the title "French Defense Policy," in *Survival* (January 1968), pp. 12-16.

See also the article by Raymond Bousquet, "La Force nucléaire stratégique française," *Revue de défense nationale* (May 1966), pp. 793-811.

A further reason behind the French stance was the refusal in Paris to be part of a military bloc designed "to prepare, as if it was ineluctable, a battle between the East and the West."[63] In French eyes this was not consistent with de Gaulle's policy of détente and rapprochement with the East European states and the eventual formation of some kind of all-European security system.

The climax of this development was the *tous azimuts* strategy announced by General Charles Ailleret in December 1967, and confirmed a month later by President de Gaulle. Ailleret asserted that "an *a priori* alliance" could no longer provide France with a general guarantee of her security "since it is almost impossible to forsee what could one day be the cause of a serious conflict, and what would be the distribution of the powers between the various sides, or what hold, even unauthorized, any power would have over the territory of any other power." His conclusion was that over the coming decades France must build a complete defense system, to include "a significant quantity . . . of megaton ballistic missiles, with a world-wide range." Such a system, which would not be directed against anyone but aimed at all points of the compass, would allow France "to wield the maximum power afforded by its national resources."[64]

The theme of General Ailleret's statement—that France must have an independent defense based on a nuclear force deployable anywhere in the world—was not new. In a sense it was simply a restatement of de Gaulle's École militaire address in November 1959, discussed earlier in this study. However, Ailleret's strong attack against the whole concept

[63] See "La France et l'Alliance Atlantique," *Note d'information*, no. 17 (August 1966).

[64] Général d'armée Ailleret, "Défense 'dirigée' ou défense 'tous azimuts.'" The quotations are from the English translation which appeared in *Survival* (February 1968).

On January 27, 1968, General de Gaulle endorsed the *tous azimuts* strategy in a speech at the École militaire; he linked it to the strategy of Marshal Sebastien Vauban in the reign of Louis XIV and asserted that the same strategy was valid for France today in the realm of nuclear deterrence. See *Le Monde*, January 30, 1968.

of France's participation in alliances for security purposes went beyond de Gaulle's 1959 speech and seemed to augur France's withdrawal from the Atlantic alliance (the natural consummation of the 1966 withdrawal from NATO commands) in the not-too-distant future. Furthermore, his call for the expansion of France's nuclear force to include ICBMs with thermonuclear warheads promised to place an enormous strain on France's limited resources. At a time when no country was threatening France, Ailleret's conception seemed to be aimed solely at extending France's world influence on the assumption that nuclear weapons could be used as a threat in the diplomatic game of world politics. This seemed logically to correspond with de Gaulle's long-range design for France as the key continental nuclear power which could assume the role of a guarantor in a future pan-European security framework.

Ailleret's proposals for the addition of ICBMs to the French nuclear arsenal as the basis for a *tous azimuts* strategy became part of the preliminary planning for the third military program law for 1971-75. According to Defense Minister Messmer, several options were being prepared in early 1968 to fulfill this new strategic mission, which might be implemented either with surface-to-surface rockets with a range of 5,000 to 6,000 miles, with submarine-based missile systems, or by a combination of the two.[65] These possibilities sparked an interservice debate as the French navy urged the government to concentrate on developing new nuclear submarine-based missiles with thermonuclear warheads, while the air force held out for an intercontinental land-based missile.[66] The idea of a *tous azimuts* extension of

[65] Pierre Messmer, "L'Atome, cause et moyen d'une politique militaire autonome," *Revue de défense nationale* (March 1968), pp. 395-402.

[66] See *Le Monde*, September 20, 1968, and February 23/24, 1969. In an article entitled "Défense tous azimuts? Oui mais . . . ," retired General Edmond Combaux argued forcefully that a *tous azimuts* strategy was beyond French resources and made sense only in the context of a larger European defense system including France and

France's nuclear capability provoked considerable criticism, both at home and abroad.[67]

As explained earlier, the budgetary pressures caused by the May–June events and the monetary crisis of 1968 undercut any such ambitious expansion of the *force de dissuasion*, while the Soviet invasion of Czechoslovakia caused a reassessment of Kremlin policy toward Europe. By the closing months of General de Gaulle's tenure of office, French strategy—as reformulated by Chief of Staff General Michel Fourquet—had dropped all reference to *tous azimuts* (more a political doctrine than a strategy) and was again directed against a preferred enemy "coming from the East."[68] Consonant with a warming up in France's attitude toward NATO begun the previous fall, Fourquet also indicated that French forces would now "normally act in close coordination with the forces of our allies." And cost studies had by now convinced analysts in the Defense Ministry that the question of constructing French intercontinental missiles would have to be postponed into the far distant future.

General Fourquet's restatement of French defense policy provided evidence of another significant change in French strategy—a moving away from "all-or-nothing" thinking about the use of nuclear weapons toward a doctrine of graduated response. Although timed to mesh with an overall foreign policy retrenchment, this change reflected a gradual evolution in strategic thought unrelated in itself to political dogmas, as the day approached when French armed forces would have operational tactical nuclear arms.

---

other countries of an expanded European Community; *Revue de défense nationale* (November 1968), pp. 1600-18.

[67] See, e.g., Alfred Grosser, "Doubts About Defence," in *Survival* (February 1968), pp. 43ff., translation from an article in *Le Monde*, December 21, 1967; also Alastair Buchan, "Battening Down Vauban's Hatches," *Interplay* (May 1968), pp. 4-7.

[68] General Fourquet's address before the Institut des hautes études de défense nationale on March 3, 1969, was reprinted as "Emploi des différents systèmes de forces dans le cadre de la stratégie de dissuasion," *Revue de défense nationale* (May 1969), pp. 757-67; an English translation appeared in *Survival* (July 1969), pp. 206-11.

The issue can be traced back to an interservice debate which began in 1964.

Following General Ailleret's June 1964 speech referred to earlier, stressing a strategic nuclear response as the key to a successful strategy of deterrence in Europe, a controversy ensued between the French army and air force over tactical nuclear warfare and the role of each of these services in such warfare. The army contended that ground forces had a mission in deterrence strategy and should be equipped with tactical atomic weapons for use on the front line against an invading enemy.[69] The air force, in rebuttal, asserted that it only had a logical mission in tactical nuclear strategy, since it could hit the enemy's support areas behind the lines of battle. In the air force view, the army should be confined to the role of a *sonnette*, sounding the alarm in case of aggression by an invading force, and of protecting nuclear delivery systems.[70] In reply, an unnamed group of officers of the army general staff disputed the air force position; they maintained that an invading enemy force must be attacked with tactical nuclear firepower at the front line, not just in the rear, and that the army must have such a capability. Moreover, nuclear artillery was alleged to be superior to aircraft-delivered atomic charges, and also cheaper.[71]

This interservice rivalry provoked the intervention of General Ailleret, probably on the insistence of President de Gaulle. Ailleret came up with a compromise *aero-terrestre* formula under which both the army and the air force would receive tactical atomic arms.[72] But just how and

[69] General Le Puloch, "L'Avenir des armées de terre," *Revue de défense nationale* (June 1964), pp. 947-60.

[70] "L'Armée de l'air dans le contexte nucléaire," *Revue de défense nationale* (October 1964), pp. 1499-1517.

[71] "L'Armée de terre et l'armement atomique tactique," *L'Armée: Revue périodique des armées de terre* (January 1965), pp. 6-12. See also the article summarizing the military debate by Jean Planchais in *Le Monde*, January 19, 1965.

[72] See General Ailleret, "Evolution nécessaire de nos structures militaires," *Revue de défense nationale* (June 1965), pp. 947-55; also the article in the *Journal de Genève*, February 12, 1965.

when these weapons would be used, and their relationship to the strategic nuclear deterrent in an attack and post-attack situation if overall deterrence failed, was left obscure.

Defense Minister Messmer focused attention again on this question at the end of 1968 in a brief statement before the National Assembly. The action of the ground, air, and naval forces, he declared, would permit the government and military commands to judge the intentions of an enemy and oblige him to escalate the levels of conflict. This would confirm the adversary's aggressive intent and expose him to a massive strategic nuclear riposte.[73] It is this function, known in earlier NATO parlance as the "trip wire," that General Fourquet clarified in French strategy for the first time.[74]

The keystone of the Fourquet doctrine, the result of a major policy review begun in the autumn of 1968, is its acceptance of the principle of graduated or flexible response (*la réplique graduée*) in place of the earlier all-out, massive retaliation strategy. Implementation of the new doctrine depends first and foremost on the use of tactical nuclear weapons, to be ready about 1972, while holding in reserve the strategic nuclear force as the ultima ratio weapon.

The essentially tripartite functional division of French forces previously described is maintained, but the missions of the *forces de manœuvre* and the *défense opérationnel du territoire* (DOT) are redefined. The combined land-air battle force constituting the *forces de manœuvre*, which will have tactical nuclear arms, now has the task of "testing the enemy's intentions" and demonstrating "our [France's] will not to submit, whatever the consequences." This testing will occur first with conventional weapons, then with tactical atomic charges (the Pluton battlefield missile or air-

[73] *Journal officiel*, Assemblée nationale, December 5, 1968, p. 5128.

[74] See also the report on the mission of the ground forces according to General Cantarel, army chief of staff, in *Le Monde*, February 8, 1969; and the unsigned article entitled "L'Armée de terre dans l'appareil militaire français," in *L'Armée*, no. 85 (March 1969), pp. 2-9.

dropped tactical bombs) as the stakes are gradually raised in an effort to halt the enemy's advance, thus affording governmental authorities time to weigh the necessity of resort to a strategic nuclear strike. The primary task of the conventional DOT forces is the protection of missile bases, airfields, and communications facilities of the strategic nuclear force; it also opposes any invasion forces that have penetrated French territory and, with the gendarmery, helps to maintain internal order. All French forces are thus related to the general strategy of deterrence. "Deterrence," in Fourquet's words, "must be equally manifested at all conceivable stages of combat so that our will to resist any aggression appears quite clear, and marks our determination to have, if necessary, rapid and inevitable recourse to the ultimate weapon."[75]

The Fourquet strategy provides the basis for increased French cooperation with NATO in the post–de Gaulle era. First, in terms of strategic doctrine, France approached for the first time the "flexible response" principle practiced by NATO officially since 1967 and *de facto* since the early part of the decade. The exact definition of the French nuclear threshold is still unspecified, however, and is likely to be below that envisioned by NATO forces. But for the strategy to work, given the location of French forces in Germany behind allied forces immediately stationed on the East German-Czech frontier, French forces will have to work closely with NATO units, be familiar with their organization and firepower, and coordinate contingency plans with them concerning, *inter alia*, the circumstances when the threshold between conventional and tactical nuclear weapons is to be crossed in case of an enemy attack.

Secondly, since French tactical atomic arms will not be available before 1972 at the earliest, the French government has an incentive to seek an arrangement with NATO whereby French forces might be provided with these weapons on

[75] Quotations are from the English version of General Fourquet's article in *Survival.*

a contingency basis in the interim period. (French forces lost the right to use NATO tactical nuclear weapons when France withdrew from the organization's military structures in 1966.) Indeed, such an arrangement was discussed in talks between General Fourquet and NATO Supreme Commander Lyman Lemnitzer in late 1968 and early 1969.[76] This may continue to be a subject of French-NATO and French-American dialogue under de Gaulle's successor, President Pompidou.

On the other hand, aside from political considerations, there are several strategic reasons why France may wish to remain independent from NATO command structures. First, the French believe that NATO strategy relies too heavily on the use of conventional forces and has set the nuclear threshold at too high a level for effective deterrence. This point is clearly made in Fourquet's article. Secondly, the credibility of the French deterrent is seen to depend on early and repeated contact with the enemy; yet this might be denied by NATO contingency plans and the facts of geography, given the position of French forces in Germany. In such a case the French deterrent "might only be used to protect French territory."[77] Thirdly, the French undoubtedly want to ensure that the NATO "pause" is not at the expense of their own soil, and they would be prepared in some cases of an enemy advance to escalate more rapidly to the nuclear level.[78]

French Policy on Disarmament and Arms Control

The policies of the Gaullist Fifth Republic on disarmament and arms control were also anchored in the two visions of

[76] *Le Monde*, April 4 and 5, 1969.

[77] Fourquet, *Survival*.

[78] These points are discussed briefly in Michael J. Brenner, "France's New Defense Strategy and the Atlantic Puzzle," *Bulletin of the Atomic Scientists* (November 1969), pp. 4-7.

the international system described at the beginning of this chapter. On the one hand, Gaullist France viewed with suspicion all efforts by the Soviet Union and the United States to negotiate agreements on nuclear arms. The de Gaulle government refused to participate in arms-control accords that protected the nuclear monopoly positions of the superpowers and discriminated against smaller states. This corresponded to basic Gaullist hostility toward a bipolar international system dominated by Moscow and Washington. Gaullist arms-control policies, which favored efforts toward complete disarmament and the destruction of nuclear stocks and delivery vehicles, were designed to help break down this bipolar system and move toward a multipolar world order.

Gaullist policy in this field was also influenced by the general's vision of a rebirth of France's *grandeur* and a French global political and security role. France has declined to participate in the Eighteen Nation Geneva Disarmament Conference since 1961 because it includes nonnuclear states, which could only dilute French prestige and influence and hinder the task of discussing effective disarmament measures. These could only be based on agreement among the nuclear powers. As suggested by the 1958 tripartite proposal, which would have given France equal recognition with Britain and the United States in matters of global security, France was unwilling to settle for less in international arms control and disarmament negotiations and would participate in such discussions only if her role as a global nuclear power could be clearly recognized. As de Gaulle said in 1962 when he explained France's empty-chair policy at Geneva:

> Of course, if there should one day be a meeting of States that truly want to organize disarmament—and such a meeting should, in our mind, be composed of the four atomic powers—France would participate in it wholeheartedly. Until such time, she does not see the need for

taking part in proceedings whose inevitable outcome is . . . disillusion.[79]

Similarly, Gaullist France opposed all arms control efforts that would hinder her own nuclear development and impede her assumption of the global security mission she saw for herself.

The priority placed on disarmament has been a cornerstone of French policy since World War II, as France sought to prevent discrimination against the smaller powers and to reassert her international role.[80] When de Gaulle regained power and pressed forward with the development of a French atomic arsenal, French pronouncements increasingly emphasized steps toward total disarmament and opposed any arms-control policies that might threaten the development of the French nuclear program. The general said in 1959: ". . . if the Anglo-Saxons and the Soviets agree among themselves to halt their tests, France can only approve. But, if anybody wished to ask France to renounce atomic weapons for herself, while others are in possession of them and are developing them in tremendous quantities, there is not the slightest chance that she would accede to such a request."[81] Speaking as premier in 1967 before the National Assembly, Georges Pompidou likewise spoke disapprovingly of "the system in which the two great powers, overarmed with nuclear weapons—the United States and the Soviet Union—would organize the disarmament of the others. . . ." He saw this situation, in which the disarmed countries would be forced "to separate into two blocs, each huddling under the protective wing that he would have chosen" as menacing to world peace.[82] At the same time,

[79] Press conference, May 15, 1962, *Major Addresses*, p. 182.

[80] See, e.g., Wolf Mendl, "French Attitudes on Disarmament," *Survival*, IX (December 1967), pp. 393-97.

[81] Press conference, November 10, 1959, *Major Addresses*, p. 61.

[82] Premier Pompidou before the National Assembly, April 20, 1967, *Textes et Notes*, no. 200/IP, May 2, 1967 (Paris: La Documentation française), p. 14.

Gaullist officials repeatedly stated that France would renounce atomic weapons only on the condition that the other nuclear powers did likewise and agreed to destroy their existing stocks of nuclear arms and delivery vehicles.

It followed that Gaullist France would oppose the two major international arms-control agreements of the 1960's. In refusing to sign the Test Ban Treaty of 1963, de Gaulle termed the treaty "of only limited practical importance" as long as the existing nuclear means of the United States and the Soviet Union, as well as their right to continue manufacturing more atomic arms, were not affected.[83] The treaty was also viewed as discriminatory against France, which was just beginning to acquire a nuclear arsenal. As Foreign Minister Couve de Murville said of the Moscow treaty, "What is at stake is not to disarm those who are armed, but to prevent those who are not armed from arming, and that is what we, as far as we are concerned, cannot find satisfactory."[84]

France viewed the Non-Proliferation Treaty in a similar light. When the United States and the Soviet Union submitted identical draft treaties to the Geneva conference in August 1967, France confirmed her intention not to sign the treaty since it would not represent a true measure of disarmament.[85] After Soviet-American agreement was obtained and the final version of the treaty was presented to the United Nations General Assembly, the French government expressed its sympathy for the principle of non-proliferation and its intention to conduct itself in the future exactly as would signatory states. But France abstained in the U.N. vote on the treaty and refused to sign it. Again, her representative stated that it did not touch on the real problem—the necessity for the nuclear powers to join together

[83] De Gaulle's press conference, July 29, 1963, *Major Addresses*, pp. 237-38.

[84] Interview with France-Inter radio network, January 7, 1967, *Speeches and Press Conferences*, no. 256.

[85] *Le Monde*, August 27-28, 1967.

and agree on steps toward the disappearance of nuclear arms through the prohibiting of their manufacture and the destruction of existing stocks.[86] In French eyes the Non-Proliferation Treaty was yet another measure that strengthened the monopoly positions of the superpowers at the expense of the smaller states.

The French approach to disarmament was primarily political and was linked to the Gaullist position on East–West relations and a European settlement. In the Gaullist revisionist perspective the major requirement for world peace and international stability was a political settlement by the great powers of the fundamental issues of Europe's division, especially the future of Germany. De Gaulle's policy of détente with the East was aimed at gradually creating the climate for such a settlement. In this context disarmament was subordinated to the resolution of Europe's political conflicts and was seen only as a later step toward international stability, if the nuclear powers could agree on it. In contrast to the superpowers, for whom arms-control measures represented instruments of détente, for France détente came before arms-control and disarmanent efforts.[87]

The one notable exception was the case of Germany. For it was an axiom of the Gaullist revisionist design that the stability of an all-European security system depended upon preservation of Germany's non-nuclear status and acceptance of other kinds of arms limitations. This was the one kind of arms control that France insisted upon immediately, for it was necessary that Germany be subordinate to France in the military field if France were to become a leader and guarantor of an all-European security system, as called for by the second Gaullist vision of France as a reinstated great power with special European and global security responsibilities.

[86] See the statement by Armand Berard, French permanent representative, before the General Assembly, June 12, 1968 (Ambassade de France, no. 1100).

[87] See speeches by Couve de Murville, April 30, 1959, *Speeches and Press Conferences*, no. 144, p. 6; and September 29, 1965, *Speeches and Press Conferences*, no. 229, pp. 6-7.

Opposition to the Force de Frappe—The Nuclear Debate in France under de Gaulle

The nuclear force was the object of much criticism in France in the early 1960's, both inside and outside parliament. This opposition gradually diminished as the *force de dissuasion* became a reality. The French debate on the nuclear weapons program of the de Gaulle government, which is considered only briefly here, can be discussed on several levels.

Parliamentary debate on the *force de frappe* was most vigorous in the fall of 1960 when the government presented the first military program law, in July of 1962 at the time of the supplemental appropriation request for the Pierrelatte isotope separation plant, and in the spring of 1966 following de Gaulle's announcement of France's withdrawal from NATO. During each of these three periods of debate, one or more censure motions were offered by the opposition to challenge the government's policy; all of these motions failed to pass. In addition, some parliamentary discussion of the French nuclear force frequently accompanied the annual consideration of the military budget.

The attitude of the non-Gaullist political parties and groupings was almost totally hostile, but with differences in emphasis.[88] These ranged from advocacy of abandonment of the nuclear deterrent for a policy of disarmament to the pursuit of nuclear armament, but in a European or Atlantic context rather than as a purely national effort. In the presidential election campaign of 1965, the two major challengers—Jean Lecanuet and François Mitterand—opposed the *force de frappe*. Lecanuet favored French participation in a European nuclear force coordinated with the American deterrent. He implied that he would place the French national force in a European framework, but details were not offered as to how this might be done. Mitterand,

[88] At party congresses, the Communist party, the SFIO, the Radicals, the MRP, the Rassemblement démocratique, and the Centre nationale des indépendants had all taken critical positions on the *force de frappe* by 1964. See *Le Monde*, December 12, 1964.

on the other hand, proposed to replace construction of the French force with a policy of non-proliferation, signature of the Test Ban Treaty, and participation in the Geneva disarmament conference; but he likewise was imprecise. If he had been elected, it is doubtful whether he would have abandoned the national nuclear arsenal completely, given the amount of money already spent on its construction.

In the spring 1967 parliamentary election, the nuclear force was much less an issue. The one point that did receive some attention was the technological spin-off value of the nuclear program, an argument used by Gaullists to meet opposition contentions that France should join in efforts to obtain a non-proliferation treaty. However, abolition of the *force de frappe* reemerged as a point of agreement in the joint platform issued by the Communists and Mitterand's Fédération de la gauche.

In the French press a lively debate took place on the nuclear deterrent in the early years, beginning in 1959-60. But this debate had tapered off by the end of 1964 when the question of whether or not France should construct a nuclear striking force had been resolved by the government's determination to carry out the program. Henceforth, the existence of the *force de dissuasion* was more or less accepted as a fact.

Another form of opposition to Gaullist nuclear policy was protest demonstrations by various kinds of groups. In March 1963 a Ligue nationale contre la force de frappe was formed, with Jules Moch as president.[89] It took the lead in association with other disarmament groups in issuing leaflets and organizing several protest marches during 1963-64 in various parts of the country. The Mouvement contre l'armament atomique, another group of this kind led by Jean Rostand, was active during 1966 in protests against the French nuclear tests in the Pacific and other demonstrations.[90]

[89] *Le Monde*, March 7, 1963.

[90] *Le Monde*, March 1, 1966; *Tribune Socialiste*, March 5, 1966.

French public opinion, although divided on the issue, was moving toward majority acceptance of the national deterrent by the second half of the 1960's. According to the major French polling organization, IFOP (Institut français d'opinion publique), 46 percent of Frenchmen interviewed in the spring of 1966 favored the proposition that France must have her own national nuclear force; 42 percent opposed and 12 percent abstained. In the period 1962-64 the group that favored the national force had hovered around 27 to 29 percent, while the negative respondents had increased from 27 percent to 40 percent. The 1966 figures showed a lower percentage of abstentions than in earlier years, which would seem to indicate that a number of people who had not expressed themselves on the subject had rallied to the idea of a nuclear force.[91] In July 1965, however, IFOP undertook a poll on the question of the effectiveness of the French force in its stage of development at that time; 31 percent judged the French force effective, but 37 percent considered it ineffective.[92] Thus, although a large portion of the French people accepted the *force de frappe*, many remained skeptical about the credibility of the first-generation weapons.

The French strategic debate, as revealed in studies by more specialized analysts, took some time to develop. Indeed, it was not until 1963-64 that a number of books and articles began to appear on the question of the French nuclear force. In terms of breadth or sophistication, the French strategic literature is dwarfed by the far more extensive American writings, extending back to the early 1950's. However, a number of serious political-strategic commentaries have appeared in France. Several of these have come from retired French generals, the best-known

[91] See *Le Figaro*, August 2, 1966. For more detailed information on public opinion polls, see *Sondages*, the journal of IFOP.

[92] Ibid. For other opinion data on the *force de frappe* and related issues, see the results of a 1964 survey of French elite attitudes reported in Karl W. Deutsch et al., *France, Germany and the Western Alliance* (New York: Charles Scribner's Sons, 1967), pp. 27-115.

being Pierre M. Gallois and André Beaufre, both of whom developed an extensive theoretical defense for the national nuclear deterrent.

General Gallois was probably the first Frenchman to write and lecture seriously on questions of nuclear strategy. He explained the principle of "proportional deterrence" in his first book, published in 1960.[93] Later, however, his views became rather dogmatic and extreme. He argued that since the establishment of the Soviet-American "balance of terror," no country would risk thermonuclear war to protect another, but only to defend its own territory; that middle-power states therefore must possess their own national nuclear forces to protect their security, which they can do thanks to the principle of "proportional deterrence"; and that military alliances no longer have meaning, except for minor conflicts or for a "strategy of means"—i.e., for designing and producing armaments, the use of which must remain a national decision. For Gallois, nuclear proliferation is therefore inevitable, and even desirable, and the credibility of the American commitment to defend Europe with nuclear weapons is reduced to zero.[94] The many flaws and internal contradictions of General Gallois's reasoning are perhaps best exposed by Raymond Aron.[95]

General Beaufre is greatly superior to Gallois in the rigor and subtlety of his strategic logic. A contributor to *Le Figaro* and director of the Institut français d'études straté-

[93] *Stratégie de l'âge nucléaire* (Paris: Calmann-Lévy, 1960).

[94] See, e.g., the two Gallois essays which are included in *Pour ou contre la force de frappe* (Paris: Éditions John Didier, 1963), entitled "Chaque puissance nucléaire a deux visages" and "Pierrelatte a ses raisons." Also his "La nouvelle politique extérieure des États-Unis et la sécurité de l'Europe," *Revue de défense nationale* (April 1963), pp. 566-93; "The Raison d'Être of French Defence Policy," *International Affairs* (October 1963), pp. 497-510; his many other articles, especially those in *Politique étrangère; Paradoxes de la paix* (Paris: Presses du temps présent, 1967).

[95] See *Le Grand Débat* (Paris: Calmann-Lévy, 1963). The English edition is *The Great Debate: Theories of Nuclear Strategy* (Garden City, N.Y.: Doubleday and Co., 1965), ch. 4, pp. 120-44.

giques, he founded the journal *Stratégie* in which many of his own studies have been published. His principal ideas on nuclear strategy and the French nuclear force are found in *Dissuasion et stratégie*, published in 1964 and since translated into English.[96]

General Beaufre's theory of multilateral deterrence has already been described. Unlike Gallois, Beaufre continues to see some value in alliances in the age of nuclear weaponry. In order that national nuclear forces not be dangerous and introduce disorder into the international system, he regards it as necessary that they be "coordinated," although the decision to use them must remain a national responsibility. The fact that Beaufre has been unable to define precisely the kind of "coordination" required is a weakness of his theoretical structure, although he has suggested that two committees be formed in NATO to cooperate on targeting and on general contingency planning or crisis management.[97]

In analyzing General Beaufre's work, it is necessary to distinguish between Beaufre as a strategic theorist and Beaufre as a Gaullist.[98] Although he defended the idea of a French nuclear force, he did so from the basis of a theoretical framework which must be recognized as a significant contribution to strategic thought. It is likely that Beaufre, in reality, disagreed with many aspects of Gaullist nuclear policy, even though he did not publicly express his dissent; his views were certainly more pro-Atlantic alliance and pro-American than those of de Gaulle, as was reflected

[96] *Dissuasion et stratégie* (Paris: Armand Colin, 1964). Beaufre's other major works on strategy are *Introduction à la stratégie* (Paris: Armand Colin, 1963); *Stratégie de l'action* (Paris: Armand Colin, 1966); and *L'Otan et l'Europe* (Paris: Calmann-Lévy, 1966), available in translation as *NATO and Europe* (New York: Alfred A. Knopf, 1966).

[97] See his article entitled "Le problème du partage des responsabilités nucléaires," *Stratégie* (July-September, 1965), pp. 7-20.

[98] For a discussion of this problem, see Edward A. Kolodziej, "French Strategy Emergent—General Beaufre: A Critique," *World Politics* (April 1967), pp. 417-42.

by his book on NATO, *L'Otan et l'Europe,* published in 1966.

Next to Generals Beaufre and Gallois, the third most important writer on nuclear strategy in France has been Raymond Aron, the widely known political and social commentator who writes for *Le Figaro* and was for a long time professor of sociology at the Sorbonne. In his grand treatise on international relations, *Paix et guerre entre les nations,* Aron devoted considerable space to an analysis of the political implications of strategy and its bearing on diplomacy.[99] *Le Grand Débat,* another of his works, is a detailed examination of questions of nuclear strategy and how they have affected the Atlantic alliance.[100]

Aron considered an Anglo-Saxon nuclear monopoly in the Alliance intolerable and therefore defended the French force. Moreover, possession of nuclear weapons seemed to him to have some prestige and diplomatic value. And it gave France an option, both technologically and militarily, for an uncertain future (should the United States, for example, decide to withdraw its troops from Europe and retreat to an isolationist posture). However, Aron would have preferred solution of France's nuclear problem through the Alliance, rather than a strictly national deterrent. He voiced support on several occasions for the concept of a European nuclear force, and he expressed disappointment that de Gaulle did not take steps in that direction during the period

[99] *Paix et guerre entre les nations* (Paris: Calmann-Lévy, 1962). The English edition is *Peace and War: A Theory of International Relations* (Garden City, N.Y.: Doubleday and Co., 1966), trans. Richard Howard and Annette Baker Fox. For Aron's discussion of small nuclear forces, see esp. pp. 624-29.

Another author who has treated nuclear strategy in a broader context is Léo Hamon, *La Stratégie contre la guerre* (Paris: Bernard Grasset, 1966).

[100] Chapter 4 of *The Great Debate: Theories of Nuclear Strategy* is devoted to a discussion of the French deterrent force. See also the *Bulletin SEDEIS,* no. 910 (February 10, 1965); this special issue was devoted to a discussion of Aron's book and includes articles by Pierre Hassner, W. W. Kaufmann, Bernard Brodie, Michel Massenet, Raoul Girardet, Alfred Grosser, and Raymond Aron.

1962-63. While defending the French force on balance, Aron opposed France's withdrawal from NATO in 1966.[101]

A European nuclear force has been supported by others who favor a French nuclear capability but oppose the nationalistic framework in which de Gaulle developed the *force de frappe*. Notable in this group is General Paul Stehlin, the former air force chief of staff who resigned in 1963—in part because of his opposition to Gaullist nuclear policy. Stehlin accepts the need for French nuclear armament, but only if it has real military value and can serve as a nucleus for a European deterrent at a later time. The latter concept is the base point of his strategic thinking. He has advocated a European center of nuclear decision-making as necessary to the general health of the Atlantic alliance in order to give Europeans an equal voice in nuclear strategy. In his view, such a European force might be based on a treaty, such as the 1948 Brussels Treaty, and should operate in some kind of partnership arrangement with the United States. General Stehlin opposed the Gaullist nuclear force because of its cost, its relative military weakness, the reductions it caused in other French conventional forces, and its detrimental effect on the Atlantic alliance. He was also critical of de Gaulle for refusing to consider the French force as a stepping stone toward creation of a European deterrent. As his writings reveal, Stehlin has been a longtime advocate of European unity, and especially of Franco-German cooperation, which he would like to see much further developed in the military field.[102]

[101] Among Aron's articles in *Le Figaro*, see the following for his views on the French force and NATO: "A l'ombre de l'apocalypse nucléaire," August 17, 1966; "Force nucléaire nationale et Alliance atlantique," September 22, 1966. On the question of France and NATO, see: "Enfin seuls!," April 2-3, 1966; "Le Problème est politique," April 22, 1966; "La Situation a changé," May 7-8, 1966; "La Réforme de l'organization militaire," May 13, 1966; "Le Compromis nécessaire," June 13, 1966.

[102] Among General Stehlin's writings, see: "The Evolution of Western Defence," *Foreign Affairs* (October 1963), pp. 70-83; "French Thoughts on the Alliance," *NATO's Fifteen Nations* (August-

Among other analyses, the notion of some kind of European deterrent coordinated with American nuclear power in an Atlantic nuclear system has been advocated by the Club Jean Moulin.[103] General Carpentier, a former commander in chief of NATO forces in Central Europe and editor of the *Revue militaire générale*, was skeptical in the early 1960's of the American commitment to defend Europe with nuclear arms. He also supported a variant of a European nuclear force, an integrated nuclear deterrent to serve the Central European theater, which would include France, Germany, and the Benelux countries. But he did not offer detailed proposals on the arrangements for control of such a force.[104]

Some critics of the French national force have supported Atlantic solutions to the nuclear control problem. These include the late General Valluy, also a former NATO commander, who retired in 1960 and was an early opponent of the national deterrent. He urged instead full French cooperation with the integrated defense arrangements of NATO.[105] Another well-argued study by a socialist group, Socialisme et democratie, after an exhaustive review of the military and technical weaknesses of the *force de dissuasion*, was critical of any European nuclear alternative and recommended full French participation in defense consultation and improved allied decision-making in the Atlantic alliance, rather than a national nuclear effort.[106]

September 1964); and his two books, *Témoignage pour l'histoire* (Paris: Robert Laffont, 1964), and *Retour à zero: l'Europe et sa défense dans le compte à rebours* (Paris: Robert Laffont, 1968).

103 See Club Jean Moulin, *La Force de frappe et le citoyen* (Paris: Éditions du Seuil, 1963); also by the Club, *Pour une politique étrangère de l'Europe* (Paris: Éditions du Seuil, 1966).

104 Based on an interview with General Carpentier in 1965, and on his articles in *Revue militaire générale*, especially October 1960, December 1960, and March 1962.

105 See his book, *Se défendre? Contre qui? Pour quoi? Et comment?* (Paris: Plon, 1960).

106 *Liaison et informations* (Bulletin intérieur de l'Association socialisme et democratie): "Les Problèmes atomiques: Incidence du programme d'armement sur le développement nucléaire français,"

Finally, there have been analyses that simply reject the national *force de frappe* on the basis of economic, scientific, and technical considerations. Jules Moch, the former French arms control negotiator, stressed the technological deficiencies and the enormous cost of the French nuclear effort.[107] This was also the principal argument of studies by Marc de Lacoste Lareymondie and in *Esprit.*[108] Pierre Sudreau, a former Gaullist minister, is also the author of a skeptical analysis of French nuclear capability. He urged greater attention to civil defense.[109]

Two Gaullist groups—the Club de Grenelle and the Cercle d'études de l'armée nouvelle—attempted to refute these criticisms.[110] Aside from the late General Charles Ailleret, the most passionate Gaullist advocate of the French deterrent was Alexandre Sanguinetti who, in 1964, urged the establishment of a total nuclear defense system for France and the virtual abandonment of conventionally armed forces.[111]

(July 1964); "La Force de frappe: Les Données techniques" (November 1964); "La Force de frappe freine la recherche scientifique" (May 1965). An analysis of the costs of the *force de frappe*, to which we have already referred in the preceding chapter, was published in *Le Monde*, July 17, 1964.

[107] Jules Moch, *Non à la force de frappe* (Paris: Robert Laffont, 1963).

[108] Marc de Lacoste Lareymondie, *Mirages et réalités: l'arme nucléaire française* (Paris: Éditions de la SERPE, 1964). *Esprit* (special issue on the *force de frappe*, December 1963). See also the studies by Socialisme et democratie, cited in n. 106 above.

[109] Pierre Sudreau, *L'Enchaînement* (Paris: Plon, 1967).

[110] Club de Grenelle, *Siècle de Damocles: La Force nucléaire stratégique* (Paris: Éditions Pierre Couderc, 1964).

For the Centre d'études de l'armée nouvelle, see "La Force de dissuasion nucléaire et les contradictions du Club Jean Moulin," *Nouvelle Frontière*, no. 5 (January 1964), pp. 56-57; and "Les réalités de M. de Lacoste Lareymondie sont des mirage," *La Nation*, June 15 and 16, 1964.

[111] Alexandre Sanguinetti, *La France et l'arme atomique* (Paris: Julliard, 1964).

5 · *The Technology and Economics of the French Nuclear Force*

THE development of the French nuclear force since 1960 has been based upon three budgetary *lois de programme*, or program laws, which set forth plans for the modernization of all France's armed forces. The first law, covering the period 1960-64, laid the foundation for the first-generation nuclear weapons system—atomic bombs carried by Mirage IV aircraft. It also provided initial funding for France's first atomic submarine, for research and development of missiles, and for construction of the Pierrelatte isotope separation plant. Military program goals and outlays for the period 1965-70 were defined in a second program law. Although not all its objectives were realized on account of budgetary cutbacks, it supported the completion of the Mirage IV force, development and initial production of second-generation atomic weapons to be carried by surface-to-surface ballistic missiles, and the start of construction work on two more nuclear submarines. Initial research and development of hydrogen bombs, a submarine ballistic missile system, and tactical atomic armament were also financed.[1] A third program law passed in 1970 establishes production guidelines for 1971-75 for submarine ballistic missiles and development of thermonuclear warheads—the third-general weapons system—as well as for a fourth atomic submarine vehicle, initial work on a fifth, and tactical nuclear weapons.

This chapter, which treats French military nuclear development from 1960 to 1969 (the year of General de Gaulle's resignation), will provide a minimum of technical information about the various components of the evolving

[1] A good general description of the first two program laws and the elements of French military modernization is found in *France and Its Armed Forces* (New York: Ambassade de France, Service de presse et d'information, 1964).

force de frappe.[2] It will also describe command and control features of the French force and address the cost of French nuclear armament. Finally, the chapter attempts a preliminary assessment of arguments relating to the impact of military nuclear programs on French science and technology, an important point in the Gaullist defense of the French nuclear effort.

The First-Generation Weapons: Mirage IV Aircraft and A-Bombs

The Mirage IV-A, the basic delivery vehicle in France's nuclear arsenal in the second half of the 1960's, is a delta-winged fighter-bomber built by the Dassault aircraft company and powered by two Atar 9K jet engines manufactured by SNECMA (Société nationale d'étude et de construction de moteurs d'aviation). An effective aircraft equipped with the French Cyrano II radar system, which allows contour flying without visibility, the Mirage IV will continue to operate into the mid-1970's. With a capability to fly at a speed of Mach 2.2 at an altitude of 26,000 feet, its range has been reported to be about 2,500 miles without refueling when flying at average speed under the most favorable conditions at very high altitudes.[3] However, it is likely that the Mirage IV's range with a full bombload under wartime conditions would be considerably shorter and on the order of 1,550 miles, as reported earlier, or just under 3,000 miles with inflight refueling.[4] This is especially true since the plane would have to fly the last part of its mission at low altitudes where it is less efficient in order to avoid radar detection and minimize the effect of Soviet air defenses.

Fifty Mirage IV planes were ordered under the first pro-

[2] The third program law is discussed in Chapter 9.

[3] Pierre Messmer, "France's Nuclear Force," *Le Républicain indépendant* (July 1967); reprinted by the Ambassade de France, Service de presse et d'information (New York, 1967), no. HS-368.

[4] See *France and Its Armed Forces*, p. 9; also Pierre Messmer, "Notre politique militaire," *Revue de défense nationale* (April 1963), p. 746.

gram law and delivered between 1963 and 1966. Because of the plane's short range, inflight refueling is necessary to enable it to reach targets in Western Russia. For this reason France sought and was granted purchase rights for a dozen American KC-135F tanker planes, delivered in 1964. Under the second program law twelve more Mirage IV planes were ordered, bringing the total to sixty-two. However, several planes have been lost in accidents. The Mirage IV force now numbers about fifty-eight aircraft.[5]

Each Mirage IV can carry one atomic bomb. A 60-kiloton bomb was tested successfully in the Sahara on May 1, 1962, and entered production about 1963. It is a fission bomb, the plutonium for which is primarily produced by the Marcoule reactors (operating since 1956). At the end of 1962 it was reported that the Marcoule plant had reached an annual production rate of about 100 kilograms of weapon-grade material.[6] In 1964 this output was substantially increased by improving the capacity of the extraction process, and the plant began to handle not only the fuel irradiated in its own reactors, but also a certain amount shipped in from other sources.[7] In the second half of the 1960's the French produced a more powerful atomic weapon, and by the end of the decade bombs with an explosive force of about 70 kilotons (about four times that of the Hiroshima bomb) were available to arm each of the Mirage IV planes of the first-generation nuclear force.

The Mirage IV force would be used in a countercity strategy.[8] A special parachute has been devised for the atomic bomb carried by each plane in order to slow its rate of descent at low altitudes and prevent it from rebounding.

[5] *Journel officiel*, October 7, 1970.

[6] Bertrand Goldschmidt, "The French Atomic Program," *Bulletin of the Atomic Scientist* (September 1962), p. 42. The actual production rate may have been higher and in the range of 130 to 140 kilograms per year.

[7] Commissariat à l'Energie Atomique, *Developments and Programs* (Paris: Service des relations publiques du CEA, 1965), p. 20.

[8] Messmer, "Notre politique militaire," p. 747.

Equipped with these devices, the Mirage planes can operate effectively at the low altitudes where they would have to fly in order to avoid enemy radar.[9] The planes themselves have been organized into two bomb wings (the 91st and 93rd), each of which numbers several small squadrons, dispersed over nine airfields, located away from large cities. Of the total force, thirty-six aircraft are deployed at all times. The remaining number are used as trainers, electronic counter-measure aircraft, and reserves. The entire force is under the direction of the Commandement aérien stratégique (CAS) with headquarters at the underground base at Taverny, about twenty miles from Paris. An alternate command post is under construction near Lyons.

Taverny is the command and control center for the nuclear striking force; it also houses the Air Defense Command (Centre d'opérations de la défense aérienne or CODA).[10] These two commands are directly linked. Information about a hostile attack would be received either via the NATO early warning network (NADGE), in which France still participates, or via seven French radar detection stations. It would be processed automatically by a Strida II computer[11] and relayed immediately to the Strategic Air Command and the chief of state. In the case of an attack by Soviet air forces, the warning time available would be on the order of fifteen minutes before French targets are hit. French air defenses, consisting mainly of nine interceptor squadrons, would then be mobilized. The warning from a Soviet missile attack would be reduced to about five minutes, perhaps only enough time to get part of the Mirage IV strategic force into the air.

By an executive decree of January 1964, the president of the Republic himself gives the command to activate the

[9] *New York Times*, February 15, 1967.

[10] For a good description of the Taverny complex and its operation, see Jean Planchais in *Le Monde*, December 14 and 16, 1963.

[11] STRIDA: Système de transmission des informations de défense aérienne. Information on this computer system can be found in Nicolas Vichney's report in *Le Monde*, December 14, 1962.

strategic nuclear force, or the premier if the president is disabled.[12] As a security measure, there are two distinct command chains between the president, the commander of the CAS, and the Mirage IV pilots. Separate sets of orders must be issued to activate the planes and later the atomic weapons. Detailed war plans apparently exist to send the planes first to points over friendly or neutral countries for aerial refueling, before they proceed to preselected Soviet targets. The planes are also equipped with "black boxes" that can be activated directly by remote control signals from the civilian political authority to neutralize the atomic bombs, as an added safety measure.

The deterrent value of the Mirage IV nuclear force has been widely questioned. First, it is handicapped by a very short warning time and is extremely vulnerable to a surprise attack that could wipe out many of the planes on the ground. To counter this weakness the French have said they will place a large number of planes on airborne alert during a serious international crisis. Another criticism relates to the uncertainty whether the Mirage aircraft could penetrate Soviet air defenses. But, in addition to its low-altitude flying capability, the Mirage IV is said to possess electronic countermeasure systems to foil Soviet radar defenses, although the quality and effectiveness of these systems is not publicly known. The Soviet defense system is based largely on the SAM III missile. Critics claims that this system is effective and would intercept most of the Mirage IV aircraft. The French response, however, is that the SAM III system still has weaknesses against attacking planes flying at low altitudes and undertaking evasive maneuvers.[13]

Although not a strong deterrent system, the Mirage IV force probably cannot be ignored by Soviet leaders, for penetration of their territory by even a few of these aircraft

[12] *Le Monde*, January 21, 1964. An earlier decree in 1962 had given this authority first to the premier.

[13] See, e.g., Joël Le Theule, "La force nucléaire stratégique française," in *France Forum* (March-April 1963), p. 9.

could endanger Russian cities. However, little is known about actual Soviet reactions to the French deterrent, especially its more advanced systems.[14]

Second- and Third-Generation Weapons: Land- and Sea-Based IRBMs

It is anticipated that the Mirage IVs will be gradually phased out in the mid-1970's as two types of intermediate-range ballistic missiles (IRBMs) enter service. The second-generation weapons system, the land-based strategic missile or SSBS (Sol-Sol balistique stratégique), will carry a "doped" atomic warhead in the 150 kiloton range. These missiles will be placed in underground silos one hundred feet deep on the Albion plateau in the Haute Provence area in southeastern France. Twenty-seven of these nuclear-tipped missiles were scheduled for deployment by 1969 in silos spread over an area of about 89,000 acres, with one fire control post for every nine silos. However, budgetary cutbacks and technical difficulties in 1968-69 caused both a postponement and a reduction in these plans. The 1970 military budget provided funds for only eighteen land-based missiles, yet to be deployed, although more may be added later.[15] These two-stage missiles, powered by T-10 solid fuel, will have a range of approximately 1,500 nautical miles. A longer-range first stage for this missile is being developed.

A more powerful and more invulnerable third-generation weapons system is planned for the nuclear force of the 1970's: a nuclear-powered missile-launching submarine carrying sixteen sea-to-surface missiles (MSBS: Mer-Sol balistique stratégique). *Le Redoutable*, first one of the se-

[14] In the early 1960's the *force de frappe* was viewed as a much less serious threat to Soviet security than the possibility that it might facilitate West German access to nuclear arms. See Thomas W. Wolfe, *Soviet Commentary on the French "Force de Frappe,"* RM-4359 (Santa Monica, Calif.: The Rand Corp., 1965).

[15] See *Le Monde*, November 7, 1969.

ries, was launched on March 29, 1967, and is due to become operational in late 1971. A second submarine, *Le Terrible*, was launched in December 1969, and is scheduled to enter service in early 1973. A third, *Le Foudroyant*, should be operational with thermonuclear warheads by 1975, to be followed by a fourth and probably a fifth vessel in the late 1970's.

MSBS missiles, advanced forms of the SSBS, are tested at the Landes test center and on board the experimental submarine platform *Gymnote* at Toulon. The first missiles will carry fission warheads, reported to be in the 500-kiloton range, over a distance of 1,200 to 1,300 nautical miles. More powerful thermonuclear warheads of about one megaton should be available by the mid-1970's after the necessary miniaturization is accomplished, along with a new second stage which will lengthen the range of the missile. The first hydrogen bomb was tested on August 24, 1968 at the Pacific Test Center in French Polynesia. After a year's hiatus due to budgetary pressures, thermonuclear tests were resumed in the summer of 1970. The thermonuclear warheads require highly enriched uranium 235, which the Pierrelatte isotope separation plant began producing when its high enrichment stage became operational in 1967.

By the end of 1969 France had tested the two strategic missile systems that will complement her first-generation nuclear force. But neither of these systems was yet in service. However, if government plans are successfully implemented, France will have by the mid-1970's a small nuclear force of approximately eighteen rather vulnerable land-based missiles and three missile-carrying submarines.

The history of the French missile program goes back to 1945-46 when a ballistic-missile research program was begun by the French army.[16] Early efforts were focused on studies of the German V-1 and V-2 weapons and the estab-

[16] For a historical synopsis see Judith H. Young, "The French Strategic Missile Programme," *Adelphi Papers*, no. 38 (London: Institute for Strategic Studies, 1967), upon which the following pages are based.

lishment in 1949 of the Laboratoire de recherches balistiques et aérodynamiques (LRBA) at Vernon to develop the liquid-propellant *Véronique* rocket. The *Véronique* program made use of German scientists and personnel who had worked on the V-rockets at Pennemunde. The first rocket was launched in 1950 and launchings continued until 1954, at which time the program was abandoned for lack of funds. Henceforth until General de Gaulle resumed power, French military attention focused on the research and development of basic atomic weapons, the Mirage IV aircraft, and small guided missiles.

After a survey in 1958, it was determined that France possessed the requisite resources and know-how for the development of ballistic missiles, and work began on the manufacture of solid propellants for missile motors. In 1959 the government consortium SEREB (Société pour l'étude et réalisation d'engins balistiques) was formed to manage the missile effort. During that year the French government had high hopes of obtaining American assistance in the development of solid-fuel missile launch vehicles. Both Lockheed and Boeing were approached for licensing privileges involving Polaris and Minuteman technology, but this cooperation was denied by the State Department. The French then proceeded with plans for development of solid-propellant missile vehicles on their own. By early 1960 a plan had been formulated for constructing a series of test vehicles; and launchings began later the same year. The 1960 military program law included initial research and development allocations for the strategic missile program which has since emerged.

SEREB has acted as the prime management contractor of the SSBS and MSBS for the Ministry of the Armed Forces. These complex programs are carried out by a large part of the French aerospace industry, including companies working on computers and guidance systems, electronics, and metallurgy.[17] The largest concentration is located in the

[17] By early 1970 France had merged its three nationalized aerospace forms—SEREB, Sud-Aviation, and Nord-Aviation—into a

Bordeaux area and includes the St. Médard industrial complex and the missile test center known as Centre d'essais des Landes (CEL). At St. Médard, a large factory manufactures solid-propellant grains. Motors and complete missiles are assembled and inspected at the Centre d'essais des propulseurs et des engins. There are also four aerospace companies: a Sud-Aviation plant which manufactures filament-wound glass-fibre cases for missile motors, a Nord-Aviation plant that constructs missile airframes and complete missile stages, a SNECMA facility for testing large motors and stages, and a research and fabrication plant of the Société d'étude de la propulsion par reaction for work on both solid and liquid propellants. All of these facilities have major responsibility for the SSBS and MSBS, but they also work on related research rockets and the *Diamant* satellite launcher for the French space program.

Completed by early 1966, the Landes Test Center is situated to the west of the St. Médard complex, near the coastal city of Biscarosse. It is designed primarily for flight-testing of strategic missiles and, as such, replaces French launch facilities in the Sahara on Algerian territory (Colomb-Béchar and Hammaguir) which were evacuated as called for by the 1962 Evian accords. There is also a French launch site on the Ile de Levant in the Mediterranean. An agreement with Portugal allows the use of an island in the Azores as a tracking facility for the Landes Center.

The French have made excellent progress in rocket technology. They have developed over thirty types of research rockets, primarily since 1958. Five experimental ballistic rockets were constructed after 1960 to gain experience in missile technology (the *Aigle*, *Agate*, *Topaze*, *Emeraude*, and *Saphir*), as well as a special rocket reentry test vehicle (the *Bérénice*). Both the SSBS and MSBS missiles have two inertially guided stages and are driven by a solid propellant.

---

new conglomerate, the Societé nationale industrielle aerospatiale (designated SNIAS). See *Aviation Week & Space Technology*, January 26, 1970, pp. 21-22.

The French missile program has been assisted by a number of production licenses granted by American companies.[18] Most important is probably the agreement with the Kearfott Division of General Precision, Inc., under which a French firm has been producing inertial guidance instrumentation (such as miniaturized gyroscopes and stabilized platforms) with the benefit of American technology. Other agreements concern the technology of filament-wound glass-fibre motor cases (Rocketdyne–Sud Aviation, 1962), Vascojet steel (Vanadium Alloys Steel Company), and missile tracking equipment (the American company is Cubic Corporation).

In 1968 the missile testing program was reported to have run into technical problems.[19] Thus, the cancellation of the 1969 series of nuclear tests (ostensibly for budgetary reasons) tended to bring the nuclear warhead program back into phase with the somewhat lagging missile development. Greater difficulties may lie ahead in the testing of thermonuclear weapons which are also behind schedule and have yet to be miniaturized and "militarized" (i.e., reduced in size and weight, made mechanically solid and resistant to physical and thermal vibrations). The reliability of French missiles and their accuracy (CEP—circular error probability) are undoubtedly below British and American standards. Less accuracy is required, however, for a counter-city strategy. So far, the French have been conducting a minimum-test operation on their vehicles and warheads in order to save time and money.

Development and testing of thermonuclear warheads has been the joint task of the Direction des applications militaires (DAM) of the CEA and various departments of the Armed Forces Ministry. Nuclear material for these weapons is provided by the enormous and very costly isotope

[18] Young, "The French Strategic Missile Programme," p. 9.

[19] See Defense Minister Messmer's remarks before the National Assembly, reprinted in *Le Monde*, November 1, 1968; Jacques Isnard in *Le Monde*, November 28, 1968. The French air force was reported to have successfully tested a final version of the SSBS in the spring of 1969; see *Le Monde*, April 25 and June 26, 1969.

separation plant at Pierrelatte in southeastern France, the fourth and final high-enrichment section of which began operation at the end of March 1967.[20] The Pierrelatte facility employs the method of gaseous diffusion to separate out U-238 and U-235 isotopes from natural uranium ore. Four separate sections of the plant repeat the process to obtain the highly enriched grade of U-235 necessary for nuclear submarine propulsion reactors and thermonuclear weapons. The decision to construct the plant dates back to 1957 and actual work on it began in 1960. The first stage began operation in late 1964. The exact rate of output is secret, as is the grade of enrichment yielded (probably about 93 percent).[21]

During 1966-67 work was completed on the large nuclear test center in French Polynesia in the Pacific, which replaced the Saharan test areas. Two series of tests in the summer of 1966, designed mainly to check the new facilities, also included explosions of a second version fission device, a tactical atomic device, and a "doped" atomic bomb.[22] Tests are conducted on the Mururoa and Fangatofa atolls. An apparatus has been devised which permits the explosion of devices from balloons. During the summer of 1967 several small bombs were tested, ostensibly in an effort to perfect a triggering device for future hydrogen bombs. As already mentioned, the first series of thermonuclear tests was conducted in the summer of 1968.[23]

[20] *New York Times,* April 7, 1967. General de Gaulle dedicated the final section in November 1967. See the *New York Times,* November 7, 1967.

[21] For more detail on Pierrelatte, see Nicolas Vichney in *Le Monde,* June 27, 1962; *Pierrelatte: Usine de séparation des isotopes de l'uranium* (Paris: Commissariat à l'énergie atomique, 1964).

[22] Commissariat à l'énergie atomique, *Rapport Annuel,* 1966 (Paris: Commissariat à l'énergie atomique, 1967), pp. 89-91. See also *The French Nuclear Tests in the Pacific* (New York: Ambassade de France, Service de presse et d'information, 1966).

[23] *New York Times,* August 25 and 28, 1968. See also the analysis by Nicolas Vichney, *Le Monde hebdomadaire,* no. 1,035, August 22-28, 1968.

Available evidence indicates that the French nuclear submarine program has made good progress. The first missile-launching submarine (SNLE: *sous-marin nucléaire lance-engin*), the *Redoutable*, is 423 feet long, has a surface displacement of about 7,900 tons and will have two rotating crews of 130 men each. Built for cruises of an average duration of two months, it can travel at a speed in the range of 20 to 25 knots while submerged. The craft is powered by a nuclear reactor similar to the prototype operated at Cadarache under the direction of the CEA. This reactor employs enriched uranium, now furnished by the plant at Pierrelatte, in conjunction with zirconium. Pressurized water is heated to produce steam which drives the turbines. The submarine will carry computer guidance systems and other advanced electronic detection and communications apparatus.[24] The eventual submarine fleet will be based in the area of the Ile Longue and Crozon near Brest on the Breton coast, where installations are under construction. Special communications stations are planned at Rosnay in the department of Indre and at Pencran in Finistère. A minimum fleet of five nuclear submarines has been recommended by the French navy.

The French nuclear submarine force will be a more credible deterrent than the first- and second-generation nuclear systems. However, this force will have significant shortcomings. It is estimated that, of a French fleet of four nuclear submarines, only two would be on alert patrol at any given moment. The others would either be in port for crew changes and supplies or major overhaul (required every three years), or en route between port and their patrol routes. In entering and leaving the ports the submarines will be particularly vulnerable to air and naval attack and will undoubtedly have to be escorted by other submarines

[24] For more technical information on the French nuclear submarine, see the reports by Nicolas Vichney and Jacques Isnard, *Le Monde hebdomadaire*, March 20-April 5 and December 7-13, 1967, and *Le Monde*, December 13, 1969.

and naval craft. It is an open question whether Soviet forces could constantly follow the two submarines on alert patrol, keep track of their positions, and destroy them without warning. The rapidly growing Soviet force of hunter-killer submarines will present a serious threat; so far France has no plans to add any such hunter-killer vessels to its arsenal.

The number of planned French submarines is, of course, small by comparison with the American fleet of forty-one nuclear missile-carrying submarines and the large and varied Soviet submarine force, about fifty-three of which can fire ballistic missiles.[25] About half of the American fleet is on alert patrol and about three-fourths will soon be equipped with the advanced Poseidon missile with its multiple, independently targeted warheads (MIRVs). A new class of Soviet nuclear-powered, ballistic-missile submarines, roughly similar to the American Polaris type, is now coming into service.

Other weaknesses of the French nuclear submarine force will be the limited range of its missiles, the fact that only one submarine base (at Ile Longue) will be available, and the probability of only one VLF communications center (at Rosnay). Moreover, the French force may also be severely challenged by new developments in superpower weapons technology—especially anti-ballistic missiles (ABMs), unless the U.S.–Soviet strategic arms limitation talks (SALT) produce an agreement limiting their deployment.

Tactical Atomic Weapons

France is also developing tactical weapons to supplement its strategic nuclear deterrent and to bolster the strength of its conventionally armed services, but these weapons were not yet ready for deployment at the end of the 1960's. Two

[25] *The Military Balance, 1969-70* (London: Institute for Strategic Studies, 1969).

tactical weapons systems are scheduled for service beginning about 1973. The army will receive the Pluton battlefield missile, a rocket launched from a ramp mounted on the chassis of an AMX-30 tank. Carrying a warhead of about 20 kilotons, the range of this missile is reported to be approximately 75 miles. The air force and the naval air force will employ tactical atomic bombs with identical warheads, to be carried by Mirage III and Jaguar aircraft. Funding of these programs began with the second program law and will be continued under the third law for the period 1971-75. So far about 150 tactical nuclear arms are projected, two-thirds of which will be assigned to the army's mechanized divisions.[26]

As discussed elsewhere, tactical atomic weapons will be directly related to the overall French strategy of nuclear deterrence which is now moving away from all-or-nothing thinking toward a flexible or graduated response strategy designed to test out the enemy before resort to strategic nuclear arms. Control over the use of tactical nuclear arms will therefore remain in the hands of the head of state and will not be delegated to field commanders.

The advent of tactical nuclear armament can be expected to make the strategic nuclear deterrent more credible. These weapons will fill a gap in France's deterrence spectrum. A potential enemy invasion force will soon have to reckon with immediate atomic resistance—both within French borders and probably in front of them, i.e., by French ground forces stationed in Germany. If an invading enemy were not halted, he would have to face the risk of French escalation to a strategic nuclear response. Moreover, tactical atomic arms may provide a basis for greater French cooperation with NATO, which already places considerable emphasis on a tactical nuclear strategy in Europe.

[26] See Pierre Messmer, "L'Atome, cause et moyen d'une politique militaire autonome," p. 399; Jacques Isnard in *Le Monde*, January 28, 1970.

THE COST OF THE NUCLEAR FORCE

Gaullist officials have frequently argued that nuclear armament is less expensive than the production of conventional weapons and is not beyond French resources. We shall now turn to an examination of the cost of the *force de frappe* and its relationship to other military and overall state expenditures, in an attempt to assess the Gaullist case. We shall also seek to determine the effects of France's 1968 domestic crisis on military spending and to ascertain whether French financial and production goals for nuclear armament over the period 1960-70 have been achieved.

Some perspective on the magnitude of French military spending is provided by the following table which compares defense expenditures of France with those of the superpowers and other West European countries in recent years. Using corrected figures to take account of nuclear program costs not shown in the budget of the Defense Ministry, Table 1 reveals that overall French defense spending has been running slightly higher in absolute terms than that of Germany and Great Britain since 1968. It also indicates that French military expenditures as a percentage of GNP have been declining since 1965. This is confirmed by Table 2, which is based on official French government figures for defense spending as a percentage of the annual state budget and of the French GNP.

The 1960-64 military program law authorized a total of NF11.8 billion (or $2.36 billion) in research and development and capital equipment expenditures, of which approximately NF6 billion ($1.2 billion) was allocated to the development of the nuclear force.[27] Most of these funds went toward production of the first fifty Mirage IV aircraft and atomic bombs. However, these appropriations were soon found insufficient, especially on account of the grow-

[27] Assemblée nationale, *Projet de loi de programme relative à certains équipements militaires*, no. 784 (Paris: Imprimerie nationale, 1960), p. 12.

TABLE 1
DEFENSE EXPENDITURES AND GNP COMPARISONS

Country	*Defense Expenditures (U.S. $ billion) 1968*	*1969*	*Estimated GNP 1968 ($ billion)*	*Defense Expenditure per capita ($) 1968*	*Defense Expenditure as a Percentage of GNP 1965*	*1966*	*1967*	*1968*
U.S.A.	79.576	78.475	861	396	8.0	9.2	9.8	9.2
USSR	39.780	42.140	430	169	9.0	8.9	9.6	9.3
France	6.104	5.586	115	121	5.6	5.4	5.3	5.3
Britain	5.450	5.438	103	98	6.3	6.0	5.7	5.3
W. Germany	5.108	5.301	132	87	4.4	4.8	4.3	3.9

SOURCE: *The Military Balance, 1969-1970* (London: Institute for Strategic Studies, 1969). Figures for France include ISS estimates of some items of the military nuclear program not shown in the official French defense budget. The 1969 figure is calculated at the post-August 1969 devaluation rate of exchange.

TABLE 2
FRENCH DEFENSE EXPENDITURES SINCE 1965 (OFFICIAL FIGURES)*

	1965	*1966*	*1967*	*1968*	*1969*	*1970*
Military expenditures as percentage of GNP	4.5	4.35	4.37	4.34	4.08*	3.4
Military expenditures as percentage of national budget	22.6	21.8	20.7	20.0	17.8*	17.6

* The 1969 figures were actually slightly less, since a further cut in the budget was made after the November monetary crisis.

ing costs of the Pierrelatte isotope separation plant and the research and development costs of the missile program. In 1962 a substantial *loi de finance rectificative* was required. The cost of construction of the Pierrelatte plant, originally forecast in the 1960 program law as NF1.750 billion, had been revised in 1962 to the figure of NF4.536 billion (in part because it had been determined that a larger plant was required), and the government made provision to pay the first installment on the difference (NF200 million) out of the 1962 military budget.[28] This caused an uproar and a vigorous debate in the French parliament, which led to a censure motion in July 1962, criticizing the government for its costly nuclear program and urging instead that a European solution be sought to the nuclear weapons problem.[29] But the censure motion failed to obtain the requisite number of votes and the government received the additional credits it requested.

The major allocations for the nuclear striking force were made under the second program law for 1965-70. According to official figures, NF28.242 billion (about $5.72 billion) was authorized for the strategic nuclear force out of a total amount of NF54.898 billion ($11.11 billion). The breakdown is shown in Table 3.

These program authorizations included production of twelve additional Mirage IV aircraft; development, production, and deployment of about twenty-five SSBS missiles; development of the MSBS and production and deployment of sixteen of these missiles in conjunction with the first nuclear submarine. Heavy expenditures were also earmarked for the completion of the Pierrelatte plant, the Landes missile test center, and the Pacific nuclear weapons test center.

[28] Assemblée nationale, *Projet de loi de finances rectificative pour 1962*, no. 1809 (Paris, 1962).

The reader is referred to two interesting reports of parliamentary commissions on the political, technical, and financial aspects of the revised allocations for the military program law: (1) Henri Dorey, "Observations sur les crédits militaires" (au nom des rapporteurs spéciaux des budgets militaires), in Assemblée nationale, *Rapport au nom de la commission des finances, de l'économie générale et du plan*, by Marc Jacquet, no. 1,830 (Paris: Assemblée nationale, 1962), pp. 119-60; (2) *Avis présenté au nom de la commission de la défense nationale et des forces armées sur le projet de loi de finances rectificative pour 1962*, by M. le Theule, no. 1,871 (Paris, 1962).

See also the explanation provided by Gaston Palewski, minister of state in charge of atomic questions, before the National Assembly, *Journal officiel*, Débats parlementaires, Assemblée nationale, July 12, 1962, pp. 2,324-27.

[29] For the debates and the text of the censure motion, see *Journal officiel*, July 11-25, 1962.

TABLE 3

NUCLEAR PROGRAM ALLOCATIONS FOR 1965-1970

Nuclear weapons and propulsion: production of nuclear materials; weapons development and production; weapons experimentation and testing; nuclear propulsion.	$3.222 billion
Missile vehicles: solid fuel manufacture; development of strategic missile boosters and new solid fuels; production of ballistic missile components common to the different types of missiles; production of surface-to-surface strategic ballistic missiles and their operational deployment; development and production of sea-to-surface strategic ballistic missiles; firing ranges and missile tests; military uses of space.	1.085 billion
Air transport and launching means: completion of the manufacture of Mirage IV aircraft, purchase of spare parts of KC 135F tanker planes, development of the electronic environment for the strategic nuclear force.	0.594 billion
Naval transport and launching means: start of work on three nuclear submarines, each armed with 16 strategic ballistic missiles; production of supply and support means.	0.399 billion
General studies: improvement of weapons performance; miniaturization, yield, range, operating security; development of different thermonuclear cycles, direct triggering of fusion, resistance to enemy countermeasures.	0.304 billion
Research:	0.174 billion
Total	$5.718 billion

SOURCE: Adapted from *France and Its Armed Forces* (New York: Ambassade de France, Service de presse et d'information, 1964), p. 52.

For some time it has been clear that actual nuclear expenditures under the second program law exceeded the original allocations. Opposition critics frequently seized on this point, and several private groups published their own estimates of actual outlays at various times.[30] By the end of 1969, the year of General de Gaulle's resignation, it was possible to set down a picture of the cost of the *force de frappe* over the decade of the 1960's using earlier government figures plus the outlays provided for in the 1970 military budget (see Table 4).

Although based on government figures that are not all-inclusive, Table 4 permits several important observations. First, it is possible to calculate the approximate cost of the French deterrent force up to 1970. Taking the figures of NF12.2812 billion for 1960-64 and NF32.0992 billion for 1965-70, one arrives at the amount of *NF44.3804 billion.* There were some outlays on atomic research prior to 1960, which have been estimated at $200 million (about NF1 billion) by one analyst.[31] Adding in these figures yields a total of approximately NF45.3 billion or *9 billion dollars* to the end of the second program law.[32]

In all likelihood these figures represent low estimates. They do not take account of maintenance and personnel costs associated with the operation of the Mirage IV weapons system and the construction and operation of various testing facilities. It is known, moreover, that the French government conceals some allocations related to the nuclear

[30] The Club Jean Moulin published a study in 1963 which estimated the probable cost of the nuclear force at between NF40 and 50 billion for the period 1964-70. See *La Force de frappe et le citoyen* (Paris: Éditions du Seuil, 1963), pp. 85-92. A study by another group, l'Association socialisme et democratie, concluded from an analysis of the second program law that actual costs would be at least NF18 billion more than projected, and probably much more. See *Le Monde*, July 17, 1964.

[31] Young, "The French Strategic Missile Programme," p. 6.

[32] Estimates for nuclear and related expenditures under the third program law, 1971-75, come to approximately NF31 billion. *Le Monde*, July 31 and August 8, 1970. See Chapter 9.

TABLE 4

French Military Spending for the Period 1960-1970

	Program Authorizations (millions of francs)			
	Projected 1960-1964 (NF 1960)	*Appropriated 1960-1964 (actual values)*	*Projected 1965-1970 (NF 1965)*	*Appropriated 1965-1970 (actual values)*
General studies			1,500	1,397.2
Production and testing of nuclear arms	4,928	8,516	15,915	14,917
Missiles and propulsion		1,705.8	5,362	9,465.7
Mirage IV bombers	1,420	1,768	2,932	3,228
Strategic missile submarines		291.4	1,674	3,061.3
Total: strategic nuclear force	6,348	12,281.2	27,383	32,099.2
Ground forces:	1,778.5	2,498.3	13,212	8,469.4
of which AMX-30 tanks	—	—	2,140	2,180
helicopters	—	—	1,064	1,595.55
Air force:		1,868	9,500	12,173.65
of which tactical aircraft (Jaguar)		—	700	2,865
Transall transport plane		—	1,100	1,512
Navy:		1,790.1	3,944	3,450.8
of which naval aircraft Bréguet-Atlantic		—	613	719
Super-Frelon helicopters		—	215	240
warships		—	778	972.9
Total: conventional forces	5,442.5	5,156.4	26,656	24,093.85
Research			859	1,014.9

Source: Adapted from *Le Monde*, December 5, 1969.

program in the budgets of other agencies (e.g., the budget of the CEA). Joël le Theule, a former chairman of the National Defense Committee of the National Assembly, estimated in 1967 that the costs directly or indirectly related to the nuclear force may be as high as 35 percent of the military budget. Government figures, however, have consistently been much lower; for example, nuclear expenditures were said to comprise approximately 25 percent of the 1967 military budget and 20 percent in 1969.[33] In the 1970 budget Defense Minister Messmer indicated that nuclear program costs amounted to 17.2 percent of military expenditures, or about NF4.7 billion. A higher estimate along the lines of le Theule's calculations would increase this amount to somewhere in the neighborhood of NF9 billion.[34] In view of these factors, the total financial outlay for the nuclear force up to 1970 may have been as high as NF60 billion or approximately *$12 billion*.

A second conclusion from Table 4 is that cost overruns for nuclear programs have been considerable in both the first and second program laws. Indeed, for the period 1965-70 allocations for development and production of missiles exceeded earlier estimates by about 75 percent, while nuclear submarine systems cost approximately 83 percent more than anticipated. At the same time, the goals of the second program law were not attained. As noted earlier, the French government has had to reduce the number of SSBS missiles planned for initial deployment in silos in the Haute Provence from twenty-seven to eighteen. It has also postponed by one year the operational status of the first nuclear submarine, the *Redoutable*, now scheduled for the end of 1971. Construction of a nuclear hunter-killer submarine was again relegated to a much later time. Explana-

[33] See *Le Monde*, June 13, 1969; also the report of Le Theule contained in the *Avis* présenté au nom de la commission de la défense nationale et des forces armées, sur le projet de loi de finances pour 1968, Assemblée nationale, no. 469, annexed to the proceedings of October 19, 1967, pp. 5-9.

[34] *Le Monde*, November 12 and 19, 1969.

tion of the rising costs of the nuclear program presumably lies in a combination of factors, including technical difficulties, higher industrial salaries following the 1968 economic crisis in France, a rapid rate of inflation, and poor estimates by program planners.

Of particular importance has been the setback in the modernization of the conventionally armed services under the second program law due to the priority given the nuclear arsenal. According to the government report submitted with the presentation of the 1970 military budget, the second law had envisioned three mechanized divisions with new armored equipment by 1970, such as AMX-30 heavy tanks and helicopters. In fact, only two divisions are so outfitted. As for light tanks and armored vehicles, the government admitted a major failure in not meeting program authorizations for 1,400 vehicles; the first hundred vehicles will only be ordered in 1970. The air force and the navy have had to endure similar sacrifices.[35] Thus, the professed French objective of a full panoply of nuclear and conventional weapons is not being met, and there are major gaps in France's conventional armory, as well as delays in elements of the nuclear force.

Without question the pressures on the French economy unleashed by France's economic and social crisis in May-June 1968 forced a reduction in military spending and are responsible for several of the postponements mentioned above in the increasingly expensive nuclear weapons program. Table 2 reflects this development. In the autumn of 1968, faced with new demands for civilian expenditures, the French government presented the National Assembly with an austerity military budget for 1969, totaling NF26,362 billion. This was only 17.8 percent of the total state budget, as compared with 20 percent the previous year. A further cutback of NF400 million in the military budget came later

[35] See the *Compte rendu sur le programme d'équipement militaire présenté par le gouvernement, 1969* (Paris: Imprimerie Nationale, 1969).

in 1968 as part of the emergency measures announced by Premier Couve de Murville to combat pressures against the franc in the November monetary crisis. This action included cancellation of the 1969 series of nuclear tests.[36]

In spite of rising costs and competing demands for social expenditures, it must be concluded that the realization of the French nuclear force as envisioned at the end of the 1960's is within the limits of French resources, given the willingness and the ability of the government to make the appropriate budgetary choices and to overcome opposition in parliament. The end of the Algerian war made sharp reductions possible in military manpower, which declined sharply from over a million men in 1961 to about 332,000 in 1967.[37] These reductions produced obvious savings. At the same time, few remaining overseas commitments and her advantageous geographic position in Europe have allowed France to get by with weakened conventional forces, as priority is given to nuclear armament. Moreover, as we have seen, the overall military budget has declined proportionately in recent years. There will be delays in meeting the objectives of France's present nuclear goals, but these goals will probably be met. The real question is whether budgetary constraints will permit the modernization of conventional forces, as well as nuclear forces, in the years ahead. More sophisticated nuclear systems, such as MIRV and ABM, are likely to be out of reach, given France's limited resources, unless the French cooperate with other countries in their development.

Nuclear Weapons and French Science and Technology

While arguing that a nuclear weapons capability assures France of military strength and hence political independence, Gaullist leaders have also been mindful of the civilian

[36] For discussion of the 1970 military budget, see Chapter 9.
[37] Messmer, "France's Nuclear Force," p. 4.

benefits of the military atomic program. It is true that advanced nuclear and space technologies have been viewed as an end in themselves, as an essential element of modern nationhood and a prerequisite for influence in the world.[38] They have also been considered the catalyst for modernization of French science and technology generally. In French eyes there is a clear link between advanced scientific technology and national security; for dependence on other nations for technology can be as much a threat to a country's sovereignty as reliance on others for defense.

As de Gaulle said in 1964, "the vast research, invention and production activity that atomic development itself involves, introduces a most effective stimulus into our scientific, technical and economic life."[39] On another occasion he put the issue as follows: "For us the question was therefore to know whether we would possess these (atomic) means of deterrence and this new ferment of economic activity, as we are well able to do, or whether we would give up to the Anglo-Saxons on the one hand our chances of life and death, on the other certain aspects of our industrial possibilities."[40] Georges Pompidou, speaking as prime minister before he became the general's successor, echoed the same theme when he remarked: "To abandon the atomic effort is to condemn France to becoming an underdeveloped country within the next ten or fifteen years."[41]

The de Gaulle government viewed national defense, especially the nuclear program, as a key agent to promote French scientific and technical programs. According to its

[38] Robert Gilpin, *France in the Age of the Scientific State* (Princeton: Princeton University Press, 1968), p. 284. See this excellent study for general treatment of the evolution of French science and technology.

[39] Press conference, July 23, 1964, *Speeches and Press Conferences*, no. 208, p. 8.

[40] Speech at Lyons in September 1963, as quoted in André Passeron, *De Gaulle Parle*, II (Paris: Arthème Fayard, 1966), 220.

[41] As quoted in Raymond Aron, *The Great Debate: Theories of Nuclear Strategy* (Garden City, N.Y.: Doubleday and Co., 1966), pp. 112-13.

logic, military research and development would set the pace for high levels of industrial achievement and build up key sectors of the economy, for example, electronics, aviation, and atomic power. Without governmental subsidies, it was asserted, these important research-based industries would not thrive on their own in France because of the small size of the civilian market. And these important industries were considered vital for France's international standing.

The heart of the Gaullist argument rested on the contention that the nuclear program has important spin-off benefits for the civilian economy and can yield new products and processes with social and economic applications. Defense Minister Messmer asserted in 1967 that government military contracts were making possible the expansion of the electronics, aerospace, and civilian nuclear industries; these contracts were cited as providing 60 percent of the business in the electronics industry, and 70 percent and 50 percent in aerospace and civilian atomics, respectively. Messmer also contended that the French armed forces were contributing more and more funds for research in pure science ($12.5 million in 1967) and for applied research ($90 million in 1967, $93 million in 1968), from which came scientific advances that benefitted civilian industries. He cited metallurgy as a specific example. Finally, the military nuclear program and its related activities were said to be providing considerable employment for French workers and were also stimulating the development of underindustrialized regions in France.[42]

[42] Messmer, "France's Nuclear Force."

See also the publication of the Defense Ministry entitled "Impact du programme militaire sur l'économie, l'industrie et la recherche," *Note d'information*, no. 15 (June 1966).

The Gaullist newspaper, *La Nation*, has frequently printed articles stressing the scientific, industrial, and economic benefits of the French atomic program. See, e.g., the series entitled "Ces investissements 'improductifs'—Voilà pourquoi la force de dissuasion aide le progrès économique français," October 8-10, 1963.

Gaullist critics, on the other hand, have contested the alleged spill-over effects of the military nuclear effort. They argued that the *force de frappe* diverts scarce funds and highly trained scientists and engineers, in critical short supply, from teaching and basic research to the development of technologies with no economic, scientific, or perhaps even military utility. Moreover, they asserted that spin-off from the narrowly defined military programs to civilian science and technology is minimal, especially in view of the relatively small scale of military research and development in contrast to the much larger and more diverse American effort.[43]

Much debated in France, as elsewhere, evaluation of the spin-off benefits of military programs is extremely difficult. No satisfactory analysis exists. There is only space here for a few summary observations. According to Nicolas Vichney, the well-informed science writer of *Le Monde* and one of the few people who has attempted a serious discussion of these questions, the civilian benefits of the military nuclear program are very limited.[44] He saw no significant civilian applications for military electronics, especially since much of the needed computation equipment has been purchased from the United States. In the area of atomic energy there may be some spill-over in reactor technology, but not much. The Pierrelatte plant, which might eventually produce enough enriched uranium for some to be applied to civilian purposes, is not competitive on the European market. And the future of civilian atomics would seem to lie in breeder-reactors, which use relatively small amounts of enriched uranium. There have been benefits for the French space program. But industrial spin-off was unclear in Vichney's view, although there may be some in the area of ma-

[43] See the discussion of these views in Gilpin, pp. 294ff.

[44] See Vichney's articles in *Le Monde*, February 22-24, November 28-30, and December 1, 1964. Another analysis which reaches a more positive conclusion is Claude Lemoine, "Contribution des programmes nucléaires militaires au développement technologique français," *Études* (April 1, 1968), pp. 490-510.

terials science. Since the construction of the nuclear force is primarily an industrial and engineering task, it has had little impact on pure science and the discovery of new scientific concepts.

In his recent study of French science and technology, Robert Gilpin concluded that the most beneficial aspect of the development of the nuclear striking force probably lies in its psychological impact as a symbol of France's commitment to modernize her society.[45] As a task which demands complex managerial and technical skills, the nuclear program sets high standards of performance for French technology and industry. Moreover, according to Gilpin, it provides an important and needed lever for restoration of structures and revision of attitudes that will spur the overall advancement of French science and technology. But the cost of these gains is high in financial terms; and without question needed resources have been diverted from important areas of civilian technology to military research and development, so far with little spill-over. Possibly of greatest significance, however, is the fact that France's choice for a national solution to the development of nuclear weapons and associated technologies "may impede a successful European cooperative effort in science and technology," the only kind of effort that could compete in the long run with the superior resources and technical skills of the superpowers.

[45] Gilpin, pp. 300-301.

THREE

FRANCE AND HER ALLIES

THE INTERNATIONAL IMPLICATIONS OF GAULLIST STRATEGY

6 · *The French Nuclear Force, NATO, and Franco-American Relations*

De Gaulle's nuclear policy undoubtedly had a greater impact on France's allies than on her enemies. In the 1960's France's relations with the West were greatly exacerbated by nuclear questions. Yet these differences had more fundamental causes. They were deeply rooted in de Gaulle's foreign policy objectives and the political conflicts generated when these objectives clashed with the goals of allied states. In the Franco-American case, the seeds of discord lay in contradictory French and American visions of the future orientation of Europe and the role of arms control in East–West relations and world order. Since French disagreements with NATO stemmed largely from differences with the United States, the effects of French nuclear policy on the relationship between France and NATO are also considered in the following discussion.

De Gaulle and Kennedy: Discord Continues over the Issue of the Tripartite Directorate

During the first year of the Kennedy administration, de Gaulle's 1958 tripartite proposal remained a major issue in Franco-American relations. As discussed earlier, the kind of nuclear consultation advocated by the general under this arrangement would have given France a right of veto over the use of atomic weapons by any of the Big Three anywhere in the world. Moreover, it was probably expected to lead to the sharing of nuclear secrets. This whole matter had been left in suspension by Eisenhower and the French leader, but was revived when President Kennedy visited Paris in early June 1961.

Toward the end of his extremely cordial talks with General de Gaulle, President Kennedy raised the issue of improving tripartite consultation. De Gaulle agreed on the need for such consultation and, according to Theodore Sorensen, told Kennedy that he had been frustrated by Eisenhower's habit of agreeing in principle but never following through.[1] Kennedy suggested the two leaders should meet frequently, and that a study of tripartite strategy should be conducted by military experts of the three nations and common positions be prepared "whenever possible." Kennedy proposed that specific threats to the peace, such as Berlin and Laos, be considered; de Gaulle agreed to this proposal.[2] But the study was never conducted.

There is some disagreement as to why this study of tripartite strategy never developed. The 1966 State Department account says that the French government was later asked to name a military representative, "but no response was ever received."[3] However, an earlier unpublished account indicated that it was left up to the foreign ministers to work out details of the study. When the foreign ministers met in early August, they began a year-long quarrel over President Kennedy's plan to seek negotiations with the Soviet Union on the Berlin problem. De Gaulle was very much opposed to any such negotiations under Soviet duress, and no arrangements were made by the foreign ministers to implement the earlier agreement.[4]

The crisis precipitated by the Berlin Wall moved the general to write a secret letter to President Kennedy in August 1961. The French president again raised the issue of a tri-

[1] Theodore C. Sorensen, *Kennedy* (New York: Harper and Row, 1965), p. 561.

[2] See the "Statement of the Department of State," August 1966, cited, p. 229; also the accounts by James Reston, *New York Times*, May 3, 1964; Robert Kleiman, *New York Times*, August 29, 1966; and David Schoenbrun, *The Three Lives of Charles de Gaulle* (New York: Atheneum, 1965), p. 314.

[3] "Statement of the Department of State," 1966, p. 229.

[4] See Kleiman's account, cited.

partite organization for combined political-military planning, but President Kennedy did not reply.[5] Instead he waited and sent a new letter to de Gaulle later, on December 31, 1961, in which he dealt at length with the Berlin crisis and his desire to negotiate with the Russians to obtain new Soviet guarantees for Berlin in order to reduce the danger of war. Kennedy also addressed himself in this letter to the Franco-American dispute on nuclear policy. Although manifesting some understanding of de Gaulle's desire for atomic weapons, Kennedy stressed his greater concern about the dangers of nuclear proliferation. Nevertheless, he apparently invited suggestions from France on how to satisfy French nuclear needs without creating precedents for nuclear proliferation. Nothing resulted from this overture.[6]

De Gaulle sent a second letter to President Kennedy on January 9, 1962, in which he again explained his hostility toward negotiations on Berlin and the reasons behind the French nuclear effort. He also repeated his proposal for a permanent tripartite political-military planning group and a combined military staff to prepare "common decisions and common actions," and he suggested a new focus for such planning, namely the third world. De Gaulle evidently promised to send Kennedy a memorandum giving further details on the possibilities of working out common policies

[5] Ibid.; also Reston, cited; Schoenbrun, pp. 315-16.

[6] See C. L. Sulzberger in the *New York Times*, January 17, 1962; also Schoenbrun's account. There are few public details about this Kennedy letter. Schoenbrun says that during negotiations which followed it a special American "formula" was devised to provide de Gaulle with an atomic capacity if he would agree to abandon any further French atomic tests. But de Gaulle turned it down (p. 316). Brief reference to such a "formula" is also made by Paul-Marie de la Gorce in "De Gaulle et les Américains," *La Nef*, no. 26 (February-April 1966), p. 73, and in his book *La France contre les empires* (Paris: Grasset, 1969), p. 74. De la Gorce suggests that Kennedy was ready to give de Gaulle some atomic bombs if France would renounce its national nuclear force, but de Gaulle declined the offer.

in this area, but this memorandum was never received. President Kennedy, for his part, did not reply to this second letter from General de Gaulle.[7]

The 1966 State Department account does not mention these last two letters from de Gaulle (August 1961 and January 1962). It simply concludes: ". . . the French Government throughout this period wished to establish tripartite arrangements that went far beyond the consultations the United States considered possible in the light of its own responsibilities and free world interests."[8] But Robert Kleiman, in noting that President Kennedy did not respond to de Gaulle's two letters after their meeting in June 1961, suggests that the United States might have done more to explore the possibilities of compromise with de Gaulle on the issue of tripartite consultation.[9] While at first glance the available evidence might seem to lend some support to this argument, it is doubtful in retrospect that any Franco-American agreement, if reached at all, would have lasted very long, given the two leaders' different conceptions of negotiation with the Soviets, and a host of other conflicting foreign policy goals that were to emerge in subsequent years.

The de Gaulle letter of January 1962 was the last communication on the tripartite question. After President Kennedy failed to respond, discussions on the matter were not resumed. In the spring of 1962 it seems that de Gaulle gave up all hope of obtaining American agreement on his proposal to include France in a potentially formalized Western strategic planning group. Instead he turned his attention to the construction of Europe under French leadership—first with the Fouchet plan, later by means of the Franco-German treaty after the Fouchet negotiations failed—and to the elaboration of a more active and independent French

[7] Schoenbrun, pp. 316-17; Sulzberger, cited; also de la Gorce, "De Gaulle et les Américains," pp. 73-74.

[8] "Statement of the Department of State," 1961, p. 230.

[9] Kleiman, cited.

diplomacy toward the Communist bloc and the third world. The settlement of the Algerian problem in 1962 strengthened de Gaulle's position in the development of his new policies. The simultaneous elaboration of President Kennedy's "grand design" for an Atlantic partnership ensured that French policies would become increasingly opposed to those of the United States, since the Kennedy design was at loggerheads with de Gaulle's vision for an independent Europe. French hostility to NATO increased in intensity, and Franco-American relations began an abrupt decline.

De Gaulle and Kennedy: Conflicting Grand Designs

Increased Franco-American tension beginning in 1962 was deeply rooted in the two countries' differing perceptions of the international system, their images of each other, and their changing international roles, as well as in contrasting foreign policy processes and diplomatic styles.[10] However, there was no more important factor in these differences than the conflicting visions held by each country for the future of Europe. As it happened, many of the conflicts between France and the United States and France and NATO in this period turned on questions of nuclear weapons. But at the heart of these nuclear disagreements lay a basic political conflict between the European policy objectives of Kennedy and de Gaulle.

In Chapter 4 we have already described the main elements of the Gaullist revisionist design in European-Atlantic policy, which sought the creation of a "European" Europe free from superpower influence as the prerequisite for a new European and world equilibrium. Various phases of Gaullist policy were also discussed. It was in the second phase of that policy, focused on the construction of an in-

[10] See Stanley Hoffmann's incisive analysis, "Perceptions, Reality, and the Franco-American Conflict," *Journal of International Affairs*, XXI, no. 1 (1967), pp. 57-71.

dependent confederal grouping of states in Western Europe on the model of the Fouchet plan, that de Gaulle's European vision clashed with President Kennedy's "grand design" for an Atlantic-oriented Western Europe linked closely to the United States.

As it was evolving by 1962, the American notion of an Atlantic partnership was based on the idea that the European Common Market, strengthened by the admission of Great Britain, would become the nucleus of an eventual West European political federation of states as advocated by Jean Monnet. By adjusting American policies it was anticipated that the United States might join with this reinvigorated Western Europe to form a partnership in common pursuit of economic progress and Western defense.[11] The Atlantic partnership model, which took on the labels of the "dumbbell" concept or the "twin pillar" theory, was to be implemented in the economic sphere by the passage of the Trade Expansion Act of 1962, which provided new authority to reduce American tariffs on products imported from the European Economic Community. However, a significant part of this law hinged on the assumption that Britain would indeed join the Common Market.

As the Kennedy administration's European policy was further delineated, it soon became clear that the European-American partnership did not apply to military affairs. Washington was unreceptive to the idea of fostering a European defense grouping, including both the British and French nuclear forces, as part of the Atlantic partnership model. Instead the United States continued to impose its policy and strategy on the European NATO allies. The most that was offered the Europeans in the nuclear field

[11] The American vision of an Atlantic partnership is described in Joseph Kraft, *The Grand Design: From Common Market to Atlantic Partnership* (New York: Harper and Brothers, 1962); see also Arthur Schlesinger's lucid account of "The Not So Grand Design" in *A Thousand Days* (Boston: Houghton Mifflin Co., 1965), ch. 32, pp. 842ff. President Kennedy's principal statement of the idea was his address at Philadelphia on July 4, 1962.

was a role in the Multilateral Force (MLF) which—had it become reality—would have remained subject to an American veto. A major part of the explanation for the American stance—which provoked years of debate on defense relationships in the Alliance—was Secretary of Defense McNamara's insistence on American central command and control of all nuclear weapons in NATO. The U.S. position was also influenced by the development of the American strategy of "flexible response" (which became *de facto* NATO strategy in spite of European objections), and the growth of American hostility toward nuclear proliferation.

Washington's failure to move toward a transatlantic military partnership led to a conflict between the Kennedy "grand design" and the Gaullist vision of an independent Europe with its own defense system; it also fanned the general's feelings of hostility toward NATO and must have contributed to his decision to withdraw France from NATO military commands in 1966.[12] However, before the period of détente began to achieve wide recognition in 1965-66, it is possible that an American policy more friendly to the strengthening of Europe's own defense role might have considerably attenuated the Franco-American dispute over Europe and provided the basis for greater French agreement with NATO, at least for a time.

In the conflict which unfolded between the French and American visions of Europe, nuclear questions occupied a central place. De Gaulle resented America's deprecation of the French nuclear force, which Washington proclaimed "dangerous," especially in view of continued U.S. assistance to the British deterrent. The general viewed the American non-proliferation doctrine as another sign of superpower condominium at the expense of smaller states. He saw the MLF as an instrument designed to bring the French *force*

[12] As analyzed in Chapter 4, de Gaulle probably planned such a withdrawal anyway when a more relaxed East–West climate would permit it, since it was a logical step in his Eastern policy.

de frappe under American control. French nuclear strategy clashed with the McNamara doctrine. It is to an examination of these disputes that we now turn our attention.

Non-Proliferation vs. Nuclear Sharing with France: the Nuclear Aid Controversy, 1962

In the early period of the Kennedy administration, the U.S. State Department seriously underestimated General de Gaulle and his policies in several respects.[13] One illusion was that the general would not be long in office and that the incompatibility of his views and American policies was, therefore, not a matter of great concern. A successor to the general, it was thought, would soon be on the scene. A second illusion was that de Gaulle would probably not be able to solve the Algerian problem. (This was removed by mid-1962, when the Evian accords laid the basis for a Franco-Algerian settlement and greatly bolstered the international prestige of the French president.) A third misconception led to the belief that, in spite of his hostility to integration in NATO and his persistent support for some form of tripartite directorate on NATO and world strategy, de Gaulle would not make any drastic moves to withdraw completely from the NATO structure. Finally, it was thought that de Gaulle was developing his nuclear force primarily to gain prestige, and that the project would soon be discontinued because of its rising costs and general unpopularity in the French parliament and among the French people. This last illusion was removed in 1962, when it became clear that de Gaulle was seriously committed to the *force de frappe* and could overcome parliamentary opposition to obtain the necessary supplementary appropriations for it (as he did in July 1962 on the bill to provide more funds for Pierrelatte).

[13] See, e.g., the comments of President Kennedy's first ambassador to France, General Gavin, in his article "On Dealing with de Gaulle," *Atlantic Monthly* (June 1965), pp. 50-51.

President Kennedy had taken office with the intent of improving relations with de Gaulle, whom he respected as one of the great European leaders. He instructed his ambassador to Paris, James M. Gavin, to seek a better working relationship with the general. In his meeting with de Gaulle in June 1961, Kennedy had made a good start toward more cordial Franco-American relations.[14] The failure to agree on de Gaulle's tripartite directorate provided the first reason why such a relationship did not develop; nuclear differences provided another.

One of Ambassador Gavin's first steps to improve relations was the negotiation of a bilateral atomic agreement with France, similar to agreements already signed with other NATO allies in 1959, authorizing the release of nuclear information to assist in the training of French forces assigned to NATO with nuclear delivery systems. Signed on July 27, 1961, this agreement was passed by the Congress later in the year after hearings before the Joint Committee on Atomic Energy. In testimony before that committee, Undersecretary of State U. Alexis Johnson emphasized that the agreement did not provide for the exchange of information "for the purposes of designing, developing or fabricating atomic weapons. . . . Thus, the agreement will not contribute to the further development of independent national nuclear weapons capabilities."[15] This agreement removed a major irritant, since before it was passed the United States had not been treating France equally with Germany, Italy, and other NATO allies.

As implied by Undersecretary Johnson's statement, a nonproliferation principle was developing in American policy. This had its roots in the Eisenhower administration. As we have noted in Chapters 2 and 3, Eisenhower and Dulles had

[14] See the description of the Kennedy–de Gaulle talks in Schlesinger, *A Thousand Days*, pp. 349-58.

[15] See U.S. Congress, Joint Committee on Atomic Energy, *Hearings on the Proposed Agreement for Cooperation for Mutual Defense Purposes with the Republic of France*, 87th Cong., 1st sess., September 12, 1961, p. 11.

used the non-proliferation argument, for example, in explaining their refusal to give nuclear assistance to France in 1958. In fact, however, the Eisenhower policy had retained considerable flexibility in the future use of nuclear weapons in the Alliance, and resistance to the spread of nuclear weapons had only been selective. That President Kennedy awarded non-proliferation a higher priority was demonstrated in his first year in office when he included a non-proliferation proposal in his speech on disarmament before the U.N. General Assembly on September 25, 1961, as well as an appeal for a nuclear test ban. At the same time, however, the Kennedy administration began experimenting with nuclear relationships in the Alliance to give non-nuclear allies some voice in nuclear strategy. This was the president's aim when in May 1961, in a speech at Ottawa, he repeated an earlier proposal made by Secretary of State Herter for a NATO multilateral nuclear force (MLF), should it be desired and found feasible by America's allies. Kennedy was to have difficulty in effectively interweaving these two strands in his European policy.[16]

In the spring of 1962 a reappraisal of American nuclear sharing policy toward France was prompted by new evidence that the French government was seriously intent on pressing forward with the development of its own nuclear force. In a speech in February, General de Gaulle restated his goal of a French nuclear arsenal, whose first units were to become operational by the end of 1963, as well as his desire to build Western Europe into an organized union of states which he hoped would become "the most powerful, prosperous and influential political, economic, cultural and military complex in the world."[17] There were also reports from Paris that U.S.-French relations would remain unsettled and French opposition to NATO would continue as

[16] For further treatment, see William B. Bader, *The United States and the Spread of Nuclear Weapons* (New York: Pegasus, 1968), pp. 44-45ff.

[17] Broadcast over French radio and television, February 5, 1962, text in *Major Addresses, Statements, and Press Conferences*, p. 159.

long as the United States opposed French ambitions to become a nuclear power.[18] Soon the American ambassador in Paris and other members of the U.S. government, especially Pentagon officials, were counseling that American policy be modified to allow some assistance to the French nuclear effort.

After his meeting with Dulles in July 1958, described in Chapter 2, General de Gaulle never personally sought American atomic aid again; it was not his style to play the role of *demandeur*. But his government officials requested such assistance from the United States on several occasions. De Gaulle probably never intended that French nuclear development be dependent on foreign atomic aid; indeed, he undoubtedly took great pride in the fact that France entered the atomic club largely on her own. Nevertheless, his government attempted several times to purchase American equipment auxiliary to the French atomic program in order to save the money and effort involved in duplication. Thus, General Gaston Lavaud led a French purchasing mission to Washington in March 1962, and presented a "shopping-list" totaling about $250 million. It was said to include information on the construction of atomic submarines, equipment for a gaseous diffusion plant, missile guidance packages, propellants, and other missile parts.[19] This mission may have been encouraged by the Pentagon, which was interested at that time in the sale of arms and equipment to help reduce the balance-of-payments deficit. Before Lavaud's arrival, his shopping list was cabled to Washington by Ambassador Gavin with the recommendation that it be seriously considered.

Gavin's position can be explained in part by his personal background, in part by his assessment of the French military atomic effort. As a former chief of research and development on the army staff at the Pentagon during the 1950's,

[18] See, e.g., Robert C. Doty in the *New York Times*, February 27, 1962, reporting views of the Quai d'Orsay.

[19] *New York Times* and *Le Monde*, April 18, 1962.

he had considerable background in the field of nuclear weapons science. He had also written two books and several articles on military strategy. After his arrival in Paris, he spent considerable time during 1961 entertaining French scientists and evaluating the French nuclear program; his conclusion was that the scientists were both capable and determined to develop a French atomic force, with or without American assistance. Gavin himself believed that it was impossible to withhold for very long the secrets of nuclear technology, many of which could be found anyway in the trade journals. He therefore tended to discount arguments for not assisting the French atomic program on grounds of opposition to nuclear proliferation. He supported some kinds of American assistance to the French nuclear effort to remove a major irritant in Franco-American relations and French attitudes toward NATO; such assistance would also help President Kennedy's balance-of-payments program and promote trade expansion. In particular, Gavin recommended American aid at the end of 1961 for the construction of a French gaseous diffusion plant (Pierrelatte) to produce enriched uranium in return for French support of a liberal trade policy in the Common Market.

According to Gavin, Kennedy was sympathetic to his argument. But the State Department remained adamantly opposed to nuclear sharing with France, refusing to contribute to early nuclear delivery capabilities (the premise of the 1958 amendments to the McMahon Act). When in the spring of 1962 Gavin recommended favorable Washington action on Lavaud's "shopping-list," which included many non-nuclear items not prohibited by the 1958 legislation, he received support from the Pentagon. But the European regional bureau at State dissented. This provoked a full-scale interagency debate in Washington.[20]

General Maxwell D. Taylor, a close military adviser to President Kennedy who had just returned from a fact-finding trip to Europe, filed a report favoring nuclear as-

[20] *New York Times*, April 18, 1962.

sistance to France. In his view, the French had progressed far enough in their military nuclear program to qualify for U.S. aid, which, he believed, might induce a more cooperative French attitude in NATO.[21] Taylor was supported by the joint chiefs of staff, who wanted to encourage France to make a greater contribution to NATO conventional forces by reducing the cost of the *force de frappe*. Other advocates of nuclear aid included Department of Defense officials Roswell Gilpatric and Paul Nitze, Secretary of the Treasury Douglas Dillon (who presumably had an eye on the balance of payments), CIA Director John McCone, several analysts at the Rand Corporation, NATO Ambassador Thomas Finletter and Ambassador Gavin. In the opposing camp was the European bureau of the State Department backed by Secretary of State Dean Rusk; they doubted that de Gaulle's conflicts with NATO could be resolved in this manner and expressed concern about fostering the proliferation of nuclear weapons. This view was supported by the president's national security adviser, McGeorge Bundy, his disarmament advisers, the Joint Committee on Atomic Energy, and NATO's supreme commander, General Lauris Norstad, who had been urging the administration for some time to accept his plan for a land-based MRBM force in Europe which would make NATO, and not France, the world's fourth nuclear power.[22]

After several weeks of debate President Kennedy decided toward mid-April to reaffirm existing practice; and the National Security Council concluded that opposition to the proliferation of nuclear weapons should be a fundamental tenet of American nuclear policy. This was a clear shift from the "substantial progress" doctrine of the 1958 McMahon Act amendments, which theoretically permitted sharing with countries that had achieved an advanced stage

21 See the *New York Times*, April 15, 1962.

22 See John Newhouse, *De Gaulle and the Anglo-Saxons* (New York: Viking, 1970), pp. 154-161; Robert Kleiman, *Atlantic Crisis*, (New York: W. W. Norton and Co., 1964), pp. 56-57; and André Fontaine in *Le Monde*, April 18, 1962.

in their atomic programs on their own. President Kennedy's decision certainly reflected his great concern about the risks of nuclear war in a world of many atomic powers and his desire to pursue arms-control agreements with the Soviet Union to reduce those risks, with a nuclear test ban as a first step. But it was also based on a judgment that nuclear aid, in Theodore Sorensen's words, "would not win General de Gaulle to our purposes but only strengthen him in his." As Sorensen explains:

> While minor military benefits might have been received in return, the General's desire to speak for all Europe, free from British and American influence, would not have been altered. His desire to be independent of NATO, and to form a three-power nuclear directorate outside of NATO, would only have been encouraged. And the West Germans, more pointedly excluded than ever, would surely have reappraised their attitude toward the Atlantic Alliance and toward the acquisition of their own nuclear weapons.

But, he added, "It was an uneasy conclusion, which he [Kennedy] privately re-examined often."[23]

The result was a standoff. In the middle of May General de Gaulle issued a strong challenge to the credibility of the U.S. commitment to European defense in light of U.S.–Soviet parity in nuclear power and delivery capability, and he defended the French nuclear deterrent.[24] Two days later President Kennedy said in a press conference:

> We do not believe in a series of national deterrents. We believe that the NATO deterrent, to which the United States had committed itself so heavily, provides very adequate protection. Once you begin, nation after nation, beginning to develop its own deterrent, or rather feeling it's necessary as an element of its independence to develop

[23] Sorensen, pp. 572-73.

[24] Press conference held by General de Gaulle, May 15, 1962, text in *Major Addresses, Statements, and Press Conferences,* p. 180.

its own deterrent, it seems to me that you are moving into an increasingly dangerous situation.

First France, and then another country and then another, until a very solid and, I think effective defense alliance may be somewhat weakened. That, however, is a decision for the French. If they choose to go ahead, of course, they will go ahead, and General de Gaulle has announced that they are going ahead. We do not agree, but he cannot blame us if we do not agree any more than we blame him if he does not agree with us.[25]

Despite President Kennedy's decision in April not to assist the French, debate on the issue continued. Ambassador Gavin persisted with his argument on behalf of a policy permitting sales to France of items related to her nuclear force, although not nuclear weapons themselves. To him, the State Department's "non-proliferation" argument missed the central issue in the French case, in view of U.S. atomic cooperation with the British and French intentions to press ahead with their military nuclear program in any case, building upon a long history of French nuclear science. Indeed, the timing of Ambassador Gavin's retirement from his post in Paris (announced at the end of August 1962) may well have been due to his differences with administration policy on this issue, although he was expected to leave soon to return to private business.[26]

American nuclear policy toward France was unfolding, meanwhile, in a rather inconsistent manner; and clumsy

[25] From the text of the president's news conference of May 17, 1962, in *Public Papers of the Presidents of the United States*, 1962 (Washington: U.S. Government Printing Office, 1963), p. 402.

De Gaulle is said to have commented at least once that, although he did not agree with the American policy of nuclear monopoly, he would probably have pursued the same policy if he were in our place (Gavin, p. 50).

[26] See the interviews with General Gavin in *Le Monde*, May 5 and September 27, 1962. In the second interview on the eve of his return to the United States, Gavin implied that America's discriminatory policy against the French nuclear program might change with time.

American diplomacy must have reinforced French, and probably other European, suspicions that the United States was not interested in cooperating with elements of West European defense not directly under American control. In an important speech at Ann Arbor, Michigan, on June 16, Secretary of Defense McNamara bluntly attacked small nuclear deterrents as "dangerous, expensive, prone to obsolescence, and lacking in credibility."[27] This passage may have been intended to provoke further public debate in France on the *force de frappe*. As should have been clear, such hortatory comment did not have the slightest effect on de Gaulle and only further exacerbated Franco-American relations.

The message of Secretary McNamara's address was that France and the other allies should place their nuclear weapons under NATO where the United States would possess a veto power over their use. Whatever the value of McNamara's strategic logic, this was not a realistic way to treat a question of national sovereignty. The secretary's sharp tone was even picked up by President Kennedy himself in a news conference a few days later when he referred to the French deterrent as "inimical to the community interest of the Atlantic Alliance."[28]

Just before the Ann Arbor address, an element of inconsistency appeared in American policy when it became known that the U.S. government was authorizing the Boeing Aircraft Company to sell France a dozen KC-135 jet tanker planes, to be used to refuel the Mirage IV bombers of the French *force de frappe*.[29] This represented an impor-

[27] Text in Richard P. Stebbins, ed., *Documents on American Foreign Relations, 1962* (New York: Harper and Row), p. 233.

[28] Press conference of June 27, 1962, in *Public Papers of the Presidents of the United States,* 1962 (Washington, D.C.: U.S. Government Printing Office), p. 513.

[29] *Le Monde*, June 15, 1962. This press report may have been a bit premature; it is likely that the final agreement with France on the tanker sale was completed later in the summer. See also the *New York Times*, September 22, 1962.

tant contribution to the development of the nuclear force at a critical time, since the French did not have other tanker planes immediately available to extend the short range of the Mirage IVs so that they would be capable of reaching Soviet targets.

The tanker sale must have done much to make the *force de frappe* a credible enterprise in the eyes of Frenchmen. The planes had presumably been one of the items on General Lavaud's list presented in Washington the previous spring. The amount of the sale was about $50 million, and its positive effect on the American balance of payments was probably an important factor in its approval by the administration. Nevertheless, the tanker sale did not reflect a consistent policy. It represented active assistance to the development of a French independent nuclear capability—which McNamara had so strongly opposed at Ann Arbor.[30]

Further confusion resulted when it was revealed in October that the administration had offered to sell France an atomic submarine.[31] Preliminary arrangements for the sale had evidently been made by Roswell L. Gilpatric, then deputy defense secretary, in Paris in September. This overture was reminiscent of the submarine offer made by Secretary Dulles to France four years earlier. It had later been dropped at the expense of considerable ill-feeling in Paris, which had been genuinely interested in the offer. The primary reason for its withdrawal was that Secretary Dulles had failed to consult the JCAE before making it. That powerful watchdog committee turned out to be opposed to the dissemination of sensitive nuclear submarine technology. Then, in 1962, the whole story seemed to be repeating itself. Immediately after press reports had revealed the new offer by the Kennedy administration for the sale of a nuclear attack submarine (not a Polaris type), it became clear that

[30] Actual delivery of the tanker planes was not to begin until the spring of 1964. The last plane was delivered in October 1964. See the *New York Times*, October 11, 1964.

[31] Jack Raymond in the *New York Times*, October 17, 1962.

once again the JCAE had not been consulted in advance. Chairman Chet Holifield's position had not shifted on the issue. He opposed the transfer of nuclear information "to nations whose political structure is unstable and whose security capability is questionable."[32] As a result, President Kennedy quietly withdrew his submarine offer. Once again there was bad feeling in Paris.[33]

The last example of unskillful American diplomacy toward France in this chain of events in 1962 was the Nassau proposal for a multilateral nuclear force and the subsequent Polaris offer to France. But we shall return to these confused developments in a moment.

Differences over Nuclear Strategy

The decision of the Kennedy administration in spring 1962 not to contribute to the proliferation of national nuclear forces was but one reason for the American government's opposition to the French nuclear force. Another important factor was the strategic doctrine elaborated by Secretary of Defense McNamara on how the North Atlantic alliance might best be defended and, particularly, on the control of NATO nuclear weapons. The McNamara doctrine had been evolving since 1961; it was unveiled before the NATO allies in the private sessions of the Athens ministerial meeting in May 1962, and then publicly in the secretary's June speech at Ann Arbor. Never accepted by France, this doctrine also provoked opposition from other European members of

[32] *New York Times*, October 18, 1962. The *New York Times* favored the submarine sale in an editorial on October 19.

[33] At a meeting in Washington of the Industrial Atomic Forum, Bertrand Goldschmidt, who is charged with external relations and programs for the French CEA, said that it was still not possible for France to have access to American atomic submarine secrets in spite of the long-standing offer made by President Eisenhower. He regretted that French laboratories "have been obliged to reproduce exactly the same process and the same techniques held secret by our American and British allies, and long since in the hands of the Soviet rival" (*Le Monde*, November 30, 1962).

NATO, as well as from its supreme commander, General Norstad.[34] When the doctrine was officially adopted by the Kennedy administration, however, it became *de facto* NATO strategy because of the predominant position of American forces in the Alliance.[35] In the Franco-American strategic debate which followed, two main points were at issue. They are perhaps best explained by referring once again to Secretary McNamara's Ann Arbor address.

The first point was Secretary McNamara's formal announcement of the shift in the role of conventional and nuclear weapons in American strategy. The heart of McNamara's new doctrine of "flexible response," which henceforth became the official strategy of the Kennedy and Johnson administrations, was the need for strong conventional forces in Europe to complement the nuclear deterrent and to deal with situations of a limited, non-nuclear attack by the enemy, "situations where a nuclear response may be inappropriate or simply not believable."[36] McNamara indicated that American and other Alliance nuclear forces in being were powerful enough to deter general nuclear war. What was needed was a greater allied contribution to the strength of the conventional forces of the Alliance. Such increased allied contributions, joined with the American divisions already in Europe, would allow NATO to meet any Soviet attack at any level and would thus reinforce the powerful nuclear deterrent largely in American hands.

[34] See the article by Charles J. V. Murphy, "NATO at a Nuclear Crossroads," *Fortune* (December 1962), pp. 88ff.

[35] Only after the French withdrawal from NATO in 1966 was "flexible response" adopted as the "official" NATO strategy by the remaining fourteen members at the ministerial session in May 1967. The Dulles "massive retaliation" strategy was finally dropped, although it had not actually been followed since 1961. See Henry Tanner in the *New York Times*, May 10, 1967; also George C. Wilson in the *Washington Post*, May 12, 1967.

[36] From the text of the Ann Arbor speech, June 16, 1962, in *Documents on American Foreign Relations*, p. 236. For an illuminating discussion of the background of the McNamara doctrine, see William W. Kaufmann, *The McNamara Strategy* (New York: Harper and Row, 1964), esp. ch. 3.

The second point concerned the manner of using nuclear weapons in the event of war. McNamara described the new American strategy as one of "controlled nuclear response" (often referred to popularly as "counterforce strategy"). The object of this strategy is to hit first at the enemy's military targets, e.g., his nuclear missile sites, while keeping some forces in reserve to hold enemy cities as hostages and thus, it is hoped, to compel restraint on his part and to prevent an all-out nuclear catastrophe. As explained by an astute American analyst, Malcolm Hoag:

> If a nation is sure that hitting the enemy all-out will lead to intolerable counter-retaliation, then it must gamble on inducing restraint in the enemy rather than on reducing his capability. It may well choose to do so by restrained counter-military attack even when most enemy forces are thought to be invulnerable, as the best of bad gambles in a situation desperate by assumption.[37]

The important corollary here is that, in order to apply this strategy effectively, there can be no competing and conflicting strategies for nuclear war in the Alliance. There must be one system of targeting. For if nuclear war should occur, according to McNamara, "our best hope lies in conducting a centrally controlled campaign against all of the enemy's vital nuclear capabilities, while retaining reserve forces, all centrally controlled."[38]

Both of these notions conflicted with French strategy. France was developing a national nuclear force which would be independently controlled (although the possibility of coordination with allied nuclear forces was never excluded), and employed in a *countercity* strategy against the Soviet Union. Furthermore, French doctrine, according

[37] Malcolm Hoag, "Nuclear Strategic Options and European Force Participation," in *The Dispersion of Nuclear Weapons*, ed. R. N. Rosecrance (New York: Columbia University Press, 1964), pp. 228-29.

[38] *Documents on American Foreign Relations*, p. 234.

to General Ailleret's June 1964 speech, continued to reject "flexible response" and invoked instead the old Dulles "massive retaliation" strategy, emphasizing an immediate atomic riposte to any attack against Europe as the cardinal principle for the deterrence of war. Opposing a purely conventional defense or even an early recourse to tactical nuclear weapons as unsatisfactory to Europeans, since either would turn Europe into a battlefield, Ailleret concluded that only strategic nuclear weapons could have "a strong deterrent effect" on the enemy by threatening to hit his war potential and break the will of his people.[39]

These fundamental differences of strategic theory were compounded by opposition to the McNamara doctrine in France, and elsewhere in Europe, on broader political grounds. Professor Raymond Aron argued the case most eloquently in an article published in the United States in 1962, and in his book, *Le Grand Débat*, which appeared in France a year later. Aron objected to McNamara's opposition to the French nuclear arsenal on grounds of the need for "centralized command and control" of Alliance nuclear weapons.

> The American theory of atomic monopoly which the experts in Washington are tireless in justifying on technical grounds, raises political difficulties which these same experts stubbornly disregard. It amounts to entrusting the United States with the major responsibility for the defense of Europe; of conferring on one man, the President of the United States, the almost superhuman task of charting the deterrent strategy on which depends the choice between peace and war. Great Britain was unwilling to accept this situation, and there is nothing to prove

[39] "Opinion sur la théorie stratégique de la 'flexible response,'" speech delivered before the NATO Defense College, June 26, 1964, reprinted in *Revue de défense nationale* (August 1964), pp. 1323-40. An English translation appeared in *Survival* (November-December 1964), pp. 258-65. See also the discussion in Chapter 4.

that either France or western Europe will accept it tomorrow.[40]

States, like people, do not wish their security to depend on others, concluded Aron. Europe should not resign itself to the status of an atomic protectorate, which is what the McNamara doctrine implied. The McNamara strategy aimed at minimizing the risk of employing the only weapons to which American soil was really vulnerable. To keep hostilities from escalating to this level, the conclusion was unavoidable that America intended to turn Europe into a conventional battlefield and make her the principal victim of any war.

Although he himself essentially agreed with the strategic rationale for "flexible response," Aron explained very clearly how political factors must be taken into account in the transatlantic strategic debate. As he put it, "Geostrategy . . . favors disagreement, whether groundless or well founded, between the partners on either shore of the Atlantic."[41] McNamara's speech did not explain to Frenchmen how their nascent *force de frappe* could be "dangerous" while at the same time "lacking in credibility as a deterrent." Nor did it clarify why the United States continued to bestow upon Great Britain favored atomic assistance which was denied France. As Raymond Aron was to write later, the privileged position of Britain in the atomic field would never be acceptable in Paris, no matter who might be in power.[42]

[40] Raymond Aron, "De Gaulle and Kennedy: The Nuclear Debate," *Atlantic Monthly* (August 1962), p. 36.

[41] From the English translation of *Le Grand Débat* entitled *The Great Debate: Theories of Nuclear Strategy*, trans. Ernst Pawel (Garden City, New York: Doubleday and Co., 1965), p. 168.

[42] "De Gaulle and Kennedy," pp. 34-36. To the argument that if France were accorded aid in this area, West Germany would have to be given equal treatment, Aron replied by emphasizing that the government of the Federal Republic renounced all claim to the manufacture of atomic arms as part of the Paris treaties in 1954. "Why should the policy makers in Washington assume in advance that at

> . . . the Kennedy Administration, like the preceding Eisenhower Administration, has refused to face up to a major truth: that neither General de Gaulle nor any other French leader can admit the official Washington thesis according to which the dissemination of atomic weapons becomes dangerous when these weapons cross the Channel, but not when they cross the Atlantic.[43]

Nassau and the MLF

In the autumn of 1962 a complex series of events occurred in Atlantic diplomacy which brought French-American nuclear differences to a head. At the same time, the underlying political conflict between the two visions for the future of Europe held by Kennedy and de Gaulle was set in bold relief. In this sequence, strategic issues interacted with political and economic relationships in alliance politics in a manner totally unforeseen. The key elements of the drama were the Nassau agreement of December 1962, in which the United States agreed to continue assistance to the British nuclear deterrent and raised the question of a NATO multilateral force; the post-Nassau offer of Polaris missiles to France on the same terms as Great Britain; and General de Gaulle's announcement at his January 14, 1963 press conference of his refusal of the American offer and his veto of Britain's application to join the European Common Market. The result was the demise of President Kennedy's "grand design" for an Atlantic partnership, which had been based on the premise that Britain would gain entry into the EEC. It was a stormy winter!

The trouble started in November when the Defense Department informed the British government that the United States was about to cancel development of the Skybolt air-to-surface missile. Since Britain had been counting on Sky-

---

some future date the West German government will try to renege on this commitment?"

[43] Ibid., p. 34.

bolt to extend the strategic life of its obsolescent V-bomber force, a major crisis ensued in Anglo-American relations. At stake was the life of the British nuclear deterrent. The problem was thrust into the hands of President Kennedy and Prime Minister Macmillan at their meeting at Nassau in late December, a conference scheduled much earlier for a general discussion of the international situation after the Cuban missile crisis.[44]

After four days of talks Kennedy and Macmillan reached an agreement which reaffirmed the special Anglo-American nuclear relationship and produced a muddled formula for relating the British deterrent more closely to NATO and reorganizing all Alliance nuclear forces. In place of Skybolt, the United States agreed to make available to Great Britain Polaris missiles, to be fitted with British nuclear warheads. This missile system would then be installed in British nuclear-powered submarines, which were committed to the defense of the Alliance "except where her Majesty's Government may decide that supreme national interests are at stake." They were assigned, along with other contingents of existing British and American strategic forces, to a "NATO nuclear force"—the multinational force contemplated under Article 6. But then there was also confusing talk about an agreement to promote the development of a "multilateral NATO nuclear force" in consultation with other NATO allies (Article 7), to which British and American Polaris submarine forces might also be made available.[45] As Arthur Schlesinger later remarked, "The drafters outdid themselves in masterly ambiguity."[46]

[44] For a full account of Skybolt and the Nassau meeting, see Schlesinger, pp. 856-66; also Henry Brandon, "Skybolt: the Full Inside Story of How a Missile Nearly Split the West," *Sunday Times* (London), December 8, 1963, pp. 29-31; Richard Neustadt, *Alliance Politics* (New York: Columbia University Press, 1970), ch. 3, pp. 30-55; and John Newhouse, *De Gaulle and the Anglo-Saxons*, pp. 213-37.

[45] The full text of the Nassau "Statement on Nuclear Defense" is reprinted in the *Department of State Bulletin* (Washington, D.C.: U.S. Government Printing Office), January 14, 1963, pp. 43-45.

[46] Schlesinger, p. 864.

The resurrection of the mixed-manned multilateral force was primarily the work of a group of State Department planners who had become attached to the concept. The idea had not aroused much enthusiasm in Europe when President Kennedy first mentioned it at Ottawa in 1961, but it never lost its appeal for some planners at State. They saw in it a way to give America's European allies a greater role in the management of the Alliance's nuclear defense, while at the same time meeting a long-recognized need for MRBM forces in the European theater. Moreover, the MLF, it was hoped, would discourage further proliferation of national nuclear forces—especially to West Germany. Some also viewed the MLF as a step toward a fully collective European nuclear force, which would correspond to the movement toward European unity. It soon became apparent that the MLF could never realize all the diverse, and sometimes conflicting hopes of its supporters. Not surprisingly, it had a short life.[47]

At the end of the Nassau conference it was also decided to offer Polaris missiles to France on the same terms as to Great Britain, i.e., assignment to NATO but with an escape clause permitting withdrawal in time of a national emergency. Thus, the Nassau agreement was transmitted to General de Gaulle with a covering memorandum, but only after it had been made public. According to Arthur Schlesinger, this offer to de Gaulle "was an entirely genuine proposal, though made publicly, formally and without the ceremony

[47] For more on the MLF, see Alastair Buchan, "The Multilateral Force: An Historical Perspective," *Adelphi Papers*, no. 13 (London: Institute for Strategic Studies, October 1964); Henry A. Kissinger, *The Troubled Partnership* (New York: McGraw-Hill for the Council on Foreign Relations, 1965), ch. 5; also Wilfrid L. Kohl, "Nuclear Sharing in NATO and the Multilateral Force," *Political Science Quarterly*, LXXX (March 1965), pp. 88-109.

In some respects the MLF was similar to an earlier unsuccessful American attempt to promote European unity through the European Defense Community. See Robert McGeehan, *The German Rearmament Question: American Diplomacy and European Security after World War II* (Urbana, Ill.: University of Illinois Press, 1971), chs. 3 and 4.

the General might have expected. The president himself and others—Bundy and Tyler especially [the reference is to McGeorge Bundy and William R. Tyler, the assistant secretary of state for European affairs]—hoped that it might throw the French a bridge back to NATO." Further, according to Schlesinger, "Kennedy and Macmillan did not exclude the thought of a British offer of Polaris warheads to Paris in exchange for French nuclear cooperation," presumably to make the Polaris offer technically feasible for France to accept.[48]

After Nassau the president called his ambassador to Paris, Charles E. Bohlen, to Palm Beach and briefed him on what to say to de Gaulle. Bohlen was told to blur the issue of nuclear warheads and leave the matter open to further negotiations, thus giving de Gaulle the chance to accept the Polaris offer to France in spite of the technological problems, if he was really interested. This is what Bohlen did when he saw de Gaulle on January 5, 1963. Bohlen left the General thinking that he would want to explore the matter thoroughly.[49] Theodore Sorensen notes that President Kennedy "had been prepared after Nassau to open full discussions with de Gaulle on nuclear matters, to recognize France as a nuclear power and to provide assistance on weapons, and perhaps even on warheads, if the French aligned their force with NATO under something like the Nassau formula."[50] Those in Washington who saw that formula primarily in terms of Article 6 remained optimistic about the chances of France joining a NATO multinational force.[51]

A few days later de Gaulle rejected the Nassau Polaris offer with one sharp stroke in his famous press conference of January 14, 1963. He also vetoed British entry into the European Common Market and thus knocked out an essen-

[48] Schlesinger, p. 865. This author found no evidence to substantiate the point that any serious consideration was given to the possibility of British nuclear cooperation with France at Nassau.

[49] Ibid., pp. 865-66.

[50] Sorensen, p. 573.

[51] Schlesinger, p. 866.

tial pillar of President Kennedy's vision for an Atlantic community. What had happened? And what, if any, was the link between these two issues?

There were several conceivable reasons for de Gaulle's rejection of the Polaris offer. First, it was not very appealing in Paris because France lacked both the submarines to carry the Polaris missiles and the warheads. These items, according to the schedule of the French nuclear program, would not be available before 1970. Neither the United States nor Great Britain made a specific offer to assist France in filling this gap in her technology. As de Gaulle noted in his press conference, Great Britain received privileged assistance from America on nuclear warhead and submarine technology and France did not. As the general put it, "in terms of technology, this affair is not the question of the moment."[52]

In terms of tactics, American diplomacy had been unusually maladroit. The Nassau agreement was a plan for revising the organization of the Atlantic alliance's nuclear defenses, yet it had been drawn up in a bilateral Anglo-American meeting. This served only to underline the kind of Anglo-American domination of the Alliance which de Gaulle had for so long deplored. The general had neither been invited to Nassau, nor consulted beforehand about the new NATO multinational or multilateral nuclear formulas. To make matters worse, the post-Nassau offer to France was made publicly; de Gaulle probably read about it first in the newspapers. This was not the way to treat a man so sensitive to protocol and status as the general. At the very least, the Nassau communiqué could have left the Polaris offers to Britain and France in vague terms, to allow time for consultation and further negotiation privately through diplomatic channels.

The most fundamental reason of all for de Gaulle's negative reaction related to the status of French nuclear weapons and the proposed NATO multilateral force. When

[52] *Major Addresses*, pp. 218-19.

Under Secretary of State George Ball visited Paris on January 9 on his way to Germany, his explanation of Nassau shifted the emphasis from that of Bohlen talks with the general a few days before. Ball's mission was to stress the MLF of Article 7 of the Nassau accord, and to reassure the West German government that it would be included in the concept of a multilateral, integrated Western deterrent. The message delivered by Ball was in terms of what France could contribute to the further integration of NATO, not what the United States could do for France.

The general must have sensed an American maneuver to bring the evolving French *force de frappe* under American management. In his press conference he strongly reaffirmed France's intention "to have her national defense" and "to equip herself with an atomic force of her own." In the domain of atomic armament, the general continued, for France "integration is something that is unimaginable." De Gaulle rejected French participation in the MLF, which he foresaw would be dominated by the Americans and would not include the bulk of American nuclear weapons anyway. As he explained:

> . . . this multilateral force necessarily entails a web of liaisons, transmissions and interferences within itself, and on the outside a ring of obligations such that, if an integral part were suddenly snatched from it, there would be a strong risk of paralyzing it just at the moment, perhaps, when it should act. In sum, we will adhere to the decision we have made: to construct and, if necessary, to employ our atomic force ourselves.[53]

A French nuclear force was necessary, and this was the heart of de Gaulle's argument, because "American nuclear power does not necessarily and immediately meet all the eventualities concerning France and Europe." If the United States objected to the independent French nuclear effort, this was understandable. The general concluded: "In poli-

[53] *Major Addresses*, p. 219.

tics and in strategy, as in the economy, monopoly quite naturally appears to the person who holds it to be the best possible system."[54]

In vetoing Britain's bid for entry into the Common Market, de Gaulle was moved by a concern that an enlarged European Community would be strongly influenced by London's special ties with Washington. This factor was undoubtedly more important to the French leader than the narrower questions of economic advantage treated in the long Brussels negotiations. The general clearly feared that the entrance of Britain and other associated states would so transform the nature of the EEC that in the end European identity, as well as French influence, would be challenged and "there would appear a colossal Atlantic Community under American dependence and leadership."[55]

There has been much debate on the question whether the Nassau pact was the principal cause of de Gaulle's veto of Britain's Common Market application. There were other factors militating against the success of the entry negotiations, as Chapter 8 will describe. But Nassau must have convinced de Gaulle, if he had not already made up his mind, that Britain was not yet ready to give up her "special relationship" with America. It placed the issue of British entry into the European Community in the worst possible light. For, at a crucial time in the negotiations, London had chosen a Polaris pact with the United States rather than a nuclear tie with Europe (the possibility of which de Gaulle had hinted at in his conversation with Macmillan at Rambouillet).[56] As André Fontaine wrote at the time, "From a profound study of the Bahamas accord, our leaders would conclude that Britain has accepted in fact to integrate completely her national defense in the American system." The tightening of "special links" between London and Washing-

[54] Ibid., p. 217.

[55] From de Gaulle's January 14, 1963 press conference, *Major Addresses*, p. 214.

[56] See Chapter 8 for more detailed treatment.

ton had led to the conclusion in Paris that British entry into the Common Market would carry a great risk of opening the doors to an American Trojan horse.[57]

The sequence of events which began with the cancellation of Skybolt and led to the Nassau agreement and de Gaulle's January 1963 veto is a fascinating case study of how nuclear issues can exacerbate an already existing political conflict between nations. In this case they helped to cause the demise of President Kennedy's vision of a united Europe, including Britain, in an Atlantic partnership with the United States. Although never clearly articulated, it had become apparent that America wanted an Atlantic-oriented Europe that would follow American leadership in questions of high politics and defense. De Gaulle saw the future of Europe differently and sought a Europe with its own defense and its own voice in world affairs. Because of nuclear disagreements discussed earlier in this chapter, the conflict lines were clearly drawn by the end of 1962.

Could the United States have done anything differently in 1962 to explore a *modus vivendi* between the de Gaulle and Kennedy designs? Hindsight is difficult, but perhaps the United States missed an opportunity earlier when it failed to test de Gaulle's limits in the area of international cooperation and to probe the possibilities of Franco-American agreement. First of all, the Kennedy administration could have demonstrated greater understanding for France's nuclear aspirations. It could also have provided certain kinds of limited assistance to the French nuclear effort, which was clearly going ahead anyway, instead of dogmatically opposing it. This would have at least toned down the irritant of our special nuclear relations with the British. Furthermore, Washington might have proposed the coordination of European national nuclear forces with our own through some kind of multinational force in the Alliance. The forces could have been coordinated through

[57] *Le Monde*, January 10, 1963.

NATO, but control over their nuclear triggers might have remained in national hands, thus meeting French desires to preserve sovereignty. Instead, the United States chose to thrust upon the Europeans a multilateral Atlantic nuclear concept which perpetuated American dominance through a veto power. Some kind of European nuclear formula, based on the British deterrent and the evolving French nuclear force with coordinated strategic planning and political consultation, would have contributed far more to European unity and come closer to realizing President Kennedy's idea of an Atlantic partnership. It might have promoted British entry into the Common Market, instead of impeding entry as did the Nassau pact and the MLF.[58]

There were only two indications that this approach was even considered by the American government. At the end of June 1962, Secretary of State Rusk is reported to have proposed to French Foreign Minister Couve de Murville that France coordinate her atomic force with American and British nuclear forces in NATO. The French responded that discussion of this question was "premature" since their force was not yet in being.[59] But perhaps Rusk's proposal did not go far enough. A few months later in a speech at Copenhagen, presidential adviser McGeorge Bundy suggested that the United States would consider sympathetically any plan for a European nuclear force "genuinely unified and multilateral, and effectively integrated with our

[58] Henry A. Kissinger, who later became President Nixon's adviser on national security affairs, was suggesting such an approach at the time. See his "The Unsolved Problems of European Defense," *Foreign Affairs* (July 1962), pp. 532-37. He was misidentified in France as an adviser to President Kennedy, which at that point he was not. Later, Kissinger elaborated his ideas for coordination of alliance nuclear forces in greater detail in *The Troubled Partnership*, esp. ch. 6.

[59] See Robert C. Doty in the *New York Times*, June 21, 1962; and *Le Monde*, June 22, 1962. It should be noted that official French pronouncements on the *force de frappe* always left open the possibility of coordination with allied nuclear forces.

own necessarily predominant strength in the whole nuclear defense of the alliance."[60] But this notion was never followed up by the Kennedy administration.

The MLF after Nassau

After de Gaulle's refusal of the Nassau Polaris offer and French participation in the MLF, as well as his veto of British entry, the Kennedy administration decided to press ahead anyway with discussions in NATO on the establishment of the multilateral force. Although himself retaining "a certain skepticism about the MLF," Kennedy recognized the need "to reassure the Germans and show NATO that there were alternatives to Gaullism."[61] After the general's January press conference, the MLF was one of the few remaining instruments that could be applied in support of U.S. Atlantic policy, which opposed de Gaulle's bid for leadership of a "third force" Europe that excluded Britain and might base its future defense hopes on a Franco-German nuclear arrangement. There was particular concern in Washington about the latter after the Franco-German friendship treaty, signed in January, although the possibility was much exaggerated at the time. Several State Department officials were persuaded that it was desirable to press the MLF as an alternative in order to preserve the American–West German relationship. The implication was that Bonn might be forced to "choose" between Washington and Paris.

As a result, high diplomatic missions were dispatched to Europe (several headed by Ambassador Livingston T. Merchant) to explain MLF to the NATO allies. Consultations continued throughout the spring. After some confusion following Nassau about the nature of the proposed MLF, it became clear that the administration's proposal was for surface ships—as had actually been discussed in

[60] Text in *Department of State Bulletin*, October 22, 1962, pp. 604-605.

[61] Schlesinger, p. 872.

staff-level talks with the European allies in 1962—and not submarines, the impression left by the Nassau accord. These surface ships (twenty-five were proposed) would carry Polaris A-3 missiles and would be jointly financed by participating allies and operated by mixed-manned crews.

European reactions to the MLF were varied. West Germany was the most enthusiastic and agreed in the spring of 1963 to support 40 percent of the costs. Great Britain was skeptical, but willing to consider the matter. The British Conservative government was more interested in its own nuclear deterrent and in the Nassau multinational force, later formalized as the Inter-Allied Nuclear Force (IANF) in May 1963. Furthermore, elections were approaching. Italy endorsed the concept, but faced uncertainties in a new coalition government based on the "opening to the left." At any rate, by October 1963, a working group composed of the NATO ambassadors of eight interested countries began technical discussions on the MLF in Paris; these talks continued throughout 1964.

Following de Gaulle's sharp rejection of the MLF idea in January 1963, the French government remained aloof from the project. France pressed forward instead with the development of her own independent nuclear arsenal. French non-Gaullist opinion was also critical of the MLF. Doubts were expressed in many quarters as to whether the principle of mixed-manning of the crews could work in practice, as well as about the strong West German role, which might draw Germany closer to acquiring her own nuclear weapons. Indeed, the whole idea was branded by many as a "multilateral farce." The MLF seemed to unite Gaullists and the opposition. As one observer wrote:

> Frenchmen are divided into three categories regarding the atomic policy of Gaullism, this policy being the essence of the regime. Some are opposed in any case to the national bomb. Others favor it in any case. Finally, the remaining, probably the most numerous, are torn by

doubts; they are opposed to the national bomb as a matter of principle but they are sensitive to the defects of the present nuclear strategy in NATO. The American project of MLF tends to align the third group with the second and even to draw closer a portion of the first group (Communists) toward the second group.[62]

Most French and many other European observers viewed the MLF as a costly gimmick that gave the appearance of a greater European role in the nuclear affairs of the Alliance, but did not really change the heart of the problem—i.e., that America still had a veto over Alliance nuclear weapons. As André Fontaine put it, "If the veto is retained permanently, the MLF is in fact what de Gaulle says it is, an American naval foreign legion."[63] Most Frenchmen, Fontaine emphasized, did not think it possible to rely forever on the United States for the defense of Europe. They were partial to the idea of a European nuclear force which might be independent, but linked to the American force.[64]

This point was not overlooked in official American MLF pronouncements, which hinted that the MLF might later evolve into a European or Atlantic nuclear force without an American veto. President Kennedy referred to this possibility in his speech at Frankfurt on June 25, 1963. Later, a few weeks before he became president, Lyndon Johnson said at Brussels: "Evolution of this missile fleet toward European control, as Europe marches toward unity, is by no means excluded."[65] But the "European clause" in the draft MLF

[62] Maurice Duverger, "Une solution fausse," *Le Monde* (weekly ed.), no. 801, February 20-26, 1964, as cited in W. W. Kulski, *De Gaulle and the World* (Syracuse: Syracuse University Press, 1966), pp. 146-47.

[63] André Fontaine, "The ABC of MLF," *The Reporter*, December 31, 1964, p. 13. This is a good summary of the history of the MLF from a French viewpoint. The article is a condensed version of a series published by Fontaine on the MLF in *Le Monde* in November 1964.

[64] Ibid., p. 14.

[65] Speech of November 8, 1963, reprinted in the *Department of State Bulletin*, December 2, 1963, pp. 853-54.

treaty prepared by the technical working groups in Paris at the request of West Germany and Italy, was little more than an agreement to review the voting procedure if and when Europe might achieve political union. The possibility of the United States renouncing its veto in favor of the formation of a European force was not taken very seriously by State Department policy planners, although they frequently stressed it in conversations with Germans. Indeed, the opposite impression was given the British and the Soviets, to whom the United States persistently emphasized its opposition to all forms of nuclear proliferation.

When in the autumn of 1964 the MLF again became a hot issue on the Atlantic political stage, the French government readdressed itself to the problem. By this time it had become an issue in German domestic politics, and the Erhard government eagerly sought an agreement. Moreover, the new Labor government had been installed in Great Britain and was turning its attention to Alliance nuclear problems. Beginning in November, French officials made a series of statements accusing the United States of trying to isolate France in the Alliance, implying a further reduction of France's participation in NATO if the MLF were actually established.[66]

Robert Bowie said before the Assembly of the West European Union on December 3, 1963: "Such a force might evolve in either of two ways: it might become an integrated Atlantic force with the United States still a member but without a veto. Or it might develop into an integrated European force without the United States as a member. . . ."

Similarly, Walt Rostow, chairman of the Policy Planning Council of the State Department, commented before the WEU Assembly on June 24, 1964: "We have wished to leave the structure of the MLF sufficiently flexible to adjust as Europe moves toward unity."

[66] The tone was set by Premier Georges Pompidou on November 5: "If the Multilateral Force should result in a sort of German-American military alliance, our first reaction would be that we could not consider this arrangement truly compatible with the present relations which we have with the Federal Republic and which are defined in the Franco-German Treaty. . . . In brief, we may ask ourselves whether this kind of project, this Multilateral Force, would not de-

The thrust of the French anti-MLF campaign was directed against West Germany. As described in the next chapter, de Gaulle applied pressure in an attempt to force Bonn to align with Paris rather than Washington. The French president seemed to be suggesting, especially in his November 22 speech at Strasbourg, that West Germany should forego the MLF and accept instead the concept of a more independent European defense organized around the emerging French *force de frappe*.

The climax of this new flurry of MLF debate in the Alliance was the December Johnson-Wilson meeting in Washington. The president and the new prime minister reviewed the whole problem of Alliance nuclear sharing and the British proposal for an Atlantic nuclear force (ANF). The latter arrangement, suggested as an alternative to MLF, was to include all British strategic nuclear forces, an equal contribution of American Polaris submarines, and a multilateral element allowing participation of the non-nuclear powers. (The door was to be left open for French participation, in case France should choose to come in later.) The Johnson-Wilson communiqué, issued on December 8, revealed no decisions. Other consultations were to follow in the Alliance.[67] But then a few days later President Johnson decided firmly to postpone indefinitely all action on the MLF-ANF problem.

This move, prompted by a detailed review by McGeorge Bundy assisted by Richard Neustadt, marked in effect the final burial of the MLF idea.[68] A National Security Council memorandum went out instructing all officials of the gov-

stroy Europe, whether it would not be a challenge to some other countries, and finally, whether it is not more or less directed against France." (*Le Monde* [weekly ed.], no. 838, November 5-11, 1964, as cited in Kulski, pp. 145-46.)

[67] See the *New York Times*, December 9, 1964.

[68] See the illuminating account of President Johnson's decision-making on the MLF issue by Philip Geyelin, *Lyndon B. Johnson and the World* (New York: Frederick A. Praeger, 1966), ch. 7, pp. 159-80; also the *New York Times*, December 21 and 22, 1964.

ernment to cease pressure on the European allies for the formation of an Alliance nuclear force. It also stated that no NATO nuclear arrangement would be acceptable if it was not agreeable to both Britain and Germany, and at least discussed with France. By the end of December the State Department MLF Task Force was abolished. Subsequent British-West German talks in 1965 on the ANF made little headway and were finally stalled by the coming West German elections.

The French government was pleased by President Johnson's stand and American assurances that the United States no longer sought to isolate France in NATO, but wanted consultations. At the December NATO meetings there were reports that France wanted to discuss coordination of the French nuclear force with the American Strategic Air Command. American officials showed a new willingness to talk about such coordination, although no agreement was reached. Accord may have been prevented by the difficulty of reconciling France's strategy of immediate "massive retaliation" in case of aggression in Europe with the United States' doctrine of "flexible response";[69] or the French may simply have decided that any talks on this subject were still premature, since their force was still coming into being.

Although Chancellor Erhard and his defense minister, Kai-Uwe von Hassel, continued to seek some kind of a "hardware solution" to the Alliance's nuclear-sharing problem in their talks with President Johnson in December 1965, there was no urgency or willingness to take any concrete action. The Johnson administration began to focus instead on the possibility of achieving a non-proliferation treaty with the Soviet Union, which had continually opposed the establishment of any MLF-ANF plan in NATO for fear it might bring West Germany closer to nuclear weapons. It was soon clear that arresting the problem of nuclear spread

[69] See the *New York Times*, December 17 and 22, 1964; and *Le Monde*, December 18, 1964.

took higher priority in American policy under President Johnson than new efforts at solving the perplexing problem of Alliance nuclear sharing.

In retrospect, the MLF episode revealed most sharply the deep political cleavage that underlay Franco-American nuclear differences. American and French designs for the organization of European defense, and more fundamentally for Europe's orientation in the world, had grown irreconcilable. The original Kennedy notion of an Atlantic partnership was not implemented in the field of European-American security relations. Instead, the American government insisted on centralized control of all allied nuclear weapons and failed early on to suggest any serious plan allowing European nations their own defense identity, and hence political voice. Subject to a clear American veto, the MLF demonstrated most clearly American unwillingness to share its power with Europe. Perhaps the nature of an alliance between a global superpower and smaller states, or the apocalyptic nature of atomic weapons, precluded any other outcome; but perhaps not. As we have argued earlier, the United States might have proposed another course of action along the lines of a NATO multinational formula in 1962 which would have gone farther to meet French and other West European concerns.

Another reason for the demise of the MLF was the advent of a new approach to NATO nuclear problems suggested by Secretary McNamara in May 1965: a special committee for consultation on Alliance nuclear strategy. Soon dubbed the "McNamara Committee," this was an attempt to institutionalize serious dialogue and joint strategic planning between the United States and its European allies on the use of NATO nuclear weapons. The special committee met for the first time as a whole in November 1965, and the Nuclear Planning Group began meetings in February 1966. At the December 1966 NATO meeting, the Nuclear Planning Group (NPG) gained formal status within NATO when, meeting without France, the fourteen members of the Alliance decided to establish it on a permanent basis. It was composed of four permanent members (the U.S., Britain, West Germany, and Italy) and three rotating members.[70] Since its establishment, the NPG has proved an excellent educational device and has alleviated many allied concerns for an increased voice in NATO strategy.[71]

France rejected the idea of the McNamara nuclear committee soon after it was proposed.[72] In her eyes, the committee appeared to be an attempt to associate France, along with other non-members of the nuclear club, in decision-making on secondary nuclear problems. The French government apparently did not believe that participation in the committee would give France the political recognition she sought as a full-fledged nuclear power, especially since West Germany and other non-nuclear countries would be involved. Presumably only a tripartite consultative structure of the nuclear powers along the lines of General de Gaulle's proposal of 1958 would have been acceptable to Paris. However, France did not oppose the existence of the McNamara Committee for consultations between other NATO members.

Differences over Arms Control I: The Test Ban Treaty

With the signing of the Test Ban Treaty in Moscow on July 25, 1963, President Kennedy achieved one of his most important foreign policy goals. Clearly haunted by the specter of nuclear proliferation, he had said earlier that year ". . . by 1970, unless we are successful, there may be ten nuclear powers instead of four, and by 1975, fifteen or twenty. . . . I see the possibility in the 1970's of the President of the United States having to face a world in which fifteen

[70] *New York Times*, December 15, 1966.

[71] See Harlan Cleveland, *NATO: The Transatlantic Bargain* (New York: Harper and Row, 1970), pp. 53-65.

[72] *New York Times*, July 10, 1965.

or twenty nations may have these weapons. I regard this as the greatest possible danger."[73] Kennedy made a sincere effort to persuade France to sign the treaty, which banned nuclear tests in the atmosphere, under water, and in outer space. He realized that, to be effective, the broadest possible acceptance of the treaty was necessary. But the president's effort failed, and the test ban became another issue in a series of Franco-American nuclear disagreements. It was also used unwisely by the United States to further its policy of nuclear discrimination against France.

Noteworthy, however, are the efforts Kennedy made to persuade France to accept the test ban. As soon as the treaty was initialed, he offered de Gaulle newly discovered knowledge on techniques of underground nuclear testing in return for French signature.[74] Then in his press conference on August 1, President Kennedy declared publicly that France was a nuclear power "in terms of the Atomic Energy Act." At the same time he made it clear that any future assistance to France would depend not only on France's meeting the requirements of the McMahon Act, but also on her political cooperation in NATO. Kennedy was still trying to reopen a dialogue with de Gaulle on this subject. In the president's words, the problem of nuclear assistance to France really depended on "the organization of the defense of the West, and what role France sees for herself, and sees for us, and what kind of a cooperative effort France and the United States and Britain and other members of NATO—and this is important, the non-nuclear powers of NATO—join in."[75]

De Gaulle rejected Kennedy's offer on August 4. He

[73] As quoted in Schlesinger, p. 897.

[74] See Schlesinger, p. 914; also Robert Kleiman, *Atlantic Crisis*, pp. 135-36.

[75] *Public Papers of the Presidents, 1963*, p. 618. The Kennedy administration's policy of not assisting the French nuclear or missile programs unless France assigned her nuclear force to NATO under something like the Nassau formula was formalized in a National Security Council memorandum issued in the spring of 1964.

stressed instead his intention to continue French nuclear tests and to make no arrangements that would jeopardize the independence of the French deterrent. Whether the general would have given the same response to such an offer a year or so earlier, perhaps in combination with a proposal for the coordination of European nuclear forces in a multinational NATO framework, remains an open question. De Gaulle had already dismissed the Test Ban Treaty in his press conference on July 29, calling it "of limited importance" since it did nothing to alter the overwhelming nuclear capabilities of the two superstates. In his view, the test ban was a form of arms control aimed against smaller powers. In effect, it would preserve the enormous power of the Soviet Union and the United States at their existing levels and "prevent France from equipping herself with the same kind of means, failing which . . . France's own security and her own independence would never again belong to her."[76] Arthur Schlesinger wrote later, "As Kennedy told Macmillan, de Gaulle's answer made it clear that he wished neither Anglo-American nuclear assistance nor even a serious discussion. But though the President was not surprised, he was nonetheless bitterly disappointed. The French declination, on top of the Chinese, meant that the treaty would fail as a means of stopping major proliferation."[77]

Bertrand Goldschmidt, a high official of the French Atomic Energy Commission, has offered the following defense of France's refusal to sign the Test Ban Treaty:

[76] *Major Addresses*, pp. 237-38.

[77] Schlesinger, p. 914. Kleiman has a slightly different version. He gives the date of de Gaulle's reply as August 2 and says that it was made in terms which did not close the door on further Franco-American discussion on nuclear cooperation. Kleiman believes that conditions were right for the revival of Franco-American dialogue at the planned Kennedy–de Gaulle meeting in early 1964. See "Background for Atlantic Partnership," in *NATO in Quest of Cohesion*, ed. Karl H. Cerny and Henry W. Briefs (New York: Frederick A. Praeger, 1965), p. 447.

Up to the last moment the United States had persisted in efforts to get France to associate itself with the new treaty. Our successive disappointments in our attempts at a military atomic rapprochement with the Americans, in particular for a submarine, along with the lesson learned from the history of the failures of Anglo-American nuclear collaboration unceasingly repeated, sufficed to prevent us from taking into consideration all offers made at the last moment, whatever their importance, to convince us to sign the treaty. It was of greater concern to France than to any other nation, since she had arrived at the stage of (developing) powerful bombs which can only be tested in atmospheric tests, a stage which the two Great Powers had just abundantly explored.[78]

In addition to the substantive disagreement between the two countries on the treaty itself, the very strict American interpretation of Article 1, paragraph 2, soon after the treaty was signed introduced a new irritant into Franco-American relations.[79] For this provision henceforth became the basis of an American refusal to provide a wide variety of equipment to France that might in any way have assisted the French in carrying out their own nuclear tests. The U.S. government invoked this provision in urging Canada to persist in refusing to sell uranium to France for use in the French military atomic program. An embargo was also imposed in Washington on such items as electronic measuring devices wanted by the French for monitoring their nuclear tests. The French government thought this embargo was rather extreme.

[78] Bertrand Goldschmidt, *Les Rivalités atomiques* (Paris: Arthème Fayard, 1967), p. 262.

[79] Article 1, paragraph 2 of the Test Ban Treaty committed all signatories "to refrain from causing, encouraging, or in any way participating in, the carrying out of any nuclear weapon explosion, or any other nuclear explosion, anywhere which would take place in any of the environments [covered by the Treaty]. . . ." (From the text as reprinted in the *Department of State Bulletin*, August 12, 1963, pp. 239-40.)

The biggest controversy erupted during 1965-1966 over the delivery to France of large, complex American computers, such as the Control Data Corporation Model 6600, which could be used in both civilian and military nuclear research. The U.S. government refused export licenses for any computers which might assist the French thermonuclear weapons program. Again, there was strong reaction in Paris, for some of these computers had been ordered for specifically civilian purposes, including one for the civilian nuclear research center at Saclay. Even though other French orders were for military applications by the CEA, it was argued that these computers were not indispensable for the development of hydrogen weapons; they would only accelerate the development program and save France time and effort.[80] The French saw themselves the victims of spite exercised against them by the government of the United States, supposedly an ally of France. In the words of Goldschmidt, "The efforts pursued by the United States to prevent us from perfecting our atomic armament, to the extent of placing an embargo on civilian equipment, are contrary

[80] See Goldschmidt, *Les Rivalités atomiques*, pp. 262-63; C. L. Sulzberger, "When the Atom Splits Friends," *New York Times*, July 2, 1965; and Nicolas Vichney in *Le Monde*, May 20, 1966; *New York Times*, February 11 and May 22, 1966.

On May 20, 1966, the State Department spokesman, Robert McCloskey, issued the following statement on U.S. policy:

> Our general policy for many years has been not to license equipment that would directly contribute to the development of an independent nuclear weapons capability or would be used in connection with nuclear weapons tests by countries not party to the Nuclear Test Ban Treaty. The U.S. has for some time refused to authorize the sale of very high performance computers that would be used in foreign atomic weapons research. We have recently licensed the export of a number of U.S. manufactured computers which are not to be involved in the French atomic weapons program. We will continue to review license applications for the export of such computers on their merits. However, we will continue *again* to deny export licenses for the sale of high performance computers that we believe will be used for nuclear weapons research.

to the spirit of the North Atlantic Treaty."[81] In his view, membership in the North Atlantic alliance carried with it a commitment of mutual assistance to maintain and increase the individual and collective capacities of all members to resist an armed attack. By its nuclear policy, the United States was reneging on its treaty obligations.

Later in 1966, after policy had been clarified in Washington, the American government did reach agreement with France on the sale of several advanced computers on the condition that they would not be used in violation of U.S. commitments under the Test Ban Treaty.[82] This cleared the way for delivery of Control Data Corporation and IBM equipment to Electricité de France and the Saclay nuclear research center, respectively. A sensitive point of Franco-American dispute had been softened, for the time being at least. One of the reasons for Washington's action was undoubtedly the fact that the previous embargo had prompted the French government to take initial steps to organize a national computer industry, which threatened the loss of a substantial market to American firms.

In a related development, it was revealed by French government sources in April 1966 that the United States had ignored official French requests since 1964 for additional enriched uranium atomic submarine fuel under the terms of the 1959 Franco-American agreement. That agreement, mentioned earlier in Chapter 3, had provided for the sale to France over a ten-year period of up to 440 kilograms of enriched uranium. The first delivery of 171 kilograms of 90 percent enriched fuel was made at that time for use in the French submarine prototype reactor at Cadarache. A second delivery, apparently requested in late 1964, was ignored by the U.S. government—probably as a punitive measure against de Gaulle's anti-NATO policies. France was now using the enriched uranium fuel in her program to develop missile-launching submarines for the third stage

[81] Goldschmidt, *Les Rivalités atomiques*, p. 263.
[82] *New York Times* (European ed.), October 22-23, 1966.

of the *force de dissuasion,* which the American government continued to oppose.[83] At any rate, the result was further French resentment at this new American atomic discrimination.

Finally, the United States announced in November 1966, that it was ending formal cooperation with France in peaceful atomic energy following the expiration of a 1956 Atoms for Peace Agreement, similar to agreements with many other countries. In the future France would have to apply for any civilian nuclear assistance, particularly reactor fuels, through Euratom, whose role in the field of international atomic control the American government wished to strengthen. The French government was again annoyed, especially since the United States had extended a similar civilian bilateral atomic agreement with Great Britain.[84]

France's Withdrawal from NATO

In a message to President Johnson on March 7, 1966, followed by an *aide-mémoire* to the fourteen governments of NATO countries on March 8 and 10, General de Gaulle announced his intention to withdraw all remaining French military forces under NATO commands, to terminate French participation in all NATO command structures, and to require the transfer from French territory of all NATO bases and installations, including the headquarters of the supreme allied commander in Europe and the Central European Command. A subsequent French government declaration on March 29 indicated that the withdrawal of French forces (two divisions and several air squadrons stationed in Germany) would take place effective July 1, 1966. NATO headquarters and base installations had to be removed from French territory by April 1, 1967. As a consequence of this decision, France unilaterally denounced five bilateral

[83] See the *New York Times* (European ed.), April 18, 1966; *New York Herald Tribune* (European ed.), April 19, 1966.

[84] *New York Times,* November 20, 1966.

agreements with the United States concerning American bases, an important pipeline, and communications networks on French territory.[85]

France's disengagement from NATO had been forewarned. In his press conference of September 9, 1965, de Gaulle had admonished that "in 1969 by the latest" (i.e., the date when the North Atlantic Treaty could be denounced upon a year's notice by any signatory no longer desiring to be a party) "the subordination known as 'integration' which is provided for by NATO and which hands our fate over to foreign authority shall cease, as far as we are concerned."[86] Similarly, in a press conference on February 21, 1966, the French president had gone further and stated that by April 4, 1969, France intended to reestablish "a normal situation of sovereignty" over her territory and claim control over all foreign military bases.[87] By his action in March 1966, de Gaulle was merely consummating earlier moves to reduce France's NATO participation, such as the withdrawal of the French Mediterranean and Atlantic fleets in 1959 and 1963, respectively. The whole process had proceeded as forewarned in his September 1958 Memorandum.

The reasons given for France's action against NATO in March 1966 are worthy of examination. In the initial memorandum NATO governments were reminded of France's longstanding dissatisfaction with the state of the organization and her belief that NATO no longer fitted the prevailing conditions of world politics.[88] Specifically, de Gaulle

[85] For other analyses of France's withdrawal from NATO, see Guy de Carmoy, *Les Politiques étrangères de la France, 1944-66* (Paris: La Table ronde, 1967), pp. 372-99; W. W. Kulski, *De Gaulle and the World* (Syracuse: Syracuse University Press, 1966), pp. 178-88; Harlan Cleveland, *NATO: The Transatlantic Bargain* (New York: Harper and Row, 1970), pp. 100-109; and Francis A. Beer, *Integration and Disintegration in NATO* (Columbus: Ohio State University Press, 1969), pp. 85-92.

[86] *Speeches and Press Conferences*, no. 228 (New York: Ambassade de France, Service de presse et d'information).

[87] *Speeches and Press Conferences*, no. 239, p. 5.

[88] *Documents officiels*, nos. 13 and 14 (Paris: Ministère des affaires étrangères, 1966), pp. 121-23.

contended that owing to several changes in the international environment the situation was different from that of 1949: first, the external threat facing Western Europe had lessened and European nations had revived since World War II; secondly, France "is equipping herself with atomic armament, the very nature of which precludes her integration"; thirdly, there was a new nuclear balance between the Soviet Union and the United States, which had transformed the conditions of Western defense; and finally, the focus of international crisis was no longer in Europe, but in Asia where not all Atlantic countries were involved. The last point seemed especially predominant in de Gaulle's mind. He had expressed grave concern in his February press conference that the American involvement in the Vietnam war could expand into a general conflagration into which American allies in Europe, closely tied to the United States through the system of NATO commands, might be drawn against their will. On the other hand, the Vietnam conflict was a convenient excuse for the general's final rupture with NATO, a move which he had clearly contemplated for a long time.

The French decision was a strictly unilateral one. De Gaulle was not interested in discussing or negotiating changes in the NATO structure. In his view, all France's partners appeared to favor the existing system, which was unacceptable to France. However, the general did proclaim that France would remain a member of the North Atlantic alliance, which, as he put it, "must continue as long as it appears to be necessary," and that she was only withdrawing from the integrated military organization (thus maintaining his usual distinction between the two). But he left his options open when he said that "barring events that in the years to come might modify in a fundamental way the relations between East and West," France did not plan to make use of Article 13 of the treaty to leave the Alliance after 1969.[89] He also asserted that France's withdrawal from

[89] Ibid.

NATO did not exclude common military actions on the side of its allies in time of war. The U.S. government was invited to discuss with France the question of making available military facilities on French territory in case of a future conflict in which both countries might be involved by virtue of the North Atlantic Treaty.

De Gaulle's announcement unleashed a crisis in the Alliance. It provoked a vigorous debate in the National Assembly, including an unsuccessful motion of censure. In that April debate, Premier Georges Pompidou vigorously defended the actions of the government. A catalogue of Gaullist grievances against NATO, his two principal speeches explained the French withdrawal primarily as an anti-American action.[90]

Viewed from Paris, several of Pompidou's arguments had substance. As a result of American domination of the organization, the premier contended, NATO's strategic doctrine had been changed from "massive retaliation," officially adopted by the North Atlantic Council in the 1950's, to the McNamara concept of "flexible response," in spite of objections by France and other European governments. Although he only alluded to it in his speeches, the United States' persistent opposition to and refusal to assist the independent French atomic force, despite the aid awarded Britain in the nuclear field, had also contributed significantly to de Gaulle's dissatisfaction with the NATO framework. At the same time, the French objected to the privileged position of the United States in NATO's nuclear defense; 95 percent of the American nuclear deterrent remained outside of NATO and the remaining 5 percent, though formally committed to NATO, could only be employed at the wish of the American president.

The French charge that integration in NATO was destroying France's identity and hampering her freedom of action was more suspect, since the actual amount of integration under NATO commands is very limited, especially

[90] *Speeches and Press Conferences*, nos. 243A and 245A.

in peacetime. Under Article 5 of the North Atlantic Treaty, France was free to decide what kinds of action she wished to take in case of hostilities. Less easy to refute, given the fact that under NATO arrangements American bases were stationed on French soil, was the argument that France might be implicated if American involvements outside of Europe (such as in Vietnam) were to provoke a war that escalated and extended to Europe.

But in retrospect the most fundamental reason for the French action was rooted in Pompidou's comment that NATO integration "is the daughter of the cold war and helps to perpetuate it." With the decline of the Soviet threat in Europe, de Gaulle had already turned his attention to developing the third phase of his European policy (described in Chapter 4): détente and gradual rapprochement with the East. In view of his June trip to Moscow, the time was opportune to reduce France's Atlantic commitments so that the French president could speak with greater independence and authority in Russia about his hopes for eventual French-Soviet agreement on pan-European security and a European settlement.

The timing of de Gaulle's sudden démarche of March 1966 caught most people unaware. American officials had known since at least mid-1965 that the general was planning to move against NATO sometime; but de Gaulle was said to have told the American ambassador in Paris in the early months of 1966 that no immediate actions were planned by the French government because of the deep American involvement in Vietnam. The Quai d'Orsay had prepared plans for the reform of NATO in late 1965 and passed them on to the Elysée; but de Gaulle rejected them and demanded new ones on short notice early in the spring.[91] True

[91] Some of the ideas of the Quai d'Orsay may have been reflected in the unsigned article which appeared in *Politique étrangère*, no. 3 (1965) entitled "Faut-il reformer l'Alliance atlantique?" The article suggested that NATO be replaced by a European alliance system with a considerable degree of integration in nonnuclear facilities only. West Germany would be included in the system, but

to his tactics of surprise and swift diplomatic action, the general gave the appearance of having suddenly changed his mind.

De Gaulle's final timetable must have been influenced by other factors. For example, he was concerned about losing a majority in the 1967 parliamentary elections. Withdrawal from NATO beforehand would leave sufficient time for the shock on public opinion to have diminished. Similarly, he probably waited until after the December 1965 presidential elections in order to ensure his reelection to a second seven-year term. But age and declining health undoubtedly were incentives for the general to make his NATO policies irreversible soon before he might be forced to depart the French political scene. Finally, de Gaulle had waited until the first generation of the *force de dissuasion* was deployed before making his move, in order to bolster his diplomatic hand.[92] This was the case by early 1966, when Mirage IV planes were in operational readiness.

During the second half of 1966 representatives of the United States and France discussed possible use by American military forces of facilities on French territory (e.g., airfields, depots, communication and port facilities, and the petroleum pipeline) in time of a crisis or the outbreak of war in Europe. These conversations were not successful, as the French government insisted that reentry rights would be granted for use of such bases and facilities only following the outbreak of a conflict in which France had decided to participate under Article 5 of the North Atlantic Treaty. Any kind of allied standby arrangements were rejected. As a result, U.S. and NATO planners have had to proceed with alternative plans for support facilities, since French facilities cannot be counted on and would be of little value un-

---

would have no nuclear role; it would have to be content with a French nuclear guarantee. This European alliance would then be linked to the United States by a looser treaty of alliance which would allow much greater freedom of action to the European member states.

[92] Premier Pompidou confirmed this point in his speech to the National Assembly on April 20, 1966, cited.

less available in advance of an actual conflict. The one exception is the petroleum pipeline running from Saint Nazaire to Metz, which the United States has been allowed to use in peacetime under the condition that it be operated by a French company. The question of use of the pipeline in case of hostilities, however, has also been reserved by the French government.[93]

The French withdrawal seriously altered the defense plans and organizational infrastructure of NATO, but the effect on overall NATO military capabilities was less than first feared.[94] By April 1, 1967, all NATO headquarters and military bases in France had departed for new locations—mostly in West Germany and Belgium.[95] The new headquarters of SACEUR moved to Casteau, Belgium. The financial burden of the costly move has yet to be settled, and it is unclear whether France will pay her part of the bill. In spite of her withdrawal from the Alliance's military organization, France requested permission to continue as a member of certain NATO technical projects—such as the NADGE early warning system (which would be vital for the French *force de frappe*), the Allied Military Communications-Electronics Committee and Long Lines Agency in Paris, and the SHAPE Technical Center in The Hague. Other NATO members granted the French request. France also continued to allow NATO planes to use French air space—first on a monthly basis and then, beginning in January 1968, on an annual basis. And in December 1966 the French government reached an agreement with West Germany permitting

[93] See the *New York Times*, December 7, 1966; also the State Department Memorandum on "Results of Recent Bilateral Discussions Between the United States and France," attached as an appendix to *Our Changing Partnership with Europe*, U.S. Congress, House, 90th Cong., 1st sess., February 22, 1967, House Report no. 26, pp. 38-39.

[94] The military effects are examined in Brigadier K. Hunt, "NATO Without France: The Military Implications," *Adelphi Papers*, no. 32 (London: Institute for Strategic Studies, December 1966).

[95] See the *New York Times*, March 15 and 31, and April 1, 1967.

French forces to continue to be stationed there—although without a formal NATO commitment.[96]

France's action has made a conventional defense of Europe more difficult and has required a review of NATO strategy. Although France's withdrawal enabled the Fourteen to agree formally on the adoption of "flexible response" as the official strategic concept of the Alliance in May 1967,[97] the fact that NATO can no longer count on the use of French forces and French territory means that NATO must now contemplate earlier escalation in any potential conflict to the use of nuclear weapons. Ironically, this represents a step back toward the "massive retaliation" strategy of the 1950's, the strategy preferred by France. Unilateral reductions by member governments in their contributions to NATO forces could further reinforce this development.[98]

By disengaging from NATO, France aggravated relations with her European allies and, especially, her relations with the United States. The French action also served to enhance the status of Germany in matters of European defense and hence her political importance in European and Atlantic affairs. Because of her geographic position, however, France actually continued to enjoy the protection of NATO military forces stationed on the German frontier, as well as the benefits of the American nuclear umbrella. For a time there was uncertainty whether the French defection would lead to reduced commitments to NATO—both political and military—by other member states. By 1967, however, it was clear that the Alliance had withstood the crisis and that the other fourteen members had reaffirmed their allegiance to

[96] See the exchange of letters between the French and German foreign ministers, reprinted in *Survival* (February 1967).

[97] *New York Times*, May 10, 1967.

[98] See General Lemnitzer's observations to the North Atlantic Assembly, reported in the *New York Times*, November 21, 1967. The NATO defense ministers agreed on new guidelines for the use of tactical nuclear weapons at their meeting in December 1969; see the *New York Times*, December 4, 1969.

collective defense under an integrated command system and their intention to proceed without France in the reshaping of the Alliance's military structures.

Differences over Arms Control II: the Non-Proliferation Treaty

By the end of 1966 the focus of American policy toward Europe had shifted. President Johnson had put an end to the MLF and American efforts to achieve a "hardware solution" to Alliance nuclear sharing; and references to the Kennedy "grand design" for an "Atlantic partnership" had practically disappeared from official American pronouncements. Instead, Johnson began formulating a policy of détente and "bridge-building" with the East.[99] Détente began to take precedence over new efforts toward Atlantic unity. On the face of it, this new American stance should have been more compatible with the European policy of General de Gaulle. But this did not turn out to be the case. Franco-American differences over nuclear weapons, NATO, and Vietnam were too deeply rooted. There was also considerable disagreement between France and the United States on approaches to détente. One example of this divergence was the American attempt to coordinate Western détente policies on a multilateral basis through NATO, an approach with which the French obviously did not agree.[100] But of greater importance was the high priority assigned by the United States to agreement with the Soviet Union on a nonproliferation treaty as part of American efforts to achieve détente. This subject once again brought U.S.-French differences over nuclear weapons and arms control to the fore.

In his first message to the Geneva Disarmament Conference in 1964, President Johnson had called for an interna-

[99] The clearest statement of the policy of bridge-building was President Johnson's speech on October 7, 1966; see the *New York Times*, October 8, 1966.

[100] See, e.g., Cleveland, *NATO: The Transatlantic Bargain*, ch. 7.

tional agreement on the non-proliferation of nuclear weapons and the application of international safeguards to transfers of nuclear materials for peaceful purposes. The first American draft treaty was submitted in August 1965. It contained a "European clause" that would have allowed for the future development of a joint European nuclear force with U.S. support. For the next two years American policy was caught between trying to keep the door open for future nuclear-sharing arrangements within the Alliance while at the same time seeking a global accord against nuclear spread. The European clause became a major stumbling block in efforts to achieve agreement with the Soviet Union; it was finally removed from the American draft in 1967 and non-proliferation became the centerpiece of American nuclear policy.[101]

After lengthy American consultations with the NATO allies and negotiations with the Soviet Union, identical Soviet and American drafts were agreed on in January 1968 (including an article on safeguards); this version received the approval of the United Nations General Assembly the following June and was signed in Washington on July 1, 1968, by the United States, Great Britain, the Soviet Union, and fifty-three other states. After a delay following the Soviet invasion of Czechoslovakia, the treaty was finally ratified by the U.S. Senate and approved for deposit by President Nixon in 1969.[102]

[101] The NPT will not bar succession by a future European federation to the nuclear status of one of its components, i.e., the "European option." But it places a major obstacle in the path of American assistance to the development of a joint nuclear deterrent by a prospective European federation. See *Message from the President of the United States transmitting the Treaty on the Non-Proliferation of Nuclear Weapons*, U.S. Congress, Senate, 90th Cong., 2nd sess., Executive H. 1968, p. 6; also Executive Report no. 9, ibid., pp. 3-4. Various assurances have been given the Federal Republic of Germany regarding the "European option." See the *New York Times*, March 30, 1967 and November 27, 1969.

[102] For general treatment of the background of the NPT, see Bader, *The United States and the Spread of Nuclear Weapons*, passim; and Elizabeth Young, "The Control of Proliferation: The

Was the NPT worth the effort? Will it really prevent countries with potential nuclear capabilities from mounting atomic weapons programs? Or is it merely a U.S.-Soviet agreement to refrain from doing something the superpowers would not have done anyway? We will not attempt to answer these questions here, but will merely note that the NPT carries with it political costs to the United States in terms of its alliance relationships. Although the United States consulted extensively with its allies about the treaty, it was essentially the product of a bilateral Soviet-American negotiation. This gave the impression to many that the treaty was a superpower accord presented to the rest of the world as a *fait accompli*; and new strains have appeared as a result in our relations with Western Europe, and with non-aligned countries, such as India.

In terms of substance, the NPT prohibits nuclear-weapons states from transferring "to any recipient whatsoever nuclear weapons or other nuclear explosive devices or of control over such weapons or explosive devices directly, or indirectly." By accepting this prohibition, the United States has given up an option in its alliance nuclear policy. It cannot strengthen its allies by making nuclear weapons available to them directly. However, the treaty does not prohibit assistance to nuclear states for development of nuclear weapons if those states agree not to use such assistance to encourage or induce non-nuclear states to develop or acquire such weapons. Cooperation in the area of nuclear delivery systems is not at all affected by the treaty.

As already described in Chapter 4, France abstained from discussions on the NPT and refused to sign it. Although expressing agreement with the non-proliferation principle, France has differed with the United States about the value of the treaty on at least two interrelated grounds. First, the French contend that the United States has been obsessed with the dangers of nuclear spread. Two succes-

1968 Treaty in Hindsight and Forecast," *Adelphi Papers*, no. 56 (London: Institute for Strategic Studies, 1969).

sive presidents—Kennedy and Johnson—have viewed nuclear proliferation as a grave threat to world peace, and have sought international agreements to remove this danger. In general, the American view assigns high priority to arms-control measures in improving international stability. France, on the other hand, has not agreed with this priority. In the face of long-time American opposition to the development of a French atomic arsenal, Gaullist France tended to view the NPT as another measure of superpower arms control aimed at preserving their monopoly positions and curtailing challenges by smaller nuclear states. Implicit in the French position is the view that nuclear proliferation is not universally a bad thing, and that smaller states can act responsibly too in their international obligations and contribute to strengthening world peace which might one day be threatened by hostility between the nuclear superpowers. De Gaulle saw both the Test Ban Treaty and the NPT as efforts by the strong to disarm the weak, and he continued to argue that only true measures of disarmament affecting all nuclear powers would be acceptable to France.

A related reason for French disagreement with the NPT lies in her different approach to détente. Unlike America, France does not see arms-control agreements as stepping stones to détente with the East. In the Gaullist view, détente must emerge from a warming-up of political and other relations and must proceed through settlement of Europe's division. Only when progress is made on such issues would France contemplate discussion of matters of disarmament and arms control. For the United States, on the other hand, the NPT became a major instrument of détente as President Johnson sought to pursue a policy of gradual warming-up of relations with Russia despite differences over the war in Vietnam. Indeed, the United States has tended to view progress on arms control as a milestone on the way to settlement of larger political questions in Europe and elsewhere. SALT confirms this assumption.[103]

[103] As President Nixon said at his first news conference: "What I want to do is to see to it that we have strategic arms talks in a way

The 1968-69 Thaw in Franco-American Relations

The far-reaching effects of the Soviet invasion of Czechoslovakia and France's political and social crisis in 1968 on de Gaulle's European design have already been described. One result of these events, which ushered in the final phase of Gaullist foreign policy, was a warming-up of France's relations with NATO and the United States. This was caused in part by de Gaulle's reassessment of Soviet behavior, in part by the dramatic escalation of France's domestic problems, which undermined the credibility of an independent Gaullist foreign policy. The beginning of the Vietnam peace negotiations in Paris and American backing of France in the November monetary crisis also helped to bring French and American views closer together.

In the months after Czechoslovakia, France quietly increased her military liaison with NATO and her cooperation in air surveillance and naval maneuvers in the Mediterranean. This cooperation was both an indication of France's concern about NATO's strength in the face of uncertain Kremlin policy in Central Europe and of French anxiety caused by increased Soviet naval activity in the Mediterranean and expanding influence in Algeria. At the NATO ministerial meeting in Brussels in November 1968, a communiqué was agreed upon which stated that "any Soviet intervention directly or indirectly affecting the situation in Europe or the Mediterranean would create an international crisis with grave consequences."[104] France associated herself with this strong declaration, although at the previous NATO meeting in Reykjavik at the beginning of the year she had refused to endorse a much less specific resolution on the Mediterranean naval buildup by the Soviet fleet.

---

and at a time that will promote, if possible, progress on outstanding political problems at the same time—for example, on the problem of the Mid-East and on other outstanding problems in which the United States and the Soviet Union, acting together, can serve the cause of peace."

[104] Text of the communiqué in *NATO Letter* (December 1968), pp. 18-19.

By the end of the year, Pierre Messmer had stated unequivocally before the National Assembly that France planned to remain in the Atlantic alliance. It was reported that French officials had approached NATO to discuss conditions under which France, which lost the use of American tactical nuclear weapons after her withdrawal from NATO military commands, would be guaranteed tactical nuclear protection in case of a European conflict.[105] There were also rumors that France had made overtures to Washington offering to coordinate targeting of the *force de dissuasion* with American nuclear forces. That these subjects could even be raised was due to the removal of several important Franco-American differences. Especially important was American willingness to negotiate a settlement of the Vietnam war and the disappearance of American Atlantic policy initiatives such as the MLF, designed to keep Europe dependent upon the United States. The warm New Year messages exchanged by de Gaulle and Johnson seemed to signal the beginning of a new Franco-American rapprochement.

The advent of the Nixon administration underscored this change of atmosphere. President Nixon made the improvement of relations with France an early objective of his administration. Having enjoyed a relationship of mutual respect with de Gaulle for some time based on personal contacts dating back to the 1950's, Nixon went to see the general soon after his inauguration. During his friendly visit in Paris, the president publicly lauded the French leader. Their discussions were reported to have touched on defense, and possibly even nuclear-related cooperation. As demonstrated by his European trip, Nixon's willingness to listen to the viewpoints of allies and to consult with them naturally helped create a better foundation for dialogue between Washington and Paris. The new Nixon tone—i.e. greater willingness to tolerate independent West European identity—must have been due in part to the president's national security adviser, Henry A. Kissinger, who had fre-

[105] *Le Monde*, April 4 and 5, 1969.

quently criticized previous administrations for not consulting sincerely with European governments. A shift in the American stance was reflected also in presidential statements. Upon his return from Europe, Nixon—in commenting on his frank talks with de Gaulle—said he shared the general's view "that Europe should have an independent position in its own right." The president continued: "I think the time when it served our interest to have the United States as the dominant partner in an alliance . . . that time is gone."[106]

The final sign of the Franco-American thaw in de Gaulle's last year in office was the shift in French defense strategy announced in March 1969 by General Michel Fourquet, which appeared to be another signal of French interest in renewing some kind of relationship with NATO. As discussed elsewhere, by declaring that henceforth French military doctrine would contemplate "a series of graduated actions" to test out the strength of an eventual aggressor before recourse was made to a "strategic response," Fourquet seemed to move French strategy toward a "flexible response" doctrine based on the use of tactical nuclear weapons, a concept which NATO had adopted many years earlier in spite of French opposition.[107] Dropping the *tous azimuts* strategy of his predecessor, the late General Ailleret, Fourquet envisioned instead an enemy "coming from the East" and stated that French forces would act "in close coordination" with allied forces in meeting an aggressor.

[106] *New York Times*, March 5, 1969. Nixon also said: "We will be dominant because of our immense nuclear power and also because of our economic wealth. But, on the other hand, the world would be a much safer place and, from our standpoint, a much healthier place economically, militarily, and politically, if there were a strong European community, to be a balance basically, a balance between the United States and the Soviet Union, rather than to have this polarization of forces in one part of the world and another."

[107] "Emploi des différents systèmes de forces dans le cadre de la stratégie de dissuasion," *Revue de défense nationale* (May 1969), pp. 757-67; an English translation appears in *Survival* (July 1969), pp. 206-11.

Presumably this French shift was linked, at least in its timing, to General Fourquet's approaches to General Lemnitzer concerning the use of NATO tactical nuclear weapons by French forces until French tactical nuclear arms were ready sometime after 1972. However, in many respects, clearer definition of the role of tactical nuclear weapons in French strategy was inevitable as the time approached when these weapons would become operational parts of the French arsenal. At any rate, Fourquet's speech provided the basis for a much more modest French strategy and laid the foundation for new moves toward French cooperation with NATO in the period after de Gaulle. It was testimony to a French reassessment of the Soviet threat in Europe, as well as a recognition of the need for allied defense cooperation in a period when new domestic demands on the French budget were postponing the realization of a panoply of French atomic weapons.

7. *The French Nuclear Force and Franco-German Relations*

In de Gaulle's design for an enhanced European role in world politics, France occupied a special place; the general was determined that his country not lose her leadership to Germany. Development of a nuclear force was, in part, adjudged an effective way to ensure that the Federal Republic would remain a second-rank European power subordinate to France. Fear of revived German militarism was not de Gaulle's primary concern.[1] Rather, it was the political consequences of West Germany's growing economic strength that he felt the need to counterbalance. Since the Bonn Republic had renounced the right to manufacture atomic weapons in 1954, France was assured a dominant military position over Germany in Europe. That fact had political consequences. As the only continental nuclear power, France could expect to play the leading role in any future discussions on the organization of European security.

In Gaullist diplomacy toward Germany, the nuclear card was played most intensely during 1962-64, as France sought to loosen Bonn's security links with the United States and to obtain German support for a European defense system based on a French nuclear core. No real dialogue developed as a result of the French overtures, because of divergent French and German security perspectives and politi-

[1] At his press conference on March 25, 1959, de Gaulle said that "Germany, as it is, in no way threatens us. We even think that with its capabilities, its energy, its resources, it constitutes an essential element in the life and progress of Europe and the whole world. Even more, as is normal for two old adversaries who have given up fighting and destroying each other, France and Germany have resolved to cooperate" (*Major Addresses, Statements, and Press Conferences of General Charles de Gaulle, May 19, 1958–January 31, 1964* [New York: Ambassade de France, Service de presse et d'information, 1964], p. 42).

cal goals. But these overtures are important for the insights they offer into the objectives and style of Gaullist nuclear diplomacy in Europe. Moreover, they may provide precedents for future developments after de Gaulle, should French and German political-strategic objectives in Europe later correspond more closely, as they have already begun to do. The general's attempt to achieve German support for his European design began during the unsuccessful Fouchet negotiations on a European political union in 1961-62; it was given further impetus by the Franco-German treaty of 1963.

The Fouchet Negotiations on a European Political Union

In the spring of 1962, after a year of intense negotiations, representatives of the six Common Market countries failed to reach agreement on a plan for a political union that would have started Europe along the path toward a European confederation. A new initiative for increased European political cooperation was suggested by General de Gaulle as early as 1959, but by 1961 it had become the centerpiece of the second phase of his European-Atlantic policy, as already sketched in Chapter 4. Part of the general's objective in supporting a West European political grouping was to coordinate European—and especially German—defense policies under French leadership, and to achieve a consensus on a more independent European stance in security matters. Such a consensus could then be used to support a fundamental reform of NATO to enhance the European role, or to promote a West European withdrawal from the organization.

In June 1959 de Gaulle had proposed that the Six establish a central secretariat to further their political cooperation. The initial reaction was one of skepticism. But later the same year the foreign ministers of the Six agreed to consult every three months on foreign policy questions and to discuss the possibility of extending the activities of the European Communities into the political realm.[2] The French plan to elevate these consultations, several rounds of which were held during 1960, to the level of heads of state or of government, and to institutionalize them in a formal political union, was launched at a meeting of de Gaulle and Adenauer at Rambouillet in July. Shortly before, the general had explained before a television audience France's desire to "contribute to building Western Europe into a political, economic, cultural and human group, organized for action, progress and defense." He termed such a Europe "the indispensable condition of the equilibrium of the world." At the same time, he emphasized that the nations involved must not cease to exist as individual states. What he envisioned was a period of "organized cooperation between states, while waiting to achieve, perhaps, an imposing confederation."[3]

At Rambouillet the French president outlined before the German chancellor his views on a European political union. He gained Adenauer's support for his plan, which called for regular periodic meetings of the six Common Market countries at the highest level, as well as at ministerial level. These meetings were to be prepared by a permanent secretariat and four commissions dealing with foreign policy, defense, and economic and cultural affairs, respectively. A parliamentary assembly, composed of members of the national parliaments, was to be created. De Gaulle advocated a popular referendum to ratify the new structure of political cooperation. This initiative was to be accompanied by a reform of NATO which would take the European political union into account, a point upon which de Gaulle insisted because France was not planning to remain much longer in the organization as it then existed.

[2] See, e.g., Achille Albonetti, *Vorgeschichte der Vereinigten Staaten von Europa* (Baden-Baden: Verlag August Lutzeyer, 1961), pp. 215-16.

[3] Address of May 31, 1960, in *Major Addresses*, p. 78.

France and Germany were to prepare a joint NATO reform proposal, an intention which was never carried out.[4]

These proposals were considered at a Paris conference of the government heads of the Six in February 1961, and a study commission (the "Fouchet commission," named after its chairman, French Ambassador Christian Fouchet) was established to develop a plan for political cooperation.[5] The commission's work was reviewed at a meeting of the heads of government at Bad Godesberg in July, where a declaration was issued expressing the common will of the Six to promote political unification and to hold regular meetings in pursuit of that objective. The Fouchet commission was authorized to prepare a draft of a European political statute. Foreseen in the declaration was a "united Europe, allied to the United States," as a means for "strengthening the Atlantic Alliance."[6]

In the autumn of 1961 the Fouchet commission began serious negotiating. France submitted a draft treaty for the establishment of a "union of the European peoples" in November which contained many of the ideas de Gaulle had presented to Adenauer at Rambouillet the year before. The union was to promote common foreign and defense policies

[4] See Konrad Adenauer, *Erinnerungen, 1959-1963: Fragmente* (Stuttgart: Deutsche Verlags-Anstalt, 1968), pp. 59-67; also Albonetti, pp. 224-25.

[5] For more comprehensive treatment of the ensuing Fouchet negotiations, see Alessandro Silj, *Europe's Political Puzzle: A Study of the Fouchet Negotiations and the 1963 Veto*, Occasional Papers no. 17 (Harvard University: Center for International Affairs, 1967); also Suzanne J. Bodenheimer, "The 'Political Union' Debate in Europe: A Case Study in Intergovernmental Diplomacy," *International Organization*, XXI (Winter 1967), pp. 24-54, and her subsequent book.

A useful selection of documents is contained in *Toward Political Union* (Luxembourg: Political Committee of the European Parliament, 1964).

[6] The text of the Bonn declaration is reprinted as Appendix 1 in Silj, pp. 133-35; see also Heinrich von Brentano, "Die Bonner Erklärung vom 18. Juli 1961," *Europa Archiv*, no. 17 (September 1961), pp. 463-66.

and cooperation in cultural and scientific affairs. There was to be a council, formed by the heads of state or of government and the foreign ministers; a parliament (already existing under the Rome treaties); and a European political commission, consisting of senior foreign ministry officials of each member state and located in Paris. Decisions in the council, to be taken by unanimous vote, were to be prepared and implemented by the political commission. There was provision for strengthening the Union after three years, a point which several of France's European partners wished to push further by stipulating the gradual introduction of a majority vote. Under de Gaulle's plan, the European union would remain separate from the three existing European Communities, an arrangement which would have allowed British entry into the Common Market without immediate participation in the European political organization.[7]

The rather liberal first French draft was suddenly withdrawn in January 1962, to be replaced by a more conservative second draft aimed at much looser European cooperation along the lines of a *Europe des patries*. This was much less acceptable to France's partners. Chances for evolution toward majority voting were eliminated in the second French proposal. Supranational features of the existing European Communities were placed in question by the inclusion of economics as one of the council's fields of competence. The new French draft was immediately rejected by the other five members. They put forward their own alternative proposal, preserving many of the elements contained in the original Fouchet draft, and even going beyond it. Economics was dropped from the council's authority; a court of justice and an independent secretary-general were added; the unanimity rule was watered down; and provision was made for the gradual introduction of the majority principle. The Five insisted that the powers of the existing

[7] *Die Zeit*, November 10 and December 1, 1961; *Die Welt*, November 4, 1961; also Silj, pp. 11-13.

European Communities remain unimpaired, and that the European union should be tied to NATO.[8]

Suspicions had been aroused by the new French draft and by the nationalistic tone of de Gaulle's television speech early in February, and once again the general held a meeting with Adenauer to calm his fears and to try to break the impasse. De Gaulle made a few concessions to the German chancellor. They reached agreement on all major questions, notably on two important points: Adenauer supported de Gaulle's wish that the European political union seek a reform of NATO to bolster the European role; but he persuaded the general that the union should support the continued existence of the Atlantic alliance and be compatible with it. The chancellor also won de Gaulle's assent to a provision that the European political union not weaken the existing European Communities.[9]

Despite the renewed Franco-German agreement and de Gaulle's successful meeting with Italian Premier Fanfani several weeks later, the Fouchet commission was unable to resolve the differences that remained and produce an agreed draft statute. When the foreign ministers of the Six met in Paris on April 17, 1962, Belgium and the Netherlands refused any further discussion of a European political union until Great Britain had been admitted to the Common Market. A final Italian mediation effort failed to produce any further progress. By the end of the summer the Fouchet negotiations had collapsed.[10]

In supporting institutionalized cooperation between the West European states on the Fouchet model, de Gaulle had sought the formation of an independent West European grouping that France could lead, thereby augmenting France's international role. This was the same goal pursued

[8] See *Die Welt*, January 29, 1962; *Europa Union*, January 26, 1962; *Die Zeit*, February 9, 1962; also Silj, pp. 13-19.

[9] See the account of the meeting at Baden-Baden, February 14, 1962, in Adenauer's memoirs, *Erinnerungen, 1959-1963*, pp. 136-50, 195.

[10] See the works by Silj and Bodenheimer, cited.

earlier by the general in his unsuccessful bid for French participation in the tripartite nuclear directorate in 1958. By taking charge of defense, a West European political union, according to his reasoning, would automatically place France—the sole continental power developing a nuclear capability—in the front-rank. Moreover, it was the French leader's hope that a European union would lead to a strengthened European position in a reformed NATO, or eventual European withdrawal from the organization and its replacement by a West European defense structure based on a nucleus of French atomic armament. The Fouchet plan, even after its demise, remained a model for the kind of West European cooperation sought by de Gaulle in subsequent years.

As revealed in public and in the fourth volume of his memoirs, Adenauer supported the Fouchet plan. This was partly due to de Gaulle's consummate diplomacy, which succeeded in blurring several fundamental differences of view. By the spring of 1962, the German government was behind de Gaulle's initiative and saw no contradiction between it and the European Communities, nor any incompatibility with NATO. Participation in such a political union would have enhanced Germany's international status in the same way as joining NATO and the Common Market in the 1950's. It would have represented a further step toward Adenauer's goal of reinstating German respectability in the eyes of the world. But the chancellor also viewed the French plan as a way to strengthen NATO and the American commitment to European security. To him, this was the objective of NATO reform, not European self-sufficiency and the reduced dependence on America desired by de Gaulle. As Adenauer explained several times to the French president, Dulles had counseled him that if the Germans did not remain loyal to the Alliance, the Americans would leave Europe.[11] As the leader of a divided and threatened country on the East–West frontier, this was not advice

[11] Adenauer, *Erinnerungen, 1959-63*, p. 139.

which Adenauer dismissed lightly; and indeed he always followed it.

De Gaulle had also won the chancellor's understanding of the importance of French nuclear weapons for the future defense of Europe. Although French nuclear armament was still in its developmental phase, the general went into some detail in July 1962 to explain to Adenauer its purpose—primarily in terms of America's weakening nuclear commitment to Europe. France, asserted de Gaulle, did not aspire to be a nuclear power by the same standards as the United States and the Soviet Union. What she sought was a small deterrent which nevertheless would present a risk to the Soviet Union and could unleash a nuclear war in which America would have no choice but to participate. Adenauer, despite his earlier skepticism, found the proportional deterrence argument persuasive. Although he reiterated Germany's desire to convince the United States to place atomic weapons at the disposal of NATO, he did not oppose de Gaulle's suggestion that the subject of European defense be carefully reexamined in light of future French nuclear weapons if a new framework of European political cooperation were achieved.[12]

The considerable support de Gaulle gained from Adenauer was possible because of the skillful way the general had concealed basic French and German differences on the security implications of a European political union. Adenauer apparently failed to grasp the French distinction between NATO and the Atlantic alliance, a distinction which became so important a few years later. Following the Rambouillet meeting in the summer of 1960, Adenauer had run into opposition from members of his government and political party, who saw the defense committee of the proposed European political union as a threat to NATO. Further clarifications were sought in Paris, and in October the chancellor had a long discussion on this point with French Premier Michel Debré and Foreign Minister Couve de Murville in

[12] Ibid., pp. 168-72.

Bonn. The Adenauer–Debré talk revealed sharp differences of approach to NATO. Debré reiterated Gaullist attacks against NATO integration, the monopoly position enjoyed by the United States in the organization, and the American refusal to coordinate three-power Western strategy in other parts of the world. He pressed the need for NATO reform, and for European control over nuclear weapons. Adenauer disagreed on many of these points. While sharing French misgivings about the American monopoly of nuclear control, he placed great hopes on General Norstad's plan for a NATO nuclear force.[13] But at the end of the two-day meeting the Germans seemed satisfied with the French pledge to remain in the Western alliance.

The communiqué stated that "the closest possible cooperation between European members and the North American members of the Alliance is vital to the defense of the free world." In German eyes, such close cooperation could only be achieved through NATO. Thus, the Germans felt reassured that any European defense discussions would be compatible with NATO. Thereafter, they supported the French initiative to develop a new political framework among the Six. The French had cleverly succeeded in clouding a fundamental difference. The seeds of later Franco-German discord on European security issues had been sown.[14]

De Gaulle first responded with bitterness to the failure of his plan for the political organization of Europe. In his press conference of May 15, 1962, he insisted he had never used the phrase *Europe des patries* (which was Debré's), but then went on to justify the concept. His remarks included a lengthy rebuttal of the proponents of a "supranational Europe." De Gaulle stressed once again the importance of Franco-German solidarity:

[13] Ibid., pp. 70-76; also Silj, pp. 7-8.

[14] See Silj, pp. 7-8. Unfortunately, Adenauer's notes, as presented in the fourth volume of his memoirs, do not cover the second day of this meeting.

On this solidarity depend all hopes of uniting Europe on the political and defense levels as on the economic level.

On this solidarity depends, in consequence, the destiny of the whole of Europe, from the Atlantic to the Ural Mountains; for if a structure, a firm, prosperous, and attractive organization, can be created in Western Europe —then there reappear the possibilities of a European balance with the Eastern states and prospect of a truly European cooperation. . . .

In such an event, we could and we should, I believe, resolve the German problem in an objective manner. In such an event, I have already said it and I repeat, France would be ready to make solid proposals.[15]

By the summer it became clear that de Gaulle had decided to conclude with Germany alone the political union he had offered but could not at that moment obtain from the Six. But he still hoped for agreement later on his plan to institutionalize West European political cooperation along the lines of a "Europe of the states" (*Europe des états*), as he preferred to call it.

The Franco-German Treaty of January 1963

During de Gaulle's visit to Germany in September 1962, he and Adenauer decided to seek an agreement that would strengthen the already existing ties between their two countries and facilitate the coordination of their policies. Adenauer was especially anxious for a tangible result of his long-time efforts to promote Franco-German rapprochement.[16] Popular support for such a step was evident in the enormous success of Chancellor Adenauer's tour of France in July and General de Gaulle's return visit to Germany in

[15] *Major Addresses*, p. 179.

[16] Adenauer, pp. 177-81. Another factor underlying Adenauer's interest in a treaty with France may have been the change in the Bonn–Washington relationship, not nearly as close under Kennedy as during the Eisenhower-Dulles years.

September. It was agreed that a protocol would be the appropriate form of such a Franco-German accord, and that the French government would prepare a draft outlining the provisions of such a document.

Soon after de Gaulle returned to Paris, the French government sent a memorandum to Bonn on September 19 proposing bilateral consultation and cooperation in the fields of foreign policy, defense, education, and youth affairs.[17] In many respects the French proposal followed the outline of the earlier Fouchet plan. Regular meetings of the heads of government and cabinet ministers were suggested. The West German government replied in November, accepted the French proposition in principle, but proposed some changes that were incorporated into a new expanded draft. Bonn's position on military cooperation was particularly cautious, and it was urged that such cooperation be related to the NATO framework. In mid-December the French and German foreign ministers, Couve de Murville and Gerhard Schröder, agreed on a framework of interministerial committees in Paris and Bonn to deal with questions of cooperation.

Only at the last moment was it decided to draft a formal treaty.[18] Adenauer had favored a protocol, but for constitutional reasons the German Foreign Ministry recommended a treaty. The final wording was drawn up during Adenauer's visit to Paris, just before the formal signing of the document on January 22, 1963, under strained circumstances. A few days before, de Gaulle had announced his decision to veto Britain's bid for entry into the Common Market, a bid that Adenauer's government had supported.[19] The French leader had acted without consulting Adenauer

[17] The background of the treaty is discussed in F. Roy Willis, *France, Germany and the New Europe, 1945-1963* (Stanford: Stanford University Press, 1965), pp. 309ff.; and in Alfred Grosser, *La Politique extérieure de la Ve République* (Paris: Éditions du Seuil, 1965), pp. 91ff.

[18] Grosser, p. 92; Adenauer, p. 198.

[19] However, Adenauer, as revealed in his memoirs, was personally not a strong proponent of British entry. Ibid., pp. 177-78, 181, 201-10.

beforehand. Nevertheless, the German chancellor proceeded with the scheduled signing of the treaty, which crowned his long efforts on behalf of Franco-German reconciliation.

In general, what the treaty did was to establish a formal mechanism for consultation between the two countries. Biannual meetings of the heads of government were provided for, and even more frequent conferences at the ministerial levels, including quarterly meetings of defense ministers. Consultations were to be coordinated on each side by an interministerial commission, headed by a high-ranking foreign ministry official. They were to encompass "all-important questions of foreign policy," including questions relating to the European Communities, East–West relations, NATO, and other multilateral organizations of which both countries were members. Aid to the developing countries, youth matters, education, and cooperation in general economic policy were also mentioned.[20]

In the area of defense, the treaty listed objectives rather than areas of agreement. Efforts were to be made to harmonize strategy and tactics, to increase already existing exchanges of personnel between the armed forces of the two countries, and to study possibilities of cooperation on civil defense. Most important, both governments agreed to organize a joint research and development program in the field of armaments.

The treaty did not mention nuclear cooperation. But at the time many observers thought this was implied. They pointed, for example, to de Gaulle's Hamburg speech at the Führungsakademie der Bundeswehr the previous September, especially his remarks on the necessity for "organic co-

[20] For further analysis of the treaty, see Alfred Grosser, pp. 92-95; for a German view, see Ernst Majonica, *Deutsche Aussenpolitik* (Stuttgart: W. Kohlhammer Verlag, 1965), pp. 210-14. An English text of the treaty is conveniently included in *The Atlantic Alliance: Treaty and Related Agreements*, U.S. Congress, Senate, Subcommittee on National Security and International Operations, Committee on Government Operation, 89th Cong. 2nd sess., 1966.

operation of our armies, with the goal of one and the same defense." "The modern requirements of military power and the art of war" were important reasons, de Gaulle contended, for close military cooperation. "Armaments," he observed, " . . . now require for effectiveness . . . the mobilization of scientific, technical, industrial, and financial resources and capacities whose limits are extending every day. France and Germany can assure themselves of these means of power especially if they join their possibilities."[21]

A more plausible interpretation of this speech, and of the treaty, is that de Gaulle may have been interested in utilizing German technology and resources in connection with some French nuclear-arms projects—a question he would raise later in 1964—but without allowing Germany any access to such weapons or say over their use. Following signature of the treaty, a West German government spokesman emphasized that Franco-German military cooperation would not extend to atomic armament.[22] According to his memoirs, Adenauer told de Gaulle clearly in January 1963 that Germany did not want atomic weapons.[23]

In a discussion of European defense at the time the treaty was signed, de Gaulle and Adenauer agreed on the uncertainty of American defense policy and the American nuclear commitment. Europe, de Gaulle hoped, would one day achieve its own defense capability and would be able

[21] Speech delivered on September 7, 1962; text in André Passeron, *De Gaulle parle*, II (Paris: Arthème Fayard, 1966), pp. 332-34.

[22] The German statement was as follows: "In the military points [of the Treaty] it was not explained that cooperation in this area does not extend to atomic armament. A corresponding reserve in the text was not necessary, because the West German government took on the obligation in 1955 to undertake atomic armament. . . . The French government has full confidence in the German government and agreed to forego any such reservation in the text of the Treaty" (*Bulletin* of the West German Government, no. 4, January 29, 1963).

[23] Adenauer, p. 202. In an earlier conversation with de Gaulle, however, Adenauer had indicated he viewed the 1954 German renunciation of the right to produce atomic weapons as not binding forever and subject to an eventual *rebus sic stantibus* interpretation, as Dulles had once pointed out to him. Ibid., pp. 59, 167.

to defend herself. An important step toward this end would be strong French and German national defense forces. The Franco-German treaty was seen as a basis for coordinating French and German defense policies. France's desire to reform NATO and reduce European dependence on American strategy was also reaffirmed. The general hoped that a collective European view on defense matters and a NATO reform proposal might also be objectives of Franco-German cooperation. Adenauer seems to have assented to all these points. He again supported the development of French atomic armament, but asked that de Gaulle understand if the German government did not foreclose participation in any eventual NATO multilateral force. Finally, the two leaders agreed that Britain, in light of the Nassau agreement, was not yet thinking like a continental power in strategic matters.[24]

In Washington, the Franco-German treaty had given rise to suspicions of an impending Franco-German nuclear arrangement. As a result, the Kennedy administration stepped up its efforts in 1963 to achieve European acceptance of the MLF as an alternative to de Gaulle's European design, but the fear of Franco-German nuclear cooperation proved unfounded. Those who saw the treaty as an anti-American gesture on the part of the Federal Republic were somewhat misled, for the timing was due more to a loss of command over events than acceptance by Adenauer of all de Gaulle's views on the future of Europe. As events unfolded, the Franco-German treaty was not the first step in a shift of West German allegiance from the United States to France. Instead, the year 1963 saw the Bonn government renewing its transatlantic loyalties.

As one analyst put it:

> The shock of January 1963 led to a German reappraisal of priorities, from which, by the end of the year, there crystalized an official consensus that European independ-

[24] Adenauer, pp. 199-206.

> ence was not of immediate relevance and that it should not be pressed at the expense of Atlantic ties. In the short run, the first priority had become a strengthening of German-American relations.[25]

European autonomy was, in effect, relegated to the status of a long-term goal in Bonn's calculations. This was evident from West German support of the American position on several major issues—the multilateral nuclear force, the Test Ban Treaty, and preparations for the Kennedy Round. Germany also did more to intensify military cooperation with the United States than with the French. The "German preamble," which the Bundestag added to the Franco-German treaty in May, also toned down the appearance that Bonn was adhering to Gaullist concepts. It reasserted Germany's commitment to an integrated Western defense in NATO, close ties with the United States, and a united Europe with Great Britain included.[26]

Nuclear Issues in Franco-German Relations and the Question of a European Nuclear Force, 1963-64

If the Federal Republic soon had second thoughts about the degree of its commitment to France, General de Gaulle sincerely hoped the Franco-German treaty would yield intensified bilateral cooperation upon which he might build his hopes for an "independent Europe." Defense cooperation was one of the first areas to get attention. There had already been some cooperation between the two countries in military matters: the institute at Saint-Louis for theoretical weapons studies, development of the Transall cargo plane dating from 1959, discussions on the development of a common tank, and French provision of some training grounds and air fields for use of West German military contingents.

[25] James L. Richardson, *Germany and the Atlantic Alliance* (Cambridge, Mass.: Harvard University Press, 1966), pp. 63-64.
[26] Ibid., pp. 68ff.

Paris now hoped to breathe new life into this area of collaboration.

French Defense Minister Messmer visited Bonn for talks in June 1963, followed by de Gaulle himself in early July; on both occasions there was discussion of NATO strategy and talk of common projects. It was agreed to prepare final decisions for production of the Transall and to consider the joint development of a helicopter and a vertical take-off aircraft. French and German war colleges had already exchanged military officers, and plans were now made for exchanges of military units in the fall. But these were modest results. Franco-German differences over NATO, skillfully blurred by General de Gaulle in previous talks with Adenauer, reemerged more sharply in this bilateral summit meeting. This was, in part, the result of President Kennedy's June trip to Europe and the reassurances he gave the German chancellor that America was prepared to risk destruction of its cities to uphold its commitment to defend Europe.[27]

Meanwhile, Germany was preparing to expand her military cooperation with the United States. Since 1958 the West German government had bought American F 104-G Starfighter aircraft, instead of the French Mirage III. After an attempt to arrive at a common Franco-German tank had failed in the summer of 1963, Defense Minister von Hassel and Secretary McNamara announced agreement in August on joint development of a German-American heavy tank for the 1970's. This was a serious blow to de Gaulle's hopes to substitute defense cooperation with France for Bonn's security links with Washington.[28]

In the nuclear field, a series of hints began to come from Paris about French interest in an eventual European nuclear deterrent which would use the French force as a

[27] See Adenauer, pp. 221-30.

[28] See *Le Monde*, June 21 and July 7-8, 1963; also Jean Planchais, "La Coopération militaire Franco-Allemande demeure encore extrémement limitée," *Le Monde*, August 17, 1963.

nucleus. These overtures were perhaps directed at disappointed advocates of European integration in all countries of the Six, and must have been aimed especially at West Germany. In 1962, Premier Georges Pompidou, in speaking about the defense implications of a European political union, broached the question of "a nuclear force within the European framework" as a topic for Europe's future agenda. He alluded to the important contribution that French nuclear weapons could make to such a force. Limitations would have to be placed on Germany's participation, however, because of her situation and previously contracted obligations (an allusion to the 1954 renunciation).[29] In the spring of 1963, French Defense Minister Messmer commented that "in order for Europe to exist, it will be necessary that she assume the burden and the responsibility of her defense, and that she possess nuclear arms for that purpose." The developing French nuclear arsenal was, in his view, a *pièce maîtresse* in the future construction of Europe.[30]

Other high-ranking French officials echoed these themes. In a vigorous defense of the budgetary allocations for the *force de dissuasion*, Minister of Information Alain Peyrefitte reaffirmed French interest in the creation of a European nuclear deterrent, but only when Europe possessed a political authority which could make the necessary decisions concerning the use of such a force. He referred to the earlier French initiative, the Fouchet plan, for the construction of "a European confederation." Foreign Minister Couve de Murville made a similar statement.[31]

These references were vague and ambiguous. They also contained an inherent contradiction, since the Gaullist idea

[29] *L'Année politique*, 1962, p. 90.

[30] "Notre Politique militaire," *Revue de défense nationale* (May 1963), p. 761.

[31] *Le Monde*, May 30, 1963; Couve de Murville's interview on German television, June 28, 1963, as reprinted in *French Affairs*, no. 191 (New York: Ambassade de France, Service de presse et d'information, July 1, 1963), p. 3.

of a confederal Europe of cooperating, but not integrated, states is hardly compatible with the kind of centralized European political authority required to make decisions about the eventual use of any European nuclear armament. A confederal Europe would not so easily provide a credible process of decision-making on the employment of atomic weapons.

Nevertheless, French suggestions of a possible Europeanization of the *force de frappe* continued. The remark of State Secretary Habib-Deloncle before the Council of Europe in Strasbourg in September 1963 commanded particularly wide attention. He suggested that France would outline how her nuclear capability could be "utilized by all the European nations for common defense"—including possibly Great Britain—when Europe's political structure had been strengthened.[32] This time there was an official German response. Adenauer praised France for her "important and noteworthy" suggestion, but the proposal was viewed in Bonn as having no immediate relevance until a European political union could be achieved.[33]

The West German position on the French overtures in the fall of 1963 was not entirely clear for several reasons. First, the retirement of Konrad Adenauer and the accession of Ludwig Erhard to the chancellorship had introduced a transition period and some obvious flux in West German policies. When Erhard traveled to Paris in November for his first official visit with General de Gaulle, he is said to have emphasized Germany's ties to NATO and his interest in the MLF, while at the same time listening to de Gaulle's position on French nuclear policies and European defense. Secondly, although the Federal Republic had been one of the first countries to express interest in the MLF after Nassau and was deeply involved in the exploratory talks in spring 1963, Adenauer and Kennedy had "shelved" the MLF, at least temporarily, in June because of the uncertain

[32] As quoted in the *New York Times*, September 25, 1963.
[33] Ibid.; also *Le Monde*, October 31, 1963.

interest of Britain and other allies. Finally, there was evidence that Franz Josef Strauss and Freiherr von Guttenberg, leaders of the CSU—the Bavarian partner of the CDU, Bonn's ruling political party—were beginning to press the Erhard government to sound out France on the meaning of the Habib-Deloncle speech.[34] As yet Erhard had probably determined neither the seriousness of the Strauss-Guttenberg challenge nor the character of French intentions.

The vagueness of the French position was an additional confusing factor. If the Habib-Deloncle and earlier speeches did represent invitations to join a European defense system based on French nuclear capability, it was surprising that the question of how control in any such European nuclear force might be shared had not been addressed. French official comment during the fall only raised further doubts about French sincerity regarding "Europeanization" of the *force de dissuasion*. Thus, Defense Minister Pierre Messmer, speaking at the end of October, stressed that nuclear arms could only be at the disposition of one man at the head of a state or a "federation of states," and that a European *force de frappe* would only have military significance if the question of control were solved by European political unity.[35] (Again this statement contradicted the professed Gaullist vision of a confederal Europe.) A series of articles in *Le Figaro* in November reported a debate between Professor Raymond Aron and Gaullist Michel Debré in which Aron probed many aspects of Gaullist policy,[36] among them government willingness to consider sharing control of the French nuclear force under some kind of European arrangement. Debré, of course, gave no indication that such a possibility was contemplated

[34] See *Le Monde*, November 20, 1963, and *Combat*, November 21, 1963. The emergence of a kind of German "Gaullist" group will be further discussed below.

[35] Speech before the Anglo-American press, reported in *Le Monde*, October 26, 1963; also *Combat*, October 25, 1963.

[36] See *Le Figaro*, November 5, 7, 9-10, and 14, 1963.

in official circles. The German Foreign Office took careful note of this debate.

At the end of 1963 the new Erhard government was, on balance, moving, like its predecessor, in the direction of strengthening Germany's Atlantic ties. The proposed NATO multilateral nuclear force was a most important instrument available for reinforcing German-American relations. Bonn's considerable interest in the MLF, as opposed to a European nuclear arrangement, was confirmed at the time by Defense Minister Kai-Uwe von Hassel as follows:

> The major importance [of the MLF], however, would be its political aspect. It would provide an additional political link between the European and the American partners to the Alliance. Its close interlacing with the nuclear potential of the United States would result in strengthening the deterrent on the one hand, and establishing strong ties between Europe and America on the other. This is its definite advantage as compared to other concepts which envisage a *European* nuclear force. In my opinion, the establishment of a European nuclear force of this kind would be more likely to slacken than to strengthen the ties between Europe and the United States. It has become apparent, with greater clarity than a few years ago, that Western Europe cannot assume a truly European responsibility for the use of nuclear weapons before it has become a political entity; in other words, it can assume this responsibility only after unification, i.e., after the careful and gradual integration of national sovereignty in a political community.[37]

Differences on nuclear defense exerted the greatest stress on Franco-German relations in 1964. In part the result of debate within the Alliance on the MLF, these differences also arose from Bonn's lack of enthusiasm for several fur-

[37] Kai-Uwe von Hassel, "Détente through Firmness," *Foreign Affairs* (January 1964), p. 189. (Italics added.)

ther French overtures aimed at drawing the German neighbor into a strictly European defense conception.

In mid-February, after successful visits with President Johnson in Texas and Prime Minister Wilson in London, Chancellor Erhard returned to Paris with five cabinet officers for a round of "working consultations" under the Franco-German treaty. French recognition of Communist China and the kidnapping in Munich (presumably by the French secret service) of OAS terrorist Colonel Antoine Argoud a short time before, must have created a somewhat strained atmosphere. De Gaulle and Erhard discussed a number of topics. They differed on Asian matters (both on French recognition of Communist China and on Vietnam), but they agreed on the need to merge the executive authorities of the three European Communities into a single European Commission and the importance of the Kennedy Round of tariff negotiations.[38] On defense matters, West German Defense Minister von Hassel insisted on the need to reinforce the Atlantic alliance and to bind together the United States and Europe in all possible ways. He also restated the German government's interest in the MLF. The French did not object too strenuously, but de Gaulle assured the German chancellor that France would stand firmly on the side of the Federal Republic—both politically and militarily—in case of a conflict over Germany or Berlin. Moreover, the general is reported to have promised that the French nuclear force would be employed "in the first moment of a conflict for the defense of Germany."[39] As an alternative to German participation in the MLF, de Gaulle had offered Germany the protection of his *force de frappe*.[40]

[38] See *Le Monde*, February 18, 1964.

[39] *Frankfurter Allgemeine Zeitung*, report of Paris correspondent and editorial page, February 17, 1964.

[40] According to an informed French source, General de Gaulle's staff had tried to get him to accept a provision in the Franco-German treaty of 1963 for the use of the French nuclear force for the protection of Germany. An early draft of the treaty included this point, but

If one can believe an interview given by Erhard in 1967, after his retirement, his conversation with de Gaulle in February 1964 went even further on nuclear matters. According to Erhard, he asked de Gaulle whether France would be interested in an agreement with the Federal Republic on the joint possession of atomic weapons. De Gaulle firmly declined. If Erhard's revelations are true, they indicate a serious German interest in a deal with France in the atomic field and an equally serious French resolve against any German access to nuclear arms.[41]

After the rather meager results of this February meeting with de Gaulle, the German chancellor insisted throughout the spring that amity with both the United States and France were basic policies of his government, and that the Franco-German treaty was not meant to be exclusive. This was not enough for one group in the CDU-CSU. By the spring of 1964 a firm split had developed in Bonn's ruling party. On the one side were the Atlantiker led by Foreign Minister Schröder, who based his foreign policy on close ties with the United States. On the other were the so-called Gaullisten, led by Adenauer and former Defense Minister Strauss; they gave priority to a close understanding with France, although they did not share all of de Gaulle's ideas about the future of Europe.[42]

The German "Gaullists" agreed that Europe must cease to depend on the United States for defense. Thus, Baron

---

the general must have overruled it. Apparently de Gaulle had changed his mind by February 1964.

[41] Interview with the *General-Anzeiger* (Bonn), as reported in the *Neue Zürcher Zeitung*, March 8, 1967.

[42] Adenauer began attacking Erhard in March for disrupting Franco-German relations. See, e.g., his speech in Bonn reported in the *New York Times*, March 6, 1964. Strauss began a campaign of attacks against Schröder in a series of articles in the *Bayern-Kurier*, of which Strauss was the editor, and Adenauer backed Strauss's stand. See, e.g., *Die Welt*, May 17, 1964. Another forum for the German "Gaullists" was the *Rheinischer Merkur*. Adenauer wrote in that paper on July 3, 1964, urging that steps finally be taken to make the Franco-German treaty the basis for a European political union.

Guttenberg, a CSU member of the Bundestag, argued for the formation of a European atomic force based on the nucleus of the French atomic arsenal.[43] At about the same time Strauss, after a visit in Washington, spoke in favor of the MLF, but only on the condition that it could later evolve into a European nuclear force independent of the United States but coordinated with American nuclear power in NATO. He admitted that a European political authority was necessary before such a European deterrent could be created.[44]

Erhard was under increased pressures from the "Gaullist" faction of his party at the time of his important meeting with General de Gaulle in Bonn in early July 1964. The influence of this faction was partially offset by the apparent progress toward realization of the MLF project, potentially a major irritant in Franco-German relations. After talks in Washington in June, Chancellor Erhard and President Johnson had agreed to proceed with preparation of an MLF treaty for signature by the end of 1964.[45] The slow pace of Franco-German military cooperation was also detrimental to the talks—results so far were limited to accords on joint production of the Transall cargo plane and on a NATO air defense control system.[46]

When de Gaulle arrived in Bonn on July 3, 1964, the major issue was that of broadening Franco-German cooperation and relating it to European unification. In an after-dinner speech, the general spoke of an independent Europe with its own policy as a common goal to be sought by the French and German governments, a Europe "based on itself with respect to security, economics, culture and, naturally, foreign policy."[47] On matters of nuclear defense, this Franco-German summit meeting turned out to be most

[43] Interview on the Bayerischer Rundfunk, June 10, 1964; *Die Welt*, June 11, 1964.

[44] *Die Welt*, June 11, 1964.

[45] *New York Times*, June 13, 1964.

[46] *Le Monde*, June 6, 1964.

[47] *Bulletin*, no. 106 (Bonn: Presse und Informationsamt der Bundesregierung, July 7, 1964).

significant. Leaks to the press thereafter, and interviews, revealed that the two leaders discussed possible German participation in the French nuclear force and the eventual use of the latter for continental defense.

De Gaulle is reported to have told Erhard that France and Germany must have a European policy independent of the United States. For this reason, the French leader said, France was constructing her own nuclear armament. When the general then asked if Germany supported France in this endeavor and hinted at an interest in West German assistance to the French nuclear program in the financial and technical areas, Erhard inquired whether the *force de frappe* was intended as a French or a European weapon. De Gaulle hesitated, then affirmed that it would be first of all a French weapon. Erhard then asked whether Germany could have some say in controlling the use of the *force de frappe*? He is said to have referred to the prospective German role in the MLF, arguing that it was important for Germany to have at least an equivalent role in decision-making on the use of the *force de frappe*. De Gaulle's reply was reportedly ambiguous, giving no indication that France was willing to consider sharing control over the use of such a Europeanized French force.[48]

After this exchange, officials of the Erhard government concluded that the object of de Gaulle's defense policy was to make Germany a satellite of France. Since it had serious doubts anyway about the military value of the French deterrent, at least the first-generation weapons system, Bonn clearly preferred the superior nuclear protection provided by the United States and even the limited nuclear sharing offered under the MLF plan. The Erhard–de Gaulle exchange in July all but dissolved the interest of the German government in the Europeanization of French nuclear armament. The SPD opposition took the same view, pre-

[48] Based on several interviews, this reconstruction is supported by press stories. See the *New York Times*, July 25, August 4, and September 16, 1964; also *Die Welt*, November 24, 1964.

ferring German ties to NATO and the United States as guarantees of German security to any protection which the French *force de frappe* might provide.[49]

The German "Gaullists," however, continued to attack Erhard for not going far enough to explore what de Gaulle had in mind concerning German participation in the French nuclear force. Presumably to squelch such attacks and rumors, Erhard told the *General-Anzeiger* after he had left office that as chancellor he had received no offer from General de Gaulle for military atomic cooperation.[50] The facts certainly seem to support his statement. In the same interview Erhard mentioned a second proposal he had made to de Gaulle for joint development of a rocket system designed to use French nuclear warheads, which would remain under French control. Erhard may have presented this idea in his July 1964 meeting with the general in a last attempt to smoke him out before committing the Federal Republic to the MLF at a considerable financial cost. Whenever it was raised, and assuming accuracy in Erhard's account, de Gaulle's refusal of the joint rocket development scheme only serves to reconfirm the strict limits de Gaulle had set for any Franco-German atomic cooperation. He seemed primarily interested in German help for the French nuclear force without strings attached.

De Gaulle did not conceal his strong disappointment with his treaty partner across the Rhine. In his press conference of July 23, 1964, the French president ticked off the many areas in which France and Germany had failed to coordinate their actions:

> . . . one could not say that Germany and France have yet agreed to make together a policy and one could not dispute that this results from the fact that Bonn has not believed, up to now, that this policy should be European

[49] SPD leader Fritz Erler was expressing doubts both about the present and even the future military value of the French deterrent. See SPD press release no. 334/64, July 24, 1964.

[50] As reported in the *Neue Zürcher Zeitung*, March 8, 1967.

> and independent. If this state of affairs were to last, there would be the risk, in the long run, of doubts among the French people, of misgivings among the German people and, among their four partners of the Rome Treaty, an increased tendency to leave things as they are, while waiting, perhaps, to be split up.[51]

Germany, de Gaulle implied, was among the advocates of a Europe "linked to an Atlantic system," in defense, economics, and foreign policy, "and consistently *subordinate* to what the United States calls its leadership." This statement, not unsurprisingly, caused strong reactions in Bonn.

In spite of the negative West German reaction to the general's July overtures, nuclear matters were raised again in the autumn against a background of heightened Franco-German tension on several fronts. Bonn and Paris were disagreeing on the Common Market's agricultural policy (which led to a French threat to leave the Market unless Germany reduced grain support prices)[52] and on an Erhard proposal for renewed discussion of a European political union.[53] Rather than seeking new joint projects with France, the German government had signed an extensive accord committing it to large offset arms purchases in the United States, plus other kinds of military cooperation.[54] Perhaps most serious of all, the MLF was entering a new active phase of Atlantic negotiation with full German sup-

[51] *Speeches and Press Conferences*, no. 208, pp. 6-7.

[52] See the *New York Times*, October 22, 1964. This issue was resolved by December when the German government agreed to make the necessary concessions.

[53] *New York Times*, November 7, 1964.

[54] Under the McNamara–von Hassel accord, Germany agreed to make offset arms purchases of about $700 million annually in the United States and to order three modern guided-missile destroyers, to be built in American shipyards. The two defense ministers also agreed on NATO forward defense strategy, on the characteristics of a new joint German-American tank, on cooperation in the development of a VTOL aircraft, and on their joint support for the multilateral force which was to be implemented "as soon as possible." (Text of the agreement in the *New York Times*, November 15, 1964.)

port. A diplomatic blunder by Erhard, who suggested in early October that the United States and the Federal Republic might form the multilateral force by themselves if other countries were reluctant to join, underlined the basically German-American character of the project.[55] This prompted a new French campaign to prevent the MLF's establishment, a campaign directed especially against Germany. For if the MLF were launched with German participation, this would greatly diminish France's nuclear advantage in future political bargaining with Bonn.

On November 5, French Premier Georges Pompidou warned in a speech in Paris that any accord between the United States and West Germany on the MLF would be incompatible with the Franco-German treaty of 1963. He also suggested that the MLF would hurt European unity and provoke the Soviet Union, and that it was "directed more or less against France."[56] When former Chancellor Konrad Adenauer visited Paris a few days later to be honored with membership in the French Académie, de Gaulle was said to have impressed on his distinguished friend both France's distaste for the MLF and the dangers that it posed not only for the Franco-German treaty but for the chances of German reunification.

Later the same month de Gaulle applied further pressure on the Germans. Speaking in Strasbourg on the twentieth anniversary of the city's liberation, the general again voiced his hopes for the construction of a "European" Europe, in his view the ultimate justification of Franco-German reconciliation. Europe, he stressed, must have its own defense organization. Germany, he suggested harshly, was on the way to renouncing European union and becoming an "auxiliary" of the United States. As friendly as the U.S. might be, the general pointed out, it was still "a power situated in a different world . . . whose destiny, by nature and by history,

[55] *New York Times*, October 7, 1964.

[56] *Le Monde*, November 7, 1964; *New York Times*, November 6, 1964.

could not be identified with that of Europe."[57] In essence the French leader was counseling West Germany to place its alliance with France ahead of its ties to the United States, especially in military matters. Acceptance of this advice implied a "no" to the MLF.

Several German observers saw in de Gaulle's remarks a new French offer to discuss a European defense organization that might include the French nuclear force. Any such offer was thought to be motivated in part by financial considerations. The French had just announced their program to construct intermediate-range ballistic missiles to bolster France's nuclear armory, and it was believed that they wanted financial help for their IRBM program. The West German reaction was a mixture of caution and disappointment. The Bonn government's press spokesman reaffirmed Germany's view that Europe must continue to have close defense ties with the United States. However, he added, the Strasbourg speech had touched on new points and Chancellor Erhard had asked to see the French ambassador in Bonn, Roland de Margerie, to discuss them. In the CDU-CSU party in the Bundestag, on the other hand, there were expressions of regret because de Gaulle had offered no concrete thoughts about German participation in a European nuclear force.[58]

It soon became clear that the French had no intention of following up de Gaulle's Strasbourg speech with firm proposals for a European defense organization. Indeed, in retrospect the speech seems to have been primarily a tactical maneuver to help bury the MLF. There were further French statements about the necessity for a "European" defense and the "European" vocation of French nuclear armament. But none were very revealing. Thus, Premier Pompidou told the French National Assembly that the

[57] Text of the speech delivered in Strasbourg, November 22, 1964, in *Speeches and Press Conferences*, no. 212.

[58] *Frankfurter Allgemeine Zeitung*, November 24, 1964; *Die Welt*, November 24, 1964.

French atomic force provided "the only certain deterrence" that Europe possessed. It would be employed "fully and automatically for the benefit of Europe," whose defense, he maintained, was inseparable from that of France. The implication was that French nuclear weapons would be used to protect West Germany and France's other European neighbors. The creation of a European nuclear force, according to Pompidou, posed a certain number of problems —especially the participation of Germany, in view of the hostile reactions that would cause, and the absence of a European political organization. The premier obviously opposed the idea that an international *fonctionnaire* at the head of a supranational authority, patterned after one of the existing European Communities, could take a decision to use European atomic weapons. Such a decision had to rest with the states. But Pompidou illuminated no further the kind of European organization France envisaged as a basis for possible Europeanization of the French *force de frappe*.[59] Discussions at a Franco-German conference in December likewise produced no clarification of this question, despite considerable probing from the German side.[60]

[59] Pompidou's speech of December 2, 1964, reported in the *Journal officiel*, Débats parlementaires, Assemblée nationale, December 3, 1964, esp. pp. 5,781 and 5,800.

In his response to Pompidou's remarks, the noted military analyst of *Le Monde*, Jean Planchais, was skeptical that French nuclear armament would really be employed to defend Berlin, for example. He wrote that the French system of alert was so organized that the *force de frappe* could only be used when the enemy crossed the Rhine, i.e., to protect vital "national interests." (See his article "À Berlin ou sur le Rhin?" *Le Monde*, December 4, 1964.)

[60] At the eighth Franco-German conference, which included private as well as governmental personalities, there were vigorous exchanges on the MLF and the *force de frappe* as a possible core of a future European nuclear deterrent. French statements on the latter continued to be ambiguous. One argument used against the MLF by the French was that the cost of German participation in it would be so high that Bonn might not be able to afford a contribution to a future European nuclear force. This point seemed to support rumors that France was still interested in a German financial contribution to the French nuclear effort as a basis for future European nuclear defense.

French denunciation of the Franco-German treaty was supposedly the price Germany would pay if she agreed to participate in the MLF. At least that is what de Gaulle told U.S. Ambassador Charles Bohlen in Paris.[61] In Bonn, however, the German government claimed it had never been officially informed of de Gaulle's intention to take this step. Later it was reported that Secretary of State Rusk, during a visit in Paris for the NATO ministerial meeting, had received personal assurances from General de Gaulle that France had no intention of giving nuclear weapons to West Germany or cooperating with Bonn in any atomic matters.[62] This démarche may have been designed to remove any fears in Washington of eventual Franco-German nuclear cooperation, one of the original concerns behind U.S. interest in the MLF.

Writing at the time, Ernst Majonica—a leading CDU foreign policy spokesman—confirmed that the Germans remained unconvinced by France's professed intentions to turn over her *force de frappe* to a European political authority. Of de Gaulle's Strasbourg speech, Majonica said:

> The French President spoke of a European solution, but without indicating what it might look like. Considering the Gaullist attitude toward supranational arrangements in Europe, it will be difficult, even nearly impossible, to Europeanize the *force de frappe*. That would mean a change in French policy on the question of integration, which would be desirable, but which is scarcely to be expected. . . . At any rate, it would lie with France, the possessor of national atomic forces, to make concrete suggestions which so far have not been forthcoming; hints are not enough.[63]

See *Die Welt*, December 7, 1964; also the report of the conference, *Deutsche-Französische Freundschaft in der Bewahrung*, VIII, German-French conference, Paris December 4-6, 1964 (Bonn: Heft 17, Schriftenreihe des Deutschen Rates der Europäischen Bewegung).

61 *New York Times*, December 7, 1964.

62 See the brief report in *Newsweek*, January 4, 1965, p. 6.

63 Majonica, p. 242.

Majonica supported German participation in the MLF, but with an open invitation for France to join at a later time. He was interested in the MLF's "European clause," which provided for future evolution toward a European nuclear force at a later time. Unlike de Gaulle, however, Majonica advocated that any such future European force be closely linked to the superior American nuclear arsenal on which ultimate deterrence depended.[64] This was also the view of the Erhard government.[65]

In January 1965, Erhard met again with de Gaulle for consultations, this time at Rambouillet. German reunification and a new Erhard plan for steps toward European political union (his model was very similar to the earlier Fouchet plan) were the principal subjects on the agenda. Defense and nuclear problems received only brief attention, but were nevertheless central to the meeting. Since the United States had taken the pressure off the MLF in December as a result of a personal decison by President Johnson, de Gaulle probably wondered whether Bonn would give up its interest in the Atlantic nuclear fleet and rally to his notion of autonomous European defense. Erhard did not comply; he merely explained that the project was shelved for the moment and nothing would be done until after the German elections in the fall. At the same time he reemphasized Germany's desire to participate in Alliance nuclear planning. According to the French press spokesman, de Gaulle recognized the Federal Republic's interest in the latter as normal and legitimate. But the general emphasized that German access to nuclear weapons in any form (including the MLF or the British alternative, the ANF) would be incompatible with German reunification.[66]

Erhard left the Rambouillet talks with the impression that de Gaulle had consented to cooperate with new Ger-

[64] Ibid., pp. 242-54.

[65] See, e.g., Kai-Uwe von Hassel, "Organizing Western Defense," *Foreign Affairs*, XLIII (January 1965), pp. 213-14.

[66] See *Le Monde*, January 22, 1965; *Die Welt*, January 21, 1965; *New York Herald Tribune*, January 21, 1965.

man initiatives toward reviving four-power negotiations with Moscow on German reunification and toward re-launching discussions among the Six on a European political union. He was wrong on both counts. Given Bonn's unwillingness to reduce its security links with the United States in favor of a European defense conception, France rejected two months later a foreign ministers' conference of the Six planned to consider next steps in political integration. And in his February news conference the general made the solution of the German problem dependent on the organization of the Six "in the political domain as well as in that of defense," and on the limitation of German armament to the nonnuclear field. Moreover, he stressed, German reunification was above all a European problem and should be tackled without the participation of the United States.[67] De Gaulle had linked the defense question to French support for German reunification and was applying new pressure on Bonn to choose between Paris and Washington. As discussed earlier, he was also laying the groundwork for the development of his Eastern policy.

France and Germany in 1965-66: Divergent Security Perspectives

By the spring of 1965 the Federal Republic had clearly rejected French overtures designed to lure Germany into a West European defense system constructed around French nuclear armament. Bonn also disagreed with de Gaulle's exclusion of the United States from a European settlement. On all fronts, the German government had chosen once again to reaffirm its Atlantic security connections. It had committed itself to expanded military cooperation with Washington (the 1964 McNamara–von Hassel accord) and persisted in its support for Atlantic nuclear sharing under the MLF plan. When the MLF began its diplomatic

[67] Press conference of February 4, 1965, *Speeches and Press Conferences*, no. 216.

descent and the Atlantic nuclear-sharing debate gave way quietly to the formation of the "McNamara Committee" for nuclear consultation—later to become the NATO Nuclear Planning Group (NPG)—Germany became an important member. After France's withdrawal from NATO military commands in 1966, the Bonn government did not follow suit but continued as a staunch supporter of the Atlantic military organization. By these actions Germany renewed her loyalty to the concept of a strong and united West, based on close ties with the United States, as the best instrument for pursuit of her political goals—especially German reunification.[68]

Another area where the Federal Republic had demonstrated its pro-American commitment was that of NATO strategy, an additional point of Franco-German nuclear disagreement. Bonn had accepted the "flexible response" doctrine introduced into NATO by the Kennedy administration, whereas the French had not. However, the German commitment was not without reservation, for the German government was much more interested than its American ally in a forward defense of Germany, accompanied by the earliest possible use of nuclear weapons, to deter Soviet aggression. On this point, the German view was actually closer to French strategic doctrine, as described in 1964 by General Ailleret, than to American strategy with its stress on a conventional defense of Europe with a higher atomic threshold. The Bonn government chose to play down these differences, however, especially after 1963, and to support American strategic policy, at least in public discussion.[69]

The foreign policy objectives of France and Germany

[68] For a review of Western policies toward German reunification, see Charles R. Plank, *The Changing Status of German Reunification in Western Diplomacy, 1955-1966* (Baltimore: The Johns Hopkins Press, 1967).

[69] For further treatment, see Richardson, *Germany and the Atlantic Alliance*, esp. pp. 73-87. Uwe Nerlich also discusses some of these points in his "Die Nuklearen Dilemmas der Bundesrepublik Deutschland," *Europa Archiv* (September 10, 1965), pp. 637-52.

diverged in several areas,[70] but the basic reason why Bonn did not follow the French lead in reorganizing West European defense lay in the two countries' contrasting security perspectives. Here there were several factors and conditions at work. Exposed geographically on the East–West frontier, West Germany has always been most conscious of any threat of aggression from the East, even in periods of thaw in East–West relations. This situation was intensified by the problem of defending West Berlin, the enclave surrounded by militant Communist East Germany, a problem which added an ideological dimension to Bonn's views of threats from the East. Furthermore, as a divided country, the Federal Republic was particularly sensitive to the need to maintain the confidence of the Big Three powers—especially the United States—who retained under the 1954 agreements the legal responsibilities for German reunification.

Since its founding, the Federal Republic has been obsessed with security, her fundamental foreign policy goal next to reunification and West European unity. The Bonn government has continually looked to the United States, through NATO, as the key ally that could fulfill her security needs. America has provided Germany with a nuclear deterrent umbrella and bolstered her conventional defenses by stationing large numbers of American troops on German territory, where they would immediately be engaged in case of Soviet attack. Moreover, West German defense policy has always been based on an integrated NATO defense and determined by NATO strategy (largely formulated by America). Staunch commitment to NATO stemmed partly from a belief that any other than an integrated defense system was impossible in the present age, and also from the fact that the German army was totally integrated into the NATO structure.

[70] See Alfred Grosser, "France and Germany: Divergent Outlooks," *Foreign Affairs* (October 1965), pp. 26-36; also the discussion in W. W. Kulski, *De Gaulle and the World* (Syracuse: Syracuse University Press, 1966), pp. 280-390.

France, on the other hand, was in a very different position. Geographically not directly exposed, she was also ideologically much less preoccupied by concern over the Communist threat. Unlike the Federal Republic, France continued to pursue worldwide political objectives. Europe, therefore, was only one area of her interest. While working toward an independent nuclear force, France has also had a national army which, under General de Gaulle, she always held somewhat aloof from NATO, and in 1966 totally withdrew from the organization. For some time de Gaulle considered the threat of aggression from the East to be minimal. Since France enjoyed the ultimate protection of the American nuclear umbrella anyway, in case of a large scale conflict in Europe, the general was able to disengage from NATO military commands and follow an increasingly independent course in his diplomacy toward the West and the East. Moreover, in Gaullist eyes, American troops were becoming less and less necessary in Europe. In case of a small-scale Soviet aggression, the French atomic force would serve as a detonator and should convince the Russians that the risk of escalation to a nuclear conflict involving the United States was great.

More sensitive to any Soviet threat and without nuclear armament, the Germans, however, took great pains never to offend Washington and to ensure that the United States remained fully engaged in the cause of German security. American troops in Germany were one guarantee of such an American commitment; in German eyes, the MLF represented another device to tie the United States even more firmly to Germany's security needs. Indeed, as Alfred Grosser wrote at the time, "the question of confidence in the United States scarcely presents itself to the French, while for the Germans it is at the center of their foreign-policy preoccupations."[71]

Of key importance, of course, to German security policy in 1965-66, was the perception in Bonn of the negligible

[71] Grosser, "France and Germany: Divergent Outlooks," p. 31.

military worth of the French *force de frappe*, as well as its political purposes. Interviews with German government officials in 1966 revealed a substantial consensus on the low military value of French nuclear armament as a credible deterrent of the Soviet Union, at least in its first-generation weapons system. This view was confirmed by several West German publicists.[72] On purely strategic grounds, it was felt that the Federal Republic had no choice but to rely primarily on the deterrent protection of America's superior nuclear capability. Some Germans went so far as to describe the French nuclear force as "dangerous," since it conflicted with NATO strategy and could only be used for "massive retaliation" strikes against cities, thus increasing the probability that a conflict might escalate rapidly into an all-out nuclear holocaust. A few German officials noted the military advantage the French force gave France with respect to Germany, although they were uncertain of French intentions in that regard.

As for the potential military value of French second-generation nuclear weapons, the missile-carrying submarines planned for the 1970's, German opinion was divided. Some officials believed that the French would eventually develop an effective force, whereupon it might aug-

[72] See, e.g., Helmut Schmidt, *Verteidigung oder Vergeltung* (Stuttgart: Seewald Verlag, 1965). One of the few German politicians knowledgeable on defense questions, Schmidt termed the Mirage IV force "militarily almost worthless" due to its high vulnerability (pp. vii-viii, 98ff.). Another West German analyst, Georg Picht, termed the *force de frappe* a "gigantic bluff" and "one of the most costly prestige symbols of world history, but . . . no instrument of deterrence." He saw it as weakening, rather than strengthening, Western defense, because its vulnerability might invite preemptive strikes. See his chapter entitled "Die Force de Frappe als politisches Strukturproblem," in *Die Force de Frappe: Europas Hoffnung oder Verhangnis?* by Hans Dieter Müller (Olten und Freiburg/Breisgau: Walter Verlag, 1965), pp. 9-35.

See also "Force de Frappe: Keule im Keller," *Der Spiegel*, November 24, 1965, pp. 110-30; Joachim Schwelien, "Wieviel Bomben hat de Gaulle?" *Die Zeit*, November 27, 1964; Alfred Frisch, "Der Atomknuppel des Generals de Gaulle," *Süddeutsche Zeitung*, December 19-20, 1964.

ment Western deterrent strength provided it was coordinated with American nuclear forces. Other Germans were even skeptical on this point.

The West German leadership seemed largely unimpressed by vague French pronouncements that French atomic weapons would be used to protect the Federal Republic. Instead, most Germans tended to believe the maxim of General Gallois (whom they falsely considered the "father" of French strategic doctrine) that in the atomic age no state can depend on another for defense, and that the "sanctuary" to be defended is only the national territory.[73] There were some notable exceptions, however. For instance, in October 1964, Bundestag President Eugen Gerstenmaier is reported to have remarked in a Paris interview that "De Gaulle . . . würde, wenn wir angegriffen werden, sofort schiessen. Mit allem was er hat."[74] Similarly, Adenauer is supposed to have said that France will answer "any Soviet attack" (against West Germany) with "an immediate, even if a small atomic strike."[75] Yet, these statements did not command much attention or support in Bonn; they were more often the object of derision and sarcasm.

Many West German officials did, on the other hand, acknowledge the political value of the French force—in their eyes primarily a Gaullist instrument for enhancing French political influence in Europe. Bonn was aware that possession of a military nuclear capability was placing France in a more advantageous political position than Germany. Some went so far as to say that France was trying to use her nuclear force to dominate Germany and to make her dependent on France.

From a German perspective, at least three factors supported this contention. First, France had made her support

[73] Georg Picht and the article in *Der Spiegel* of November 24, 1965, both express doubt that France will risk national suicide to defend the territory of the Federal Republic with nuclear weapons.

[74] "De Gaulle . . . would, if we were attacked, let go with everything he has." As quoted in *Die Zeit*, November 27, 1964.

[75] Quoted in *Der Spiegel*, November 24, 1965, p. 122.

of German reunification since 1964 practically dependent on German non-participation in Alliance nuclear-control arrangements, such as the MLF. Secondly, she had pressed for a common defense policy among the Six, and made further progress toward a European political union (a goal supported by Bonn) contingent upon achievement of a European defense policy. Were a common defense policy ever realized, France would automatically assume a predominant position due to her nuclear capability, which, Paris had made clear, would remain under French national control. Thirdly, France had indicated a willingness to guarantee West Germany's non-nuclear status in agreements with the Soviet Union, thus consolidating France's position of leadership over Germany within the Six, and in relations with the Soviet Union as spokesman for the Six. This policy was manifest both during Soviet Foreign Minister Gromyko's talks in Paris in April 1965, and General de Gaulle's visit to Russia in June 1966.[76]

Perhaps the principal political effect of the French nuclear force from a West German viewpoint was that it was impeding European integration. Because France was unwilling to embrace what were mainly American-sponsored plans for a common Atlantic defense policy, the problems of nuclear control became structural problems of European unity and European-American relations. By the winter of 1964-65, controversies over the MLF had thrust the West German government into the precarious position of trying to balance between Paris and Washington. To the Germans at that time, it looked as though European unity was possible only under French domination in the defense field and at the cost of German-American relations and German security interests. Despite its reluctance to say so, the Bonn government was inclined to choose Washington over Paris. When at the end of 1964 President Johnson withdrew his

[76] Some of these points are discussed in Nerlich, "Die Nuklearen Dilemmas der Bundesrepublik Deutschland."

support for the MLF, however, the pressure to make such a clearcut decision was lifted.

West German officials regarded defense as one of the last steps in the process of European integration, not one of the first, as the French were implying by the end of 1964. Germany has clearly never found the *force de frappe* acceptable as a unifying factor, in spite of French attempts to present it as such. The Bonn government chose to retain its security connections with Washington and not to gamble on a weaker European defense arrangement headed by France. Still, there was considerable German interest in preserving the option of a European nuclear force for the future. This was evident in West Germany's support for the "European clause" in the MLF. Later, it was part of Bonn's position in the negotiations on the Non-Proliferation Treaty.

One German group, the so-called Gaullist faction headed by Franz-Josef Strauss (the CSU leader who became a minister in the Kiesinger government in 1966), was more vocal in support of the idea of a European deterrent. As early as 1964, Strauss proposed a nuclear-armed European defense community in place of the MLF. A book by Strauss in 1965 suggested the formation of a European confederation over a six-year period.[77] Under this scheme, Britain and France would pool their nuclear forces, though initially nuclear weapons would remain under national control. Then, as integration progressed toward a federal political structure and a formal defense community, a European nuclear council of defense ministers would be established to elaborate a common defense policy for an integrated European nuclear force. Such a force, according to Strauss, would have to be closely coordinated with the nuclear arsenal of the United States in NATO; it could not hope to operate independently. As far as he was concerned, a confederal Europe (such as de Gaulle advocated) was

[77] *The Grand Design: A European Solution to German Reunification* (New York: Frederick A. Praeger, 1965); see esp. chs. 1 and 3.

only an intermediate step on the way to a true federation, which he believed to be the only political pattern under which Europe could ultimately develop its resources and play an effective role in world politics.

Strauss did not support the exchange of American protection for the French *force de frappe*. He explained his thinking as follows:

> Germany does not want atom patronage, but atom partnership, and we are certainly not prepared to exchange American atom patronage, which from its size and technical efficiency is at least a determining instrument, for French atom patronage. But if the General or his successors show themselves willing to make the French atomic weapon a basis for a European atomic weapon, if possible in combination with the British element, then here is a foundation for political integration which we could support.[78]

Germany, stressed Strauss, would have no national control over nuclear weapons under his plan. Control would be in the hands of a European federal authority.[79]

France and Germany, 1966-69: Less Divergent Security Outlooks

In the period between the installation of the Grand Coalition government at the end of 1966 and the resignation of General de Gaulle from the French presidency in April

[78] Ibid., p. 64.

[79] Strauss later repeated his proposal for a European nuclear authority in a second book, *Challenge and Response* (New York: Atheneum, 1970). See also Strauss's interview in *Der Spiegel*, September 1, 1969, pp. 29-30.

Apart from Strauss and his close associate Freiherr von Guttenberg, other German politicians who have expressed an interest in the European nuclear force idea include former Bundestag President Gerstenmaier, former FDP leader Erich Mende, and CDU politicians Birrenbach, Krone, and Barzel.

1969, several factors narrowed the security differences previously described, while other basic divergences remained. Rooted partly in the gradual transformation of the international environment, these changes were also due to shifts in French and German policies that were internally inspired.

The decline of Bonn's earlier obsession with security was the first major change on the German side. After 1966 the pursuit of détente with the East increasingly captured the attention of the Federal Republic and other Western governments, and of NATO as well. By now, efforts to strengthen the Alliance—for example, through nuclear-sharing schemes—had lost all previous urgency. Germany abandoned her interest in a "hardware solution" to the problem of NATO nuclear control and contented herself with a role in the consultations of the Nuclear Planning Group while keeping open a future "European option" in the NPT. Meanwhile, Chancellor Kiesinger and Foreign Minister Brandt began to assert a more active German policy in both the East and the West.

In Western Europe Kiesinger moved to improve relations between Bonn and Paris and to reduce Bonn's dependence on Washington. Despite painstaking efforts and agreements in 1967 to set up Franco-German study commissions on European defense policy and on industrial and technological cooperation, the rapprochement with France yielded only modest results. The joint study of European security needs never took off, doubtless undercut by France's persisting hostility toward NATO, and the uncertainties for Germany implicit in General Ailleret's *tous azimuts* strategy. The major fruit of Franco-German consultations was an agreement to disagree without unnecessary recrimination on issues where the views of Bonn and Paris remained far apart.

With regard to the United States, the major German policy shift was one of tone rather than substance. Kiesinger moved nearer to de Gaulle's position on European-American relations when he called for an independent Europe outside "a North Atlantic imperium."[80] However, he refused to endorse criticism of American policy in Vietnam, while perpetuating Bonn's basic security ties to Washington.

Of greatest significance in the narrowing of the Franco-German gap was the appearance of the German Ostpolitik. Inspired in no small part by de Gaulle's Eastern initiatives, this new German policy was officially adopted by the Grand Coalition government (although the groundwork had been laid previously by the Erhard-Schröder "policy of movement"). The basis of Ostpolitik was a change in German priorities on the "German question." Reunification was no longer viewed as a prerequisite for a relaxation of tensions with the East; instead, it was admitted that German unity was not imminent and could come about only at the end of a long and gradual process of détente. Moreover, this process of détente was one in which the Federal Republic could play an active role. With little promise of further progress in the spheres of West European integration or Atlantic security (Bonn's other foreign policy concerns), the new German government assigned Ostpolitik top priority among its foreign policy objectives.[81]

As elaborated by Foreign Minister Willy Brandt, Ostpolitik involved discarding several anti-Communist doctrines, as Bonn now sought to normalize its relations with the Soviet Union and the East European states. Previously, Bonn's Eastern relations had been governed by the principle that only the Federal Republic was entitled to speak in

[80] Addressing the West German parliament in 1968, Kiesinger said: "Strong as our ties in the Atlantic Alliance are, friendly as our relations with the United States are, we may not seek our own future, and, we believe also, the future of a united West Europe in the firm structure of a North Atlantic imperium. Such a solution would transform the demarcation line that divides Germany and Europe into a permanent border wall. Such a solution could also increase the danger of a world conflict in a dramatic way" (*New York Times*, March 12, 1968).

[81] The background and initial development of Ostopolitik is well described in Karl Kaiser, *German Foreign Policy in Transition* (London: Oxford University Press, 1968).

the name of all Germans (the *Alleinvertretungsanspruch*). Thus, the Federal Republic had refused to enter into diplomatic relations with East European and other governments which recognized the East German regime (the Hallstein doctrine). Both these tenets were abandoned when Bonn established full diplomatic relations with Rumania in 1967 and Yugoslavia in 1968. Meanwhile, a trade mission was given consular status in Prague. The range of Bonn's political, economic and cultural contacts in Eastern Europe was expanded enormously. Furthermore, the Kiesinger-Brandt government manifested a spirit of reappraisal on the question of German borders. A concession was made to Czechoslovakia by declaring the 1938 Munich agreement invalid, and there were signs of eventual compromise on the Oder-Neisse issue with Poland.

There was also a friendlier tone toward the Soviet Union, although it produced few immediate results. Bonn continued to pursue the matter of pledges renouncing the use of force, which it wanted to initiate first with Moscow and then with other East European countries. Foreign Minister Brandt publicly expressed interest in the Soviet-proposed all-European security conference (France had done likewise) when adequate preparation could be achieved, and in the idea of "balanced force reductions" in Central Europe.

Perhaps the most significant and far-reaching aspect of Ostpolitik was the change in approach toward East Germany. Here, too, Bonn sought to normalize its relations, or at least to obtain a *modus vivendi*. In declarations soon after he took office, Chancellor Kiesinger made clear that West Germany now accepted the Ulbricht regime as the effective government of East Germany, although she still disclaimed its legitimacy. Further, Kiesinger now sought an improvement in the living conditions of the "other half" of the German people and a gradual liberalizing of the GDR regime, rather than early reunification. In an exchange of letters with East German Prime Minister Willi Stoph in

1967, Kiesinger proposed talks between the two parts of Germany at any level on the practical measures that could be taken to promote détente within Germany and ease the suffering caused by the division of the German people. Although the West German government still refused to recognize the GDR, a trend in German thinking had started which did not exclude that possibility in the future and which might lead to an eventual solution of the German problem based on an association of two separate German states, rather than the earlier notion of either reunification or the *status quo*.

Although the results that could be achieved were uncertain, the new German Ostpolitik clearly brought French and German perspectives on European security and the process of East–West reconciliation more closely into phase. The Soviet invasion of Czechoslovakia in 1968 was a setback for both French and German Eastern policies. It pointed up the desirability for greater coordination of détente initiatives. By early 1969, however, it was clear that Germany, like France, was intent on continuing its Ostpolitik in spite of the hardening Soviet attitude reflected in the Czech affair.

The most important change in French policy during the period 1966-69 was the shift of emphasis to domestic priorities following the crisis of May-June 1968.[82] The resulting economic and social difficulties—highlighted further by the November crisis of the franc—weakened the sinews of the Gaullist political regime and reduced France's prestige abroad and her room for international maneuvering. The Soviet intervention in Prague had undermined de Gaulle's Eastern initiatives and encouraged him to improve his relations with the United States. Consequently, there occurred a certain equalizing of French and German political positions in Europe, both because of France's internal troubles and the removal of pressure on Bonn to choose between

[82] See Grosser, "France and Germany: Less Divergent Outlooks," pp. 235-44.

Paris and Washington. As their similar Eastern policies and the improvement in France's relations with NATO during de Gaulle's final year demonstrated, French and German diplomatic influence and European security perspectives were closer in the spring of 1969 at the time of the general's retirement. However, in Bonn there was still little interest in a West European defense unit built around French nuclear armament, as urged earlier by de Gaulle. The already questioned credibility of the *force de frappe* was further diminished by construction delays when pressures for domestic expenditures increased after the 1968 crisis.

The shifting diplomatic constellation caused by France's internal upheavals and economic disruption set against Germany's continuing prosperity and industrial strength was beginning to raise a new possibility in Europe—that of rising German political power. The case was amply demonstrated in November 1968 at the international monetary conference in Bonn when, despite considerable pressures, the German government refused to revalue the mark—which placed the burden of the crisis on France and the French franc. This specter may have been a key factor in de Gaulle's overture to British Ambassador Soames in early 1969 for the creation of a looser grouping of European states, including Great Britain which, together with a weakened France, might be able to balance and control Germany's ascendance.

The French Nuclear Force and Germany's Nuclear Prospects

France's nuclear policy is fraught with contradictions and could even be dangerous in its potential impact on the Federal Republic. Two basic Gaullist arguments for the French national nuclear force were: (1) nuclear weapons are essential if a nation is to have the political prestige and diplomatic status required to pursue an active foreign policy; and (2) atomic discrimination is not tolerable within an alliance (referring to American assistance to the British, but not to the French nuclear effort). Yet France discriminated against West Germany by refusing to give Bonn a share in any joint European atomic venture and by supporting the Soviet demand that West German renunciation of nuclear weapons for all time be a condition for German reunification. By setting an example, France also provided an incentive for the Federal Republic to pursue more nationalistic policies of its own.

The problem was stated succinctly by Raymond Aron in 1966:

> If the possession of nuclear arms has all of the value which General de Gaulle attributes to it, why should the Germans accept indefinitely to remain an inferior nation and to be deprived of them? . . . France is in the process of adopting with regard to the Federal Republic the attitude which the United States and Great Britain adopted with regard to France ten years ago. We are condemning the Federal Republic to a permanent discrimination.[83]

At this time the Federal Republic continues to abide by its unilateral declaration in 1954 "not to manufacture in its territory" any atomic, biological, or chemical weapons (the so-called ABC weapons).[84] However, France has made it easier for any future West German government to employ a

[83] Raymond Aron, "Force nucléaire nationale et Alliance atlantique," *Le Figaro*, September 22, 1966; see also the article to which Aron is replying, Alfred Fabré-Luce's "Le Mythe de la dissuasion," *Le Monde*, September 1, 1966.

[84] Declaration made by Chancellor Adenauer, Annex I, Protocol No. III on the Control of Armaments, signed in Paris, October 23, 1954, amending the Brussels Treaty of 1948. A text is contained in *NATO: Facts About the North Atlantic Treaty Organization* (Paris: NATO Information Service, 1965), p. 256. In the declaration Germany also agreed to limitations and restrictions on other categories of armaments, which can, however, be modified upon request if approved by the Brussels Treaty Council of Ministers. It should be noted that the German renunciation of domestic atomic weapons manufacture does not preclude purchase of these weapons or their manufacture elsewhere.

rebus sic stantibus argument and renounce the 1954 pledge. The de Gaulle government did this by choosing to ignore an important provision of a 1954 Western European Union agreement on the control and limitation of European nuclear-weapons stocks by the WEU Council of Ministers.[85] Under the arms control protocol, the WEU has the power to supervise the levels of production of French atomic weapons. By bypassing her obligation to abide by WEU controls, France has, in effect, renounced—or at least downgraded—the very instrument which governs the limitations on German nuclear armament.

So far, however, the evidence strongly suggests that West German politicians and government officials are not interested in a national nuclear-weapons program. Although political concerns of status and influence in the Alliance have influenced the German approach to nuclear issues (to wit, the long debate over the MLF), the Bonn government has focused more on its security needs than on the kind of national prestige that motivated France's independent policy. Theo Sommer, an astute German political analyst, wrote in 1966 that both public and published opinion in the Federal Republic would not support a call for German nuclear armament. Citing public-opinion polls, he concluded there was actually "an aversion to nuclear weapons" in Germany. He predicted no sudden change in this attitude as a consequence of resurgent nationalism. In Sommer's words, "the ideological, mythical and symbolical furniture of nationalism does not mean much any more in Germany. It is hard to see how anything could restore it to its pristine

[85] Article III of the 1954 arms control protocol to the Brussels Treaty, already cited, states: "When the development of atomic, biological and chemical weapons in the territory on the mainland of Europe of the High Contracting Parties who have not given up the right to produce them has passed the experimental stage and effective production of them has started there, the level of stocks that the High Contracting Parties concerned will be allowed to hold on the mainland of Europe shall be decided by a majority vote of the Council of Western European Union" (text in *NATO: Facts About the North Atlantic Treaty Organization*).

glory—certainly not the bomb, which would tear the nation asunder rather than cement it."[86] Moreover, as Sommer pointed out, British and French national deterrents have been the subject of mild derision in Germany, rather than objects of envy, in view of their cost, inefficiency, and doubtful prestige value.

After 1966 the debate over the Non-Proliferation Treaty raised some voices on these issues. But that debate centered mostly on the implications of the NPT for bargaining on the reunification question and for future German civilian nuclear technology and nuclear fuel supplies, rather than creating any new interest in national nuclear arms. The question of inspection by Euratom or the IAEA was also an issue. After the 1969 elections, however, the new government headed by Chancellor Willy Brandt signed the treaty.[87]

The future is uncertain in spite of the NPT. Germany will probably continue to hedge its bets. It might pursue a below-the-threshold program of civilian nuclear development that could be shifted to military applications within a very short time.[88] So far the Bonn government has maintained a modest civilian program of nuclear research and reactor development. It may soon expand its efforts and investments in the area of fast-breeder reactors, which could provide the necessary plutonium for atomic weapons.

There are, on the other hand, important factors militating against a German decision to embark on the development of a national nuclear force. First, possession of nuclear arms by Bonn would greatly hinder the West German Ostpolitik and the chances for success of any eventual German reunification formula. Moreover, German nuclear arma-

[86] Theo Sommer, "The Objectives of Germany," in *A World of Nuclear Powers?* (Englewood Cliffs, N.J.: Prentice-Hall for the American Assembly, Columbia University, 1966), pp. 52-53.

[87] *New York Times*, November 29, 1969.

[88] For some discussion of this problem, see Bennett Boskey and Mason Willrich, ed., *Nuclear Proliferation: Prospects for Control* (New York: Dunellen Co., 1970), esp. ch. 4.

ment would probably be as unacceptable to Bonn's Western partners as it would be to the Soviet Union.[89] In view of Bonn's new flexibility on the reunification question and apparent readiness to consider various frameworks, the achievement of some kind of confederal association of the two Germanies coupled with a non-nuclear status is gaining more and more acceptance in German political circles.

But since reunification is still a long way off, and might finally be excluded as a real possibility, what about the more immediate future? As long as German security is more or less achieved through NATO, there is little reason for any change in the Federal Republic's present nuclear policy. In case of a total breakdown of NATO and/or a withdrawal of the American nuclear umbrella, Germany might be moved to reconsider its position—especially if French nationalism persisted and prevented further steps toward European integration. But even under these extreme circumstances, it is difficult to imagine what Germany might gain from a national nuclear policy. Such a policy would surely breed resentment in the West and tend to isolate Germany from her allies. At the same time, it would arouse immense hostility in the East and perhaps even cause the Soviet Union and Eastern European countries to launch a preventive attack on Germany. Indeed, it appears that no policy would be more ruinous for German reunification than one based on a decision to build a national nuclear force.[90]

Whether this situation will look different in the future remains to be seen. If several more nations acquire a nuclear capability, and if the governments of Great Britain and France continue to spend substantial amounts on their nuclear deterrent programs, these factors are bound to influence West German government thinking. Some German

[89] See Nerlich, p. 648.

[90] Helmut Schmidt offers a number of arguments against a German nuclear capability from the standpoint of purely German interests. See his *Verteidigung oder Vergeltung* (Stuttgart: Seewald Verlag, 1965), chs. 6 and 10.

observers, such as Uwe Nerlich, fear that if France and Britain do not take pains to assure Bonn's participation in European security planning, the Federal Republic may experience a resurgence of nationalism. Says Nerlich:

> The danger here is not so much that the Federal Republic decides to become a nuclear power, but rather that, disappointed by its previous policy of integration, it will turn to a course which emphasizes nationalistic egoism as much as de Gaulle does—a course that would not only leave the problems of the Federal Republic's external security unresolved, but would seriously endanger its domestic stability.[91]

Others who take an even more pessimistic view believe that Germany will be unable in the end to resist pressures for the development of a German nuclear deterrent. They note the country's advanced civilian nuclear technology and the possibility of rapid conversion to military uses.[92]

Assuming that she does not choose to contravene the NPT and seek national nuclear arms, Germany's future security options are essentially three: unarmed neutrality (which is difficult to imagine, given the Federal Republic's economic importance and key location in Central Europe); acceptance of guarantees of protection from friendly nuclear states; or participation in a collective European nuclear force. Many Germans retain an interest in the latter alternative, in spite of the difficulties posed by accelerating weapons technology (especially ABM).[93] If Britain succeeds in joining the Common Market, such a force might be formed on the basis of a Franco-British nuclear core, with German financial and industrial support and a role for

[91] Nerlich, p. 651.

[92] See e.g., Timothy W. Stanley, *NATO in Transition* (New York: Frederick A. Praeger for the Council on Foreign Relations, 1965), p. 188.

[93] See Catherine M. Kelleher, "The Issue of German Nuclear Armament," *The Atlantic Community Reappraised, Proceedings of the Academy of Political Science*, XXXIX (November 1968), pp. 103-104.

Bonn in consultations on nuclear strategy. This prospect would require a considerable revision of French policy. Although not very likely, a change might be forthcoming in the post–de Gaulle era, based on the belief that it would represent the only course open to European nations if they want to have any world influence. In that case, France might revert to the precedent set in the 1957-58 discussions between Strauss and Chaban-Delmas, two personalities who continue to play important political roles in their respective countries, on possible joint atomic armament production.

8 · *Nuclear Issues in Franco-British Relations*

At the start of the 1960's Great Britain persisted, with diminishing success, in trying to wield her power and influence in three major spheres, as she had done since the war. Britain saw herself as a global power with troop deployments and obligations in far-flung Commonwealth countries of Asia, Africa, and the Middle East. At the same time, she sought to be a major European power and to maintain her "special relationship" with the United States. Unlike France, which had almost completed the process of disengagement from earlier colonial commitments, Britain did not yet consider Europe as the center of her foreign policy preoccupations. Nor had Britain declared any interest in joining the European Common Market. Britain—like France—had developed an atomic bomb and was ahead of the French in deploying an operational nuclear force.[1] Indeed, Britain was already the first European nuclear power, although she had benefited from American technology and atomic secrets. As noted earlier, the discrimination inherent in the special Anglo-American nuclear relationship—originating in World War II and revived during the 1950's—had long been a source of French grievances.

Britain's activities in military atomics never went unnoticed in France. First, the British decision to develop an independent nuclear deterrent set an example and sup-

[1] On the development of the British deterrent see R. N. Rosecrance, *Defense of the Realm* (New York: Columbia University Press, 1968) and Andrew J. Pierre, *Nuclear Politics: The British Experience with an Independent Strategic Force, 1939-1970* (London: Oxford University Press, 1972); also H. A. DeWeerd, "British-American Collaboration on the A-bomb in World War II," and "The British Effort to Secure an Independent Deterrent, 1952-1962," in *The Dispersion of Nuclear Weapons*, ed. R. N. Rosecrance (New York: Columbia University Press, 1964), chs. 2 and 5.

ported the arguments of those Frenchmen who urged that France, too, should have her own nuclear force. Britain's yielding to American pressure to reject French proposals for nuclear cooperation was also important during the 1950's. In early 1955 France had made known her eagerness to cooperate with England, and negotiations were under way regarding the possible construction of an isotope separation plant in France. The French were interested in gaining access to British technological know-how in the nuclear field; Britain was also agreeable to such cooperation—for diplomatic as well as trade reasons. But then the United States intervened on the basis of earlier Anglo-American accords and opposed any British atomic sharing with third parties where military applications might become involved. Consequently, Britain felt obliged to discontinue her negotiations with the French in the interest of preserving her own special nuclear relationship with the United States.[2] That privileged relationship was further extended in 1958 by amendments to the American Atomic Energy Act and by an Anglo-American bilateral agreement which provided London with a nuclear submarine propulsion plant, together with the necessary nuclear fuel and other classified information.[3]

Relations between London and Paris in the 1960's were dominated by Britain's decision to seek a new relationship with Europe through admission to the European Economic Community. Defense and nuclear questions became corollary issues in Britain's ensuing "European drama," which is the subject of this chapter. In London's successive bids to join the Common Market—first in 1961-63, later in 1967—questions of Britain's future military-political relationship to an evolving Europe lurked in the background of relations between Britain and France, although they were not

[2] See Bertrand Goldschmidt, *L'Aventure atomique* (Paris: Arthème Fayard, 1962), pp. 118-19; for more details see also his more recent book, *Les Rivalités atomiques, 1939-1966* (Paris: Arthème Fayard, 1967), pp. 225-27.

[3] See Chapter 2.

brought to the surface by the British government. This latter fact explains in part why two attempts at British entry floundered on the veto of General de Gaulle. Because London insisted on maintaining her previous commitments to the Commonwealth and to the United States, Britain had not yet demonstrated, in his view, the necessary readiness to wear the cloak of a genuine European.

Developments within the United Kingdom in the latter part of the 1960's led to a searching reexamination of Britain's global role and prompted decisions to withdraw from bases East of Suez. This evolution, discussed in the last section of the chapter, reduced the areas of contradiction between London's earlier global mission and her more recent choice for an increased role in Europe. It also tended to align British and French views on European defense, and this change placed the third British effort to join Europe in the period after de Gaulle in a much more favorable light.

The Nuclear Issue and de Gaulle's Common Market Veto of January 1963

Prime Minister Harold Macmillan went before the House of Commons on July 31, 1961, to announce a major change in British policy: the decision of his government to apply for membership in the EEC. This action, which broke a decade of British aloofness toward integration efforts on the Continent, was preceded by extensive diplomatic soundings in Europe and considerable debate within the cabinet and the Conservative party. Of interest here is not the background of the British decision, nor the lengthy economic negotiations which followed in Brussels,[4] but rather the manner in which defense, and particularly nuclear questions, became intertwined with the question of British entry into the Common Market.

[4] See Miriam Camps, *Britain and the European Community, 1955-1963* (Princeton: Princeton University Press, 1964); also Nora Beloff, *The General Says No* (Baltimore: Penguin Books, 1963).

At the time of Macmillan's announcement there had been signs that France was favorably disposed toward the prospect of British accession to the European Communities. After a meeting with de Gaulle at Rambouillet the previous January when questions of EEC–EFTA relations and European political cooperation were discussed, Macmillan returned to London with the impression that de Gaulle was not adverse to considering full Common Market membership for Britain.[5] This impression was strengthened by the following remark made by French Foreign Minister Couve de Murville to the Council of Europe on March 2: "Our partners of the Six and ourselves have always said that the Common Market itself is and will always remain open to any other European country desiring to join."[6] Speaking at Metz at the end of June, de Gaulle himself had commented: "It is necessary also that England come into the Common Market, but without posing conditions."[7]

After announcing his decision, Macmillan must have been encouraged by the general's positive reaction:

> All along the members of the Common Market, the six of them, have wanted other countries, and in particular Great Britain, to join the Treaty of Rome, to assume the obligations involved in it and, I think, to obtain the advantages deriving therefrom. We know very well how complex the problem is, but it appears that everything now points to tackling it, and as far as I am concerned, I can only express my gratification, not only from my own country's point of view, but also from the point of view of Europe, and consequently of the world.[8]

[5] See Beloff, p. 104; also Robert Kleiman, *Atlantic Crisis* (New York: W. W. Norton and Co., 1964), pp. 63-64.

[6] As quoted in Beloff, p. 106.

[7] As quoted in André Passeron, *De Gaulle parle*, I (Paris: Plon, 1962), 433.

[8] Press conference, September 5, 1961, in *Major Addresses, Statements and Press Conferences of General Charles de Gaulle, May 19, 1958-January 31, 1964* (New York: Ambassade de France, Service de presse et d'information), p. 147.

Furthermore, at a conference with Macmillan at Birch Grove in November, the general is reported to have emphasized that Britain had to choose between the Commonwealth and Europe, but he repeated that England "would be welcome" in the Common Market as *un pays sérieux*.[9]

But despite several talks with Macmillan, many believe that it was not until after de Gaulle's very cordial meeting with the British leader at the Chateau de Champs in June 1962 that the general really became convinced of Britain's determination to join the Community. Although some kind of British participation in Europe may have fitted into his long-term plans for a European confederation, de Gaulle was not ready to accept the English in 1962-63. British membership and the British view of Europe conformed with neither of the general's two visions of Europe's future at that time: a loose West European grouping with an independent role in world politics, and a Europe in which France would have a special position of leadership. Between the summer of 1962 and his press conference of January 1963, de Gaulle made up his mind to reject the British application. Events in the intervening months allowed him to use nuclear issues and questions of Britain's future relationship to European defense to demonstrate that the British government was indeed not yet "European" and therefore not ready to join Europe.

During 1961 and 1962, British policy planners gave some attention to the question of whether or not to increase the European orientation of England's defense policies. Officials involved were generally of the opinion that Britain had to maintain its defense ties with the United States before all else. Only a few considered it important for Britain to extend its European policies to the area of defense as part of its bid to join Europe. In a rare reference to the political-military aspects of British entry into Europe, Edward Heath, then London's chief negotiator in Brussels, suggested in a speech to the Council of the Western European

[9] As quoted in Kleiman, p. 67.

Union on April 10, 1962, that the British government might profitably join discussions among the Six on a European political union (a reference to the Fouchet commission). The British felt, said Heath, that such a European political union would inevitably be concerned with defense matters and a common European outlook on defense questions would certainly emerge. He went on to stress that any European defense arrangements must be placed within an "Atlantic" context and related to NATO.[10] Peter Thorneycroft, the minister of defense, and Julian Amery, the minister of aviation, were of a stronger European persuasion and had dropped appropriate hints in Paris that they would even be interested in exploring a nuclear partnership with France. But none of these questions relating to the security implications of Britain's effort to enter the Common Market were followed up by the British government in the ensuing months.

In addition, there were suggestions in the British press before the de Gaulle–Macmillan meeting at Champs that Britain, in order to bolster her case for admission to the Communities, ought to consider proposing some kind of nuclear agreement with the French. An *Economist* editorial urged Macmillan to try to arrive at a "preliminary understanding with General de Gaulle about how Britain

[10] See *New York Times*, April 11, 1962; also the discussion in Camps, pp. 420-21. The following excerpts from Heath's speech are of particular interest, as taken from the full text reprinted as Appendix C in Camps, pp. 525-30:

> We quite accept that the European political union, if it is to be effective, will have a common concern for defence problems and that a European point of view on defence will emerge. What is essential, however, is that any European point of view or policy on defence should be directly related to the Atlantic Alliance. We must make it clear beyond all doubt that the object of our common policy is to defend and strengthen the liberties for which the Atlantic Alliance is the indispensable shield. . . .
>
> This new Europe will be a great power, standing not alone but as an equal partner in the Atlantic Alliance, retaining its traditional ties overseas and fully conscious of its growing obligations towards the rest of the free world.

might dispose of its nuclear armoury if and when it joins the common market." It even suggested an *"entente nucléaire* . . . a joint Anglo-French nuclear arm which might provide a credible deterrent for the whole of Western Europe."[11] Other British press stories reported that de Gaulle was actually demanding an Anglo-French nuclear deal as the price of British entry into the EEC. As recounted by one analyst, de Gaulle was warned by his advisers before the Champs meeting that this might be a British "maneuver" to blame him for a breakdown of the Brussels negotiations. Consequently, the French president called in the British ambassador in Paris, Sir Pierson Dixon, and made it clear to him that he was not asking for nuclear cooperation as a condition for British entry into the Common Market.[12] This action did not, of course, mean that the French leader was uninterested in the possibility of some Franco-British nuclear arrangement; it only meant that he would not place himself in the position of *demandeur.*

At Champs, Macmillan and de Gaulle discussed the economic issues of the Brussels negotiations, and the prime minister spoke with great optimism about his hopes to solve the problems of agriculture and the Commonwealth. The two leaders reached considerable agreement on the idea of a European political union, based essentially on the Fouchet model. Macmillan was reported relieved that de Gaulle's idea of a more independent Europe did not mean a neutral Europe. The British leader, in turn, said that Britain looked forward to political as well as economic union with the Six and would cooperate not only in foreign policy but also in defense.

With regard to the latter, French interviews confirmed that Macmillan spoke for the first time of the need to strengthen European, as opposed to NATO, defense policy. There was discussion in broad terms of possible Anglo-

[11] *Economist,* May 12, 1962, p. 536; a similar idea was advanced in the issue of April 28, 1962.

[12] Kleiman, p. 68.

French defense cooperation after Britain had entered the Common Market. In particular, Macmillan suggested the two countries might coordinate plans for the use of their nuclear forces in case the United States should ever decline to come to Europe's aid with American nuclear strength. De Gaulle never asked directly for British assistance in the nuclear field, and Macmillan never made any specific offer in this direction. But Macmillan did leave the impression he was considering a more European orientation in his defense policies. De Gaulle, in turn, explained French nuclear policy to Macmillan, and the prime minister, apparently to the French leader's surprise, expressed no objection to it.[13]

A short communiqué issued at the conclusion of their very cordial talks underlined the two leaders' agreement on the "community of interests which unites Britain and France." Obviously impressed with Macmillan's presentation, de Gaulle went away convinced for the first time that the British were serious in their desire to join Europe. Indeed, the two leaders probably were in closest accord at the time of the Champs meeting. But this friendly atmosphere was deceptive. No doubt their meeting would have been far less amicable if they had discussed in detail the highly important defense and nuclear questions, rather than simply skirting these issues.[14]

After Champs Macmillan acknowledged publicly that France had become a nuclear power and would probably remain one. He said that he and his government fully understood the reasons for French policy.[15] This was the first public recognition by the British government of France's new nuclear status. In the same June speech, Macmillan emphasized his government's intention to preserve the independent British deterrent, created after fifteen years of effort. (At Ann Arbor earlier the same month Secre-

[13] See André Fontaine's article of June 5 and Henri Pierre's reports of June 6 and 7, 1962, in *Le Monde*; also Leonard Beaton in *The Times* (London), June 5, 1962.

[14] Camps, p. 429.

[15] *Le Monde*, June 28, 1962.

tary McNamara had condemned all small national nuclear forces). Macmillan also made a vague statement interpreted by some to mean that the British government was ready to consider a European defense system, but he gave no details.

On the French side, Defense Minister Pierre Messmer said in an interview with the *Observer* a short time later that the French government was interested in cooperation with Great Britain and other members of the European Community in a European deterrent force, once the French *force de frappe* had been created.[16] His statement came shortly after the vigorous defense debate in the French National Assembly on the Pierrelatte project and its rising costs. As noted in an earlier chapter, that debate produced a motion of censure against the French government criticizing de Gaulle's policy of a national nuclear force and urging instead the creation of a European Community deterrent. Thus, Messmer's comment may well have had domestic political motivations.

The Brussels negotiations made considerable progress in the summer of 1962, and most of the Commonwealth preference issues were settled by the time of the August adjournment. Apparently the "spirit of the Champs" had had some effect. After the Commonwealth Prime Minister's meeting and the Conservative and Liberal party conferences, the final round of negotiations began in October.[17] It quickly bogged down, however, on the problem of agriculture. British negotiating tactics became dilatory, as months were spent arguing about administrative details relating to Britain's transition to the Common Market agricultural system. By the end of the fall, the prevailing mood in Brussels was one of disenchantment with Britain and with the slow pace of the negotiations.

Meanwhile, developments on the French domestic political scene were strengthening General de Gaulle's hand in

16 Anthony Verrier in the *Observer*, July 15, 1962.

17 See Camps, ch. 14, for a detailed account of the final round of the accession negotiations.

foreign policy. In October 1962 de Gaulle won—albeit by a narrow majority—a constitutional referendum approving popular election of the president. Then, in the November legislative elections, the Gaullist UNR gained an unexpected landslide victory and, with the aid of a few Independents, won an absolute majority in the National Assembly. This gave de Gaulle a free hand, especially in French policy toward European integration and the question of British entry. Before the elections any acts of obstruction in this area would have made him vulnerable to the European-minded center-left and center-right opposition, but now this was no longer the case.

On the international scene, an important strategic-diplomatic development—the Cuban missile crisis in October—had made Europeans both more aware and more wary of their nuclear dependence on the United States.

It was against this setting that the issue of nuclear defense reemerged in December to complicate the problem of British entry into Europe. During talks between de Gaulle and Macmillan that month at Rambouillet, the security implications of Britain's choice for Europe first became apparent; and the Anglo-American defense conference at Nassau a few days later—to which France was not invited—only exacerbated the situation.

The Macmillan–de Gaulle meeting at the Chateau de Rambouillet outside Paris on the weekend of December 15-16 was by all accounts a chilly affair, very different from the cordial encounter at Champs the previous June.[18] The two leaders first exchanged views on the international situation following the Cuban missile crisis. They then focused on two subjects: the Common Market negotiations and defense questions associated with the coming Nassau talks. De

[18] The following summary of the Rambouillet conversations is based on interview sources and on the following secondary accounts: Kleiman, pp. 48-51, 96-98; Camps, pp. 468-70; Beloff, pp. 157-58; John Newhouse, *De Gaulle and the Anglo-Saxons* (New York: Viking, 1970), pp. 205-12; and Don Cook, *Floodtide in Europe* (New York: G. P. Putnam's Sons, 1965), pp. 267-71.

Gaulle gave a rather pessimistic appraisal of the Brussels negotiations and expressed grave doubts about whether Britain could actually make the adjustments necessary for entry into the EEC. Macmillan was shocked by the general's remarks. He especially resented de Gaulle's explanation of how Britain's entry would change the entire balance of the Community and fundamentally alter France's position in it. The prime minister reportedly asked the French leader whether he was now raising a matter of principle after fourteen months of negotiations. No agreement was reached on the economic issues. According to at least one account, de Gaulle may have proposed British "association" with the EEC instead of full membership.[19]

With regard to defense, Macmillan briefed de Gaulle on the background of America's decision to scrap the Skybolt missile, on which the British had been counting for further development of their nuclear deterrent.[20] Macmillan told the general he was determined to obtain an "effective alternative" when he saw President Kennedy in Nassau. The prime minister apparently saw no inconsistency between any agreement he might conclude with the Americans at Nassau and Britain's declared policy of willingness to join Europe, including European defense arrangements.

Contrary to later reports, the question of merging the British and French nuclear efforts was mentioned by neither side at Rambouillet, though there was a brief discussion of Anglo-French cooperation. De Gaulle cited the agreement the two nations had recently signed to develop the Concorde supersonic aircraft and twice alluded to the possibility of similar cooperation on the development of strategic missiles.[21] Although raising the matter very cautiously, since he did not take to the role of supplicant, the

[19] Kleiman, p. 97. [20] For details see Chapter 6.

[21] Confirmed to me by a high French official, de Gaulle's interest in missile cooperation is corroborated by André Fontaine, "What is French Policy?" *Foreign Affairs* (October 1966), p. 74, and Newhouse, pp. 207-208.

general was apparently proposing that Britain revive the Blue Streak missile in collaboration with France. As the French saying goes, de Gaulle may have been "holding out a perch" for Macmillan to seize and thus prove himself a true "European" by agreeing to develop a strategic weapon with France instead of depending upon the United States. Macmillan did not respond to these overtures. Either he did not understand the general's intentions, or he simply chose not to commit himself.

Two days later, Macmillan met President Kennedy for the four-day conference in Nassau. As described previously, the two leaders agreed that the United States would make Polaris missiles available to Britain as a substitute for Skybolt. Installed in British submarines and fitted with British nuclear warheads, these missiles eventually became part of a NATO nuclear force to serve the defense needs of the Western alliance, except when Britain might decide that her "supreme national interests are at stake." A similar U.S. Polaris offer was made to France at the close of the Nassau conference.

By tying the British Polaris nuclear forces to NATO and offering the same missiles to France, British and American officials at Nassau felt they were diminishing the long standing special Anglo-American relationship in nuclear matters. Pleased by the results of Nassau, they had no inkling of any possible adverse effects on the British entry negotiations. But General de Gaulle's reaction was precisely the opposite. The Nassau agreement gave him the final pretext he needed for his dramatic veto of British entry, announced in his famous press conference of January 14, 1963.

A number of myths grew out of the Rambouillet-Nassau events. For example, Gaullists claimed subsequently that Macmillan was not completely candid with de Gaulle at Rambouillet, and that the British leader then proceeded to make a "secret deal" with Kennedy at Nassau. The record does not bear this out, since Macmillan did tell de Gaulle at Rambouillet of the impending Nassau conference. As the prime minister later said himself at Liverpool on January 21, 1963:

> . . . it has been suggested that by making the Polaris arrangement with President Kennedy a few days after I had seen General de Gaulle himself at Rambouillet I did not treat him with absolute sincerity. On the contrary we discussed this question and I explained that if the Americans decided to abandon Skybolt as unlikely to prove satisfactory I would do my utmost at Nassau to obtain an effective alternative. I explained to him in some detail my view of the relations between interdependence and independence, and said that we must have a British deterrent available for independent use if need be. I am sure he fully understood our position. This impression was confirmed through diplomatic contacts after the Nassau agreement had been announced.[22]

Another myth was that Macmillan had suggested a merger of the British and French nuclear forces at Rambouillet. This was what de Gaulle is reported to have said at an Elysée reception for a group of parliamentarians in February:

> Mr. Macmillan came to tell me [at Rambouillet] that we are right to develop our *force de frappe*. "We also have our own force," he said to me. "We should try to unite them in a European framework, independent of America." Thereupon, he left me to go on to the Bahamas. Naturally, what occurred there changed the tone of my press conference on January 14.[23]

The record simply does not confirm any serious British offer or discussion of a European nuclear force at Rambouillet.

Having disposed of these myths, one can still comprehend the reasons for de Gaulle's violent reaction to this chain of

[22] As quoted in Camps, p. 487.
[23] As quoted in *Le Monde*, February 7, 1963.

events. The technological unattractiveness of the Polaris offer to France and the tactical clumsiness of the Anglo-Saxons in not inviting de Gaulle to a meeting which considered a major reorganization of nuclear weapons in NATO have already been described.[24] The rapid cancellation of Skybolt and the confused nature of the Nassau conference, whose political ramifications were grasped by British and American officials only on the eve of the talks, are partial explanations of these negative factors. But another element was simply the short-sightedness of British diplomacy. Macmillan evidently "thought it better to get the agreement [at Nassau] first and smooth things over afterwards."[25] And then the letters sent to de Gaulle from Nassau outlining the American Polaris offer contained nothing more than the general had already read in newspaper reports of the conference, since Macmillan had insisted that the Nassau agreement be announced before he returned to London.[26] The result was to present de Gaulle with a *fait accompli.* As Nora Beloff observed, "It was a strange way to treat a man widely known to suffer from a acute persecution mania, amounting almost to paranoia, about the 'Anglo-Saxons.' "[27]

Most important, however, was de Gaulle's conclusion that Macmillan had sacrificed Britain's nuclear independence at Nassau, in spite of British claims to the contrary. Because London had chosen a Polaris pact with the United States, rather than proposing new defense links with Europe, the French easily surmised that Britain preferred her "special relations" with Washington and was not yet ready for full membership in Europe. As noted earlier, it was felt in Paris that British entry into the Common Market would "carry a great risk of opening the doors to an American 'Trojan horse.' "[28]

[24] See Chapter 6. [25] Beloff, p. 160.

[26] Evidently the American officials at Nassau had favored opening discussions with France before announcing the agreement. See Kleiman, p. 60.

[27] Beloff, p. 159.

[28] André Fontaine in *Le Monde,* January 10, 1963.

Whether the Nassau agreement actually precipitated the general's decision to reject British entry, or was only a contributing factor, has been a subject of much debate. Evidence presently available would seem to favor the latter interpretation. After her detailed analysis of the British accession negotiations, Miriam Camps concluded that "the Government of General de Gaulle advocated membership for the United Kingdom when they were confident that there was no chance that the British Government would apply to join, and that they subsequently acted on the assumption that the British Government would not, in fact, be willing, or politically strong enough, to accept the terms which a strict reading of the Treaty of Rome and of the subsequent decisions of the Community implied."[29] When the seriousness of British intentions became manifest after his meeting with Macmillan at Champs, de Gaulle was ready to stiffen his terms and allow the Brussels negotiations to run on indefinitely without attempting to reach any agreement. Certainly the general's tough stance at Rambouillet was evidence that probably he had decided by then that Britain's application was not going to succeed.[30]

It is doubtful, however, that de Gaulle was contemplating the sudden veto he announced at his January press conference. The Nassau agreement gave him a convenient excuse for such a dramatic action. Strengthened by the strong Gaullist victory in the fall French elections, and by the knowledge that Chancellor Adenauer likewise had reservations about British entry and would offer little or no resistance,[31] the general was able to carry it off.

In his press conference de Gaulle negatively exaggerated

[29] Camps, p. 500.

[30] Newhouse contends that de Gaulle's mind was made up at Rambouillet. See *De Gaulle and the Anglo-Saxons*, pp. 211, 226-28.

[31] Adenauer had expressed his reservations to de Gaulle at their meeting in September 1962. See Konrad Adenauer, *Erinnerungen, 1959-63: Fragmente* (Stuttgart: Deutsche Verlags-Anstalt, 1968), pp. 177-78, 181.

the state of the economic negotiations; although several troublesome problems remained to be solved (e.g., alignment of British agriculture, arrangements for New Zealand and for other EFTA countries), they were not incapable of solution.[32] But this was merely the general's way of supporting his fundamental argument—i.e., that the British had one concept of Europe and he another. In the general's eyes, the British were not ready to accept a strong and independent European identity in the political and military spheres, as well as in the economic domain. De Gaulle's principal stated objection to British admission was that the United Kingdom was too closely tied to the United States. Were the Common Market to approve British accession under those conditions, to be followed by other EFTA countries, it would run the risk—as the general put it—of being "swallowed up" in "a colossal Atlantic Community under American dependence and leadership."[33]

As stated earlier, British membership in the European Communities was compatible with neither of the general's visions of European construction in 1962-63, although it is likely that he contemplated a European role for Britain later on.[34] First, British entry would have challenged de Gaulle's hopes for a West European political and economic union dominated by France. Secondly, it would have threatened the Gaullist vision for an independent "third force" Europe, since the British clearly intended that Western Europe be Atlantic-oriented and open to American influence. Although most Europeans did not accept the Gaullist vision of a Europe under French leadership, there were many who were sympathetic to the second vision and the need for a European viewpoint in world affairs that could compete with the United States'. The Anglo-American Nassau accord

[32] For a discussion of the state of the Brussels negotiations at the time of the breakdown, see Camps, pp. 494ff.

[33] Text of the press conference of January 14, 1963 in *Major Addresses*, p. 214.

[34] See the discussion of the Soames affair later in this chapter.

was sufficient proof that Britain still placed her links with the United States ahead of her relations with Europe; it was therefore a credible reason for rejection of British entry in the eyes of non-Gaullist Europeans. Thus, the course of events at the close of 1962 allowed de Gaulle to use nuclear issues to defend his political-strategic conception of Europe; those issues had brought most clearly to light the differences between London and Paris about Europe's future orientation.[35]

The Macmillan government's major miscalculation in 1961-62 was that it regarded entry into Europe as primarily an economic problem. Somehow the British failed to grasp the political-strategic implications of such a new alignment. Even after the cancellation of Skybolt—a natural opportunity for Britain to rethink its defense relationships with its European neighbors—London plodded along its former course and sought an American substitute for Skybolt rather than a replacement in Europe. Moreover, Britain agreed to a new nuclear plan for NATO with the United States at Nassau without consulting France, the other European nuclear power. As Henry Kissinger has written:

> In retrospect, the failure of Britain to consult with France and its other European allies before committing itself to the Nassau Agreement seems a crucial missed opportunity. It will never be known what the reaction would have been if Britain had made such an overture before

[35] In subsequent statements de Gaulle referred to both the state of the economic negotiations and the Nassau agreement as reasons for his veto of British entry in January 1963. In his press conference on July 23, 1964, he said: ". . . Great Britain having shown throughout the interminable Brussels negotiations that it was not in a position to accept the common economic rules and, by the Nassau Agreement, that its defense force, particularly in the nuclear domain, would not be European for lack of being autonomous in relation to the United States. . . ." (*Speeches and Press Conferences*, no. 208 [New York: Ambassade de France, Service de presse et d'information], p. 6). He made a similar comment in his press conference of October 28, 1966 (ibid., no. 253A, p. 4).

the Bahamas meeting. Even had it failed, it would have placed the subsequent debate in a far better context.[36]

British Attitudes and Policies on Nuclear Force After the Veto

After General de Gaulle had forced the British entry negotiations to a halt in January 1963, there was some feeling in Britain and among Europeans close to Jean Monnet that London should make a counterinitiative. It was suggested that the United Kingdom might put forward a plan for a European defense arrangement, utilizing its strongest bargaining card, namely the nuclear deterrent. But such a move was not politically feasible for the Macmillan government, which needed time to recover from the shock of the French veto and was in no mood to search for ways to overcome it.[37]

Although many people in Britain questioned the need for an independent British nuclear deterrent, there was no consensus on what to do about it. To Macmillan himself, the Nassau agreement seems to have been a desperate effort to retain a semblance of independence in nuclear matters, after the collapse of Skybolt, and to postpone the politically explosive question of changing Britain's nuclear role. In this respect, American Polaris missiles were an attractive way out on generous terms. Although there was good cause for questioning just how much independence Britain would re-

[36] *The Troubled Partnership* (New York: McGraw-Hill, 1965), p. 86.

[37] Miriam Camps, *European Unification in the Sixties* (New York: McGraw-Hill, 1966), pp. 125ff.

Based on deliberations of a study group at Chatham House in late 1963 and early 1964, Kenneth Younger recommended in his *Changing Perspectives in British Foreign Policy* (London: Oxford University Press, 1964) that the British government propose to place its nuclear weapons in some kind of collective European nuclear arrangement, since the nuclear area was the only one "where early action is possible, which could be seen to place Britain squarely at the side of her European neighbors on a footing of complete equality" (pp. 127-28).

tain with Polaris, at least the terms of the agreement seemed palatable enough to the British public at large.

Certainly the 1964 election campaign must have dismayed Britain's European friends when they heard both major parties enunciate their respective positions on defense matters. The Conservative government continued to emphasize the importance of preserving an independent British nuclear deterrent. Ironically, the arguments it used echoed those employed frequently by de Gaulle to justify the development of the *force de frappe*. Nonetheless, the Conservatives supported the strengthening of NATO; they were willing to move toward integrating the British deterrent only into a NATO framework. They failed, however, to take a clear stance on the MLF.

Much less disposed toward British nuclear armament, the Labor party even went so far as to promise that, if elected, it would denegotiate the Nassau pact and renounce the national nuclear force. Hostile toward the MLF and any form of European nuclear deterrent that might provide Germany with a nuclear role, Labor party leaders appeared to give priority to East–West relations and the possibility of arms-control agreements in Europe. Neither the Conservative nor the Labor campaign positions on defense seemed consistent with a primarily "European" role for Britain over the long run.[38]

After Nassau the Macmillan government continued its defense ties with Washington and its adherence to Atlantic defense concepts, both deeply rooted orientations. Thus, when French Foreign Ministry official Habib-Deloncle suggested the eventual formation of a European nuclear force in 1963, the Foreign Office, recalling Edward Heath's April 1962 speech to the WEU, indicated that Britain wanted no part of a European nuclear effort isolated from the United States and not directly related to the Atlantic alliance.[39] And throughout the MLF debate of 1963-64 the Conservative government, although not enthusiastic about the plan, con-

[38] Camps, *European Unification in the Sixties*, p. 130.
[39] See the *New York Times*, September 25, 1963.

sidered its Atlantic framework and built-in U.S. veto to be one of its principal strengths. Unlike German officials and some other Europeans, the British did not urge a "European clause" in the proposed MLF treaty. They preferred the American veto, in their eyes a guarantee that no European nuclear force would be developed outside of NATO.

Following Labor's victory in October 1964, Harold Wilson, the new prime minister, was faced with honoring his campaign commitment to reduce defense expenditures and abandon the "independent nuclear deterrent." Once in office, Labor began to see nuclear issues in a new light. In fact, it proved easier to move in the direction of placing Britain's nuclear capacity under an international arrangement than to relinquish atomic weapons altogether. A number of reasons were given for continuing the nuclear force: construction of the nuclear submarines had advanced to the point where cancellation would have been costly and difficult; a Polaris force was needed to provide a nuclear guarantee for India; and the generous terms for the acquisition of Polaris missiles had weakened the contention that Britain could not afford a nuclear force. Labor leaders soon admitted that their earlier arguments about Britain's contributing to nuclear spread had lost validity. British actions now could be expected to have little effect on nuclear programs already under way in Asia and the Middle East. Moreover, Labor was coming to realize that nuclear weapons were an asset in diplomacy, that self-abnegation would leave France the only European nuclear power, and that a British nuclear capability might well assist Britain's future entry into the European Economic Community.[40]

The Wilson government soon proposed an Atlantic nuclear force (ANF) as an alternative to the MLF (once American and German determination to act on the latter plan had become clear). Indeed, the ANF's main purpose may well have been to help kill the multilateral nuclear fleet. Because it was to include the greater part of the Brit-

[40] Andrew J. Pierre, "Britain's Defense Dilemmas," *Proceedings of the Academy of Political Science*, XXIX (November 1968), 74-75.

ish V-bomber force and the Polaris submarines under construction, the ANF would, it was held, serve to internationalize Britain's defense structure. A small mixed-manned element was to allow participation of the non-nuclear powers, and the whole force was open to any future French contribution.[41]

The Atlantic nuclear force was to be directed by a single authority, representing the participating nations, and closely linked to NATO. British forces were to be committed "for as long as the Alliance lasts." In effect not much different from the emergency withdrawal formula of the Nassau agreement, this commitment nevertheless allowed Wilson to make good his campaign pledge to give up the national British deterrent. The United States, Britain, and France—if she took part—were each to have a veto power over the use of all elements in the force. Other participating European countries might possibly exercise a veto as a single group. But Wilson strongly opposed any kind of "European clause," which might weaken the American veto. Future renegotiation of the veto arrangement by a politically united Europe was *not* a possibility under the ANF plan, in contrast to the MLF.

Prime Minister Wilson made no attempt to conceal his hostility for the idea of a European nuclear force. At Guildhall on November 16, 1964, he stated: "We reject categorically any idea of a separate European deterrent." The latter, he believed, would divide NATO, prompt the U.S. to reappraise its attitude toward Europe, and be "a grave step in the proliferation of nuclear weapons." "In a nuclear world," said Wilson, "safety lies in collective security al-

[41] The main features of the ANF proposal were first revealed in an article in *The Times* (London) by the defense correspondent, Alun Gwynne Jones (later to become Lord Chalfont and minister in charge of disarmament questions), October 24, 1964. The plan was further developed by the Wilson government during the fall and presented to President Johnson in December during Wilson's visit in Washington. See also *Hansard*, Commons, November 23 and December 16, 1964.

liances based on interdependence. There is nothing so debilitating as an alliance within an alliance."[42] Wilson did not deviate from this position.

Appearing on the surface to offer France an equal role with Britain, the ANF was in fact designed to safeguard British interests in the nuclear field. Since the Wilson government insisted upon an American veto power over the ANF for all time and rejected any evolution toward a European deterrent, any interest which Gaullists might have had in the British proposal was quickly extinguished. Indeed, the ANF plan underscored Britain's lack of interest in a future U.K. role in a European political union.[43]

The Labor government's initial defense priorities, according to its Defense White Paper, issued in February 1965, were non-proliferation of nuclear weapons, East–West agreements on arms control, and the strengthening of Britain's ability to keep the peace "East of Suez," instead of in Europe. According to that document, the ANF was central to Labor's defense policy in the European-Atlantic area. Through it, the British government proposed to collectivize the nuclear deterrent and promote strength and solidarity in the Alliance, while at the same time removing any incentive for further nuclear proliferation. In a small economy gesture, the number of planned British Polaris submarines was reduced from five to four.[44]

As the MLF-ANF debate faded away in 1965, Labor clung to the one remaining NATO nuclear initiative, the McNamara "special committee" for nuclear consultation, later to become the Nuclear Planning Group. While the 1966 Defense White Paper indicated the ANF proposal was "still on the table," it was no longer pressed by London. The consultative approach to nuclear sharing seemed amply suf-

[42] *New York Times*, November 17, 1964.

[43] Camps, *European Unification in the Sixties*, p. 149.

[44] *Statement on the Defence Estimates, 1965*, Command 2592 (London: HMSO, February 1965). The first Chinese nuclear explosion a short time before probably influenced this Labor White Paper to emphasize Britain's role east of Suez and the position on the deterrent.

ficient for the Wilson government. At that time the British were more concerned with threats to the peace outside Europe and with maintaining Britain's peace-keeping role in Asia, the Middle East, and Africa.[45]

This concern prompted the announcement that London planned to purchase fifty F-111A strike aircraft from the United States to fill the gap between the phasing out of the V bombers and the introduction of Polaris submarines and an advanced fighter-bomber. Underlying this decision was a rather vague notion about the necessity for a British nuclear role in Asia. Placed in March 1967, the order for purchase of the final forty F-111s seemed to represent a firm new British defense link to the United States. But ten months later the whole deal was canceled as part of a series of economic belt-tightening measures, the impact of which we will return to in a moment.[46]

Britain's Second Approach to Europe, 1967

Five years after Macmillan's 1961 announcement before Parliament of Britain's desire to join Europe, Prime Minister Wilson stood at the same lecturn to proclaim his government's intention to seek Common Market membership.[47] Soundings and personal consultations with the heads of government of the Six took place during the following winter and spring. Wilson's final decision to apply was approved by an overwhelming 488-62 vote in the House of Commons on May 10, 1967,[48] and formal application was made in Brussels the next day. The resounding support which this new move toward Europe received in Commons was evidence of a fundamental change in British po-

[45] See the *Statement on the Defence Estimates, 1966*, Command 2901 (London: HMSO, February 1966).

[46] *New York Times*, April 1, 1967; January 17, 1968.

[47] *New York Times*, November 11, 1966.

[48] *New York Times*, May 11, 1963.

litical attitudes since 1962. Both major political parties now favored British entry into the Common Market.[49]

In the early prenegotiation phase of this second British approach to Europe, Wilson tried to avoid some of the errors made by his predecessor. Above all, he was anxious to give the impression that his government desired to reduce its dependency on the United States and was prepared to become more "European." He spoke of his intention to join in building Europe as a "pillar of equal strength" with the United States in a speech on November 30, 1966. American economic domination of Europe should be prevented. Britain, he suggested, could provide important assistance in the forging of a technologically advanced European economy. This was followed up in the ensuing months by a more concrete proposal for a European technological community of the Six plus the United Kingdom and for the creation of a European technological institute.[50]

Once again, the question of defense and possible nuclear cooperation—especially with France—lurked in the background of Britain's drive to join Europe. In an article reminiscent of 1962, the *Economist* suggested in early May 1967 that defense issues, and in particular the nuclear deterrent, might provide the key to winning Gaullist assent to Britain's second entry bid. No hope was seen for the formation of an integrated Franco-British deterrent, but it was recommended that joint Franco-British cooperation in missile development be seriously considered. Instead of turning again to the United States for advanced missiles—such as the Poseidon—to modernize its deterrent, the British government was urged to undertake collaboration with France. The French, it was pointed out, were accomplished in rocketry, and French missile know-how might complement

[49] For an account of the revival of British interest in the European Community during 1965-66, see Camps, *European Unification in the Sixties*, ch. 5.

[50] *New York Times*, December 1, 1966; and Wilson's speech before the Council of Europe in Strasbourg, January 23, 1967, reported in the *New York Times*, January 24, 1967.

British expertise in the construction of nuclear warheads. Such an arrangement might be made in return for Britain's admission to the European Community.[51]

The possibility raised by the Poseidon issue of "another Nassau agreement" between London and Washington at a time when Britain was again preparing for Common Market negotiations seemed ominous indeed. Fortunately, however, Wilson put that to rest. On a television interview program in May 1967, he said that Britain was not likely to purchase the Poseidon missile from the United States. The prime minister was also quoted as saying that Britain should join the Common Market "to make Europe more strong, more independent, more decisive in world affairs."[52] Offering no hint as to his thinking on modernizing the British deterrent after Polaris, he was doubtless unreceptive to a European nuclear arrangement, given his party's past hostility to this idea and its loyalty to NATO.

President de Gaulle's reaction to Britain's second Common Market application was swift and negative. In his press conference on May 16, 1967, he reiterated many of the arguments he had used against Britain in 1963. In particular, de Gaulle assailed "Britain's special links with the United States," "the existence of the Commonwealth and its preferential arrangements," and "the special commitments which Britain still has in diverse regions of the world and which distinguish her fundamentally from the continentals." England's special defense ties to America obviously continued to bother the general, who went so far as to say that Britain and Western Europe could merge "only if the British became again full masters of their destiny, notably with respect to defense, or if the continental nations gave up forever their intention to create a European Europe (*une Europe qui soit européenne*)."[53]

[51] *Economist*, May 6, 1967, p. 545.

[52] As quoted in the *New York Times*, May 9, 1967.

[53] See the text of President de Gaulle's press conference in *Le Monde*, May 19, 1967.

Despite de Gaulle's virtual rejection, the Wilson government was undeterred and pressed forward doggedly to get negotiations under way in Brussels. These efforts were finally cut short by de Gaulle's announcement in his November press conference that France would oppose the opening of negotiations. The French leader again inveighed against British membership on both political and economic grounds. The devaluation of the British pound earlier the same month was not sufficient in his eyes to solve Britain's economic troubles. A "radical transformation" of her economic system, as well as substantial political realignment, was required before she would be fit to join the Continent. In effect, de Gaulle had cast his second veto against British entry.[54]

The Narrowing of the Franco-British Gulf on European Defense, 1967-69

In its first years in office the Labor government emphasized Britain's role as a world power and assigned no special priority to Britain's place in Europe. Impressed by Britain's assistance in suppressing the East African mutinies of 1964 and her contribution toward maintaining order in Cyprus, Defense Minister Denis Healey saw a continuing intervention role for Her Majesty's Government in Asia, Africa, and the Middle East—the key areas of future world instability. Just before assuming office, Healey had written:

> Britain is a world power, whether we like it or not. History has saddled her with interests and responsibilities in every continent. The structure of her economy prohibits a regional approach to international affairs. . . . We should count ourselves fortunate that we have the power to exert some influence in every continent.[55]

[54] See the *New York Times*, November 28, 1967.

[55] Denis Healey, *A Labour Britain and the World* (London, 1964) as quoted in Andrew J. Pierre, "Britain and European Security: Issues and Choices for the 1970's," in William T. R. Fox and Warner R. Schilling, ed., *European Security and the Atlantic System* (New York: Columbia University Press, 1972).

Labor's leaders clearly thought that Britain's global interests and responsibilities still afforded London a special place in world political councils and distinguished her from other European powers which had long since abandoned their military obligations in former colonies.

The retention of a global defense policy differentiated Britain sharply from France in 1965-66, and this breach in the security perspectives of the two countries was further accentuated by differences in their strategic policies toward Europe and the Atlantic.[56] Unlike France, Britain remained fully committed to NATO and accepted, in effect, U.S. domination of the Alliance's strategy and command structures, as well as the American monopoly of nuclear decision. After France's withdrawal from NATO military commands, it was the British government that took the lead in rallying the Fourteen and revitalizing NATO solidarity. In the nuclear field, the Labor government supported the McNamara committee for nuclear consultation and subsequently joined the Nuclear Planning Group; it appeared even more willing than the Conservatives to commit the British deterrent to NATO and all but relinquish its "independent" status.

On the subject of possible new arrangements for European defense, the British attitude—i.e., the greater part of both Conservative and Labor opinion—was highly reserved. Britain placed priority on Atlantic defense arrangements and on continuing, so far as possible, a "special relationship" with the United States. The problem of fitting Britain into a future European defense system was viewed as one of the last steps in Britain's changing relationship with Europe.[57] An exception was the position of Edward

[56] See, e.g., Dorothy Pickles, *The Uneasy Entente: French Foreign Policy and Franco-British Misunderstandings* (London: Oxford University Press, 1966), esp. pp. 106-14.

[57] Dorothy Pickles comments that Conservative and all but a small portion of Labor opinion would agree with the following statement by Sir Alec Douglas-Home at the Conservative party conference in October 1965: "The alliance with the United States must . . . have the strongest priority in arrangements for our security. Neither Britain

Heath, the Conservative party leader, who was beginning to urge a reorientation of British defense policy toward Europe and a merger of the British and French nuclear deterrents, although in just what manner was left unclear.[58] There were a few other influential Conservatives with so-called Gaullist views, among them Peter Thorneycroft, Julian Amery, and Duncan Sandys—all former ministers.

One area of Anglo-French security agreement was on the necessity to keep the German Federal Republic a non-nuclear power, though London was willing to support German membership in the Nuclear Planning Group. But British interest in arms control went much further and here again contrasted with French policy. The British government was an ardent supporter of the Test Ban Treaty and played an active part in negotiating the Non-Proliferation Treaty. London retained a keen interest in opposing nuclear proliferation and in seeking other kinds of East–West arms control arrangements.

Beginning about 1967, the British undertook a major reassessment of their global military commitments which led to a retrenchment and to a new emphasis on Britain's future role in Europe. This development, which tended to synchronize defense policy with Britain's desire to enter the European Community, brought her security perspectives much more closely into line with those of France. The trend started alongside London's unsuccessful 1967 Common Market application.[59]

---

nor any other country in Europe, or even Europe combined, could command absolute security unless the Western Alliance was Atlantic in scope" (p. 111).

[58] See, e.g., Heath's statement to the 1966 Vienna conference of the Institute for Strategic Studies, reprinted in "Western and Eastern Europe: The Changing Relationship," *Adelphi Papers*, no. 33 (March 1967), pp. 30-35; also Heath's statement before the House of Commons, as reported in the *New York Times*, May 10, 1967.

[59] The following discussion is based largely on L. W. Martin, "British Defence Policy: The Long Recessional," *Adelphi Papers*, no. 61 (November 1969); and Pierre, "Britain's Defense Dilemmas." See also Walter Goldstein, "British Strategy and NATO: Prospects for the

The main catalyst for the reduction in Britain's foreign defense commitments was the need to reduce defense expenditure abroad in order to avert recurring balance-of-payments crises, which were threatening the country's monetary health. Despite a sense that U.K. armed forces were overextended and underequipped, it took a while after the Labor party came to power in 1964 for hard decisions to emerge. The first visible sign was the 1966 Defence White Paper which announced the evacuation of the Aden base and highlighted the overextension of British forces. This led to a drastic curtailment of future weapons systems and a decision not to purchase a new aircraft carrier.

By 1967, a firm withdrawal from overseas bases had been set in motion. The end of Indonesia's confrontation with Malaysia weakened the rationale for forces East of Suez. The left wing of the Labor party had become increasingly dissatisfied with the government's posture in the Far East because it appeared to support the American position in Vietnam. The financial outlays required to support a presence there could, it was felt, be better directed toward social services. These factors, coupled with worsening economic conditions, resulted in the July 1967 announcement that British forces in Malaysia, Singapore, and the Persian Gulf would be reduced by half in 1971, and that all fixed bases East of Suez would be abandoned by the middle of the 1970's. Only a naval and air presence was to be retained in the area after 1975. The devaluation of sterling in November 1967 accelerated the timetable for evacuation. In January 1968 it was decided to give up all British bases and the traditional East of Suez role by the end of 1971.

The speed of this announced timetable for the phasing-out of East of Suez responsibilities was rather breathtaking, especially when one recalls that, in financial terms, Asia was the largest area of Britain's overseas military commitments

---

Seventies," in *NATO in the Seventies*, ed. Edwin H. Fedder (St. Louis: Center of International Studies, University of Missouri, 1970), pp. 89-113.

in 1966. As the 1968 White Paper declared, British defense efforts would henceforth be centered mainly in Europe and the Atlantic area. In 1969 Defense Minister Healey affirmed that the defense decisions of the last years "set the seal on the transformation of Britain from a world power into a European power."[60]

This drastic adjustment of Britain's global role and declaration of intent to concentrate her future efforts on Europe was reinforced by British initiatives within NATO. First, unlike most members of the alliance, the British began to increase their contribution to European defense, a move made possible by withdrawal of troops from East of Suez. London decided to deploy a third squadron of VTOL Harrier Strike aircraft in Germany. An additional parachute brigade was committed to NATO, and a 20,000-man strategic reserve force stationed at home was earmarked for NATO use in case of a crisis in Central Europe or on the flanks of the Alliance. The British contribution to defense in the Mediterranean was likewise stepped up with the assignment of new naval, marine, and air surveillance forces to help counterbalance the increased Soviet presence in that area.[61]

Secondly, Britain took the lead in urging the creation of a European caucus in NATO—perhaps in part to underscore London's "European commitment." Concern over possible reductions in American forces in Europe was also a factor, as was the U.K. belief that Europeans should present a collective viewpoint to the United States on issues related to the Soviet-American talks on strategic arms limitation and other questions. Moreover, a sincere British interest in a rationalization of European arms procurement was developing, as discussed below. Finally, it is interesting to note

[60] Press conference on the 1969 Defence White Paper, *British Record*, no. 3, February 21, 1969.

[61] See Healey's speech on European defense, Munich, February 1, 1969, reprinted in *Survival* (April 1969), pp. 110-19; also Healey's "Britain's Role in NATO," in *NATO Letter* (January 1969), pp. 26-28.

Defense Minister Healey's suggestion in 1969 that a reconciliation between Western and Eastern Europe would be facilitated as Western Europe became less dependent on the United States for its security.[62] Frequently espoused by General de Gaulle, this concept is also shared by his successors.

A further sign of Britain's new interest in European defense was the lead taken by London, along with the Federal German government, to develop within the Nuclear Planning Group contingency plans for the initial use of NATO tactical nuclear weapons.[63] Although France has not participated in this activity and obviously disagrees with Britain in her stance toward NATO, in reality British (and German) views on tactical nuclear strategy may turn out not to be very different from the French strategic doctrine of General Michel Fourquet, described in an earlier chapter.

An economic factor also tends to support British interest in European defense: the need for defense-related industries in the United Kingdom to find larger markets if they are to continue operating on anywhere near their present scale. Pressure from the aircraft industry, for example, has already led Britain to become involved in several bilateral and multilateral programs. A number of these—the Concorde supersonic airliner, the Jaguar trainer, and various helicopter projects—have linked Britain and France. Others, like the air bus and the proposed European multirole combat aircraft (MRCA), involve Britain with other countries, especially Germany. Rising costs and the complexity of new aircraft and associated technologies, together with the difficulty encountered by the British government (among others) in placing enough orders to keep its aerospace industry occupied and efficient have prompted this international collaboration. The report of the Plowden Committee, issued in 1966, concluded that an independent

[62] See Healey's 1969 Munich speech.

[63] See e.g., "When the Nukes Have to Go," the *Economist*, June 7, 1969, pp. 15-16.

British aircraft industry had no future and recommended far greater collaboration with Europe, especially with France. Since the British and French aircraft industries are the largest in Europe and are complementary in several respects, joint projects are a natural development. There is also a growing desire to protect and expand European technology in the face of strong American aerospace competition.[64]

In other areas of technology as well, such as computers and civilian nuclear energy, Britain can make a strong contribution to Europe and stands to gain from better access to European customers. Britain has a larger industrial research-and-development base and continues to spend more money on this than any continental power. The dynamics of advanced, large-scale technology seem, therefore, in addition to other forces, to be drawing Britain toward Europe. A logical extension of expanding technological linkages with Europe may well prove to be some kind of military nuclear cooperation.

There are several factors at work which may lead to some kind of future Anglo-French nuclear cooperation.[65] First, the British government will soon face difficult and costly decisions concerning the modernization of the U.K. nuclear deterrent. U.S.–U.K. nuclear agreements will begin to terminate in 1974, and research and development decisions for weaponry in the 1980's will have to be made. Aside from its aging V bombers, the mainstay of the British nuclear force is four Polaris submarines, all of which were opera-

[64] See Christopher Layton, *European Advanced Technology* (London: George Allen and Unwin, 1969), esp. chs. 3 and 9; John Calmann, *European Cooperation in Defence Technology: The Political Aspect* (London: Institute for Strategic Studies, 1967).

[65] See, e.g., Andrew J. Pierre, "Nuclear Diplomacy: Britain, France, and America," *Foreign Affairs* (January 1971), pp. 283-301; also Ian Smart, "Future Conditional: The Prospect for Anglo-French Nuclear Cooperation," Adelphi Papers, no. 78 (London: Institute for Strategic Studies, 1971), which only became available while this book was in press.

tional by 1971. The Polaris A-3 missiles, purchased from the United States as a result of the Nassau agreement, are outfitted with multiple reentry vehicles (MRVs) which —in contrast with the American MIRVs—are not independently targeted. The range of these missiles is 2,500 nautical miles. It is unlikely that Britain will decide to abandon her nuclear effort in the years immediately ahead, since that would mean leaving France as the only European nuclear power. But, given the long lead time necessary for nuclear programs, plans must soon be made regarding the addition of other submarines to the British arsenal and the improvement of missile systems, if the deterrent is to retain its credibility in an age of accelerating weapons technology.

Steps already taken by the United States and the Soviet Union to begin deployment of ABM systems, which will severely challenge the credibility of small European nuclear forces, increase the urgency of this question. If SALT fails to produce an agreement limiting these systems and the superpowers proceed to install medium-to-heavy ABM defenses, this will greatly undermine the effectiveness of the British and French deterrents unless their size is expanded and their warheads and penetration aids improved. The latter is a costly prospect. Yet good reasons may exist for moving in this direction. For in an ABM and MIRV age, neither superpower could be assured of invulnerable strategic systems. This could produce strong pressures for U.S.-Soviet accommodation at the expense of Europe.

Once again the possibility of nuclear cooperation lurks in the background of British entry into the European Community. Leaders in London are aware that the nuclear deterrent has important political implications if Britain joins Europe. In order to demonstrate that she has come to think in "European" terms, Britain may ultimately propose participation in a new scheme for European defense, which would include British and French nuclear forces. The

French might also be interested in some kind of nuclear cooperation with England.

There is some complementarity in the French and British nuclear programs so that each could benefit from the other's more advanced technology in certain areas. Britain is ahead in nuclear submarine technology, warhead design, and the techniques of producing thermonuclear weapons. The British are also exploring the production of enriched uranium from gas centrifuge reactors. France, on the other hand, has more experience in the field of solid fuel propulsion and missile development, since the British have had no missile program following the 1960 cancellation of Blue Streak. If one considers all areas of nuclear and related technology, Britain has a lead on France and would stand to gain less from cooperation. France presently has a more balanced program, however, and the British have considerable respect for the progress made by the French in recent years. There is therefore a basis for certain kinds of cooperation.

Faced, therefore, with both economic and political constraints, British leaders may decide not to seek renewed nuclear assistance from the United States—which might not be forthcoming anyway. Instead, they may wish to explore possible cooperation with France, though U.S. concurrence would probably be necessary for certain kinds of cooperation because of previous Anglo-American nuclear accords.

Anglo-French nuclear cooperation could, of course, take several forms. At least four types of cooperation might be envisaged: (1) technical assistance by one or both to the national weapons systems of the other; (2) joint development of new, more advanced weapons systems for individual national use; (3) common or coordinated planning of the two national forces; and (4) an actual integrated European deterrent. Then there is the additional question whether cooperation would be inside or outside the NATO framework.

As already noted, mutual technical assistance to existing

French and British nuclear forces is quite conceivable. Limited forms of such cooperation on a bilateral basis might not necessarily be inconsistent with present French and British policies toward NATO. However, the question could easily be complicated by the need for U.S. concurrence in British sharing of technology of American origin, which would make the matter a tripartite and not simply a bilateral affair.

Joint development of advanced weapons systems, such as MIRVs, might be possible. It would be based on a determination to maximize the two countries' financial and technical resources in order to expand presently existing or planned national forces. At best, however, this would be an expensive proposition. The outcome of SALT could be a major determining factor for such cooperation, because if SALT fails to produce an accord on ABMs, the British and French may need to MIRV their forces to maintain nuclear credibility. Even if they decided to cooperate to modernize their deterrents, the continuing superpower arms race would make it a difficult task for them to keep up with advancing superpower weapons technology. If SALT does yield a Soviet-American agreement limiting ABMs and other weapons systems, this would simplify the task of prolonging British and French nuclear credibility.

Coordinated planning on the use of British and French nuclear forces in wartime might be the easiest form of cooperation to arrange. The word "coordination" could imply anything from combined military staff talks about European defense to actual joint targeting—though the fact that British nuclear forces are committed to NATO would complicate any meaningful coordination on targeting, given France's unwillingness to rejoin the Alliance's military organization. But some kind of liaison with SACEUR on an informal basis might be conceivable to get around this problem. If a coordinated Anglo-French deterrent were formed, with control over each component remaining in national hands, it might even be accompanied by an associated consultative committee for non-nuclear European countries, though this would require a considerable evolution in French thinking and in NATO.

A joint nuclear force would be the most difficult to accomplish, since it would imply either an Anglo-French or a European federal government with a single authority competent to decide on its use. Moreover, such a force would raise in boldest form the delicate political issue of German participation. Either variant of such a joint European deterrent would require a substantial surrender of sovereignty by Britain and France. Given the slow pace of European integration, an integrated European nuclear force is not a likely development in the foreseeable future.

The trends in British defense policy and in technology discussed above are tentative and can be reversed by future political decisions. One of them, Britain's retrenchment from global defense commitments, has at minimum already been slowed by the decision of Prime Minister Edward Heath, following his election in June 1970, to retain some forces East of Suez.[66] However, the Conservative government has also assigned first priority to Britain's European defense role, as evidenced by an increased British contribution to NATO forces. It remains to be seen whether the 1970 Tory decision on forces East of Suez will represent a true reversal of Labor's policy, or merely a hopeless last ditch attempt to postpone Britain's retreat from world power. At this writing, Britain seems inexorably drawn toward her European destiny and prepared to play a much greater role in European deterrence and defense than she has in the past. Admission to the European Community could be expected to accelerate this tendency.

Among the many imponderables connected with Britain's European future is the question whether London will readjust her foreign policy and security perspectives in the 1970's and undertake a diplomacy independent of the

[66] See the 1971 Defense White Paper.

United States. Will England become a revisionist power, like France and Germany, with a stake in détente as a step toward changing the *status quo* in Europe? So far, the British have had no firm position on European security and political reconciliation comparable to the Gaullist vision of a Europe of states "from the Atlantic to the Urals" or West Germany's Ostpolitik. London has preferred instead summit diplomacy among the major powers, arms-control and disarmament measures, and an Atlantic conception of European security. It may be a while before the British abandon the diplomatic role of a great power on a global scale. Although trends previously described could bring about a major recasting of U.K. foreign policy priorities, it will take some time before British and French security perspectives are more closely synchronized.

9 • *Conclusion and Prospects*

In his last memoirs, de Gaulle clearly revealed what his objectives were for France when he returned to power in 1958. A West European confederation was among his primary goals. Beyond that, he explained his other aims as follows:

> My design consisted . . . in disengaging France, not from the Atlantic Alliance, which I intended to maintain as an ultimate precaution, but from the integration realized by NATO under American command; in forging with each of the states of the Eastern bloc, and first with Russia, relations aimed at détente, then at entente and cooperation; in doing the same, at the appropriate time, with China; finally, in providing us with nuclear power of such force that nobody could attack us without risking terrible wounds.

While confirming that his mind was set on leaving NATO from the moment of his resumption of office, the general also disclosed that he never expected the United States and Great Britain to accept his tripartite proposal.[1] Thus, his famous 1958 Memorandum appears to have been essentially a tactical device which allowed de Gaulle to proceed along his predetermined course of gradual disengagement from the Atlantic defense system.

De Gaulle also illuminated his 1958 conversation with Dulles. According to the general's account, he told Dulles:

> There is no France of worth, notably in the eyes of Frenchmen, without worldwide responsibility. That is why she does not approve of NATO, which does not

[1] Charles de Gaulle, *Memoirs d'Espoir: Le Renouveau, 1958-1962* (Paris: Plon, 1970), p. 214-15.

> allow France her proper role in decisions and which is limited to Europe. That is also why she is going to provide herself with an atomic armament. By that means, our defense and foreign policy will be able to be independent, on which we insist above all.[2]

In one sense, de Gaulle accepted and carried forward the atomic decisions of previous French governments to their logical conclusion. When he regained power, he inherited an extensive nuclear development program begun under the Fourth Republic. Although no high-level decision was made to prepare for the testing of an atomic bomb until April 1958, de Gaulle quickly took steps to reaffirm Premier Gaillard's decision setting the target date for the first atomic tests in the spring of 1960, and he quickened the pace of the atomic program to meet that goal. Following the first successful explosions, the general successfully exploited his strong presidential powers to force a reluctant National Assembly to pass the first military program law authorizing the initial construction phase of the French nuclear deterrent.

There is a sharp distinction, though, between the Gaullist nuclear force which subsequently developed and the more modest atomic intentions of leaders of the Fourth Republic. The *force de frappe ou de dissuasion* became a highly political instrument in support of the general's independent foreign policies. This discontinuity of nuclear motivation has been a central argument of this study.

The incentives for atomic weapons under the Fourth Republic were both political and military. France's declining influence in NATO and the frustrations caused by the loss of colonial territories provided political and diplomatic motivations. After the defeats in Indochina in 1954 and at Suez in 1956, numerous politicians, officials, and military officers saw nuclear weapons as the key to restoring

[2] Ibid., p. 221. The next sentence is: "If you agree to sell us bombs, we will gladly buy them from you, provided that they belong entirely to us and without restrictions."

France's prestige and international political respect. The need to counterbalance the political effects of German rearmament in NATO and a growing special relationship between the United States and Great Britain, especially in nuclear matters, also motivated those who advocated a French nuclear armament.

Military and strategic factors, while slightly less important in the minds of politicians, were nevertheless present and were particularly significant for the military officers who provided leadership in many parts of the atomic research program. They desired the most modern weapons for the French army, so as to restore its morale. They also wished to offset the military effects of German rearmament and to become less dependent on American military protection. Toward the end of the Fourth Republic, Moscow's acquisition of long-range strategic missiles marked a sudden change in the U.S.–Soviet strategic relationship by demonstrating the increased vulnerability of American territory to possible Soviet atomic attack. This important factor reduced the credibility of the American commitment to defend Europe and increased the strength of French arguments for diminishing their country's reliance on the American nuclear guarantee. Great Britain's decision to rely on a national nuclear deterrent, as announced in the 1957 White Paper, also had the effect of stimulating the French military atomic effort. Toward the end of the Fourth Republic a small group of military officers began to consider how the atomic bombs under development would eventually be deployed, and the notion of a deterrent force, or *force de frappe*, began to evolve.

Thus, the idea of a French nuclear force also antedated General de Gaulle. The key difference is that the *force de frappe* envisaged under the Fourth Republic was intended to be used to bolster France's security and political position *within* the Western alliance, and not independently of it as General de Gaulle later prescribed. Most military leaders were fully committed to French participation in NATO. Political leaders, such as Premier Gaillard, saw in the nascent nuclear effort a way to achieve closer cooperation with the United States and Britain and thus to enhance France's influence in the Alliance.

For de Gaulle, on the other hand, the nuclear force became primarily a political tool that served his ambitious foreign policy designs for revision of the existing European and Atlantic frameworks. Military and economic-technological considerations were also involved, but they were of lesser importance for the general. As this study has argued, Gaullist nuclear policy was, above all, an integral part of Gaullist foreign policy. The general's key foreign policy aims, partly encapsulated in the quotations opening this chapter, can be summarized in two visions: the first was a multipolar international system to replace the bipolar system and to be achieved by promoting the emergence of an independent European grouping of states—first in Western Europe, later including all of Europe—that would speak with its own voice in world affairs and act as a third world power. At the same time, de Gaulle was determined that France regain the status of an important global power, his second vision, which was to be accomplished through the establishment of her leading role in Europe. French nuclear armament supported these two frequently conflicting visions.

De Gaulle pursued both designs through several phases in his European-Atlantic policies with mixed results. In the first phase, his 1958 proposal for French equality with the Anglo-Saxons in a three-power directorate to coordinate world strategy was rebuffed. However, this was a clever maneuver; and the French president expected this result. Rejection of his demand, which had been based on impending French membership in the nuclear club, and upon the acceptance of which de Gaulle had made France's continued membership in NATO contingent, afforded the general a pretext to reduce France's NATO participation. Having scored this tactical success, he was better able to justify his long-planned withdrawal of France from NATO later in 1966—a move which was necessary to allow France to regain her freedom of action and to pursue his pan-European policy.

In the second phase, however, de Gaulle failed in his efforts to form a loose political union in Western Europe on the model of the Fouchet plan and to rally the Six to an independent European defense conception based on French nuclear armament. Other European states were either more interested in a federal Europe, closely allied with the United States and NATO, or were suspicious of French intentions and possible French domination of such a grouping. The Franco-German treaty of 1963, the general's effort to make a start nevertheless toward constructing Western Europe according to his model, likewise failed to produce close Franco-German cooperation and to loosen Germany's deep-seated political and security ties to the United States. Leaders in Bonn did not rally to Gaullist hints about French nuclear protection. Unimpressed by the strength of the French deterrent in comparison with superior American forces, they feared that, if they followed France's lead, the *force de frappe* would make Germany subordinate to France.

As a diplomatic instrument working within this larger foreign policy construct, the *force de frappe* did have considerable "nuisance value." It allowed de Gaulle, who benefited anyway from the protection of the American nuclear umbrella, to challenge successfully the Anglo-Saxon nuclear monopoly in NATO and, especially, American domination of NATO strategy. Moreover, the general skillfully employed nuclear issues to support his policy of excluding Britain from Europe—first in 1963, later in 1967. In both cases France's independent nuclear capability helped de Gaulle to resist the American design for an Atlantic-oriented Europe under strong American influence. But the nuclear force was not successful as an instrument of pressure to obtain a reform of NATO in order to elevate

France's status in the Alliance or to extend the latter's geographic scope. When France withdrew from NATO in 1966, this tended to diminish rather than increase her influence in Western allied councils: no other country followed the French lead, and France was isolated as NATO regrouped and reorganized as a defense organization of the Fourteen.

After 1965, de Gaulle began the third phase of his policy —his Eastern initiatives. Aimed at détente, entente, and cooperation with the Soviet Union and the East European states, and eventually some kind of pan-European political and security arrangements, this policy was proven premature—if not irrelevant—by the Soviet invasion of Czechoslovakia in 1968. In sending troops into Prague, Moscow showed that it still controlled the destiny of states in its East European orbit and would place strict limits on trends in those countries toward liberalization, national autonomy, and increased contacts with the West.

In his last year in office, the general was compelled to recognize the lack of realism of his foreign policy designs and his nuclear-political aspirations. The 1968 domestic convulsions which shook the foundations of the Gaullist regime were evidence that France suffered from serious internal weaknesses and was not fit for the exalted role of leadership in Europe and the renewed global influence the general had so passionately sought. The economic crisis which followed the May-June events thwarted Gaullist plans for an ambitious extension of the French nuclear weapons program that was to include intercontinental missiles and a *tous azimuts* strategy, the mainstay of Gaullist hopes for a leading French role as a guarantor of a future all-European security system. The whole Gaullist foreign policy structure appeared to be collapsing. The aging president was forced to reduce sharply the pace of French nuclear development to meet competing domestic needs, and to adopt a more modest strategy and strengthen his links with the Western alliance.

The implications of the Gaullist nuclear deterrent and independent nuclear strategy for Western alliance politics have also been examined in this study. Questions of nuclear strategy provoked heated political debates in the Atlantic alliance during the 1960's. Was French nuclear proliferation in itself a major cause of Alliance disarray? Or did all the talk about nuclear differences really derive from more fundamental causes?

A number of analysts have studied the effects of nuclear weapons on alliances and have reached different conclusions. Some have contended that alliances will dissolve under the influence of the atom, since no nation will take the risk of a thermonuclear war to defend an allied state.[3] Others have argued that nuclear weapons should reinforce the solidarity of alliances.[4] This study has suggested that basic differences in foreign policy objectives are more likely causes of exacerbated relations between nuclear allies than simple discord over nuclear strategy, as relationships in the 1960's between France and the United States and France and NATO have demonstrated. In the North Atlantic alliance nuclear weapons have in themselves yielded neither the extremes of fission nor fusion; rather, they have tended primarily to amplify already existing political trends. The

[3] This is the view of General Pierre M. Gallois, who argues that nations will use atomic weapons only to defend their own supreme national interests, i.e., their own territory, and that allies of nuclear superpowers must therefore have their own national nuclear forces. See, e.g., his *Stratégie de l'âge nucléaire* (Paris: Calmann-Lévy, 1960) and "The Raison d'Être of French Defense Policy," *International Affairs* (October 1963), pp. 497-510. In his second book, *Les Paradoxes de la paix* (Paris: Presses du Temps Présent, 1967), Gallois modified his position only slightly; see pp. 184-89, 275.

[4] General André Beaufre reaches this conclusion from his theory of multilateral deterrence. See his *Dissuasion et stratégie* (Paris: Armand Colin, 1964), pp. 103-106. Another theorist, Raymond Aron, simply postulated that in the age of thermonuclear weapons, "alliances will either evolve toward communities or else dissolve altogether; they will certainly not revert to their pre-atomic prototypes." See *The Great Debate: Theories of Nuclear Strategy* (Garden City, N.Y.: Doubleday and Co., 1965), p. 263.

evidence presented here, especially in light of the political role of nuclear weapons in Gaullist foreign policy, supports the conclusion that nuclear arms do not in themselves cause the disintegration or the integration of alliances; instead they tend to play the role of a multiplier of existing integrative or disintegrative forces in alliance relationships. In the Western alliance, as also in the Sino-Soviet alliance, "the nuclear factor has considerably sharpened the problems of independence and solidarity by increasing the leader's claim to centralized control and his distrust of his adventurous allies, and by the claim of the latter to sovereignty and their distrust of their too prudent protector."[5]

De Gaulle returned to power in mid-1958 with a strong distaste for Anglo-American domination in NATO and a desire to pursue an independent French foreign policy toward both the East and the West. Neither of his two goals —revision of Europe's role in world politics and the return of France to the ranks of the great powers—was consistent with American policy. Burdened with global peace-keeping responsibilities, the United States favored the formation of an integrated, Atlantic-oriented Europe closely linked with America, as well as superpower and middle-power arms control. Washington supported integration in NATO, centralized command and control of nuclear weapons, and one common (American) strategy; it could not tolerate independently controlled nuclear forces such as the *force de frappe*.

As we have seen, French and American policies for Western Europe proved irreconcilable and clashed openly at several junctures: first, on de Gaulle's 1958 tripartite proposal, then on President Kennedy's "grand design" for an Atlantic partnership between America and an enlarged Eu-

[5] Pierre Hassner, "The Nation-State in the Nuclear Age," *Survey*, no. 67 (April 1968), p. 6. See also ch. 2 in Hassner's paper, "Les alliances sont-elles dépassées?" (Paris: Centre d'étude des relations internationales, Fondation nationale des sciences politiques, 1966), pp. 21-27, for a related discussion; and Leonard Beaton, *Must the Bomb Spread* (London: Penguin Books, 1966), p. 125.

ropean Community, and then on NATO questions, arms control issues, and approaches to détente. Nuclear disagreements were frequently the subject of Franco-American contention; they tended to amplify underlying political differences as well as to cloud their presence.

The German Federal Republic's basic political divergence with France was her close allegiance to the United States and to NATO. This had been a persistent tenet of postwar German foreign policy because Bonn had always needed American political support—in the early years to recover sovereignty, later in her quest for German reunification—as well as American military assistance to meet her special security needs arising out of an exposed geographic position on the East–West frontier. During Adenauer's tenure, French and German views on the organization of Europe in the political and economic fields contained many points of agreement. But de Gaulle failed to win over the German chancellor on the military implications of his designs for European autonomy under French leadership. Under Erhard, Germany's political conception of Western Europe was even more Atlantic-oriented, and necessarily clashed with the general's European vision, as well as with his insistence on a special French role.

This was the principal explanation of the failure of Gaullist efforts under the Franco-German treaty to use military cooperation and nuclear issues—such as vague promises of French nuclear protection and some kind of German participation in the *force de frappe*—to woo Bonn away from its intimate defense and political ties with Washington. Instead, Germany supported the American MLF plan until its demise, and there was no question of Bonn's following France's lead when the latter withdrew from NATO in 1966. Again, nuclear issues happened to be at the cutting edge of contrasting political-strategic perspectives. They reinforced already existing political divergencies. Although these trends continued under Chancellor Kiesinger, the emergence of the West German Ostpolitik began to bring

French and German policies more closely into phase by the end of the decade.

In Franco-British relations nuclear questions arose primarily as background issues in Britain's two unsuccessful bids to join the Common Market; but they were important as indicators of quite different British and French foreign policy priorities. With political and security commitments to the Commonwealth and the United States still in place, Britain was not ready in the 1960's to readjust her defense policies to support her newly acquired interest in a European role. General de Gaulle was able to make use of Britain's special atomic relationship with America, reaffirmed in the 1962 Nassau agreement, and her failure to suggest an alternative British defense role in Europe (especially a nuclear role), as arguments to support his two vetoes of Britain's application to join the European Communities. Nuclear questions, and especially the opportunity missed by the British government in not making nuclear proposals that might have linked her more closely with France and the Continent, widened the breach that already existed between the two countries because of their dissimilar conceptions of the future orientation of Europe and the role each nation was to play there. Trends set in motion by a major shift in British defense policy and a contraction of her global role in the latter part of the decade, together with technological and other factors, began to narrow the differences between French and British perspectives on European security and may lead to closer defense cooperation across the Channel in the 1970's.

What conclusions can be drawn in retrospect regarding American policy toward the French nuclear deterrent? First, it seems clear that an American offer in the early 1960's to share nuclear secrets and missile technology with France, as President Eisenhower and General Gavin had advocated, would not have altered de Gaulle's basic hostility to NATO. The evidence presented in this study suggests that de Gaulle's attitudes toward NATO and his preoccupation with *national* defense as a fundamental feature of French sovereignty were firmly established in his thinking upon his return to power in 1958. Moreover, French withdrawal from NATO—or a fundamental reshaping of the organization to take account of a largely autonomous West European defense system—was implicit in his design for the organization of Western Europe in the second phase of his European policy. Disengagement from NATO was a prerequisite for the third phase, the pursuit of all-European reconciliation and pan-European political and security structures.

Some American aid to France in nuclear and related fields, on the other hand, would have removed a major irritant in Franco-American relations and reduced the strain on the relationship between France and NATO during the first half of the decade. It might have postponed France's NATO withdrawal. Most important, it would have set the stage for subsequent diplomacy in a much more favorable light. Such an offer of American assistance could have been linked to a proposal for coordinating European nuclear forces within NATO.

In retrospect, the non-proliferation rationale against nuclear sharing, except with the British partner, was overemphasized during the early period of the Kennedy administration. The special nuclear relationship with Britain could have been extended to include the French, once France had demonstrated that she would produce her own nuclear weapons anyway. Given the special relationship with Britain, discrimination against France was hard to defend; discrimination against Germany in the nuclear domain would, however, have been more easily justified.[6] As

[6] This author does not accept the standard argument of some State Department officials during those years that nuclear aid to France would have meant aid to West Germany as well. First, during the 1960-62 period (before the peak of the MLF debate) German interest in national nuclear weapons was minimal (with the possible exception of Strauss's interest in tactical nuclear weapons). This was before the MLF proposal really brought the question to the fore. Further-

noted in one study, the result of American unwillingness to assist France was perhaps a delay in French nuclear and missile development. But "the longer process of domestic substitution has given France a capability and independence she might not otherwise have possessed, particularly with regard to further exports of missile technology."[7] Some nuclear cooperation with France would have enhanced the ability of the United States to influence the future of the French nuclear program; and access to American technology could have reduced the chances of French nuclear accidents.

Although hindsight prescription is admittedly uncertain and difficult, it is possible that some American aid to the French nuclear program, coupled with a proposal that Britain and France share nuclear technologies and coordinate their nuclear forces in a European defense system, might still have reoriented French policy during 1961-62. Such a policy might have helped Britain into the European Common Market. Coming before the first units of the French nuclear force were in being, it might have attracted General de Gaulle (who was a pragmatist in foreign affairs) to place his *force de frappe* in a coordinated European multinational structure, which could then have cooperated with the American nuclear force but would not have been subject to the veto of the American president.[8] The greatest

---

more, the Federal Republic was prohibited by its 1954 declaration from producing nuclear weapons on her own soil, and it had no real political interest in trying to procure the weapons elsewhere.

[7] Judith H. Young, "The French Strategic Missile Programme," *Adelphi Papers*, no. 38 (London: Institute for Strategic Studies, 1967), p. 8.

[8] Another alternative would have been to propose a NATO nuclear authority not dependent on the American veto, such as General Norstad had advocated. As outlined in a speech before the Academy of Political Science in 1963, Norstad favored a NATO nuclear executive of the three nuclear powers (the United States, Britain, and France), with which other allies could be associated. Decisions on use of the nuclear weapons would be taken by a majority vote of the executive, but dissenting nations could opt out and withhold use of their own weapons. See General Lauris Norstad, "NATO, Its Prob-

opportunity for American diplomacy to reorient France's nuclear policy arose, however, during the period 1956-58, when the United States could have supported France's interest in a European isotope separation plant, instead of opposing it. French participation in such a project then would have placed the French nuclear program in the context of a European Community effort. This might have headed off the purely national effort which later developed, especially if a leader less nationalistic than General de Gaulle had taken the reins of power in 1958.

After Nassau and de Gaulle's January 1963 press conference, it is doubtful whether any serious dialogue, let alone an agreement, could have been achieved with France on nuclear questions. Development of the first-generation weapons for the French nuclear force was too far along, and the perception gap in Franco-American relations resulting from conflicting foreign policy "grand designs" and diplomatic styles had become too acute, as well as publicly visible.

On the level of tactics, the record of American diplomacy toward France on nuclear and related issues has been weak, and has intensified already existing differences. This was true first in the case of de Gaulle's 1958 tripartite proposal. Although the American government could not have accepted de Gaulle's demands for a tripartite structure to shape world (including NATO) strategy without seriously discriminating against other NATO allies, it should have made its response clearer; the door was left open for subsequent misunderstandings. American policy was also inconsistent. After approving the sale of enriched uranium to France in 1959 for a prototype submarine reactor and of twelve KC-135 tanker planes in 1962 to refuel French Mirage IV bombers, Washington refused to license any further assistance in the fields of nuclear and missile technology. A nuclear submarine offered to France by the Ameri-

lems and Its Continuing Promise," *Proceedings of the Academy of Political Science*, xxvi (May 1963), pp. 102-14.

can government in 1958 and again in 1962 was never delivered, primarily because of objections from the Joint Committee on Atomic Energy, which had not been consulted in advance.

American diplomacy has also been hortatory. It should have been clear that public castigation of the *force de frappe* by American officials in 1962 would not have had the slightest positive effect on the attitude of General de Gaulle. Then there was the clumsy handling of the Nassau pact, a bilateral Anglo-American nuclear agreement on a subject of multilateral interest in the Alliance. When a similar arrangement was later offered to General de Gaulle, it was done in public and on technical terms which were at best unattractive. The subsequent American campaign to obtain allied acceptance of the MLF in 1963-64 was cast in a very anti-French light.

If we are to learn from the past, future American policymakers should accept France for the nuclear power she is today and consider what might be done to utilize French nuclear strength more effectively within the framework of overall Western deterrence. Coordination of France's strategic nuclear force and her impending tactical atomic weapons with the forces of her allies should be encouraged. This might be done through *ad hoc* bilateral agreements with NATO, leading perhaps to some kind of associated NATO status; or within a West European defense grouping which could become part of a restructured NATO. Some kinds of assistance to ongoing French nuclear programs might also be possible, and desirable, without contravening our legal obligations under the Limited Test Ban and Non-Proliferation treaties. There are signs that the Nixon administration is considering some of these new approaches to dealing with France as a nuclear power.

Although largely unsuccessful as an instrument of his grand political designs, de Gaulle's nuclear policy was not a complete failure in terms of French and European interests. Some weight must be given to the general's contention that "vast enterprises" are necessary to unite the French nation. Although causing initial dissension, the *force de frappe*—when it was later accepted—may have helped to hold the French army and the French people together psychologically in the difficult period following the Algerian crisis by giving them a sense that France could still be a great and respected nation. Moreover, the French nuclear weapons program has had some side benefits in assisting the modernization of French science and technology, although not as many as Gaullists have claimed. The costs have been high, but not exorbitant. But they will be higher in the future if France attempts to keep abreast of new developments in nuclear weapons technology and acquire enormously expensive multiple warhead missiles or ABM systems.

The strongest case that can be made in favor of Gaullist nuclear policy hinges on several long-term considerations. First, there is an intangible prestige associated with membership in the nuclear club. Nuclear weapons can enhance a nation's political influence, even that of a medium-sized power such as France, especially if it cooperates with other nations instead of operating in isolation as de Gaulle tended to do. A nuclear capability can increase France's influence and freedom of action in world affairs if she adopts foreign policy objectives more in tune with French means than de Gaulle's overextended international designs and chooses to coordinate her strategy with other Western allies, either through a rapprochement with NATO or on a bilateral or European basis. In such a case, nuclear weapons would give France a stronger voice in Western councils, at future East-West conferences on arms control in Europe, and in an eventual European settlement.

Secondly, nuclear weapons do give France, the only continental nuclear power, both a military and a political advantage over West Germany. Militarily, they provide some insurance against the possibility, however remote, of a resurgent and nationalistic Germany in the distant future. Politically, they could help counterbalance superior German economic strength in the process of Europe's future construction. A nuclear capability assures France of a front-rank position in any future discussions on the organization of West European defense. If European integration should accelerate and progress to the stage of a political union with defense responsibilities, France will have the basis for a leading role.

Thirdly, Europeans may conclude that there is a role for small but credible European nuclear forces in safeguarding future European security. Recent increases both in nuclear strength of the superpowers and their mutual vulnerability to each other's strategic forces might encourage them to seek tacit agreement on rules of engagement for a European conflict that would preserve them from a nuclear exchange, but might prove disastrous to West Europeans. European nuclear forces coordinated in some fashion with American forces could set limits to such strategies, since they would present a risk of triggering the American atomic arsenal. In the absence of strategic arms limitation agreements, superpower ABM deployments may reinforce these arguments, since they could weaken the American nuclear guarantee in Europe. Further, European nuclear forces do strengthen Western Europe's defense for a contingent future that might one day include the withdrawal of American troops from the Continent.

Finally, and perhaps most importantly, by supporting de Gaulle's efforts to defy America's "grand design" for an Atlantic-oriented Europe in close partnership with the United States, the *force de frappe* may have strengthened the chances of Western Europe's interesting the Soviets in the process of all-European reconciliation at some future time. It is difficult to see why the Soviets should ever withdraw their troops from the Eastern half of Europe if the Western half remains dominated by American policy and

American strategy. Although a definitive judgment is impossible at this time, small European nuclear forces placed at the service of some kind of independent West European defense system or community might play an important role in European reconciliation and the quest for an eventual system of pan-European security. Such a deterrent could also provide a bargaining counter for future negotiations on arms limitation in Europe that might include Soviet MRBMs and possibly lead to a new European strategic balance stabilized at a lower level.[9]

What of French nuclear policy under Pompidou? The early actions of his regime seem to bear out the lack of realism of Gaullist nuclear-political aspirations, at least in their most ambitious form. Any thoughts of French intercontinental ballistic missiles and a *tous azimuts* strategy, once contemplated by de Gaulle, have been discarded. Under President Pompidou the development of the French nuclear force is being continued, but on a more modest scale than once envisioned by the general, a scale compatible with French resources. However, as noted earlier, de Gaulle himself was forced to acknowledge in his last year of office that his bold designs for French *grandeur* and revision of the European system, based in large part on an augmented French nuclear capability, were overextended and unrealistic. Thus, in a sense, Pompidou's carefully measured stance toward the nuclear program followed on the general's own decisions for retrenchment in 1968-69.

Signs of more fundamental change may be seen, however, in the unfolding post–de Gaulle pattern of French foreign policy and the less prominent political role assigned to French nuclear weapons. The Pompidou government is adopting a less ambitious set of goals in its European and

[9] See, e.g., Pierre Hassner's discussion in his *Change and Security in Europe*, Part II, *Adelphi Papers*, no. 49 (London: Institute for Strategic Studies, 1968), pp. 31-35.

global policies, more consistent with France's capabilities. It is also demonstrating a willingness to enter into certain new kinds of international cooperation.

These changes have proceeded in part because Pompidou does not enjoy de Gaulle's immense personal prestige and respect, in part because France is a country with serious domestic problems, which caused even de Gaulle to adopt more modest foreign objectives before his retirement. But it also derives from the much different temperament and personal style of M. Pompidou, an intellectual and a technocrat turned politician, a man used to the procedure of pragmatic negotiation.

A few days after the formation of the new government in the summer of 1969, Premier Jacques Chaban-Delmas declared in a radio interview that French nuclear policy was both *irréversible et orientable*. Continuity was emphasized by the appointment of Gaullist leader Michel Debré as minister of defense. The term *orientable* implied two things: first, that the French nuclear effort would be cut back in view of pressing domestic economic and social needs, and great care would be taken to avoid unnecessary expenditures; second, that France might be interested in cooperation with Britain in the nuclear field. On the latter point, the premier said that if Britain entered the Common Market, a nuclear accord might be reached "which would seriously modify the conditions of the [French] national effort, which would cease to be national in order to become European."[10] The British Labor government responded negatively to this French overture. However, the subject could be reopened by the Tory government, given Prime Minister Edward Heath's longstanding interest in the idea.[11]

[10] As quoted in *Le Monde*, June 29-30, 1969.

[11] See Edward M. Heath's 1967 Godkin Lectures at Harvard, published as *Europe and the Atlantic Alliance* (Cambridge: Harvard University Press, 1970), in which he advocated a pooling of British and French nuclear forces to form a joint deterrent, to be "held in trust" for a federated Europe. The revised introduction, reaffirming Heath's interest in his earlier proposal, was printed in *The Times* (London),

The French have remained vaguely interested in possible nuclear cooperation with the United Kingdom, but are in no hurry to undertake specific discussions. As noted in the preceding chapter, such cooperation—should it develop—could take a number of forms below the level of an integrated deterrent. The latter remains an unlikely prospect for the foreseeable future. President Pompidou has made clear that France will not rejoin NATO, and this places strict limits on the possibilities for nuclear collaboration.[12] Nevertheless, the Heath government might be willing to explore certain kinds of cooperation outside the NATO framework, or possibly associated with it in some fashion. British admission to the European Community would seem a necessary prerequisite for any such development.

The tightening of budgetary constraints on the French nuclear program, begun in 1968 under de Gaulle, was carried further in President Pompidou's first military budget adopted by the National Assembly in the fall of 1969. Representing only 3.44 percent of GNP and 17.6 percent of the

---

July 14, 1970. See also the paper by Eldon Griffiths and Michael Niblock, "Anglo-French Nuclear Deterrent?" written for the Conservative party and reprinted in the *Atlantic Community Quarterly*, VIII (Summer 1970), pp. 196-209.

[12] Asked in a press conference on July 2, 1970, for his views on possible Anglo-French nuclear collaboration, President Pompidou replied: "It all depends on the manner this is done. That there may be agreements on nuclear matters between France and Britain, that is, indeed, possible. It is probably even desirable, but there are limits beyond which one must not hope to get us to go by tendering this bait; in particular we will not be made to re-enter NATO." (See Document no. 1413, New York: Ambassade de France, Service de presse et d'information.) The question was raised in general terms later the same month by British Foreign Minister Sir Alec Douglas-Home during talks in Paris. Maurice Schumann, his French counterpart, reportedly called nuclear cooperation a long-term problem "which one day would merit an in-depth discussion" (*Le Monde*, July 17, 1970). Of interest also is an article by General Pierre Gallois, "Faut-il créer une force atomique franco-britannique?" *Preuves*, no. 1 (1970), pp. 62-69. He concludes that Anglo-French nuclear cooperation is possible on the level of technical assistance for the development of new weapons. General Beaufre, on the other hand, now advocates strategic coordination of British and French forces.

total national budget, the planned 1970 expenditures on military programs (NF27.19 billion) were proportionately the lowest in over a century. Although priority continued to be given to nuclear weapons, it was the 1970 budget which announced a scaling down of missile programs. The previously announced goal of twenty-seven land-based missiles was reduced to eighteen. Nuclear tests were resumed in the summer of 1970, but the launching of the fourth nuclear submarine was postponed. According to Defense Minister Michel Debré, the 1970 budget was an austerity budget unacceptable over the long term. Debré insisted publicly that the strategic nuclear force would be "constantly adapted and modernized."[13]

Future plans for the *force de frappe* are outlined in the third military program law for the period 1971-75. Passed by the National Assembly in the autumn of 1970, this law reflects a determination to continue development of the nuclear force but at a slower pace than de Gaulle, or even his still active disciple, Michel Debré, probably would have liked. The tone was set by a high French defense official who noted that France begins the 1970's without any immediately visible threats to her security. In this context, "compromises appear possible, taking account of the available financial means, between the needs of defense policy and those of the economic and social development appropriate for the country."[14] In proportion to French GNP, the defense budget is scheduled to decline from 3.44 percent in 1970 to approximately 3.0 percent in 1975, a figure never before attained in the history of the French Republic. President Pompidou, who reportedly desires to allocate to defense "all it is due, nothing more, nothing less," has indicated that beginning in 1971 the defense budget will cease

[13] The above information is based on reports in *Le Monde*, November 7, 11, 12, 14, and 19, 1969.

[14] Marceau Long, "Financement de la politique militaire française," *Revue de défense nationale* (April 1970), p. 537. Long is secretary-general for administration in the Ministry of Defense.

to be the largest share of the national budget and will be surpassed by allocations for education.[15]

Out of a projected total of NF93.5 billion (about $17 billion) to be authorized for defense procurement and research and development under the third program law, about one third (NF30.9 billion) will be earmarked for strategic and tactical nuclear systems, according to official figures. This compares with about NF34 billion spent on nuclear programs during the six year period 1965-70.[16] The 1971-75 program budget will underwrite the production of eighteen land-based missiles to be deployed in 1971-72. Tactical nuclear arms—short-range Pluton missiles for the army and small tactical bombs to be carried by the air force's Jaguar aircraft—will be produced and are expected to come into service around 1973. Nuclear tests will be continued to "militarize" thermonuclear warheads for use in both land- and sea-based missiles. By 1975, three nuclear missile-carrying submarines should be operational, of which probably one—or at most two—could be on constant alert patrol. In the latter part of the decade the number of submarines will increase to five, by which time it is also hoped that one-megaton thermonuclear warheads will replace atomic charges in all submarine-based missiles. Within these carefully set limits, the priority given nuclear programs under the third program law will undoubtedly mean further postponement of the modernization of conventional forces, which have already suffered severely during a dec-

[15] *Le Monde*, July 30, 1970.

[16] *Le Monde*, July 31 and August 8, 1970; *Journal officiel*, October 7-9, 1970. Many of the contours of the law of 1971-75 were predetermined by projects already begun in the previous period. In terms of purchasing power, the amount budgeted for nuclear programs under the third program law would appear somewhat less on an annual average than that spent during the six-year period of the second program law. Aside from economy measures, an important reason for the decline in nuclear spending is the fact that the most expensive investment projects have been completed (e.g., construction of Pierrelatte and the Pacific test center). But cost overruns can be expected. And the actual amounts allocated can be changed in the annual defense budgets.

ade of nuclear priorities. This may cause increasing resentment among officers of the career services.[17]

The third program law was drawn up at the Ministry of Defense with the aid of new planning, programming, and budgeting techniques said to have been copied from the American model. Funds will no longer be requested directly for each of the three armed services, but for various mission objectives (*forces nucléaires stratégiques, force de sûreté, force de manœuvre, forces d'action extérieure, forces d'usage général*) and support functions. Under this new rationalized system it is hoped that a more efficient use of resources can be obtained within the strict limits set on future military expenditures.[18]

If current plans are successfully implemented, France's already existing strategic nuclear force of thirty-six Mirage IV bombers (plus additional reserve and trainer aircraft) will be complemented in the mid-1970's by under two dozen rather vulnerable land-based missiles and three missile-carrying submarines. At that point the British force of four nuclear submarines will be somewhat more imposing, in view of its superior Polaris A-3 missiles with multiple thermonuclear warheads and somewhat longer range. By the end of the decade, however, France could increase the number of its nuclear submarines to five and improve their missile warheads and penetration devices. On the face of it, such a nuclear submarine force should be moderately impressive.

Just how impressive it will be depends, of course, on how fast superpower weapons technology develops. The scale of Soviet ABM deployment will be particularly important. This will depend largely on the results of efforts by the superpowers to limit their strategic arsenals: for the greater

[17] In the spring of 1970 the chief of staff of the French navy, Admiral Patou, resigned his post after a dispute with Defense Minister Debré over a cutoff in funding for the modernization of an anti-aircraft cruiser.

[18] See *Le Monde*, April 22, 1969 and January 28, 1970; also the illuminating article by Long, passim, pp. 535-55.

their progress in arms control, the more impressive the growing French strategic force becomes. Thus, the outcome of the US-Soviet strategic arms limitation talks (SALT) will be of great interest to the French, and will determine the relative strength of the French (and the British) nuclear capability for years to come.

In his first year in office, Pompidou consolidated his position within the French political system and assured the continuation of presidential power. He has taken personal charge of policy-making in most areas, with the exception of economic and social affairs, which were designated the domain of Premier Jacques Chaban-Delmas. Although he does not act with de Gaulle's Olympian manner and undoubtedly is much more open to discussion and suggestions from his cabinet ministers, Pompidou is at the center of important governmental decision-making, especially on foreign and security matters, though in both these areas he has had to reckon with the presence in his cabinet of arch-Gaullist Michel Debré.

By his initial actions it would seem that Pompidou has continued to implement Gaullist concepts in some areas of foreign and security policy, while adapting Gaullist policy in others to changing French and world conditions. On the whole, Pompidou's foreign policy so far has been characterized by a contraction of global aspirations and a more modest conception of "national interest." As a result, French nuclear armament can be expected to serve less as a political instrument, no longer buttressing ambitious frameworks for the revision of the European order as it did in de Gaulle's times. Pompidou has concentrated on carving out an active middle-power role for France in two key areas: Europe and the Mediterranean.

The greatest departure from traditional Gaullist ideas is revealed in Pompidou's approach to Europe. De Gaulle's political vision of a Europe of states "from the Atlantic to the Urals" is not a part of the parlance of his successor. Instead of pressing for reconciliation of the two halves of Europe, Pompidou appears to assign first priority to the organization and strengthening of Western Europe so that it can resist the power of the East. His professed goal is a West European confederation, to be formed on a pragmatic, step-by-step basis. After playing a leading role in the Hague summit conference of the Common Market in December 1969, Pompidou reached a compromise with Chancellor Willy Brandt in early 1971 on the basis for launching the first stage of European economic and monetary union, to be achieved by 1980. Pompidou has already sketched how a future confederation might evolve and develop some powers of its own, building on the Council of Ministers. His goal is an independent Western Europe that can find its own place in the world. Like the general, Pompidou is cautious about infringing on the identity and sovereignty of the member states. Unlike his predecessor, Pompidou appears ready to build on the existing Community framework, extending it first in the economic, later in the political and defense fields, rather than circumventing it as de Gaulle tried to do.[19]

The other fundamental change in the attitude of the Pompidou government has been on the issue of enlarging the European Community. France agreed with her partners at the Hague conference to open negotiations with the British government in July 1970. After publicly affirming his support for British entry, the French president reached a wide-ranging understanding with Prime Minister Heath on the future of Europe at their historic meeting in Paris, May 20-21, 1971. This cleared the way for the successful conclusion of the accession negotiations at Luxembourg a month later. Agreeing on the need to develop "distinctively European policies," first in economic matters "and progressively in other fields," the two leaders also reached common views on

[19] See Pompidou's press conference, January 21, 1971 no. 71/9 (New York: Ambassade de France, Service de presse et d'information); also his June 24, 1971, television interview, reprinted in *Le Monde*, June 26, 1971.

the future development and functioning of Community institutions, based on the unanimity rule. Assenting to participation in European economic and monetary union, Britain accepted the principle of the Common Market agricultural policy and gave France assurances on the future role of sterling. Defense and nuclear matters appear not to have been part of the bargain. Cooperation in these areas, it was agreed, would be discussed thoroughly later on. For the time being Pompidou seems to have accepted London's special defense ties with the United States, but Paris probably hopes to interest the British in European defense cooperation when the construction of Europe is further advanced (and when French and British nuclear forces are more equal in strength).[20]

In accepting British entry, the Pompidou government has doubtless recognized the need for U.K. participation in the European Community to help balance rising German power —a factor which de Gaulle came to perceive before retiring from office. France's relations with West Germany have taken on a different character in the post-de Gaulle era. Although regular consultations and exchange visits have proceeded in a cordial atmosphere under the Franco-German treaty, neither country seems intent on the kind of special Franco-German relationship once sought by Adenauer and de Gaulle. The relationship now is more likely to be one of equals, in view of Germany's economic strength and Brandt's willingness to take foreign policy initiatives. Since the European policies of the two countries are now more parallel there is a basis for considerable Franco-German agreement on key issues. New hopes have been expressed for military cooperation between the two countries, as well as cooperation in industrial projects and civilian nuclear technology. Neither Paris nor Bonn is pressing for supranational in-

[20] The quotations are from the joint communiqué issued at the close of the Heath-Pompidou talks, May 21, 1971, *Le Monde,* May 23-24, 1971.

tegration in Western Europe and the French government has in principle declared its support for Brandt's Ostpolitik. However, Brandt has moved so rapidly on this front that tensions could easily develop as each country begins to compete for favored relations in the East. The new self-assertiveness in Bonn, highlighted by Ostpolitik and again by West German determination to float the mark in the spring 1971 currency crisis, has removed any possibility of French domination of a West European grouping, an objective sought by de Gaulle.

In Eastern Europe, President Pompidou has not discarded the Gaullist policy of détente and cooperation aimed at breaking down Europe's cold war division, but he seems to have no illusions about the difficulty of achieving that goal. Moreover, he has no precise blueprint for a pan-European political or security framework, nor for the role France should play in it. Although Bonn has seized much of the initiative in this area, Paris can be expected to persist with its Eastern efforts. It is not yet clear whether Pompidou will differentiate more carefully than his predecessor between relations with Moscow and those with the East European states. The French president's visit to the Soviet Union in the autumn of 1970, which produced a pro-forma French-Soviet consultation agreement but rather limited results, may have been the start of such a policy.

At the Hague conference France pressed for and obtained the assent of her partners to the principle that a Europe of the Six, eventually enlarged, should serve to promote rapprochement among the peoples of the entire European Continent. France has supported the Soviet-proposed European security conference, but only after careful diplomatic preparation and at a time when the East-West climate has evolved to the point where such a conference would promise more than a confirmation of existing blocs.

As for Atlantic relations, it is unlikely that France will rejoin NATO. But her intention to remain a member of the Atlantic alliance has been emphasized. Moreover, Pompidou, in contrast to de Gaulle, has asserted that France wants U.S. troops to remain in Europe.[21] French cooperation with NATO has recently increased in a number of areas. Building on an earlier agreement between General Ailleret and NATO Commander Lemnitzer, contingency planning has been undertaken regarding the employment of the two French divisions stationed in Germany. The French have allowed NATO the continued use of a pipeline and certain communication facilities in France and have granted rights for military overflights of French territory. French military liaison with certain NATO headquarters has increased, and the French participate in the NADGE early-warning system and, in more limited fashion, in NATO air defense planning and some NATO exercises, including naval maneuvers.

Recent statements by French leaders, including Defense Minister Debré, have underscored France's willingness to cooperate with the alliance.[22] It is possible that bilateral cooperation between France and NATO could be stepped up in the coming years without formal reentry into NATO. A clearer agreement might be reached, for example, on use in a crisis of French forces stationed in Germany and on their relationship to NATO forces and strategy. The French are already manifesting some interest in eventual coordination of their tactical nuclear weapons with those of NATO units, as France approaches deployment of the Pluton tactical missile. The French strategy elaborated by General Michel Fourquet (*la replique graduée*) should facilitate such coordination. France might even establish some relationship with the NATO Nuclear Planning Group. There

[21] *New York Times*, February 25, 1970.

[22] In his October 1970 presentation of the third military program law to the French National Assembly, Debré made repeated references to the possibilities of French cooperation with the alliance. Noting that the prevailing détente carries the risk of being "very fragile," Debré said *inter alia*: "Cooperation is a constant preoccupation because, if the circumstances require it, if there is agreement on objectives . . . we are ready to take our responsibilities in the Alliance" (*Journal officiel*, October 7-9, 1970).

are other areas of potential cooperation, including: assured availability of certain areas of French territory for support facilities and air space; assured availability of the petroleum pipeline in time of war; expanded joint maneuvers and assignment of French officers to NATO headquarters; and consultations on nuclear strategy. In a number of fields —such as tactical nuclear strategy and participation in the NATO satellite communication system—it will clearly be in France's interest to increase her cooperation with NATO.

France continues to pursue warmer relations with the United States, a trend begun by de Gaulle. Pompidou's state visit to America in February 1970 underscored this objective. There are several kinds of potential military cooperation with the United States in which the French government has shown signs of interest, ranging from conventional weapons projects all the way to the sale of computers and the sharing of missile and nuclear-related technologies. Another possibility, and one that might easily be managed, is the coordination of the *force de dissuasion* with American nuclear forces. The sharing of American information on missile guidance or nuclear warheads would obviously be a more difficult matter to resolve, given the Test Ban Treaty, the Non-Proliferation Treaty, and past American policy with its bias against France. Much will depend on the evolution of French policies toward NATO and the outcome of SALT. The Nixon administration is trying to improve Franco-American relations and may be sympathetic to cooperation in some of these areas.

In 1969-70 President Pompidou boldly seized the initiative in North Africa and the Mediterranean where he moved swiftly to strengthen France's presence. Through a series of visits by Foreign Minister Maurice Schumann, France revived friendly relations with Algeria and Tunisia and reestablished normal relations with Morocco. Weapons and military equipment may be delivered to these countries. Most spectacular, however, was the announcement that France had agreed to sell 110 Mirage jets to Libya. A smaller number of these planes will also go to Spain and possibly to Greece.

Officially, it was explained that this new thrust in French policy is designed to reinforce France's economic and cultural interests in the states of North Africa, particularly in her former colonies, with a military sphere of influence aimed at preventing further superpower (especially Soviet) penetration in the area. Libya and other countries of this region are important sources of oil for France and other European countries. For both strategic and political reasons the south shore of the Mediterranean is viewed as the vulnerable "underbelly of Europe" which France has taken upon herself to protect.[23] It remains unclear how this French initiative will affect the Arab-Israeli war and the chances for a Middle East settlement, which, France insists, depends on Four-Power accord. Pompidou's Mediterranean policy was dealt a severe blow in the spring of 1971 when nationalization of French oil company assets produced a major crisis in French-Algerian relations.

In sum, the initial policies of the Pompidou government have modified substantially the ambitious independent political role conceived by General de Gaulle for the French nuclear force. If these early signs are verified by later actions, they will accentuate the discontinuity of Gaullist nuclear policy and its role as a mainspring of France's foreign policy. It is likely that the 1970's will see a return to a conception of French nuclear armament based on more modest political aspirations, not unlike those that moved French leaders to develop atomic weapons in the last years of the Fourth Republic. In the period ahead France's nu-

[23] Pompidou's interview with C. L. Sulzberger, *New York Times*, February 15, 1970.

For further discussion, see Edward A. Kolodziej, "French Mediterranean Policy: The Politics of Weakness," *International Affairs* (July 1971), pp. 503-17; and André Fontaine, "Pompidou's Mediterranean Policy," *Interplay* (April 1970), pp. 12-14.

clear arsenal will undoubtedly be maintained and further developed, but with the principal objective of increasing France's status and security in Europe and within the Western alliance, even if France does not choose formally to rejoin the Alliance's military organization.

Bibliography

PUBLIC DOCUMENTS

France. Ambassade de France. *The First Five Years of the Fifth Republic of France, January 1959–January 1964.* New York: Service de presse et d'information, 1964.

France. Ambassade de France. *France and Its Armed Forces.* New York: Service de presse et d'information, 1964.

France. Ambassade de France. *France and the Atom.* New York: Service de presse et d'information, 1962.

France. Ambassade de France. *France's First Atomic Explosion.* New York: Service de presse et d'information, 1960.

France. Ambassade de France. *French Affairs* (series). New York: Service de presse et d'information.

France. Ambassade de France. *Major Addresses, Statements and Press Conferences of General Charles de Gaulle, May 19, 1958–January 31, 1964.* New York: Service de presse et d'information, 1964.

France. Ambassade de France. *Speeches and Press Conferences* (series). New York: Service de presse et d'information.

France. Assemblée Nationale. *Documents.* Paris: Imprimerie de l'Assemblée nationale.

France. *Le Dévelopment nucléaire français depuis 1945.* Notes et études documentaires, no. 3246. Paris: La Documentation française, 1965.

France. *Expériences nucléaires françaises dans le Pacifique.* Paris: La Documentation française, 1966.

France. *Journal officiel.* Débats parlementaires, Assemblée Nationale. Paris: Imprimerie des Journaux officiels.

France. Ministère des affaires étrangères. *Documents officiels.* Paris: Ministère des affaires étrangères.

France. Ministère des armées. *Notes d'information* (monthly series). Paris: Service d'information, d'études et de Cinématographie.

France. Premier Ministre, Commissariat à l'énergie atomique. *Bilan et Perspectives, 1965-1967.* Paris.

France. Premier Ministre, Commissariat à l'énergie atomique. *Pierrelatte: Usine de Séparation des Isotopes de l'Uranium.* Paris, 1964.

France. Premier Ministre, Commissariat à l'énergie atomique. *Rapport Annuel, 1964-1966.* Paris.

France. Sécretariat d'état à l'information. *Le Dossier de l'Alliance Atlantique.* Paris, 1966.

Germany. Bundesregierung. *Bulletin.* Bonn: Presse- und Informationsamt der Bundesregierung.

Germany. Deutsch-Französische Konferenz. *Deutsch-Französische Freundschaft in der Bewahrung*, VIII. Paris, December 4-6, 1964. Bonn: Schriftenreihe des Deutschen Rates der Europäischen Bewegung, Heft 17, 1965.

Great Britain. *Command Papers.* London: HMSO. *Statement on the Defence Estimates, 1965.* Cmnd. 2592. *Statement on the Defence Estimates, 1966.* Part I. *The Defence Review.* Cmnd. 2901. *Statement on the Defence Estimates, 1967.* Cmnd. 3203. *Supplementary Statement on Defence Policy, 1967.* Cmnd. 3357. *Statement on the Defence Estimates, 1968.* Cmnd. 3540. *Statement on the Defence Estimates, 1969.* Cmnd. 3927. *Statement on the Defence Estimates, 1970.* Cmnd. 4290.

Great Britain. *Parliamentary Debates* (5th series) (Commons).

U.S. Congress. House. *Amendment to the Atomic Energy Act of 1954, As Amended. H.R. Report No. 1849 to Accompany H.R. 12716*, 85th Cong., 2nd sess., 1958.

U.S. Congress. House. *Our Changing Partnership with Europe. H.R. Report No. 26*, 90th Cong., 1st sess., 1967. (Appendix, State Department Memorandum on "Results of Recent Bilateral Discussions Between the United States and France.")

U.S. Congress. Joint Committee on Atomic Energy. *Agreements for Cooperation for Mutual Defense Purposes. Hearings* before the Subcommittee on Agreements for Cooperation on the Exchange of Military Information and Material with the United Kingdom, France, Canada, the Netherlands, Turkey, Greece, and the Federal Republic of Germany, 86th Cong., 1st sess., 1959.

U.S. Congress. Joint Committee on Atomic Energy. *Agreement for Cooperation for Mutual Defense Purposes with the Republic of France. Hearings*, on the Proposed Agreement for Cooperation, 87th Cong., 1st sess., 1961.

U.S. Congress. Joint Committee on Atomic Energy. *Agreement for Cooperation with NATO for Mutual Defense Purposes. Hearings*, before the Subcommittee on Agreements for Cooperation, 88th Cong., 2nd sess., 1964.

U.S. Congress. Joint Committee on Atomic Energy. *Amending the Atomic Energy Act of 1954. Hearings*, before the Subcommittee on Agreements for Cooperation on the Exchange of Military Information and Material with Allies, 85th Cong., 2nd sess., 1958.

U.S. Congress. Senate. Committee on Foreign Relations. *Treaty on the Nonproliferation of Nuclear Weapons*. Executive Report No. 9, 90th Cong., 2nd sess., 1968.

U.S. Congress. Senate. Committee on Government Operations. *Atlantic Alliance*. Part 7 (supplement). *Hearings* before the Subcommittee on National Security and International Operations, 89th Cong., 2nd sess., 1966. (Contents include text of letter from President Eisenhower to General de Gaulle of October 20, 1958; "Department of State Statement Recording the Events Surrounding General de Gaulle's 'Directorate' Proposal of 1958 and the U.S. Response to It"; letter from Dwight D. Eisenhower to Senator Henry M. Jackson, May 17, 1966.)

U.S. Congress. Senate. Committee on Government Operations, Subcommittee on National Security and International Operations. *The Atlantic Alliance: Treaty and Related Agreements*. 89th Cong., 2nd sess., 1966.

U.S. Congress. Senate. *Message from the President of the United States Transmitting the Treaty on Non-Proliferation of Nuclear Weapons*. 90th Cong., 2nd sess., 1968.

U.S. *Department of State Bulletin*. Washington, D.C.: U.S. Government Printing Office.

U.S. *Documents on American Foreign Relations* (annual). New York: Harper and Brothers for the Council on Foreign Relations.

U.S. *Public Papers of the Presidents of the United States* (annual). Washington, D.C.: U.S. Government Printing Office.

BOOKS AND PAMPHLETS

Adenauer, Konrad. *Erinnerungen 1955-1959*. Stuttgart: Deutsche Verlags-Anstalt, 1967.

Adenauer, Konrad. *Erinnerungen 1959-1963: Fragmente*. Stuttgart: Deutsche Verlags-Anstalt, 1968.

Ailleret, Charles. *L'Aventure atomique française*. Paris: Grasset, 1968.

Ambler, John Stewart. *Soldiers Against the State*. Garden City, N.Y.: Doubleday and Co., 1968.

L'Année politique. Paris: Presses universitaires de France, annually.

Aron, Raymond. *The Great Debate: Theories of Nuclear Strategy*, translated by Ernst Pawel. Garden City, N.Y.: Doubleday and Co., 1965.

———. *Paix et guerre entre les nations*. Paris: Calmann-Lévy, 1962.

———. *Peace and War: A Theory of International Relations*. Translated by Richard Howard and Annette Baker Fox. Garden City, N.Y.: Doubleday and Co., 1966.

Bader, William B. *The United States and the Spread of Nuclear Weapons*. New York: Pegasus, 1968.

Ball, George W. *The Discipline of Power: Essentials of a Modern World Structure*. Boston: Little, Brown and Co., 1968.

Beaton, Leonard. *Must the Bomb Spread*. London and Baltimore: Penguin Books, 1966.

Beaton, Leonard, and Maddox, John. *The Spread of Nuclear Weapons*. New York: Frederick A. Praeger for the Institute for Strategic Studies, 1962.

Beaufre, André. *Dissuasion et stratégie*. Paris: Armand Colin, 1964.

———. *Introduction à la stratégie*. Paris: Armand Colin, 1963.

———. *L'Otan et l'Europe*. Paris: Calmann-Lévy, 1966.

———. *Stratégie de l'action*. Paris: Armand Colin, 1966.

Beloff, Nora. *The General Says No*. Baltimore: Penguin Books, 1963.

Boskey, Bennett and Willrich, Mason, eds. *Nuclear Proliferation: Prospects for Control*. New York: Dunellen Co., 1970.

Brandt, Willy. *Peace Policy for Europe*. New York: Holt, Rhinehart and Winston, 1969.

Buchan, Alastair, ed. *A World of Nuclear Powers?* Englewood Cliffs, N.J.: Prentice-Hall for the American Assembly, 1966.

———. *The Implications of a European System for Defence*

Technology. Defence, Technology and the Western Alliance, no. 6. London: The Institute for Strategic Studies, 1967.

———. *Europe's Futures, Europe's Choices.* New York: Columbia University Press for The Institute of Strategic Studies, 1969.

———. *NATO in the 1960's.* Rev. ed. New York: Frederick A. Praeger, 1963.

———. *The Multilateral Force: An Historical Perspective.* Adelphi Papers, no. 13. London: The Institute for Strategic Studies, 1964.

Calmann, John. *European Co-operation in Defence Technology: The Political Aspect.* Defense, Technology and the Western Alliance, no. 1. London: The Institute for Strategic Studies, 1967.

Camps, Miriam. *Britain and the European Community, 1955-1963.* Princeton: Princeton University Press, 1964.

———. *European Unification in the Sixties.* New York: McGraw-Hill for the Council on Foreign Relations, 1966.

———. *What Kind of Europe?* London: Oxford University Press for the Royal Institute of International Affairs, 1965.

Cerny, Karl H., and Briefs, Henry W., eds. *NATO in Quest of Cohesion.* New York: Frederick A. Praeger for the Hoover Institution, 1965.

Cleveland, Harlan. *NATO: The Transatlantic Bargain.* New York: Harper and Row, 1970.

Cleveland, Harold van B. *The Atlantic Idea and Its European Rivals.* New York: McGraw-Hill Book Co. for the Council on Foreign Relations, 1966.

Club de Grenelle. *Siècle de Damocles: La Force nucléaire stratégique.* Paris: Éditions Pierre Couderc, 1964.

Club Jean Moulin. *La Force de frappe et le citoyen.* Paris: Editions du Seuil, 1963.

———. *Pour une Politique étrangère de l'Europe.* Paris: Éditions du Seuil, 1966.

Collection Forum. *Pour ou contre la force de frappe.* Paris: Éditions John Didier, 1963.

de Carmoy, Guy. *Les Politiques étrangères de la France, 1944-66.* Paris: La Table Ronde, 1967.

de Gaulle, Charles. *Memoires d'espoir: Le Renouveau, 1958-1962:* Paris: Plon, 1970.

de Gaulle, Charles. *Mémoires de guerre.* I, *L'Appel;* II, *L'Unité;* III, *Le Salut.* Paris: Librairie Plon, 1954, 1956, 1959.
———. *Le Fil de l'épée.* Paris: Éditions Berger-Levrault, 1944. (Paris: Collection Le Monde en 10/18, 1962.)
———. *The Complete War Memoirs of Charles de Gaulle.* New York: Simon and Schuster, 1964.
———. *Vers l'armée de metier.* Paris: Éditions Berger-Levrault, 1934. Paris: Presses Pocket, 1963.
de Lacoste Lareymondie, Marc. *Mirages et realités: l'arme nucléaire française.* Paris: Éditions de la SERPE, 1964.
de la Gorce, Paul-Marie. *De Gaulle entre deux mondes.* Paris: Arthème Fayard, 1964.
———. *La France contre les empires.* Paris: Grasset, 1969.
———. *The French Army.* New York: George Braziller, 1963.
de la Malène, Christian, and Melnik, Constantin. *Attitudes of the French Parliament and Government Toward Atomic Weapons.* Research Memorandum, RM-2170-RC. Santa Monica, Calif.: The RAND Corporation, 1958.
Deney, Nicole. *Bombe atomique française et opinion publique internationale.* Paris: Fondation nationale des sciences politiques, Centre d'étude des relations internationales, 1962.
Deutsch, Karl, et al. *France, Germany and the Western Alliance.* New York: Charles Scribner's Sons, 1967.
Eisenhower, Dwight D. *Waging Peace, 1956-1961.* Garden City, N.Y.: Doubleday and Co., 1965.
Esprit. Special issue on the *force de frappe.* December 1963.
Fox, William T. R., and Fox, Annette Baker. *NATO and the Range of American Choice.* New York: Columbia University Press, 1967.
Freund, Gerald. *Germany Between Two Worlds.* New York: Harcourt, Brace and Co., 1961.
Furniss, Edgar S., Jr. *De Gaulle and the French Army.* New York: The Twentieth Century Fund, 1964.
———. *France: Troubled Ally.* New York: Frederick A. Praeger, 1960.
Gallois, Pierre M. *The Balance of Terror.* Boston: Houghton Mifflin Co., 1961.
———. *Stratégie de l'âge nucléaire.* Paris: Calmann-Lévy, 1960.
———. *Paradoxes de la paix.* Paris: Presses du temps présent, 1967.

Geyelin, Philip. *Lyndon B. Johnson and the World.* New York: Frederick A. Praeger, 1966.

Gilpin, Robert. *France in the Age of the Scientific State.* Princeton: Princeton University Press, 1968.

Goldschmidt, Bertrand. *L'Aventure atomique.* Paris: Arthème Fayard, 1962.

———. *Les Rivalités atomiques.* Paris: Arthème Fayard, 1967.

Grosser, Alfred. *La Politique extérieure de la Ve République.* Paris: Éditions de Seuil, 1965.

———. *La IVe République et sa politique extérieure.* Paris: Armand Colin, 1961.

Hassner, Pierre. *Change and Security in Europe.* Part I: *The Background.* Adelphi Papers, no. 45. London: The Institute for Strategic Studies, 1968.

———. *Change and Security in Europe.* Part II: *In Search of a System.* Adelphi Papers, no. 49. London: The Institute for Strategic Studies, 1968.

———, et al. *Le Grand débat nucléaire.* Special issue of the *Bulletin SEDEIS*, no. 910, February 10, 1965.

Heath, Edward M. *Europe and the Atlantic Alliance.* Cambridge: Harvard University Press, 1970.

Hoffmann, Stanley. *Gulliver's Troubles.* New York: McGraw-Hill for the Council on Foreign Relations, 1968.

———, et al. *In Search of France.* Cambridge: Harvard University Press, 1963.

Hunt, K. *NATO Without France: The Military Implications.* Adelphi Papers, no. 32. London: The Institute for Strategic Studies, 1966.

Institute for Strategic Studies. *The Military Balance.* London (published annually).

———. *Strategic Survey.* London, published annually.

Kaiser, Karl. *German Foreign Policy in Transition.* London: Oxford University Press for the Royal Institute of International Affairs, 1968.

Kaufmann, William W. *The McNamara Strategy.* New York: Harper and Row, 1964.

Kissinger, Henry A. *Nuclear Weapons and Foreign Policy.* New York: Harper and Brothers for the Council on Foreign Relations, 1957.

Kissinger, Henry A. *The Troubled Partnership*. New York: McGraw-Hill for the Council on Foreign Relations, 1965.

Kleiman, Robert. *Atlantic Crisis*. New York: W. W. Norton and Co., 1964.

Kraft, Joseph. *The Grand Design*. New York: Harper and Brothers, 1962.

Kulski, W. W. *De Gaulle and the World*. Syracuse: Syracuse University Press, 1966.

Laloy, Jean. *Entre Guerres et paix, 1945-65*. Paris: Plon, 1966.

Layton, Christopher. *European Advanced Technology*. London: George Allen and Unwin, 1969.

Majonica, Ernst. *Deutsche Aussenpolitik*. Stuttgart: W. Kohlhammer Verlag, 1965.

Martin, L. W. *Ballistic Missile Defence and the Alliance*. Atlantic Papers, no. 1. Paris: The Atlantic Institute, 1969.

———. *British Defence Policy: The Long Recessional*. Adelphi Papers, no. 61. London: The Institute for Strategic Studies, 1969.

Mendl, Wolf. *Deterrence and Persuasion: French Nuclear Armament in the Context of National Policy, 1945-1969*. New York: Praeger, 1970.

McGeehan, Robert. *The German Rearmament Question: American Diplomacy and European Security after World War II*. Chicago: University of Illinois Press, 1971.

Moch, Jules. *Non à la force de frappe*. Paris: Robert Laffont, 1963.

Müller, Hans Dieter, ed. *Die Force de Frappe: Europas Hoffnung oder Verhängnis?* Olten and Freiburg im Breisgau: Walter Verlag, 1965.

NATO Information Service. *NATO: Facts About the North Atlantic Treaty Organization*. Paris, 1965.

Neustadt, Richard. *Alliance Politics*. New York: Columbia University Press, 1970.

Newhouse, John. *Collision in Brussels: The Common Market Crisis of June 30, 1965*. New York: W. W. Norton, 1967.

———. *De Gaulle and the Anglo-Saxons*. New York: Viking, 1970.

Nieburg, Harold L. *Nuclear Secrecy and Foreign Policy*. Washington, D.C.: Public Affairs Press, 1964.

Osgood, Robert E. *Alliances and American Foreign Policy*. Baltimore: The Johns Hopkins Press, 1968.

———. *NATO, The Entangling Alliance*. Chicago: University of Chicago Press, 1962.

Passeron, André. *De Gaulle parle*. I, Paris: Plon, 1962. II, Paris: Arthème Fayard, 1966.

Pickles, Dorothy. *The Fifth French Republic*. Rev. ed. New York: Frederick A. Praeger, 1962.

———. *The Uneasy Entente: French Foreign Policy and Franco-British Misunderstandings*. London: Oxford University Press for Chatham House, 1966.

Pierre, Andrew. *Nuclear Politics: The British Experience with an Independent Strategic Force, 1939-1970*. London: Oxford University Press, 1972.

Planchais, Jean. *Le Malaise de l'armée*. Paris: Plon, 1958.

Planck, Charles R. *The Changing Status of German Reunification in Western Diplomacy, 1955-1966*. Baltimore: The Johns Hopkins Press, 1967.

Reynaud, Paul. *The Foreign Policy of Charles de Gaulle*. Translated by Mervyn Savill. New York: The Odyssey Press, 1964.

Richardson, James L. *Germany and the Atlantic Alliance*. Cambridge, Mass.: Harvard University Press, 1966.

Rosecrance, R. N. *Defense of the Realm*. New York: Columbia University Press, 1968.

———, ed. *The Dispersion of Nuclear Weapons*. New York: Columbia University Press, 1964.

Sanguinetti, Alexandre. *La France et l'arme atomique*. Paris: Julliard, 1964.

Scheinman, Lawrence. *Atomic Energy Policy in France Under the Fourth Republic*. Princeton: Princeton University Press, 1965.

Schlesinger, Arthur M., Jr. *A Thousand Days*. Boston: Houghton Mifflin Co., 1965.

Schmidt, Helmut. *Verteidigung oder Vergeltung*. Stuttgart: Seewald Verlag, 1965.

———. *Strategie des Gleichgewichts*. Stuttgart: Seewald Verlag, 1969.

Schneider, Fernand-Thiébaut. *Stratégie pour l'occident*. Paris: Charles-Lavauzelle and Co., 1965.

Schoenbrun, David. *The Three Lives of Charles de Gaulle.* New York: Atheneum, 1965.

Schütze, Walter. *European Defence Co-operation and NATO.* Atlantic Papers 3. Paris: The Atlantic Institute, 1969.

Siegler, Heinrich. *Dokumentation der Europäischen Integration, 1961-1963.* Bonn, Vienna, Zurich: Verlag für Zeitarchiv, Siegler and Co., 1964.

Silj, Alessandro. *Europe's Political Puzzle: A Study of the Fouchet Negotiations and the 1963 Veto.* Occasional Papers No. 17. Cambridge: Harvard University Center for International Affairs, 1967.

Sorensen, Theodore C. *Kennedy.* New York: Harper and Row, 1965.

Stanley, Timothy W. *NATO in Transition.* New York: Frederick A. Praeger for the Council on Foreign Relations, 1965.

Stehlin, Paul. *Retour à zero: l'Europe et sa défense dans le compte à rebours.* Paris: Robert Laffont, 1968.

———. *Témoignage pour l'histoire.* Paris: Robert Laffont, 1964.

Strauss, Franz-Josef. *Challenge and Response.* New York: Atheneum, 1970.

———. *The Grand Design: A European Solution to German Reunification.* New York: Frederick A. Praeger, 1965.

Sulzberger, C. L. *The Last of the Giants.* New York: Macmillan Co., 1970.

Tournoux, J.-R. *La Tragédie du Général.* Paris: Librairie Plon, 1967.

Valluy, General Jean. *Se Défendre. Contre qui? Pour quoi? Et comment?* Paris: Plon, 1960.

Weisenfeld, Ernst. *De Gaulle Sieht Europa: Reden und Erklärungen, 1958-1966.* Frankfurt: Fischer Bücherei, 1966.

Williams, Philip M. *Crisis and Compromise: Politics in the Fourth Republic.* Hamden, Conn.: The Shoe String Press, 1964.

Willis, F. Roy. *France, Germany and the New Europe, 1945-1963.* Stanford, Calif.: Stanford University Press, 1965.

Wolfers, Arnold, ed. *Changing East–West Relations and the Unity of the West.* Baltimore: The Johns Hopkins Press, 1964.

Young, Elizabeth. *The Control of Proliferation: The 1968 Treaty in Hindsight and Forecast.* Adelphi Papers, no. 56. London: The Institute for Strategic Studies, 1969.

Young, Judith H. *The French Strategic Missile Programme.* Adelphi Papers, no. 38. London: The Institute for Strategic Studies, 1967.

Younger, Kenneth. *Changing Perspectives in British Foreign Policy.* London: Oxford University Press for Chatham House, 1964.

ARTICLES

Ailleret, Charles. "Applications 'pacifiques' et 'militaires' de l'énergie atomique." *Revue de défense nationale* (November 1954), pp. 421-32.

———. "Complexe atomique du français." *Revue de défense nationale* (January 1956), pp. 3-9.

———. "Défense 'dirigée' ou défense 'tous azimuts.'" *Revue de défense nationale* (December 1967), pp. 1,923-32.

———. "De l'Euratom au programme atomique national." *Revue de defénse nationale* (November 1956), pp. 1,319-27.

———. "Evolution nécessaire de nos structures militaires." *Revue de défense nationale* (June 1965), pp. 947-55.

———. "Les études stratégiques au Centre des hautes études militaires." *Revue de défense nationale* (February 1965), pp. 193-207.

———. "Opinion sur la théorie stratégique de la 'Flexible Response.'" *Revue de défense nationale* (August 1964), pp. 1,323-40.

"L'Armée de terre dans l'appareil militaire français." *L'Armée,* no. 85 (March 1969), pp. 2-9.

Aron, Raymond. "De Gaulle and Kennedy: The Nuclear Debate." *Atlantic Monthly* (August 1962), pp. 33-38.

———. "The Spread of Nuclear Weapons." *Atlantic Monthly* (January 1965), pp. 44-50.

L'Association socialisme et démocratie. "La Force de frappe freine la recherche scientifique." *Liaison et informations* (May 1965).

———. "La Force de frappe: Les Données techniques." *Liaison et informations* (November 1964).

———. "Les Problèmes atomiques: Incidence du programme d'armement sur le développement nucléaire française." *Liaison et informations* (July 1964).

Beaufre, André. "Le problème du partage des responsabilites nucléaires." *Stratégie*, no. 5 (July-September 1965), pp. 7-20.

Bodenheimer, Suzanne J. "The 'Political Union' Debate in Europe: A Case Study in Intergovernmental Diplomacy." *International Organization*, XXI (Winter 1967), 24-54.

Bousquet, Raymond. "La Force nucléaire stratégique française." *Revue de défense nationale* (May 1966), pp. 793-811.

Bower, Michael. "Nuclear Strategy of the Kennedy Administration," *Bulletin of the Atomic Scientists* (October 1962), pp. 34-42.

Bowie, Robert R. "Strategy and the Atlantic Alliance," *International Organization*, XVII (Summer 1963), 709-32.

Brandon, Henry. "Skybolt: The Full Inside Story of How a Missile Nearly Split the West." *Sunday Times* (London), December 8, 1963, pp. 29-32.

Brenner, Michael J. "France's New Defense Strategy and the Atlantic Puzzle." *Bulletin of the Atomic Scientists* (November 1969), pp. 4-7.

von Brentano, Heinrich. "Die Bonner Erklärung vom 18. Juli 1961." *Europa Archiv*, no. 17 (September 1961), pp. 463-66.

Buchan, Alastair. "Battening Down Vauban's Hatches." *Interplay* (May 1968), pp. 4-7.

Carpentier, M. "Déclarations et réalités." *Revue militaire générale*, no. 3 (March 1962), pp. 404-10.

———. "Force de frappe." *Revue militaire générale*, no. 8 (October 1960), pp. 287-95.

———. "Force de frappe." *Revue militaire générale*, no. 10 (December 1960), pp. 565-71.

Cercle d'études de l'armée nouvelle. "La force de dissuasion nucléaire et les contradictions du Club Jean Moulin." *Nouvelle Frontière*, no. 5 (January 1964), pp. 56-67.

———. "Les réalités de M. de Lacoste Lareymondie sont des mirages." *La Nation*, June 15-16, 1964.

"Ces investissements 'improductifs'—Voilà pourquoi la force de dissuasion aide le progrès économique français." *La Nation*, October 8-10, 1963.

Combaux, Edmond. "Defense Tous Azimuts? Oui Mais. . . ." *Revue de défense nationale* (November 1968), pp. 1,600-18.

de la Gorce, Paul-Marie. "De Gaulle et les Américains." *La Nef*, no. 26 (February-April 1966), pp. 59-77.

Delmas, Claude. "La France et sa défense nationale." *Revue de défense nationale* (October 1957), pp. 1,434-48.

de Rose, François. "Atlantic Relationships and Nuclear Problems." *Foreign Affairs*, XLI (April 1963), 479-90.

Edmonds, Martin. "International Collaboration in Weapons Procurement: The Implications of the Anglo-French Case." *International Affairs* (April 1967), pp. 252-64.

Ely, Paul. "Notre Politique militaire." *Revue de défense nationale* (July 1957), pp. 1,033-51.

———. "Perspectives stratégiques d'avenir." *Revue de défense nationale* (November 1958), pp. 1,631-40.

Fabré-Luce, Alfred. "L'Espoir subsiste d'un accord interallié." *La Vie française*, October 21, 1960.

Fontaine, André. "The ABC of MLF." *The Reporter*, December 31, 1964, pp. 10-14.

———. "L'Allemagne et les armaments nucléaires." *Le Monde*, October 19, 1965.

———. "Comment avorta le dialogue franco-britannique." *Le Monde Hebdomadaire*, March 13-19, 1969.

———. "De Gaulle's View of Europe and the Nuclear Debate." *The Reporter*, July 19, 1962, pp. 33-35.

———. "Un Memorandum 'Connu' mais non 'Publié.'" *Le Monde*, October 28, 1960.

———. "What Is French Policy?" *Foreign Affairs*, XLV (October 1966), pp. 58-76.

"Force de Frappe—Keule im Keller." *Der Spiegel*, XIX, November 24, 1965, pp. 110-30.

Fourquet, Michel. "Emploi des differents systèmes de forces dans le cadre de la stratégie de dissuasion." *Revue de défense nationale* (May 1969), pp. 757-67.

Gaillard, Félix. Interview with Robert Kleiman. *U.S. News and World Report*, January 3, 1958, p. 63.

Gallois, Pierre M. "Chaque puissance nucléaire a deux visages." *Pour ou contre la force de frappe* (Paris: Éditions John Didier, 1963), pp. 43-53.

———. "Faut-il créer une force atomique franco-britannique?" *Preuves*, no. 1 (1970), pp. 62-69.

———. "L'Alliance atlantique et l'évolution de l'armement." *Politique étrangère*, no. 2 (1959), pp. 179-203.

Gallois, Pierre M. "La nouvelle politique extérieure des États-Unis et la sécurité de l'Europe." *Revue de défense nationale* (April 1963), pp. 566-93.

———. "Les conséquences stratégiques et politiques des armes nouvelles." *Politique étrangère*, no. 2 (1958), pp. 167-80.

———. "Limitations des armes à grand pouvoir de déstruction." *Revue de défense nationale* (December 1956), pp. 1,485-96.

———. "Pierrelatte a ses raisons." *Pour ou contre la force de frappe* (Paris: Éditions John Didier, 1963), pp. 113-22.

———. "The Raison d'Être of French Defense Policy." *International Affairs* (October 1963), pp. 497-510.

Gavin, James M. "On Dealing with de Gaulle." *Atlantic Monthly* (June 1965), pp. 49-54.

Goldschmidt, Bertrand. "The French Atomic Energy Program." *Bulletin of the Atomic Scientists* (September 1962 [pp. 39-42] and October 1962 [pp. 46-48]).

Goldstein, Walter. "British Strategy and NATO: Prospects for the Seventies." *NATO in the Seventies*. Edited by Edwin H. Fedder. St. Louis: Center of International Studies, University of Missouri, 1970, pp. 89-114.

Goodman, Elliot R. "De Gaulle's NATO Policy in Perspective." *Orbis*, x (Fall 1966), 690-723.

Gordon-Walker, P. C. "The Labor Party's Defense and Foreign Policy." *Foreign Affairs*, XLII (April 1964), 391-98.

Griffiths, Eldon and Niblock, Michael. "Anglo-French Nuclear Deterrent?" *Atlantic Community Quarterly*, VIII (Summer 1970), 196-209.

Grosser, Alfred. "France and Germany in the Atlantic Community." *International Organization*, XVII (Summer 1963), 32-55.

———. "France and Germany: Divergent Outlooks." *Foreign Affairs*, XLIV (October 1965), 26-36.

———. "General de Gaulle and the Foreign Policy of the Fifth Republic." *International Affairs* (April 1963), pp. 198-213.

———. "France and Germany: Less Divergent Outlooks." *Foreign Affairs*, XLVIII (January 1970), 235-44.

von Hassel, Kai-Uwe. "Détente Through Firmness." *Foreign Affairs*, XLII (January 1964), 184-94.

———. "Organizing Western Defense." *Foreign Affairs,* XLIII (January 1965), 209-16.

Hassner, Pierre. "From Napoleon III to de Gaulle." *Interplay,* I (February 1968), 12-19.

———. "The Nation-State in the Nuclear Age." *Survey,* no. 67 (April 1968), 3-27.

Hoag, Malcolm W. "Nuclear Policy and French Intransigence." *Foreign Affairs,* XLI (January 1963), 286-98.

Hoffmann, Stanley. "Cursing de Gaulle Is Not a Policy," *The Reporter,* January 30, 1964, pp. 38-41.

———. "De Gaulle, Europe, and the Atlantic Alliance." *International Organization,* XVIII (Winter 1964), 1-28.

———. "De Gaulle's Memoirs: The Hero as History." *World Politics,* XIII (October 1960), 140-55.

———. "Discord in Community: The North Atlantic Area as a Partial International System." *International Organization,* XVII (Summer 1963), 521-49.

———. "Perceptions, Reality, and the Franco-American Conflict." *Journal of International Affairs,* XXI no. 1 (1967), 57-71.

Kelleher, Catherine M. "The Issue of German Nuclear Armament." *The "Atlantic Community" Reappraised, Proceedings of the Academy of Political Science,* XXIX (November 1968), 104-105.

Kelly, George A. "The Political Background of the French A-Bomb." *Orbis,* IV (Fall 1960), 284-306.

Kissinger, Henry. "The Unsolved Problems of European Defense." *Foreign Affairs,* XL (July 1962), 515-41.

Kitsikis, Dimitri. "L'Attitude des États-Unis à l'égard de la France de 1958 à 1960." *Revue française de science politique,* XVI (August 1966), 685-716.

Kleiman, Robert. "Reports Differ on U.S.–French Rift." *New York Times,* August 29, 1966.

Kohl, Wilfrid L. "Nuclear Sharing in NATO and the Multilateral Force." *Political Science Quarterly,* LXXX (March 1965), 88-109.

———. "The French Nuclear Deterrent." *The "Atlantic Community" Reappraised, Proceedings of The Academy of Political Science,* XXIX (November 1968), 80-94.

Kolodziej, Edward A. "French Strategy Emergent—General Beaufre: A Critique." *World Politics*, xix (April 1967), 417-42.

"La Guerre que prevoit de Gaulle." *L'Express*, December 7, 1964, pp. 24-27.

Lemoine, Claude. "Contribution des programmes nucléaires militaires au développement technologique français." *Études* (April 1968), pp. 490-510.

Le Puloch, General. "Avenir de l'armée de terre." *Revue de défense nationale* (June 1964), pp. 947-60.

le Theule, Joël. "La force nucléaire stratégique française." *France Forum*, no. 47 (March-April 1963), pp. 3-10.

Lieber, Robert J. "The French Nuclear Force." *International Affairs* (July 1966), pp. 421-31.

"L'Institut franco-allemand de Saint-Louis." *Revue militaire d'information* (December 1964), pp. 18-23.

Long, Marceau. "Financement de la politique militaire française." *Revue de défense nationale* (April 1970), pp. 537.

Martin, André. "L'Armée de l'air dans le contexte nucléaire." *Revue de défense nationale* (October 1964), pp. 1,499-517.

Mendl, Wolf. "French Attitudes on Disarmament." *Survival* (December 1967), pp. 393-97.

———. "The Background of French Nuclear Policy." *International Affairs* (January 1965), 22-36.

Messmer, Pierre. "L'Atome, cause et moyen d'une politique militaire autonome." *Revue de défense nationale* (March 1968), pp. 395-402.

———. "Notre Politique Militaire." *Revue de défense nationale* (May 1963), pp. 745-61.

———. "The French Military Establishment of Tomorrow." *La Revue de deux mondes* (February 15, 1962).

———. "Why a U.S. Ally Insists on Its Own Nuclear Forces." Interview in *U.S. News and World Report*, September 24, 1962, pp. 70-73.

Moch, Jules. "Les Conséquences stratégiques et politiques des armes nouvelles." *Politique étrangère*, no. 2 (1958), pp. 149-67.

Murphy, Charles J.V. "NATO at a Nuclear Crossroads." *Fortune* (December 1962), pp. 88ff.

Nerlich, Uwe. "The Nuclear Dilemmas of the Federal Republic of Germany." Paper prepared for the Stanford Research Institute. An earlier version of this paper appeared as "Die Nuklearen Dilemmas der Bundesrepublik Deutschland." *Europa Archiv*, no. 17 (September 1965), pp. 637-52.

Norstad, Lauris. "NATO, Its Problems and Its Continuing Promise." *Proceedings of the Academy of Political Science*, XXVII (May 1963), 296-308.

Pay, Rex. "Technical Implications of BMD." *Survival* (July 1967), pp. 219-23; reprinted from *Technology Week*, March 20, 1967.

Pergent, J. "Wie weit ist die Force de Frappe?" *Wehrkunde* (August 1964), pp. 417-23.

Perret-Gentil. "Vers la force de frappe." *Revue militaire suisse* (June 1962), pp. 277-87.

Pierre, Andrew J. "Britain and European Security: Issues and Choices for the 1970's." In *European Security and the Atlantic System*, edited by William T. R. Fox and Warner R. Schilling. New York: Columbia University Press, 1972.

———. "Britain's Defense Dilemmas." *The "Atlantic Community" Reappraised, Proceedings of the Academy of Political Science*, XXIX (November 1968), pp. 64-79.

———. "Nuclear Diplomacy: Britain, France and America," *Foreign Affairs*, XLIX, 283-301.

Pleven, René. "France in the Atlantic Community." *Foreign Affairs*, XXXVIII (October 1959), 19-30.

Reston, James. "Why the U.S. and de Gaulle Have Disagreed." *New York Times*, May 1 and 3, 1964.

Scheinman, Lawrence. "Euratom: Nuclear Integration in Europe." *International Conciliation*, no. 563 (May 1967).

Schumann, Maurice. "France and Germany in the New Europe." *Foreign Affairs*, XLI (October 1962), 66-78.

Schütze, Walter. "Die franzöische Atombewaffnung im Spiegel der parlamentarischen Debatten." *Europa Archiv* (May 1961), pp. 207-18.

———. "La France et l'OTAN." *Politique étrangère*, no. 2 (1966,), pp. 109-18.

———. "Pierrelatte: Schwerpunkt und Symbol der Atompolitik Frankreichs." *Europa Archiv* (August 1962), pp. 559-70.

Stehlin, Paul. "French Thoughts on the Alliance." *NATO's Fifteen Nations* (August-September 1964).

———. "Réalités stratégiques en 1939 et vingt ans après." *Revue de défense nationale* (May 1959), pp. 749-62.

Stehlin, Paul. "The Evolution of Western Defense." *Foreign Affairs*, XLII (October 1963), 70-83.

Strauss, Franz-Josef. "An Alliance of Continents." *International Affairs* (April 1965), pp. 191-203.

Taylor, Edmund. "The Powerhouse of German Defense." *The Reporter*, April 18, 1957, pp. 25-30.

Vernant, Jacques. "Armement nucléaire français ou force de frappe 'européene?'" *Politique étrangère*, no. 6 (1959), pp. 591-605.

———. "De l'entente française-allemande à l'armée nucléaire française." *Revue de défense nationale* (August 1962), pp. 1,383-90.

———. "Stratégie et politique à l'âge atomique." *Revue de défense nationale* (May 1958), pp. 855-62.

Wohlstetter, Albert. "Nuclear Sharing: NATO and the N+1 Country." *Foreign Affairs*, XXXIX (April 1961), 355-87.

XXXX. "L'Armée de Terre et l'Armament Atomique Tactique." *L'Armée: Revue périodique des armées de terre* (January 1965).

XXX. "Faut-il reformer l'Alliance atlantique?" *Politique étrangère*, no. 4-5 (1965), pp. 230-44.

XX. "Faut-il reformer l'OTAN? Un examen critique." *Politique étrangère*, no. 4-5 (1965), pp. 324-29.

de Rose, François. "Aspects politiques des problèmes posés par l'armement nucléaire français." Lecture given at the Institut des hautes études de défense nationale, November 18, 1958. Mimeographed. Paris: Institut des hautes études de défense nationale, Direction des études, December 17, 1958.

———. "Les Aspects politiques des problèmes nucléaires." Lecture given at the Institut des hautes études de défense nationale, January 26, 1960. Mimeographed. Paris: Institut des hautes études de défense nationale, Direction des études, March 24, 1960.

Kelleher, Catherine M. "German Nuclear Dilemmas: 1955-1965. Ph.D. diss., M.I.T., 1967.

Kolodziej, Edward A. "French Strategic Policy: A Systemic Perspective." Paper presented at the annual meeting of the American Political Science Association, New York, September 2-6, 1969. Now published in *Journal of Politics* (May 1971), pp. 448-77.

Index